The Capitulations and the Ottoman Legal System

The Capitulations and the Ottoman Legal System

Qadis, Consuls and Beratlıs *in the 18th Century*

By

Maurits H. van den Boogert

BRILL

LEIDEN | BOSTON

This paperback was originally published in hardback as Volume 21 in the series Studies in Islamic Law and Society.

Cover illustration: Jean Baptiste Vanmour, 'The Meal presented to Ambassador Cornelis Calkoen by the Grand Vizier in the name of Sultan Ahmed III, 14 September 1727'; oil painting on canvas. Rijksmuseum Amsterdam.

The Library of Congress has cataloged the hardcover edition as follows:

Boogert, Maurits H. van den.
The capitulations and the Ottoman legal system : Qadis, Consuls and Beratlıs in the 18th Century/ by Maurits H. Van den Boogert.
p. cm. — (Studies in Islamic law and society, ISSN 1384-1130 ; v. 21)
Includes bibliographical references and index.
ISBN 90-04-14035-2 (alk. paper)
1. Capitulations. 2. Exterritoriality. 3. Privileges and immunities—Turkey—History—18th century. 4. Aliens—Turkey—History—18th century. 5. Merchants, Foreign—Legal status, laws, etc.—Turkey—History—18th century. I. Title. II. Series.

KKX2290.B66 2005
349.561'09'033—dc22

2005042154

Typeface for the Latin, Greek, and Cyrillic scripts: "Brill". See and download: brill.com/brill-typeface.

ISBN 978-90-04-42862-1 (paperback, 2020)
ISBN 978-90-47-40612-9 (e-book, 2020)
ISBN 978-90-04-14035-6 (hardback, 2005)

This book is printed on acid-free paper and produced in a sustainable manner.

Aan mijn ouders en Monique

CONTENTS

LIST OF FIGURES AND TABLES

Figures

Tables

ABBREVIATIONS

A.DVN.DVE	Bâb-ı Âsafî Defterleri—Düvel-i Ecnebiye Defterleri (Registers of the Grand Vizier-Registers of Foreign Nations), in *BOA*
BL	British Library, London
BNA	British National Archives, Kew (formerly: Public Record Office)
BOA	Başbakanlık Osmanlı Arşivi (Archives of Prime Minister's Office, Ottoman section), Istanbul
Bronnen II	*Bronnen tot de geschiedenis van den levantschen handel* [Sources on the History of (Dutch) Levant Trade] *Tweede deel* [Part II]: *1661–1726* K. Heeringa ed., (The Hague, 1917)
Bronnen III	*Bronnen tot de geschiedenis van den levantschen handel. Derde Deel* [Part III]: *1727–1765*, J.G. Nanninga ed., (The Hague, 1952).
Bronnen IV/i	*Bronnen tot de geschiedenis van den levantschen handel. Vierde Deel* [Part IV]: *1765–1826 Eerste stuk* [Vol. i], J.G. Nanninga ed., (The Hague, 1964)
Bronnen IV/ii	*Bronnen tot de geschiedenis van den levantschen handel. Vierde Deel* [Part IV]: *1765–1826 Tweede stuk* [Vol. ii], J.G. Nanninga ed., (The Hague, 1966)
CAS	Consulaatarchief Smirna (Archives of the Dutch consulate in Izmir), in *DNA*
CDG	*Collectie Dedem van de Gelder* (*Private Archive of F.G. van Dedem* van de Gelder, Dutch ambassador in Istanbul 1785–1810), in *DNA*
CH	Cevdet Hariciye, in *BOA*
Cod. Or.	Codex Orientalis, in *ULL*
DNA	Nationaal Archief, The Hague (formerly: Algemeen Rijksarchief)
ED	Ecnebi Defterleri (Foreign Registers), in *BOA*
Eg.	Eggerton Collection, in *BL*
EI^2	*The Encyclopaedia of Islam*—2nd edition (Leiden, 1960–2003)
HH	Hatt-ı Hümayun (Imperial Rescripts), in *BOA*

HMC	Historical Manuscript Commission (in *BNA*)
JESHO	*Journal of the Economic and Social History of the Orient*
LAT	Legatiearchief Turkije (Archives of the Dutch Legation in Istanbul), in *DNA*
LH	Levantse Handel (Levant Trade Files), in *DNA*
Propaganda	Archives of the Sagra Congregazione De Propaganda Fide, Rome
SC	Scritture Riferiti nei Congressi (Documents referred to Congregations), in *Propaganda*
SG	States General's archives, in *DNA*
SP	State Papers, in *BNA*
ULL	University Library, Leiden

ACKNOWLEDGEMENTS

This study is to a large extent based on the research I did for my doctoral dissertation, which I defended in Leiden on 8 November 2001. The focus of the thesis was much different from the present volume, however, which took me almost a year to write. Several people have been immensely important in both phases of the process, and I want to acknowledge my debt to them here.

Alastair Hamilton and Alexander H. de Groot supervised my thesis. Their expertise, enthusiasm and encouragement went far beyond the call of duty, and my debt to them is immeasurable. The same is true for Kate Fleet who has been a constant advisor and friend for years. Remke Kruk, Erik-Jan Zürcher, Han den Heijer and Jan Just Witkam raised questions at my viva that continued to resonate in my mind throughout the work on this volume. This is also the case with Léon Buskens, whose ideas I have used here, and whose friendship I value greatly.

During the rewriting process Jan Schmidt has corrected the typescript expertly in too many places to mention. His efforts have saved me many embarrassments, for which I am deeply grateful. The mistakes still left are all mine. The reason for reviewing my research from a new perspective in the first place was Ruud Peters' offer to publish my book in the present series. As an historian without any formal training in law, I felt, and continue to feel, honoured by his proposal. I greatly appreciate the opportunity to publish this series, although it is also quite daunting. I also want to thank Antonis Anastasopoulos for sending me his unpublished paper on Dimitrios Bekallas of Karaferya, and Elena Frangakis-Syrett and Colin Heywood for much encouragement and advice. At Brill Trudy Kamperveen and Boris van Gool kindly put up with the delays and kept me on track.

Four friends deserve to be mentioned here separately. When my laptop computer crashed halfway through writing this book, John Robbemond brought it back to life. He saved the project and still keeps back-ups of all my files. Laila al-Zwaini's knowledge of Islamic law has often been my safety net. Heleen Plaisier witnessed the entire process of writing the thesis, hating it, and taking up the process once again, remaining supportive throughout. Brother-in-arms Thurstan Robinson read early drafts of this book and made valuable comments.

I also want to thank my most loyal supporters. My parents, Leo van den Boogert and Jenny van den Boogert-Boslooper, unconditionally supported all my efforts and visited me wherever the archival trail took me. My brother, Leon, and his wife, Janette, sponsored a trip to China for much needed "R&R", looked after me and Monique in Singapore, and always took an interest in my obscure endeavours. Finally, I owe more to Monique Hogenkamp than words can express. *Zij maakt het verschil.*

Funding

The research for this book was made possible by a PhD-position at the Research School for Asian, African, and Amerindian Studies CNWS in Leiden. During this period I was awarded several travel grants from the Dutch Council for Academic Research (NWO) in The Hague. At an earlier stage I have benefited from grants from the Skilliter Centre for Ottoman Studies, Newnham College, Cambridge; the Dutch Institute in Rome; the Scholten Fund; and the Dr. C. Louise Thijsse-Schouten Fund.

MvdB
Leiden, March 2005

INTRODUCTION

Several hours before sunrise on Saturday, 26 January 1754, the merchant Jan Hendrik Meijer left his house in Pera, the diplomatic quarter of Istanbul, never to be seen again in the Ottoman capital. He left behind his wife and two bankrupt firms, taking with him a considerable amount of money and diamonds belonging to his business partner's father. Meijer was a member of the Dutch community in Istanbul, which he had served as treasurer for several years. The Dutch embassy was left to sort out the chaos of the two firms, to make arrangements for the deserted wife and for Cornelis van der Oudermeulen junior, the underage business partner who had been robbed of his father's capital.

The ambassador, Elbert de Hochepied, was particularly worried by the fact that the creditors of the two firms included several Ottoman subjects. The young van der Oudermeulen only made things worse by using force to retrieve jewellery and letters of credit Meijer had given his Jewish broker as surety for his debts. Although the value of the jewels was added to Meijer's estate and could thus be seen as beneficial to all creditors, the Ottomans among them were not reassured by these actions. They threatened to take van der Oudermeulen to the Islamic court, "by which action he would certainly have been imprisoned" the ambassador thought. The creditors insisted on being repaid in accordance with "the law of the land", which de Hochepied knew favoured them over foreign creditors. Moreover, the ambassador referred to an article in the French capitulations of 1740

> by which they [the French] commit themselves to compensate the people of the land [first], regardless of the other creditors. And although we do not have this article in ours, we are nevertheless obliged also to honour it, like everybody else, because our capitulations [of 1680] say that we will be allowed everything the French, English and other nations are allowed and awarded, and while we often use this to our advantage, the Court claims that in these matters we have to act in accordance with this article too.[1]

[1] DNA, States General 6957: Elbert de Hochepied to Fagel, 16 February 1754.

For the present study on the legal status of Westerners and their protégés in the eighteenth century, several aspects of the Meijer-incident are of interest. Even this brief summary of the case affords a first glimpse of the procedures and problems involved in bankruptcies of foreign merchants in the Ottoman Empire. For example, the procedures involved in bankruptcies have received surprisingly little scholarly attention. Even more important is the fact that we see the Dutch ambassador turning to the texts of the capitulations for guidance in a serious legal crisis. Not only does he mention a specific article, he also draws attention to the connections between the various charters of privileges granted to European nations. The Ottomans honoured the principle of the most-favoured-nation, which meant that the Dutch also enjoyed the privileges granted to France (and vice-versa). In this case, however, the principle evidently worked against them. The implied hierarchy between "the law of the land" and the capitulations is noteworthy as well. The creditors could claim preferential treatment on the basis of Ottoman laws for all they wanted, it was the fact that the French capitulations supported them that mattered. The ambassador emphasizes the exclusive authority of these texts and suggests that the Porte agreed with this view. These points will be discussed in more detail elsewhere in this study.

Here attention must first be drawn to a significant error in the Dutch ambassador's letter to his superiors: The article of the French capitulations of 1740 referred to by the Dutch ambassador did not exist. The only stipulation concerning bankruptcies, article 53, states that the debts of a bankrupt should be paid from the balance of his estate. It could be regarded as a specification of the more general article 22, in which the personal responsibility and liability of debtors and their guarantors are emphasized. Nobody should be forced to pay another man's debts, even if he was a fellow countryman, for example.[2] There is no reference whatsoever to any procedures for the division of the estate. De Hochepied may honestly have believed that it did, but we cannot rule out the possibility that he deliberately lied in order to cover himself against future complaints in case the incident escalated later. If circumstances called for such drastic actions, the ambassador would probably give in to the Ottoman

[2] For a more comprehensive discussion of this and other capitulatory articles, see Chapter One.

creditors' demands to the disadvantage of the European creditors. Should complaints about the ambassador subsequently be addressed to the Dutch States General, at least he would have forewarned them. Whatever his motives may have been, in an official letter to the States General of the Dutch Republic the ambassador gave an account of the capitulatory system that is incorrect on an important point.

The Dutch ambassador's mistake (or deception) does not appear to have been discovered by the States General. The Dutch government undoubtedly considered the ambassador an authority on matters Ottoman, whom there was no reason to doubt. Even if a translation of the French capitulations of 1740 were available in The Hague, it seems unlikely that anyone would have checked to see if the article was indeed in the text. Similarly misleading statements from other Western diplomats about the texts of the capitulations and the capitulatory system as a whole generally also seem to have gone unnoticed by their superiors.[3] Ambassadors' accounts were all too often accepted at face value. Many modern students of the Ottoman capitulations have done the same. Those who were interested in their legal aspects generally studied only (translations of) the texts, while those whose interests focused on diplomatic and commercial relations seldom consulted the texts to correlate practice with theory.

The three principal themes of this study are the perception, theory and practice of the capitulatory system in the Ottoman legal system in the eighteenth century. The Meijer case alone indicates that perceptions about this system found in the Western sources must be treated with caution. An examination of the text referred to by the ambassador brought to light a difference between his own ideas about the capitulations and what the texts actually said. How bankruptcies of foreign merchants in the Ottoman Empire were handled in practice was a different matter altogether again, which did not necessarily conform to the theory of the capitulations, or the perceptions

[3] In this study several examples of ambassadorial disinformation will be discussed later. For a published example, see Colin Heywood, 'The Kapudan Pasha, the English Ambassador and the *Blackham* Galley: An Episode in Anglo-Ottoman Maritime Relations (1697)' in: Elizabeth Zachariadou (ed.), *The Kapudan Pasha, His Office and His Domain* (Crete, 2002), 409–438, esp. 419.

of Western diplomats. The extent to which theory, practice and perception differed often depended on the interaction between the ambassador or consul on the one hand, and the Ottoman judiciary on the other. This interaction therefore takes a central place in the present study.

Early Studies of the Capitulations

The study of the Ottoman capitulations has long been more popular among students of international law than of history. Roughly between 1850 and 1950 a considerable number of juridical studies appeared on Ottoman foreign relations and the documents on which they were based, the *ahdnames*, or capitulations. Many were doctoral dissertations submitted at universities across Western Europe. The authors of these early works on the Ottoman capitulations had various, sometimes opposite, motives for writing them. Most Western authors justified their efforts by pointing to the Eastern Question and the good use to which diplomats might put their work. This is particularly true for diplomatic manuals that also appeared in this period, which aimed to provide a clear and concise discourse on the duties and legal capacities of consular personnel in the Levant.[4]

Around the turn of the century three Dutch students presented theses on legal issues connected with the capitulations that they considered economically and politically relevant for their time.[5] Johannes van Oordt foresaw an increase in commercial relations between his country and the Levant, which would make his work useful for Dutch

[4] See, for example, Jac. Wertheim, *Manuel a l'usage des consuls des Pays-Bas précédé d'un aperçu historique sur l'établissement du consulat néerlandais a l'étranger et de la législation depuis son origine jusqu'à nos jours suivi d'un recueil de documents officiels* (Amsterdam, 1861).

[5] van Oordt, *De privaatrechterlijke toestand van den Nederlandschen koopman in de landen van den Islam* [The status of Dutch merchants in the countries of Islam according to civil law] (Leiden, 1899); Joekes, *Schets van de bevoegdheden der Nederlandsche consuls* [Essay on the authority of Dutch consuls] (Leiden, 1911); Kramers, *Strafrechtspraak over Nederlanders in Turkije* [Criminal Justice for Dutchmen in Turkey] (Amsterdam, 1915). The works of van Oordt and Kramers were doctoral dissertations at the Faculty of Law of Leiden University. Joekes submitted his thesis in the Faculty of Political Science of the same university. Also see F.E. Embrechts, *Over den invloed van het Europesche volkenregt op de internationale betrekkingen der Ottomannische Porte* [On the Influence of the European Law of Nations on the International Relations of the Ottoman Porte] (Utrecht, 1858).

merchants and diplomats abroad. The intended readership of A.M. Joekes and J.H. Kramers, the well-known Orientalist, clearly consisted of diplomats and politicians. Their doctoral dissertations did not have an exclusively academic purpose. Their aim was aptly summarized by another author, A. Schopoff, who hoped to render a "service à la science historique, aux hommes politiques en général et aux diplomats en particulier."[6] Some of these studies focused on one particular area, like the work of G. Pélissié du Rausas, the director of the French Law School in Cairo, whose focus is on nineteenth-century Egypt.[7] The "men of politics and diplomacy" these authors had in mind were almost certainly Europeans.

Students of the capitulations from the world of Islam had a similar readership in mind. They, too, pointed to the Eastern Question to justify their efforts, but with a radically different aim. At the end of 1918, just after the end of the First World War, the Turk Mahmud Essad submitted his licentiate thesis in the Faculty of Law of the University of Fribourg. In this book the author argued for the abolishment of the capitulations, a system he considered incompatible with the dignity of his country. Essad proposed to introduce a modern constitution in the Ottoman Empire, instead. By the time the thesis was published, ten years later, the author happily noted that many of his ideas had been implemented already in the recently established Turkish Republic.[8] Another passionate advocate of the abolition of the capitulatory system was Habib Abi-Chahla. His doctoral dissertation, a fervent denunciation of the injustice of the capitulations, was published in Paris in 1924. Already in the preface the author cries out: "Combien de fois mes compatriotes se sont-ils étonnés de ce que 'ceux du dehors', qu'on appelle encore les 'francs', bénéficient des privilèges exorbitantes dont ils supportent les charges redoutables?"[9] In contrast with his Turkish colleague, the Arab Abi-Chahla saw no reason to be optimistic about the future, because,

---

[6] Schopoff, *Les réformes et la protection des chrétiens en Turquie 1673–1904: Firmans, bérats, protocoles, traités, capitulations, conventions, arrangements, notes, circulaires, règlements, lois, mémorandums, etc.* (Paris, 1904), Préface.

[7] Pélissié du Rausas, *Le régime des capitulations dans l'Empire Ottoman* (Paris, 1910–1911).

[8] Mahmoud Essad, *Du régime des capitulations ottomanes: Leur caractère juridique d'après l'histoire et les textes* (Istanbul, 1928).

[9] Habib Abi-Chahla, *L'extinction des capitulations en Turquie et dans les régions arabes* (Paris, 1924). [5].

according to him, the unjust capitulatory system continued unabated in many locations.

Their different political agenda's notwithstanding, these works about the capitulations have much in common. The *ahdname*s discussed in them are primarily those of the nineteenth and early twentieth centuries. The system these authors studied was still in operation, so they wrote predominantly about contemporary issues. Moreover, their studies display an almost exclusive emphasis on texts, the authors' views on consular jurisdiction based predominantly on the capitulations. There was consensus among these legal scholars that the capitulations were binding, and that discussions about their interpretation should be based on the texts alone. According to these works there was little difference between the legal status of Westerners and that of their protégés, who were locally recruited non-Muslim subjects of the sultan. Despite the fact that several authors had personal experience with the capitulatory system, references to practice are scarce. The discussions of consular jurisdiction generally remain abstract, and the descriptions of the system tend to be normative.

By focusing exclusively on the *ahdname*s as international treaties concluded between rulers, these authors disregarded their second function. The capitulations not only governed international political, diplomatic and commercial relations, they also regulated the Ottomans' contacts with foreigners within the Ottoman Empire.[10] Politics and trade went hand in hand from the beginning. Merchants from the West made the first contacts with "the Turk", requesting certain privileges from the sultans to guarantee their personal safety in Muslim territory. In the early period trade was more important than permanent political relations, but this gradually changed when the Eastern Mediterranean came under Ottoman rule.

---

[10] I realize that "foreigners" is a much wider category that the group I aim to study, i.e. the subjects of those, predominantly Western European, countries who enjoyed capitulatory privileges. On other foreign elements in Ottoman society, see Svetlana Ivanova, 'The Empire's "own" Foreigners: Armenians and *Acem tüccar* in Rumeli in the seventeenth and eighteenth centuries', in: Maurits H. van den Boogert and Kate Fleet (eds.), *The Ottoman Capitulations: Text and Context* (Rome, 2003), 115–148.

An Historical Survey

A brief historical survey of the development of the capitulatory system is useful at this point. Originally the Ottoman sultans granted the *ahdnames* unilaterally to the sovereigns of foreign countries who sent envoys to the Sublime Porte to apply for trade privileges. The sultans awarded capitulations on the applicants' explicit promise to maintain peaceful relations with the Ottoman Empire, on the understanding that any violation of this promise might lead to a unilateral revocation of the privileges. The *ahdnames* were intended to stimulate trade with the West, and to regulate the presence of communities of foreign merchants in the Ottoman domains. Immediately after the fall of Constantinople Mehmed the Conqueror granted capitulations to the Genoese community of Galata, across the Golden Horn.[11] Later the Venetians were also accorded commercial privileges in the Ottoman domains. Merchants from Genoa and Venice would long continue to dominate the trade between the eastern and the western parts of the Mediterranean, but the arrival of French ambassadors in Istanbul in the early sixteenth century heralded the coming of a new era of Ottoman relations with the West.[12]

In the sixteenth century the Ottoman sultans granted France and England capitulations, and the Dutch Republic followed at the beginning of the seventeenth century. The eighteenth century witnessed a dramatic increase in the number of foreign powers that applied for commercial privileges for their subjects. In 1718 the Habsburg Emperor was granted capitulations, and Sweden followed in 1737. Three years later the Kingdom of the Two Sicilies obtained its own *ahdname*. Also in 1740 France acquired considerable extensions of its privileges with the renewal of its capitulations. In 1747 the subjects of Tuscany were accorded trade privileges in the Levant, while Denmark got its own capitulations in 1746. Fifteen years later Prussia was granted an *ahdname*. Russia entered the system in 1774 after the treaty of Küçük Kaynarca, while Spain established formal relations with the Porte in 1782.[13]

---

[11] Halil İnalcık, 'Ottoman Galata, 1453–1553', in: Edhem Eldem (ed.), *Première Rencontre Internationale sur l'Empire Ottoman et la Turquie Moderne* (Istanbul, Paris, 1991), 17–105—reprinted in his *Essays in Ottoman History* (Istanbul, 1998), 271–376.

[12] Kate Fleet, *European and Islamic Trade in the Early Ottoman State. The Merchants of Genoa and Turkey* (Cambridge, 1999).

[13] Reşat Ekrem, *Osmanlı muahdeleri ve kapitülâsiyonlar 1300–1920* (Istanbul, 1934).

An important capitulatory privilege allowed foreigners to recruit Ottoman subjects as interpreters. Using Italian for communication, they acted as intermediaries in the broadest sense of the word. The Europeans knew them by the title of *dragoman*, a loan from the Arabic *tarjuman* (interpreter). Not only did the dragomans interpret and translate Ottoman speech and text into Italian, and vice versa, but they also guided their foreign employers through the mazes of Ottoman protocol, gave advice, gathered intelligence, and mediated in disputes between Europeans and Ottomans. On the basis of the capitulations and their own deeds of appointment (*berats*) the dragomans enjoyed the same fiscal privileges as the foreigners, something that made their post attractive to non-Muslim Ottoman merchants. The arrangement by which these Ottoman interpreters were affiliated to foreign embassies and consulates is commonly called the "protection system".[14]

When the balance of military power shifted to their advantage, the Western powers and Russia started to use the capitulations against the Ottoman Empire. The date of the turning point is controversial, but most authors fix it at the end of the seventeenth century, implicitly marking the eighteenth century as an era of decline. In this period the Ottoman authorities are generally believed to have felt that they could no longer revoke the privileges they had granted unilaterally, being frequently faced with foreign demands they could not refuse. The protection system is often considered symptomatic of this development. What started as a privilege that enabled foreigners to employ Ottoman subjects as their interpreters (*dragomans*) is generally thought to have evolved into a system by which embassies and consulates illegitimately extended diplomatic immunity to growing numbers of Ottoman non-Muslims. The Europeans allegedly sold innumerable *berats* to Ottoman subjects who were not actually employed as dragomans, but enjoyed their privileges nonetheless. The Ottoman treasury reportedly suffered dramatically from this state of affairs. As foreign powers became increasingly important in the governing of the Ottoman state, its subjects felt more and more disadvantaged and discriminated against, as Abi-Chahla's testimony has already illustrated.

---

[14] The system is also called the protégé system; See Salâhi R. Sonyel, 'The Protégé System in the Ottoman Empire and its Abuses', *Belleten* LV/214 (1991), 675–686.

Another result of this historical development must also be emphasized here: the unity of the capitulatory system. Each foreign nation received its own *ahdnames*, but their contents were always linked to the charters of privileges of other foreign communities. The most-favoured-nation clause, already mentioned above, guaranteed that all privileges granted to one befriended foreign community also applied to all the others. This meant that, in principle, in the eighteenth century there was no difference in legal status between, for example, a French and a Swedish merchant. As far as the capitulations were concerned, all foreigners enjoyed the same legal status in the Ottoman Empire.

The Juridical Approach

Echoing Western sources, many scholars have claimed that the Europeans enjoyed complete legal autonomy in the Ottoman Empire and were immune to the Ottoman justice system. Since their protégés enjoyed the same privileges, it has been claimed that *berats* "nullified the sultan's authority" over them.[15] One of the most recent proponents of this view is Yoram Shalit, whose book on non-Muslims and foreigners in Aleppo and Damascus in the eighteenth and nineteenth centuries sets out to prove that the Ottoman administrative and legal systems systematically discriminated against these groups.[16] Shalit also refers to the capitulations, and summarizes the articles concerning the legal status of foreigners. The author mentions the jurisdiction of the consul, emphasizing that the Ottoman judiciary had no right to interfere with the consular legal procedures, even if foreign merchants invited them to. He acknowledges the fact that some cases should be referred to the Sublime Porte, but he interprets this as a safeguard for consular jurisdiction. Shalit thus concludes that the Westerners had an "extraterritorial position on the

[15] Bruce Masters, 'The Sultan's Entrepeneurs: The *Avrupa Tüccaris* and the *Hayriye Tüccaris* in Syria', *IJMES* (1992), 579–597, esp. 579.

[16] Yoram Shalit, *Nicht-Muslime und Fremde in Aleppo und Damaskus im 18. und in der ersten Hälfte des 19. Jahrhunderts* (Berlin, 1996). This aspect of the book is similar to the central thesis of Karl Binswanger, whose work is neither referred to, nor is it found in the bibliography, however. Binswanger's views are discussed below, in Chapter Three.

basis of their exemption from the Ottoman tax and legal systems".[17] The author's discussion of the privileges of foreigners is based on the controversial first French capitulations of 1536, the existence of which has yet to be proved definitively.[18] Although several articles of this text also appear in later capitulations in a slightly different form, the text of 1536 does not accurately reflect the legal privileges of Westerners in the Ottoman Empire in the eighteenth and nineteenth centuries. Moreover, Shalit did not consult any Ottoman archival sources, relying exclusively on Arabic chronicles, and French and English archives.

This isolationist view on the legal position of Westerners in the Ottoman Empire seems to be based on a number of suppositions. The first is that the capitulations granted foreign subjects legal exemptions to the extent that they practically enjoyed extraterritoriality.[19] Consequently, Islamic courts in the Ottoman Empire had no jurisdiction over foreign nationals. It is also widely believed that the procedures by which non-Muslim Ottoman subjects could obtain foreign protection were beyond the controls of the Ottoman authorities. The protection system was a scheme devised and implemented by foreign diplomats. The privileges extended in this way to non-Muslim Ottoman subjects were the same as those enjoyed by foreigners, so these protégés also had an extraterritorial status. According to this view the Ottoman judiciary thus lost its jurisdiction over Ottoman subjects who obtained foreign protection.

An important question of this study is whether Western communities in the Ottoman Empire were part of the Ottoman legal system, or were separate from it somehow. This leads us back to the capitulations, and raises a number of additional questions about their practical limitations. Firstly, what were the practical boundaries of consular jurisdiction? Within his community the consul may be assumed to have had sufficient authority to keep its members on the

---

[17] Shalit, *Nicht-Muslime und Fremde in Aleppo und Damaskus*, 20.

[18] Ibid., 18–19. Shalit relied on J.C. Hurewitz, *Diplomacy in the Near and Middle East. A Documentary Record. Volume 1: 1535–1914* (Princeton, 1975), 502. On the controversy over this text, see J. Matuz, 'A propos de la validité des capitulations de 1536 entre l'empire ottoman et la France', *Turcica* XXIV (1992), 183–192.

[19] 'Imtiyāzāt ii. The Ottoman Empire' (H. İnalcık), *EI*², 1179–1189; Ibid., 'The Status of the Greek Orthodox Patriarch under the Ottomans', *Essays in Ottoman History*, 195–214, esp. 204 (reprinted from *Turcica* XXI–XXIII (1991), 407–436).

straight path as much as possible, but what if members of different foreign communities came into conflict with each other? How did it work when a dispute involved a foreigner and a subject of the sultan? Another important issue concerns the legal status of the Ottoman protégés of Western embassies and consulates. Was it really true that Ottoman subjects—indigenous Christians and Jews, but Ottoman subjects nevertheless—could somehow obtain extraterritoriality through foreign embassies and consulates? If this was indeed the case, how did it affect the consular legal system? And, finally, how did foreign jurisdiction interact with the Ottoman judiciary in cases involving both protected and ordinary Ottoman subjects?

Methodology

Before an attempt can be made to answer these questions issues of methodology must be addressed. Both the Ottoman and Western sources contain innumerable references to legal conflicts. The Ottoman Registers of Foreign Nations, for example, primarily consist of (summaries of) *fermans* issued in response to complaints and petitions from foreigners throughout the Ottoman Empire. The Western diplomatic records contain an equally large number of references to legal conflicts and dispute resolution. The degree of overlap is impossible to establish with certainty, but it is clear that not all complaints found in the Western records were passed on to the Porte. Sometimes ambassadors considered it unwise to file complaints at a particular time, because larger issues were on the agenda, an unsympathetic officer was about to be replaced by someone who might be more positively inclined, or too many petitions had already been filed recently.[20] Moreover, only serious problems were recorded to begin with, which means that the disputes on record probably represent only the tip of the iceberg. The invisible part consists of instances in which foreign merchants and consuls on the one hand, and qadis and other Ottoman authorities, on the other, cooperated without any problem. Conflicts are thus over-represented in our sources, which do not necessarily

[20] For an exceptionally informative letter about such considerations, see ENA, SP 110/29: 16, 15 July 1749, [Ambassador James] Porter to Consul & Factory at Aleppo.

offer a representative image of everyday contacts between foreigners and Ottomans.

This study is based on both Ottoman, Dutch and English archival sources consulted in Istanbul, The Hague and London, respectively. In the latter two archives I have also found a great deal of relevant Ottoman material. One of the principal differences between Ottoman and Western sources is their style. Ottoman *fermans*, for example, tend to be formulaic summaries of the specific circumstances in response to which they were issued. The documents commonly mention who requested their issue and for what reason. An imperial order in response to the situation then follows, along with an exhortation to comply with the command. For example, a foreign merchant somewhere in the Ottoman Empire might complain that a local tax agent forced him to pay double taxes on his merchandize imported from Europe, contrary to the capitulations, whereupon the Porte issued a *ferman* forbidding this. Such *fermans*, which are an important source for this study, thus represent the final step in a decision-making process, the earlier stages of which have often either not been recorded, or have not survived. Sometimes the Porte issued contradictory orders, making it difficult to determine its policies.[21]

The Western sources, by contrast, usually lack the focus that characterizes the Ottoman documents. Diplomatic letters to and from the Levant tend to contain a multitude of references to a wide variety of on-going affairs. Long lines of communications often meant that ambassadors and consuls had to fend for themselves and obtain approval of their actions from their superiors later, which naturally influenced their reports. Moreover, policies are generally easy to identify, but they were often short-lived, and could change rapidly on the basis of new information, rumours, or reconsideration. Contrary to the Ottoman sources, personal accounts and interpretations abound in the Western correspondence. Some ambassadors had close personal contacts with high Ottoman officers, while others preferred to fraternize only with fellow Westerners. Despite this great variety of "voices" in these sources, they convey a remarkably constant and consistent view on the capitulations in relation to the Ottoman legal system.

[21] Cf. Karen Barkey, *Bandits and Bureaucrats. The Ottoman Route to State Centralization* (Ithaca, 1994).

The Ottoman and Western text corpuses thus have radically different perspectives, something I have attempted to incorporate in this study. The European and Ottoman views on the *ahdname*s are therefore as much part of this study as the functioning of the capitulatory system itself. This is particularly true for the first three chapters.

The first chapter opens with a discussion of several aspects of the *ahdname*s that received little attention from scholars in the past, but are vital for our understanding of the capitulatory system. They include the concept of "Sacred Capitulations", the revocation of these texts, and the role of other documents. I will subsequently focus on the privileges the European communities in the Ottoman Empire enjoyed, with an emphasis on the legal position of foreigners. At the end of Chapter One I will discuss a theoretical framework within which we can interpret the legal position of foreigners in relation to the Ottoman legal system. The second chapter is devoted to the status of Ottoman non-Muslim protégés. While dragomans were the most important protégés, there were others who obtained foreign protection, too. Their privileges will be examined, as well. Furthermore, I will quantify the growth of the protection system in an attempt to establish how many people fell under consular jurisdiction throughout the eighteenth century. Finally, Chapter Two contains a discussion of the European and Ottoman policies *vis-à-vis* the extension of capitulatory privileges to Ottoman subjects. Chapter Three offers an analysis of the phenomenon of *avania*, a key term in Western accounts of the Ottoman justice system—especially its perceived capriciousness. I will analyse several case studies of incidents from all over the Ottoman Empire that were labelled *avania*s in Western sources within the context of the Ottoman administrative and legal system.

The methodology of case studies is even more prominent in the second part of this study. It consists of three detailed case studies of legal disputes involving foreigners and non-Muslim protégés. The use of case studies is normal for students of legal history, but it is not a fashionable methodology among historians of the Ottoman Empire. Edhem Eldem, for example, has argued that we should not devote too much attention to individual cases, which may be colourful, but are often not representative. It is on the structural problems and developments that the historian should focus, according to Eldem.[22]

---

[22] Edhem Eldem, *French Trade in Istanbul in the Eighteenth Century* (Leiden, 1999), 229 n. 14.

For the determination of the practical boundaries of consular jurisdiction in the Ottoman context, however, case studies are indispensable. These boundaries were defined and redefined by individual disputes that challenged (fixed ideas about) them.

Our cases have several things in common. Firstly, their principal location is Aleppo, although the Porte was important in the first two cases, and the cadi court in Basra had a major influence on the third. Because Aleppo is one of the most studied cities in the Ottoman Empire, focusing on cases there enables us to identify local circumstances that influenced the dynamics between the jurisdictions of consuls and qadis. All three cases date from the second half of the eighteenth century, a period generally believed to have been characterized by declining Ottoman control over the capitulatory system. Their number is obviously too limited to justify firm conclusions, but these cases will shed some light on the extent to which the practical implementation of the capitulations changed in this period. These cases predominantly concern the Dutch and English consulates. According to the capitulations all foreign communities had the same legal status, so in theory an analysis of Dutch and English examples are also relevant for the French, the Danes, and all other foreigners with capitulatory privileges. It is possible, however, that the implementation of these privileges was somehow affected by the geopolitical importance of these countries for the Ottomans. By the eighteenth century the Dutch Republic had long lost its political and military importance in the Eastern Mediterranean, while Great Britain would become one of the most dominant powers in the region at the end of this period. Our cases will therefore also indicate whether or not this made any difference in the practical implementation of their legal privileges in the second half of the eighteenth century.

Finally, the selection of these cases requires an explanation. To a large extent the material itself determined this choice. In both the Ottoman and European sources one finds innumerable references to legal disputes. Sometimes they are mentioned only in passing, remaining outside of the scope of the sources, and hence beyond the grasp of the historian. Other conflicts of a legal nature are described somewhat more extensively, providing us clues about the substance of the dispute, or the procedures followed. Sometimes only a complaint has remained, sometimes just the verdict, or a description of an intermediate phase. Taken together these snippets of information—maybe comparable with the pottery shards found by archaeologists[23]—provide an image of the legal status of foreigners and their protégés in the Ottoman Empire in the eighteenth century, and I have included several as context for my case studies. It is, however, the cases I found more or less complete and intact that I put on display. My aim to present three thematically different cases further narrowed down the available corpus.

Published Texts

During the nineteenth century a number of compendia of texts were published that remain valuable instruments for comparative research on the capitulatory system. The first is E. Charrière's monumental collection of French treaties and capitulations, whose text of the controversial French capitulations of 1536 I have relied on.[24] The collection of relevant documents by Ignace Baron de Testa is useful, but this compendium, too, exclusively concerns French-Ottoman relations. The same is true for the contemporary, more concise compendium by F.A. Belin.[25] For this study I have primarily used Gabriel Efendi Noradounghian's work, which, by contrast, contains the most important treaties and capitulations concerning a large number of Western European powers. Most of the texts are French translations of the original Ottoman, but some occur in Italian. A collection of texts gathered by a former Ottoman ambassador to London, Musurus Paşa, formed the basis of the work by Noradounghian, who has also done extensive research in the archives of the Ottoman state and several European states, using published texts, chronicles and the works of Hammer, d'Ohsson and other prominent authors, too.[26]

Useful as these collections are for comparative purposes, they do

[23] The comparison between archival research and archaeology has been used before, for example by Dick Douwes, *Justice and Oppression: Ottoman Rule in the Province of Damascus and the District of Hama, 1785–1841* (PhD Dissertation: Nijmegen, 1993). A reworked version, called *Ottomans in Syria. A History of Justice and Oppression* was published by I.B. Tauris in 2000.

[24] E. Charrière (ed.), *Négociations de la France dans le Levant* I (Paris, 1848).

[25] Ignace baron de Testa, *Recueil des traités de la Porte Ottomane avec les Puissances étrangers depuis le premier traité conclu en 1536*... (Paris, 1864–1898); F.A. Belin, *Des capitulations et des traités de la France en Orient* (Paris, 1870).

[26] Gabriel Effendi Noradounghian, *Recueil d'actes internationaux de l'empire ottoman I: 1300–1789* (Paris, 1897).

not offer the Ottoman texts of the relevant documents, which are indispensable for the present study, because, as Noradounghian explains, "lorsque les parties contractantes ont à invoquer ces Traités, elles ont recours au texte turc, les traductions, même officielles, n'étant pas reconnues comme faisant loi."[27] Modern editions of some texts are available. For example, Dariusz Kołodziejczyk has recently published an impressive edition of Ottoman-Polish *ahdnames*, offering transliterations of the Ottoman texts with English translations and facsimiles of a considerable number of texts. Hans Theunissen has produced a similarly learned edition of Ottoman-Venetian capitulations from their initiation to 1640, which can be consulted online.[28]

An Ottoman publication that contains various texts of capitulations is Feridun Beg's *Münşeat-i Selatin*, which was continued by others after the author's death in 1583. This work should be treated with some caution, however, because some of the texts included were fictitious. At the end of the nineteenth century a large number of relevant texts was printed in the *Muahedat Mecmuası*. Despite the fact that it is often unclear on the basis of which sources these texts were published, and that not all texts were printed in full, this is an important publication for comparative research.[29]

Alexander de Groot has published a critical edition of the Dutch capitulation of 1612, along with an analytical description of the mission of the first Dutch ambassador to the sultan's court. This text was renewed only once, in 1680, and this text remained valid until the capitulations were abolished. A comparison of the two texts shows that the latter is more accurately described as a confirmation of existing privileges, the contents being identical to the text of 1612.[30] The

[27] Ibid., Préface.

[28] Dariusz Kołodziejczyk, *Ottoman-Polish Diplomatic Relations (15th–18th Century). An Annotated Edition of 'Ahdnames and Other Documents* (Leiden, 2000); Theunissen, *Ottoman-Venetian Diplomatics: The* 'Ahd-Names. *The Historical Background and the Development of a Category of Political-Commercial Instruments together with an Annotated Edition of a Corpus of Relevant Documents* has been published on the Internet. See the Electronic Journal of Oriental Studies of Utrecht University, the Netherlands, at www.let.uu.nl/oosters/EJOS/EJOS-1.2.html. See the bibliography there for earlier editions of these texts. Also see Gökbilgin, M. Tayyib, 'Venedik devlet arşivindeki Türkçe belgeler koleksiyonu ve bizimle ilgile diğer belgeler', *Belgeler* V–VIII (1968–1971) 9–12, 1–152.

[29] Feridun Beg, *Münşeat-i Selatin* (Istanbul, 174–1275/1858); *Muahedat Mecmuası* (1294/1877–); About reliability of the former work see "Feridun Beg" (J.H. Mordtmann—[V.L. Ménage]), *EI*², 881–882.

[30] A.H. de Groot, *The Ottoman Empire and the Dutch Republic. A History of the Earliest*

first *ahdname* granted to England in 1580 has been edited by Susan Skilliter, who published other relevant documents from the earliest period of Anglo-Ottoman relations at the same time. Necmi Ülker has published transliterated texts of the capitulations granted to England in 1580, 1601 and 1675, without the Ottoman originals.[31] An excellent German edition of the first Prussian *ahdname* of 1761 exists, consisting of a translation with a facsimile.[32] Finally, an article by Viorel Panaite, whose work in general offers valuable comparative material for the present study, contains transliterations of articles about the legal status of merchants from the Ottoman-Polish *ahdnames* in the seventeenth century.[33]

No critical edition seems to exist of arguably most important text, i.e. the French capitulation of 1740. Apart from the *Muahedat Mecmuası*, I have therefore relied on the "French" *Ecnebi Defteri* 29/4 in the Başbakanlık Osmanlı Arşivi in Istanbul. Another Ottoman copy of this text, in MS 780 of the Eggerton collection in the British Library, also contains a contemporary French translation, which I have used. It is on these Ottoman primary texts that we must base our assessment of the privileges awarded by the sultans to foreigners and their protégés.

Diplomatic Relations 1610–1630 (Leiden/Istanbul, 1978). For a French translation of the text of 1680, see Noradounghian, *Recueil* I, 169–181.

[31] S.A. Skilliter, *William Harborne and the Trade with Turkey 1578–1582. A Documentary Study of the First Anglo-Ottoman Relations* (Oxford, 1977); Necmi Ülker, 'XVII. Yüzyılın ikinci yarısında İzmir'deki İngiliz tüccarına dair ticarî problemlerle ilgili belgeler', *Belgeler* XIV (1989–1992), 306–308 [1580], 309–311 [1601], 312–314 [1675]. Ülker republished the same texts, again without facsimiles, in his *XVII. ve XVIII. yüzyıllarda İzmir şehri tarihi I. Ticaret tarihi araştırmaları* (Izmir, 1994), 126 ff.

[32] Helmuth Scheel, 'Die Schreiben der türkischen Sultane an die preußischen Könige in der Zeit von 1721 bis 1774 und die ersten preußischen Kapitulationen vom Jahre 1761', *Mitteilungen des Seminars für Orientalische Sprachen zu Berlin. Zweite Abteilung, Westasiatische Studien* XXXIII (1930), 1–82.

[33] Viorel Panaite, *The Ottoman Law of War and Peace. The Ottoman Empire and Tribute Payers* (Boulder, 2000); Ibid., 'Islamic Tradition and Ottoman Law of Nations', *Archæus* IV/4 (2000), 123–140; Ibid., 'The Status of Trade and Merchants in the Ottoman-Polish *'Ahdnāmes* (1607–1699)', *Archív orientální. Supplementa VIII* (1998), 275–298; I am grateful to Dariusz Kołodziejczyk for bringing Panaite's work to my attention and to Colin Heywood for giving me some of this author's articles.

CHAPTER ONE

THE SULTAN'S PROMISE

The privileges the European mercantile communities in the Levant enjoyed were based on two promises, one from the sultan, the other from the sovereign to whom the *ahdname* in question was granted. The beneficiaries vowed that they would maintain peaceful relations with the Sublime Porte and its subjects in general, and not capture and enslave Ottoman mariners and merchants in particular. On the condition that they kept their word, the sultan in his turn guaranteed the implementation of the privileges codified in his "letter of promise".[1] This chapter focuses on several aspects of the contents of the capitulations that have not been sufficiently examined before. For this study the question of which jurisdictions the *ahdname*s recognized is particularly important, forming the subject of the second part of this chapter. The first part deals with five other relevant aspects of the capitulatory system: *berat*s and *ferman*s as additional documentary evidence; the revocation of privileges; the definition of foreign communities; and the tax exemptions granted by the sultan. First the dynamics of the system need to be examined, starting with the notion of "sacred capitulations".

Sacred Capitulations

In his study on Wallachia, Moldavia and Transylvania under Ottoman rule, Panaite has extensively discussed the Islamic legal prescripts concerning the honouring of pacts, a principle called *pacta sunt servanda* in the West. Referring to the Koran and other sources of Islamic law, the author argues that in principle pacts must be honoured according to *şeriat*. The jurists specify various reasons for which the Islamic ruler may legitimately break pacts, but Panaite empha-

[1] The Arabic *'ahd*, promise, with the Persian *nāme*, letter. On the various terms used for these texts, see Kołodziejczyk, *Ottoman-Polish Diplomatic Relations*, 32–34.

sizes that the Ottomans always felt the need to justify their actions on the basis of *şeriat* when they broke treaties.[2] This section focuses on Western ideas about the sanctity of pacts concluded by the Ottomans, which is epitomized by the recurrence of the phrase "sacred capitulations" in Western diplomatic correspondence.[3]

These words also occur in contemporary translations of Ottoman texts, which might suggest that it was used by the Ottoman chancery, too. Speaking about the late seventeenth century Panaite argues that "in this period of military decline took place the transition from the holy war to 'holy peace', due to the fact that in the Ottoman chancery the attribute 'sacred' (*mübarek*) was regularly joined to the term 'peace' [*sulh*]."[4] The word *mübarek* was undoubtedly used in this context to emphasize that the peace was in conformity with Islamic law. It would seem possible, therefore, that a similar term was used to legitimise the grant of *ahdname*s. A comparison of contemporary translations with the original Ottoman texts suggests that this is not the case however. A letter by the *Şeyhülislâm* in Istanbul to the qadi of Aleppo of 1731 is a case in point. The Italian translation of the document suggest that even the highest religious officer in the Ottoman empire attributed divine sanction to the *ahdname*s, the implementation of which he recommended to the provincial Islamic judge. However, a comparison with the Ottoman text reveals that "sacre capitulationi" is a translation of *ahdname-i hümayun*, which means nothing more than "imperial capitulations".[5] The same procedure is found in documents translated from Western languages into Ottoman. Some petitions to the Porte occasionally speak of "sacred capitulations" in the originals, but in the Ottoman translations this phrase is rendered as *ahdname-i hümayun*.[6]

---

[2] Panaite, *The Ottoman Law of War and Peace*, 284–291.

[3] Vera Constantini, 'Il commercio veneziano ad Aleppo nel settocento', *Studi Veneziani* XLII (2001), 143–211, esp. 154: "Nei documenti veneziani del Settecento, le Capitulazioni vengono raremente nominate senza l'accompagna-mento dell'aggettivo 'sacre'."

[4] Panaite, *The Ottoman Law of War and Peace*, 79.

[5] DNA, LAT 1095, 78: Letter of recommendation by the *Şeyhülislâm*, Dürri Mehmed Efendi, in Istanbul to the qadi of Aleppo [1731], Ottoman with Italian translation. The same translation of *ahdname-i hümayun* as "Sacre Capitulazioni" is found in NA, LAT 1118: *I'lâm* [1760s], Ottoman with Italian translation. On this *Şeyhülislâm* see 'Dürrīzade" (J.R. Walsh), *EI*^{2}, 629–630.

[6] DNA, LAT 1095, 52–53: Italian translation of a letter by the Dutch ambassador, Cornelis Calkoen, to the *müsellim* of Aleppo, 18 November [1731].

The phrase "sacred capitulations" is a meaningful metaphor. In the minds of the Europeans, their privileges in the Ottoman Empire were practically written in stone. They were definitive and immutable and any violation of these "sacred" texts carried the connotation of sin. The capitulatory corpus formed the sole legal basis for the status of foreigners in the Ottoman Empire, most Europeans believed, and few ever expressed any doubt that the interpretation of the *ahdnames* that was the most favourable to the foreigners was the only legitimate way of reading them.

In the eyes of the Westerners the *ahdnames* were superior to any other "law of the land". Support for this view could be found in the capitulations, which generally stated that commands of prior or ulterior date should not be listened to if they were contrary to the capitulations.[7] Despite the fact that this order was undoubtedly meant to reinforce particular privileges, taken out of context it appeared to confirm the Europeans' ideas about the primacy of the capitulations. At the same time the foreigners frequently solicited the issue of Ottoman decrees that amended and extended their privileges. Confirmations of existing privileges were also important, because their implementation by provincial and local authorities often depended on them. The *ahdnames* thus were nor immutable, and amendments, clarifications, and, sometimes, revisions were part of the on-going process of keeping the texts in tune with reality.

The fact that the *ahdnames* allowed various interpretations was an uncomfortable reality for the Europeans to face. If an interpretation of the capitulations that was unfavourable to the Europeans could be argued on the basis of the text just as easily as a favourable interpretation, they might lose the argument. This could create a precedent on the basis of which other unfavourable decisions might follow, which might lead to a gradual erosion of the privileges codified in the capitulations. This was to be avoided at all cost, the European diplomats thought. However, even the ambassadors occasionally had to admit that unfavourable interpretations were not necessarily unreasonable, or unjust. Paradoxically the solution to this problem was to avoid too specific references to the capitulations in communications with the Ottoman authorities altogether. The English ambassador,

---

[7] See, for example, article 25 in the French capitulation of 1604, quoted below on page 21.

Sir James Porter, confirms this explicitly in a letter to the English consul and factory in Aleppo. The community in Aleppo had complained to Porter about the unwarranted demands of the Ottoman collector of customs duties (*emin-i gümrük*), who wanted the English to pay the duties on silk in Dollars. Instead of 10 *akçe* he demanded three thirds of a Dollar per bale. Article 64 of the renewed English capitulations of 1675 stated specifically that the duty on silk was 10 *akçe* per bale.[8] At the time the exchange rate was 14 *akçe* to the Dollar, more or less the sum demanded by the *emin-i gümrük*, but in the meantime the exchange rate had changed. By 1747 it was 120 *akçe* to the Dollar, making the duty of 10 *akçe* not three thirds, but one twelfth of a Dollar. The devaluation of the *kuruş* (which consisted of 40 *akçe*) had been to the advantage of the English, but it decreased the revenues of the tax collector. The English community thought that an imperial decree (*ferman*) on the basis of the capitulations reiterating their privileges in detail would prevent the "customer" pursuing the matter further, so they asked the ambassador to obtain the decree. Porter agreed that this development had to be stopped, but he did not consider it wise to point to specific articles of the capitulations. He explained this as follows:

> The capitulations were renew'd by J[oh]n Finch in the year 1675 and several parts of them were amended & explain'd, this was the end of that renewal. In a translation I have [had] made here, as well as in an English one branch'd out into articles, the first branch or article is a pure recital of the duty's goods should pay as agreed upon in 1653. It is there said *specifically that silk shall pay 10 Osmanys per bale &c.*[9]
>
> In the second branch or article which seems to relate merely to 1675 one would conclude that it annuls the former, and substitutes *3 per cent for all goods* exported and imported, as if that duty implied the whole, for if that second branch is only a continuation of the recital made in the first, what doth it mean? Something or nothing, if the former it is an addition to the 10 Osmanys which were also exacted, if the latter it is absurd.
>
> This I say I suspected a delicate difficulty, for with the Reis Efendi[10]

---

[8] . . . *ve haririn her dengine onar Osmanî . . . alınup*. Ülker, 'XVII. Yüzyılın . . . belgeler', 261–320, esp. 312.

[9] Original underscoring. In the same letter Porter writes: ". . . call it Aspers [*akçe*] or Osmanys, it is the same thing."

[10] The *reisülküttab*, the Ottoman chancellor who acted as a kind of Foreign Secretary. For an overview of the development of the Ottoman chancery from c. 1700 in general, and this office in particular, see Virginia Aksan, *An Ottoman Statesman in War and Peace. Ahmed Resmi Efendi 170–1783* (Leiden, 1995), 1–23.

> full of metaphysical criticism, he is the first man in this country to lay his finger on such a dilemma, the consequence of which must have been the subjecting the whole Trade of the Levant to a duty of 3 per cent and even on that valuable branch you mention.

Porter admitted that the English had been fortunate. If the exchange rate had changed to their disadvantage, they would also have had to pay the exact sum mentioned in the capitulations. Nevertheless, the ambassador did not want to risk alerting the Porte to the ambiguous meaning of the subsequent capitulatory article for fear of negative consequences for the English Levant trade. Porter thus reported that "these considerations made me think it best to limit the complaint to general grievances, and to have the ancient custom & capitulations ascertained without entering into the consideration of the value of money, which would have led us into a long discussion and in the meantime have been a vast expense by the detention of the ships."[11]

Ambassador Porter's ideas were strongly supported by the Levant Company. So much so that the company even complained to the ambassador when he obtained from the Porte an authentic copy of the Ottoman text of the English capitulations for the consul in Izmir, Samuel Crawley. In a letter to Porter the Levant Company remarked that

> if those he [Crawley] had were legible, we could have wished that he had been contented with them, for We think that the less Use there is made of them, they have perhaps the more Force, as it is often a happy circumstance when a Turkish Governor does not exactly know the utmost extent of his Power, least he should be inclinable to go as far as ever he can.[12]

On the one hand the capitulations thus were "sacred" to most Europeans in the Ottoman Empire, and ambassadors, consuls and merchants did their utmost to uphold the privileges they thought they were entitled to. On the other hand, when they benefited from ambiguities in the texts, the same foreigners were often reluctant to base their arguments on their charters of privileges, lest the Ottoman authorities discover loopholes. This approach to the capitulations is

[11] BNA, SP 110/74 (IV): Porter to the Consul and Factory of Aleppo, 18 April 1747.

[12] BNA, SP 105/119, 1: The Levant Company, London, to James Porter, 28 July 1758.

characteristic of Europeans in the Ottoman Empire in the eighteenth century. They clung to the notion that the *ahdname*s were immutable, while incessantly seeking to extend their privileges at the same time. In practice most ambassadors and consuls took more pragmatic positions, but these are seldom reflected in the official correspondence. Only if we dig deeper, do traces appear of the ways in which the apparent gap between the Europeans' expectations and the Ottoman perception of their privileges was bridged. Before we turn to the practical aspects of the capitulations, however, I want to make two important points about the capitulatory system. Firstly, it was not based exclusively on the *ahdname*s, but on several other kinds of imperial orders as well. Secondly, the Porte retained the right to revoke all these documents at any time. These points will be discussed further in the following paragraphs.

Ferman*s and* Berat*s*

In the Introduction I have argued that the *ahdname*s formed a network of interconnected charters of privileges. The capitulations codified basic arrangements that enabled foreign merchants to reside in the Ottoman Empire indefinitely without becoming subjects of the sultan. Merchants of nations without capitulations of their own either had to obtain them, or operate under the flag of a nation that did have formal relations with the Porte. In that sense the *ahdname*s were a *sine qua non* for international trade.

Capitulations could also be "renew'd, amended & explain'd", as Porter phrased it. Upon the accession of a new sultan, he usually confirmed the orders issued by his predecessor as part of the ceremonies. This confirmation included the capitulations, which remained valid and unchanged under the new ruler. When a European power wanted to change, or, more commonly, extend its privileges, a renewal was necessary. In contrast to a confirmation, a renewal entailed prolonged discussions with the highest Ottoman officials and a considerable investment in the form of fees and gifts. When in 1680 the first Dutch capitulations of 1612 had to be renegotiated, the costs were so high and the result so disappointing, that the Dutch ambassador considered the whole procedure a form of extortion (*avania*).[13]

---

[13] DNA, SG 12578.55: "True account or report . . . in the form of a diary writ-

In the course of the seventeenth and eighteenth century only the French and the English obtained several renewals with numerous additional privileges. On the basis of the most-favoured-nation principle these privileges also applied to all other foreigners, but this was not automatically the case. Whenever a new privilege was codified in a renewed *ahdname*, the ambassadors of other nations had to apply to the Porte for *ferman*s confirming that the privilege also applied to their merchants. The other nations thus eventually profited from the numerous French renewals and extensions of privileges, but the advantage for the French was that for a short period they alone enjoyed them. The fact that it was important to have copies of the *ahdname*s of other nations is illustrated by the chancery archive of the Dutch embassy in Istanbul, which included translations of the capitulations of England (1675), Sicily (1740), and Denmark (1746).[14]

The period between the acquisition of a nation's capitulations and their renewal is also important. The Europeans applied for *ferman*s constantly, and the Ottoman registers are thus filled with summaries of them. In many cases these orders merely confirmed a capitulatory privilege, explicitly naming one or more foreigners as beneficiaries. Other imperial decrees explained ambiguous articles, or applied existing stipulations to new situations. Many concerned trade. Whenever a new tax was introduced, the Europeans had to obtain new *ferman*s exempting them. Both the Ottoman and the ambassadorial chanceries charged fees, which were paid by the individual merchants if only they profited from the *ferman*. When the orders served the interests of the entire community, the expenses were charged to the communal treasury. Recurrent problems for which new *ferman*s had to be obtained repeatedly were thus expensive for the European communities. The accumulation of such problems could be a reason for a foreign community to invest in a renewal of the capitulations, with additional articles addressing these issues.

Two forms of *berat*s, Ottoman deeds of appointment, were also part of the capitulatory system. The European consuls and vice-consuls were appointed by their home authorities, but without an Ottoman

---

ten about everything that happened after 14 August 1680, in relation to the *avania* that befell the whole Dutch nation in the Levant." The result was disappointing because the text of 1680 was virtually identical to that of 1612 and did not contain any new articles.

[14] DNA, LAT 1042.

deed of appointment they could not function. The same is true of the *berat*s issued to the dragomans in actual service and the honorary dragomans, or protégés. Generally recruited from the non-Muslim subjects of the sultan, they received extensive privileges. Every consul, dragoman and protégé needed an individual deed of appointment confirming his privileged status. They usually applied for a confirmatory *ferman*, too.[15] As an incident described in the next chapter will show, consuls who attempted to assume their office without having their *berat*, could well get in trouble with the Ottoman authorities. These consular and dragomans' *berat*s contained articles that were not in the capitulations, effectively elaborating on them. For example, the early consular *berat*s emphasized that the foreign merchants should accept the authority and jurisdiction of their own consuls, without being "obstinate and opposing" (*inad-ü mühalifet etmeyeler*).[16] By the eighteenth century consular authority was firmly established, and this article no longer occurred in consular *berat*s. Other clauses reflecting currant issues at the time then appear, like the prohibition to purchase or own real estate or land in the Ottoman Empire. This rule was only introduced in consular *berat*s at the end of the eighteenth century.[17] Any examination of the capitulatory system therefore has to take these documents into account as well.

Revocation

The right and the capacity of the Sublime Porte to revoke the privileges of foreigners and their protégés are seldom acknowledged in the relevant literature. The *ahdname*s were part of the Ottoman administrative and legal system. All official documents were issued by the

[15] See, for example, BOA, A.DVN.DVE 81/70, end Cemaziyülevvel 1183/22 September–1 October 1769; BOA, A.DVN.DVE 99/2, end Zilhicce 1195/8–16 December 1781 and DNA, LAT 1090, docs 4, 12–16, 18–20, 26, 33, 37, 47.

[16] UBL Cod. Or. 1228, f. 169; Quoted from the *berat* of Cornelis Witsen, appointed Dutch consul in Aleppo mid Safer 1039/29 September-8 October 1629. On questions of (the lack of) consular authority, see the articles by Rhoads Murphy and Merlijn Olnon in Alastair Hamilton, Alexander H. de Groot and Maurits H. van den Boogert (eds), *Friends and Rivals in the East. Studies in Anglo-Dutch Relations in the Levant from the Seventeenth to the Early Nineteenth Century* (Leiden, 2000).

[17] DNA, Collection De Hochepied, 1611–1956, no. 86: [Contemporary] traduction du Bérat du Consul de Smyrne et ses dépendances pour le Citoyen Lanmond, Consul de la Répub*lique* Fran*çaise*, 25 Rebiülevvel 1210/8 November 1795.

Imperial Chancery, and without the Imperial cypher (*tuğra*) and other Ottoman marks of authenticity, these texts had no authority. It was also in the Porte's power to revoke these documents, collectively or individually. Even individual privileges could be revoked.[18]

The capitulations were granted on the condition that the beneficiaries honoured their promise to maintain peaceful relations with the Ottoman Empire. The most serious violations of this pledge of peace generally occurred at the hands of privateers, who commonly had little regard for the laws and international agreements within which they were supposed to operate. Both the Porte and the European authorities explicitly considered acts of piracy a threat to the stability of political and commercial relations.[19] However, piracy seldom led to a breakdown of diplomatic relations, something that only happened when war broke out.

Napoleon's invasion of Egypt in 1798 shows which measures the Ottomans took against the enemy in their midst in times of war. Throughout the empire French nationals were arrested and put in prison, where many of them remained until France agreed to withdraw its troops from Egypt in 1802. The ambassador and consuls shared their fate. These developments also affected the Ottoman protégés of the French embassy and consulates, for their *berat*s were revoked collectively. The Ottoman administration of French affairs was suspended altogether between 1798 and 1802.[20]

The Dutch also suffered from the war between France and the Ottoman Empire. Meanwhile the Dutch Republic had been invaded by the French armies, and had been turned into the Batavian Republic, a satellite state of France. The Batavian Republic had its own ambassador at the Porte, but his country's ties with France dragged it into

[18] The Dutch were confronted with this as late as the beginning of the nineteenth century. See Gaspard Testa [in Istanbul] to Goldberg, 15 January 1816: "[Your Excellency] ne doit pas ignorer, que d'après nos capitulations avec la Porte existant depuis l'an 1612 ce privilège est accordé à notre pavillon sur le pied des autres nations commerçantes, mais par le laps du tem*p*s, qui s'était écoulé sans que nos navires en profitassent, cette concession était regardée comme nulle . . .", *Bronnen* IV/ii, 882.

[19] Maurits H. van den Boogert, 'Redress for Ottoman Victims of European Privateering. A Case against the Dutch in the *Divan-i Hümayun* (1708–1715)', *Turcica* 33 (2001), 91–118.

[20] BOA, CH 1309, 15 Şaban 1213/22 January 1799. The four-year gap can clearly be seen in BOA, ED 27/2.

the conflict with the sultan. The ambassador was allowed to withdraw to Belgrade to await further developments, but the situation affected Dutch communities throughout the Ottoman Empire. Consulates were closed, and consular personnel lost their privileges and risked imprisonment. These measures were not taken spontaneously by provincial authorities, but were ordered from Istanbul. The Porte sent orders to numerous Ottoman centres of trade to report about the presence of any French or Dutch subjects.[21] The central authorities also announced that the *berat*s of all protégés of these nations were revoked, a measure that is traceable in the Ottoman Foreigners' Registers, where entries for consular and dragomans' *berat*s were crossed out. Contrary to their French colleagues, the Dutch/Batavian consuls were not imprisoned in retaliation for the French invasion of Egypt, and some were able to maintain their positions to some extent.[22]

More limited measures could affect groups of protégés. At the end of 1764 the Porte wanted to curb the European practice of employing non-Muslim Ottoman subjects as vice-consuls. By this time the Ottoman authorities had fixed maximum numbers of dragomans for every capitulatory nation, but no limit was imposed on the number of vice-consulates. In the Ionian Islands, in particular, this had lead to an increasing number of indigenous merchants acquiring the status of foreign vice-consul. This development should not be overestimated, as they probably numbered only several dozen individuals per foreign power, but the Ottoman authorities objected, nevertheless. In order to end this practice the Porte literally struck their consular *berat*s from the records in 1764, but due to a lack of enforcement in subsequent years, the ranks of the vice-consuls in European service swelled again later.[23]

---

[21] See for the Ottoman documents about this procedure BOA, CH 264, beginning Ramazan 1213/6–15 February 1799; Ibid., 1140, 19 Muharrem 1214/23 June 1799; Ibid., 1246, 18 Ramazan 1213/23 February 1799; Ibid., 1309, 15 Şevval 1213/22 March 1799; Ibid., 1666, 21 Ramazan 1213/26 February 1799; Ibid., 1807, 9 Şevval 1213/16 March 1799. I am grateful to my friend and colleague İsmail Hakkı Kadı for providing me with these documents.

[22] Jan van Maseijk, the Batavian consul in Aleppo, for example, adopted Prussian protection and actively interceded with the authorities in Aleppo on behalf of the French prisoners. DNA, LAT 167, letters by Van Maseijk to (probably) ambassador Van Dedem van de Gelder dated 18 July 1799 and 11 April 1800 (in French).

[23] BOA, ED 22/1, 350/1518, 26 Zilkade 1171/1 August 1758, marginal note

The individual revocation of capitulatory privileges was also possible. In Chapter Two the example of Jirjis A'ida, a dragoman of the English consulate in Aleppo, will show that corruption charges could be a reason for the withdrawal of a dragoman's *berat*. Such incidents were rare, however. Until the early nineteenth century most dragomans held their appointments until they were dismissed, gave them up voluntarily, or died.

In 1806 numerous dragomans lost their *berat*s due to an Ottoman policy change. A sultanic writ ordered all protégés of France, Great Britain, Austria, Russia and Prussia who did not reside in the same place as the consulates with which they were formally connected to return to their stations. Disobedience would lead to the revocation of their *berat*s. Despite protests from the ambassadors of these nations, the Porte acted on its threat, and withdrew several dozen *berat*s when their holders did not comply with its wishes.[24]

The Europeans' hold on their privileges was firm, but external developments could weaken, or even break it. The Sublime Porte was able to suspend the capitulatory system unilaterally, if circumstances called for such drastic steps. It could revoke the privileges of communities as a whole, but the same was true for individual *berat*s, too. The Porte did not take these measures lightly, but the fact that it could and did take them during the second half of the eighteenth century indicates that the capitulatory system was still controlled by the Ottomans in this period. The military balance of power had certainly shifted in the Europeans' favour by this time, but the day-to-day relations between Westerners and their Ottoman environment were still ruled by the Porte's orders in the form of capitulations, *berat*s and *fermans*. It is time now to turn our attention to these texts to delineate the boundaries of the capitulatory system.

---

dated beginning Cemaziyelevvel 1178/27 October–5 November 1764 (Dutch vice-consul in Athens); Ibid., 381/1649, 12 Cemaziyelevvel 1176/29 November 1762, marginal note of the same date (Dutch vice-consul in Negropont); ED 35/1, 86/224, 14 Cemaziyelahir 1153/7 August 1740, marginal note of the same date (English vice-consul in Chios).

[24] BOA, ED 27/2, 169/806, beginning Şevval 1221/12–21 December 1806 (Salonica); 169/807, 3 Cemaziyelevvel 1221/19 July 1806 (Yanina and Narda); 169/809, end Cemaziyelevvel 1221/6–15 August 1806 (Izmir). Eleven more entries were crossed out on these pages of the register. The Ottoman measures are also mentioned in the records of the Capuchin missionaries. Archivum Generale Cappucini, Rome, A.D. 106 I (1626–1834), 208.

Müste'mins

What it was exactly that the sultans promised befriended foreigners must be determined on the basis of the *ahdnames*, supplementary *fermans* and the consular and dragomans' *berats*. Together they form the documentary basis of the capitulatory system. They cover a wide range of issues over an extended period of time. Since the focus of this study is the Europeans' interaction with the Ottoman legal system in the eighteenth century, I will focus on the legal aspects. Other aspects will be discussed in more general terms.

The privileges the Ottoman authorities granted communities of foreign merchants can be divided into three categories. The first is a group of arrangements concerning the basic conditions of foreign life in the Levant, while the second concerns trade related privileges. The third category is that of the articles regarding the position of Westerners and their protégés vis-à-vis the Ottoman legal system.

The capitulations applied to a group of merchants, the members of which were not individually named in the text, and remained valid as long as the foreigners maintained friendship and peace with the Ottoman state. This meant that, in theory, individual merchants arriving in the Ottoman Empire from countries with which the Porte maintained diplomatic relations did not have to apply for an individual safe-conduct (*aman*) anymore. Their sojourn was also not limited to a prescribed period. The controversial French capitulations of 1536 contains an article (no. 14) that limits the French merchants' stay to a period of ten consecutive years, but it appears in none of the later capitulations, French or otherwise.[25] This was a departure from the prescripts of Islamic law, which limit the validity of *aman* to one lunar year. The beneficiary of *aman, müste'min*, who stayed longer in the lands under Islamic rule, automatically became a *zimmi*, a protected non-Muslim subject of the sultan. Although this limitation does not occur in any of the capitulations granted after 1536, it remained a sensitive issue at least until the beginning of the nineteenth century. In the *fetva* collection of Mehmed el-Kadusi, which was written in 1808 and appeared in print in 1822, several opinions are found concerning foreigners buying land subject to the land-

[25] Noradounghian, *Recueil*, I, 87; Cf. Charrière, *Négociations*, 283–294.

tax. If they stayed long enough to cultivate the land and harvest the crop, in theory they became subjects of the sultan. In practice this rule does not seem to have been enforced, but people apparently continued to seek the advice of jurisconsults over the legal status of foreigners at least until the nineteenth century.[26]

The capitulations were probably not a continuation of the classical practice of *aman*,[27] but the fact that the Ottomans adopted the terminology of *aman* indicates their desire religiously to legitimise controversial practices. Judging from the diplomatic correspondence this doctrinal weakness does not seem to have provoked many Ottoman qadis or muftis to reject the capitulations.[28] Although research on *fetva* collections of Ottoman *Şeyhülislâms* from the seventeenth to the nineteenth century has not yielded any rulings on the validity of the *ahdnames*, there is evidence that *Şeyhülislâms* not only condoned them, on occasion they actively assisted the Europeans.[29] A letter by *Şeyhülislâm* Dürri-zade Mehmed Efendi in 1731 in which he explicitly recommended the qadi in Aleppo to respect the imperial capitulations has already been mentioned above, but other examples are also known. In the early seventeenth century, for example, the *Şeyhülislâm*, Yahya Efendi (d. 1053/1644), wrote a letter to the Dutch States General confirming the appointment of the first Dutch ambassador to the Porte. At the end of the eighteenth century Dürrizade Mehmed Arif Efendi, *Şeyhülislâm* from 1792 to 1798, wrote a letter to an Ottoman officer in Ankara in support of French traders there.[30] Theoretical limitations of the concept of *aman* generally seem to have been irrelevant in practice.

---

[26] M. Bianchi, 'Recueil de Fetvas, écrit en turk et en arabe, par Hafiz Mohammed ben Ahmed ben Elcheikh Moustafa Elkedousy, imprimée à Constantinople en 1822', *Journal Asiatique* IV (1824), 171–184.

[27] 'Amān' (J. Schacht), *EI*², 429–430. Also see below, p. 56.

[28] For a rare example of a qadi who did challenge the Islamic theoretical basis of the capitulations in Izmir in 1686, see Merlijn Olnon, 'Towards Classifying *Avanias*: A Study of Two Cases involving the English and Dutch Nations in Seventeenth-Century Izmir', in Hamilton et al. (eds), *Friends and Rivals in the East*, 169, 170, 172.

[29] Hilmar Krüger, *Fetwa und Siyar. Zur internationalrechtlichen Gutachtenspraxis der osmanischen Seyh ül-Islām vom 17. bis 19. Jahrhundert undert besonderer Berücksichtigung des 'Behcet ül-Fetāvā'* (Wiesbaden, 1978).

[30] UB Leiden, Cod. Or. 1090, f. 48b, (Yahya Efendi's letter, undated); ibid., Cod. Or. 1354, f. 3a [late December 1797, or early 1798] (Mehmed Arif Dürrizade's letter).

The capitulations also guaranteed foreigners safety of person and property. Protected foreigners were allowed to travel freely by land and by sea. They were not to be taken captive and sold as slaves, if they travelled on ships of hostile powers that were seized by Ottoman corsairs. If they were shipwrecked, their possessions were to be returned to them. If they wished to return to their home country, no one should prevent them from leaving, provided they had paid their debts, or made arrangements for their payment. Other articles enabled foreign merchants and diplomats to a large extent to live the lives they were used to. They were allowed to produce and consume wine in their houses, for example, although this was a capitulatory article for which many Europeans annually obtained a confirmatory *ferman*. Most foreigners retained Western dress, a privilege guaranteed by both the capitulations and the consular *berat*s. They were also allowed to conduct religious services in the privacy of their own homes and in consular chapels.

A privilege of fundamental importance concerned the establishment of consulates and vice-consulates in Ottoman centres of international trade. During the sixteenth, seventeenth and eighteenth centuries the European presence remained limited to Ottoman port cities, like Istanbul, Smyrna (Izmir), Beirut, Acre, and Sidon. Noticeable exceptions were Aleppo, the terminal of caravan routes from the Persian Gulf, and Ankara. The consuls were appointed by their home authorities, but needed to be able to show their Ottoman *berat* to the local authorities in order to be able to function in office. As long as the consuls and vice-consuls were foreigners, the Porte's confirmation of their appointment was a formality, but this changed when the Europeans increasingly appointed local non-Muslim Ottoman notables vice-consul in the course of the eighteenth century. As we have seen, at the end of the century the Porte revoked the *berat*s of a large number of these vice-consuls, but the policy did not have a lasting effect.

Tax Exemptions

Befriended foreigners enjoyed extensive tax exemptions in the Ottoman Empire. They were exempt from paying *bac*, a transit tax, the *masdariye* tax on exported goods, and all *tekalif-i örfiye*, or non-canonical taxes.[31] The exemption from these taxes was also mentioned in the consular and dragomans' *berats*. Naturally the decrease of the general customs tariff from five to three percent was of considerable importance for the foreign merchants' commercial activities. Symbolically, the most important exemption was from the poll tax levied on all adult non-Muslim male subjects. Called *cizye* in the classical terminology, the Ottomans generally referred to it as *haraç*, a land tax in the classical legal texts. Most European merchants could easily have afforded to pay the highest of the three *haraç* categories, which amounted to about eleven *kuruş* per tax-payer throughout the second half of the eighteenth century, but the symbolic value of the tax was undoubtedly more important. Paying the *haraç* was to accept Ottoman rule, and it therefore epitomized the difference between a privileged foreigner and a tributary subject of the sultan.[32]

Tax exemptions determined the foreigners' legal status, too. The Ottomans distinguished two legal classes, despite the fact that this distinction was not rooted in Islamic legal theory. The military class (*askerî*) did not have to pay taxes, in contrast to the common subject class (*reaya*) who did pay taxes. As Colin Imber states "the basic legal divide was not, as in Hanafi law, between Muslim and non-Muslim, but between taxpayers and non-taxpayers." He also calls tax-exemption "perhaps the most important marker of legal status in the Ottoman Empire."[33]

Jurisdictions

Kate Fleet has shown that in the fourteenth century four types of court ruled on matters affecting Genoese merchants in "Turchia",

[31] In Noradounghian's translation of the French capitulations of 1740 the words *tekalif-i örfiyye* are translated as "impôts arbitraires", but Bianchi notes (note V) that this is conducive to error. Bianchi points out that "l'*ourf* est le complément du *cher'i* et n'est plus arbitraire que nos lois et règlements" Noradounghian, *Recueil*, I, 301–302.

[32] 'Djizya ii-Ottoman' (Halil İnalcık), *EI*², 562–566, esp. 564. Also see Henry Grenville, *Observations sur l'etat actuel de l'empire ottoman* Andrew S. Ehrenkreuz (ed.) (Ann Arbor, 1965), 34–40. In 1755 one could buy 11 kg of rice with 11 *kuruş*, but in 1789 the same sum bought only 3 to 4 kg. DNA, Collection 46, no. 7, 'Note de la différence des prix . . . 1755 . . . 1789.'

[33] Colin Imber, *Ebu's-suʿud. The Islamic Legal Tradition* (Edinburgh, 1997), 77, 116.

the lands under Turkish rule. Firstly, there was the consul, who adjudicated all disputes between Latins. His "judicial control [over the Latins] was complete, including imposition of any punishment he thought fit including the death penalty and imprisonment." He was entitled to assistance from the beyliks of Menteşe and Aydın, if he needed it. Any claims from Turks against Latins should be addressed to the consul's court, or to the second type Fleet describes, the Genoese courts in Chios, which Turks occasionally turned to with claims against Genoese subjects. Thirdly, she has found evidence of Turkish courts ruling on complaints from Latins against Turks. Finally, and most surprisingly, Fleet has found evidence of mixed courts, a phenomenon most people associate exclusively with the nineteenth century. This arrangement, which was codified in the 1348 treaty concluded between the Sancta Unio and Aydın, entailed the joint adjudication of disputes by the consul and the *naib*.[34]

Which of these jurisdictions were relevant in the eighteenth century? When it comes to the degree of legal autonomy foreigners enjoyed in the Ottoman Empire, Western sources are generally unreliable. Merchants and diplomats from the West commonly exaggerated the solidity of the guarantees codified in the *ahdname*s. To establish what it was exactly that the sultans promised, we must examine the Ottoman texts of the capitulations and compare them with Western translations.

Consular Jurisdiction

Early works on Western mercantile communities in the Ottoman Empire invariably mention the duties of the consuls, but only in the most summary way. According to these studies the consul was "le répresentant de l'authorité royale, un juge, un protecteur, un guide."[35]

[34] Kate Fleet, 'Turkish-Latin Diplomatic Relations in the Fourteenth Century: The Case of the Consul', in Fleet and van den Boogert (eds), *The Ottoman Capitulations*, 32–43.

[35] Paul Masson, *Histoire du commerce français dans le Levant au XVIIe siècle* (Paris, 1911)—reprinted New York, 1967, 445–446. Wood's words are strikingly similar: "the consuls were thus the representatives of the Company's authority, as well as judges, protectors, and guides." Alfred C. Wood, *A History of the Levant Company* (Oxford, 1935), 219–220.

In this paragraph the boundaries of the consul's role as judge will be delineated, something that has not been adequately done before.

Article 3 of the controversial first French capitulations of 1536 established the outlines of foreign consular jurisdiction. The French king was allowed to appoint an ambassador to the Porte and consuls in provincial Ottoman centres of trade. These officers had the authority to adjudicate all civil and criminal cases among French subjects in their place of residence according to their own customs. The Ottoman qadis and *subaşıs* should not interfere with these cases, unless the ambassador or consul specifically requested Ottoman assistance to force disobedient French merchants to respect consular legal rulings. Whenever qadis adjudicated disputes between French subjects without explicitly having been asked to by the French authorities, the verdicts of the qadis were null and void.[36] This article was largely repeated in the French capitulations of 1569, and it is also found in the first *ahdname* awarded to the English eleven years later. The possibility for the ambassador and consuls to request the assistance of the Ottoman authorities to enforce their orders is not mentioned in these, and subsequent, capitulations, however. The Ottoman text of the English capitulations of 1580, for example, reads:

> *ve eğer İngilterelinin biri ile nizaları olsa mezbur elçileri ve konsolosları âdetlerince faslederler, kimesne mani olmaya.*
>
> and if the English should have disputes one with the other let their aforesaid ambassador and consul decide [them] according to their usage; let no one hinder [them].[37]

Later texts explicitly mention that cases of murder also fell under the jurisdiction of the ambassador and consuls, provided both the victim and the killer were members of the same foreign community. In the Dutch capitulation of 1612 these cases are called *dem ü diyet da'valarī*, "blood and blood money cases".[38]

Until 1740 no capitulatory arrangements existed for the adjudi-

[36] Noradounghian, *Recueil*, i, 84.

[37] Skilliter, *Harborne*, 88. Transliteration based on Ülker, 'İzmir', 308.

[38] For the French capitulations of 1569 (art. 12) and 1673 (art. 16), see Noradounghian, *Recueil*, i, 92 and 139. For the capitulations of Genoa of 1665 (art. 15) and the English one of 1675 (art. 16 and 42), see Ibid., 101, 149, 156. For the Dutch capitulations of 1612 (art. 5), see De Groot, *The Ottoman Empire*, 237 and 251.

cation of disputes among members of different European *nations*. Article 52 of the French capitulations of that year stipulated that

> S'il arrive que les consul et les négociants français aient quelques contestations avec les consuls et les négociants d'une autre nation chrétienne, il leur sera permis du consentement et à la réquisition des parties, de se pourvoir par-devant leurs ambassadeurs qui résident à ma Sublime Porte, et tant que le demandeur et le défendeur ne consentiront pas à porter ces sortes de procès par-devant les pacha, cadi, officiers ou douaniers, ceux-ci ne pourront pas les y forcer ni prétendre en prendre connaissance.[39]

This article formalised a long tradition. The European communities had long dealt with disputes among members of different *nations* by referring complicated matters to their ambassadors. On the basis of the *forum rei* principle the rules of procedure dictated that conflicts be brought before the consul of the defendant.[40] Appeals should be filed with the ambassador of the defendant. The capitulation of 1740 did not codify any of these rules, merely acknowledging the jurisdiction of ambassadors in such matters. At the same time the article allows the possibility that foreigners brought their disputes before the Ottoman judiciary. This article thus does not strengthen the legal privileges of foreigners, but subtly introduces the option of having cases between members of different foreign communities tried before the Ottoman authorities. It is especially significant that the Ottoman judiciary were only forbidden to assert their jurisdiction if both the claimant and the defendant refused the have the case tried by them. This suggests that if either party turned to the qadi or the *beylerbeyi*, the foreign ambassadors could no longer claim exclusive and automatic jurisdiction.

The Europeans tended to emphasize that these articles assigned exclusive authority over all legal disputes involving Westerners to their ambassadors and consuls, while in fact these texts clearly limit consular jurisdiction to cases exclusively involving members of foreign communities. This raises the question of how foreign communities were defined in the capitulations.

While the *ahdname*s invariably mentioned all the territories of the

---

[39] Ibid., 290.

[40] Bianchi points this out in note XXIII to Noradounghian's translation. Ibid., 304.

rulers whose subjects benefited from the privileges awarded by the sultan, the group of beneficiaries was not limited to people originating from these areas. Several capitulations explicitly allowed their beneficiaries to extend protection to merchants from nations that did not have formal relations with the Porte. They were generally referred to as "merchant strangers" in the Western sources. After France had obtained its first capitulations, every non-French merchant arriving in the Ottoman Empire automatically fell under the authority of the French ambassador and consuls, to whom they had to pay consular duties. The Venetians, who had had their own capitulations for a long time, were the only exception. When William Harborne procured an *ahdname* for England in 1580, the French diplomats in the Levant not only lost their English clientele, the English also claimed the right to allow Dutch merchants to conduct trade under the English banner. The French fervently objected to this development, and several disputes ensued over who had authority over the Dutch. The Porte settled this matter in 1604, when the French obtained a renewal of their capitulations. A separate act appended to the capitulations of 1604 determined that "all foreign nations that do not have ambassadors at our Felicitous Porte" fell under the French capitulations.[41] In the course of the seventeenth century, however, this additional clause became a dead letter. The proliferation of capitulations rapidly enlarged the circle of capitulatory nations, and those merchant strangers that remained were free to adopt the protection of any consul they liked.

Most *nations* in the Levant thus comprised merchants from the areas ruled by the sovereign who had been granted capitulations by the sultan, as well as an undefined group of other Western merchants. Apart from the fact that the merchant strangers paid higher consular duties, their status was the same as that of the regular members of foreign communities in the Ottoman Empire.

Besides these Westerners the foreign communities also comprised protected non-Muslim Ottoman subjects. They were the consular dragomans who actually served as interpreters; the honorary dragomans (*beratlıs*) who enjoyed the same status without doing the job; indigenous brokers, moneychangers and warehousemen, and the immediate family of these protégés. Their connections with the foreign

[41] Ibid., 108–110.

communities will be discussed in the Chapter Two. For now suffice it to say that they, too, belonged to the ill-defined foreign *nations* over whose internal conflicts the consuls and ambassadors tended to claim exclusive jurisdiction.

European Consular Regulations

The legal customs in accordance with which the foreign consuls and ambassadors should adjudicate disputes among members of their communities were not specified in the capitulations. In this respect the Porte thus granted the Europeans full autonomy. This did not mean that the consuls and ambassadors could resolve disputes as they saw fit. Each country had its own laws and regulations for such matters, the basic premises of which were similar. Western consuls in the Levant had several official capacities. They represented their country before the local Ottoman authorities. At the same time they were the agents of the national governing body of Levant trade, and had to enforce its regulations. They often also represented a college of admiralty in strictly maritime matters, such as the sale of corsairs' prizes.[42] Finally, they acted as judges of conflicts among members of their own communities. The *ahdname*s only mention the last of these functions, creating a framework for consular legal procedures without prescribing the legal norms that should be applied. These procedures were based on individual acts of delegation of authority by the governments of France, Great Britain, the Dutch Republic and so on, but they were nevertheless similar for all foreign *nation*s in the Levant.

In France the Levant trade was reorganised by Jean-Baptiste Colbert. Originally the French consulates in the Levant were granted by the king as hereditary appendages, but this changed with the reforms of Colbert and those of one of his successors, Louis Comte de Pontchartrain. Colbert gave the Provence the monopoly on French Levant trade. Marseilles thus became the official centre of French commercial traffic with the eastern Mediterranean. The Chambre de Commerce, a body of merchants who supervised the implemen-

---

[42] Jean-Marc David, 'L'amirauté de Provence et des mers du Levant' unpublished doctoral dissertation, Université d'Aix-Marseille, 1942, 299–305; Van den Boogert, 'Redress for Ottoman Victims of European Privateering'.

tation of national trade policies in the Levant, and the Admiralty of the Provence, which was responsible for all naval affairs, both resided in the city. In 1691 the Comte de Pontchartrain initiated another reform, after which the king appointed the French consuls in the Levant, and the Chambre de Commerce paid their salaries. In civil suits, the verdict of the French consul was provisional, as appeal was possible to the provincial parliament of Provence. In criminal matters appeal against the consul's verdict was only possible when corporal punishment was involved. In that case, the consul was only authorized to report the crime, and to send the culprit home in shackles by the first ship that set sail for France. The suspect was then judged by officers of the admiralty of Provence in the first French port where the ship would call.[43]

The English Levant trade was also a monopoly, originally held by a group of twelve merchants on the basis of a royal charter issued in 1581. The Levant Company was given the authority to make laws and ordinances in order to regulate and stimulate trade. It had to work in close cooperation with the admiralty, and it paid for the use of ships and mariners. Originally the king appointed the English ambassadors, but later this was taken over by parliament. The charter was renewed in 1592, after the Levant Company and the Venice Company had joined forces, and again in 1604. The earliest English consuls in the Levant were appointed by the ambassadors, but henceforth by the Levant Company. It was also given broader authority to punish interlopers and disobedient members, and the Company was guaranteed the assistance of England's officials in the maintenance of its rights and privileges. Disputes were to be tried by the consuls and ambassadors, with the option of appeal before the ruling body of the Levant Company.[44] In maritime affairs the High Court of Admiralty was the competent court in England.

In the case of the Dutch Republic the highest body of government, the States General, delegated authority to its consuls in a number of decrees starting in 1612, the year in which the Dutch obtained their first *ahdnames*. The foundation of the College of Directors of Levant Trade and the Navigation of the Mediterranean in 1624

[43] David, 'L'amirauté', 304–305.
[44] Wood, *A History of the Levant Company*, 219–220.

created a bureaucratic apparatus that supervised the implementation of the States General's orders. The college was located in Amsterdam, and consisted of notable merchants who generally had experience in many areas of the Dutch overseas enterprise. On the authority of the States General the Directors corresponded with the Dutch ambassador in Istanbul, as well as with consuls throughout the Mediterranean. Later similar colleges were established in other Dutch cities, but the one in Amsterdam remained the most important. In contrast with the English Levant Company (and, for that matter, the Dutch East India Company) the Colleges of Directors were not given a trade monopoly. The Directors did not have the authority to make laws, and their policies had to conform to the principles of free trade heralded by the States General. The Directors adjudicated disputes between consuls and merchants abroad, but their verdicts had to be confirmed by the States General, which also appointed the ambassador in Istanbul and the Dutch consuls. Like the Chambre de Commerce and the Levant Company, the Dutch 'Colleges of Directors' had close ties with the colleges of admiralty, with which they shared the responsibility for the safety and equipment of ships destined for ports beyond the Straits of Gibraltar. In 1675 the States General adopted a regulation for trade with Istanbul and Izmir alone, but in practice it was valid for other locations as well. Only in 1741 was a slightly extended regulation adopted that was formally valid for all Dutch communities in the Ottoman Empire.[45]

The authority delegated to ambassadors and consuls was broadly similar for all three countries. They were allowed to sequester inheritances of countrymen who had died in the Levant without leaving a will and to arrange for them to be consigned to the heirs. The ambassadors and consuls also had notary powers, enabling them to register contracts, witness statements, bills of lading, wills, and other such documents that were important for the merchants, factors and captains. These documents had the same legal validity as documents drawn up in France, Great Britain or the Dutch Republic, provided they were signed and the chancellor registered them properly in the presence of witnesses. In matters of criminal law ambassadors and consuls had very limited authority. They were only allowed to have

[45] Van Oordt, *De privaatrechterlijke toestand*, 44–53.

offenders arrested and deported home to stand trial there. The home authorities of all three nations also reserved an important role for the assembly of merchants, which should be held regularly. The consul had to consult the congregation of merchants in extraordinary circumstances, and varying numbers of them acted as assistant to the consul. These *assessors* were part of a system of checks and balances, which was meant to prevent the consul abusing his office.

The most important rule of procedure determined that in conflicts between members of different European communities the case should be brought before the consul of the defendant (the *forum rei* principle). Suits should be filed in writing, so that they could be recorded in the consular chancery registers. The claimant could do this in person, but if he belonged to a different *nation* than the defendant he could also ask his own consul formally to represent him, whereupon a dragoman would file the complaint. The defendant was subsequently given some time to respond in writing or orally. In either case a written record was made, which mentioned the date of the reply and the names of at least two witnesses of the proceedings. The European consuls accepted Ottoman legal documents as evidence. The consul could decide to deal with certain matters without a hearing, inviting further written arguments from both parties on the basis of which he would pass judgment. In most cases several written charges, counter-charges and retorts were exchanged before the consul decided that he had sufficient information to reach a verdict. The consul could also organise a hearing where the parties could present their case, or order a council of arbitrators to be established, the members of which were appointed by both parties. The consuls often chose the latter method, upon which they merely ordered the implementation of the arrangements proposed by the arbitration committee. Appeal was only possible to the ambassador of the defendant, whereby the claimant was supported by his own ambassador. The ambassadors often gave verdicts on the basis of the written statements taken during the original consular procedure, but sometimes oral arguments were also presented by proxies of the parties involved.

An example of a dispute that was first adjudicated by the consul and subsequently by the ambassador began in Izmir at the beginning of the eighteenth century. The case was filed by the heirs of the former English consul in Izmir, William Raye. They demanded payment of a sum of 4,800 *kuruş* plus interest from the first dragoman of the consulate in Izmir, Paulo Homero. The debt, which Homero refused to pay, seems to have originated from the rent of a "dwelling house" in Izmir, which must have been owned by Raye. The claim was based on a written acknowledgement of debt given by Homero to Raye on 11 March 1692. The interest demanded was ten percent per annum from 1 January 1692. On 12 November 1705 the English consul in Izmir, William Sherrard, ruled in favour of his predecessor's heirs. He ordered his dragoman to pay 11,400 *kuruş*, the original sum plus interest until 1 October 1705. Homero appealed to the ambassador, Sir Robert Sutton, who confirmed the consul's verdict in April 1706. Any revenue the heirs of Raye had received in the meantime from renting out the house to others was to be deducted from the sum Homero was ordered to pay. Although Homero lost in this particular case, a later dispute involving his heirs indicates that protégés were not necessarily at a disadvantage in such procedures.[46]

It was understood that the parties should accept the final verdict, and comply with it without delay. The involvement of the Ottoman authorities in matters under consular jurisdiction by one of the parties under consular authority—either during procedures or after them—was considered unacceptable by most European representatives, but no formal penalties existed to prevent members of the communities having recourse to a qadi.

The Qadi

In recent years the use of court records (*sicill*) has become increasingly popular among historians and students of the theory and practice of Islamic law.[47] These records shed light on the important role of the courts in Ottoman society. The Ottoman qadi was both Islamic judge and civil administrator at the same time. His primary task was to run the main *mahkema*, the court that dispensed justice according to the Hanafi school of Islamic law (*şeriat*). The judge dealt with criminal and civil matters, as well as with morals. The qadi had a

---

[46] PRO, SP 105/178: 279–280; PRO, SP 105/182: 98–100, 1 April 1732: 'His Excellency [George, Earl of Kinnoull]'s Decree & Order in the dispute betwixt Mr Consul Boddington & Sig.r Georgio Homero'.

[47] For a survey of relevant literature, see Suraiya Faroqhi, "Sidjill", *EI*², vol. IX, 539–45.

staff, the size of which depended on his post. In most centres of international trade this staff seems to have included deputy judges, interpreters, bailiffs, scribes, dividers of estates, and investigators, who were usually of local descent and held office for many years. They formed the court's stable and experienced cadre that was headed by the qadi, who was generally appointed for one year only. The judge adjudicated conflicts between spouses, heirs, business partners, neighbours, debtors and creditors, etc. After informal attempts to solve a dispute had failed, it was usual for the parties to turn to a court for a decision; litigation was common among Ottoman subjects. The qadi also supervised the administration of religious endowments (*vakıfs*), and he was the legal guardian of those who had no one else, such as orphans and brides without a guardian. One of the officers of the court arranged the division of inheritances, sealing the property of those who had died, calculating the taxes due to the state, and supervising the division of the remainder among the heirs. Finally, the *mahkema* also had a notary function. People registered all kinds of deeds and agreements there, from marriage contracts to those concerning loans and real estate transactions. Muslims and non-Muslims alike used the court for this purpose, and Europeans could do so too.

Recently Ergene has emphasized the role of the qadi as mediator. The qadi conveyed the orders of the Porte to the local community, as well as the community's complaints and petitions to the Porte. Moreover, he mediated in local disputes between the military class (*askerî*) and common subjects (*reaya*). When conflicts arose among members of the subject class, he generally also attempted mediation before the case was formally brought before the court. Ergene has also shown that not all courts had the same functions. The judicial functions of some courts were more pronounced than those of others, administrative and notary duties dominating the operations of the latter. Furthermore, Ergene has pointed to a number of lacunae in our knowledge of the Islamic courts, which cannot be filled on the basis of the court records. We know little about the actual court sessions, for example. Nor is it always clear how much time passed between the various stages of litigation, as the records generally give compressed accounts of the procedures.[48]

[48] Boğaç A. Ergene, *Local Court, Provincial Society and Justice in the Ottoman Empire. Legal Practice and Dispute Resolution in Çankırı and Kastamonu* (Leiden, 2003), passim.

While the position of non-Muslims in the Ottoman courts has received considerable scholarly attention, the use made of the Islamic courts by foreign merchants has not. This is surprising, because the court was as indispensable a part of the Ottoman commercial infrastructure for them as for their local competitors and partners. The *ahdnames* invariably contain an article recommending that Western merchants use the court to register their transactions. As we have seen the capitulations explicitly assigned jurisdiction over disputes involving both Ottoman subjects and foreigners to the qadi. Furthermore, it was specified that the qadi should only accept written proof in claims against Europeans. The relevant articles read:

> *ve İngiltere ve ana tabi olan yerlerin bazargânları ve tercümanları ve konsolosları memalik-i mahrusemizde bey ü şira ve ticaret ve kefalet hususlarında ve sair umur-u şer'îyye oldukta kadıya varup sebt-i sicil ettirüp veya hüccet alalar, sonar niza olursa hüccet ve sicille nazar olunup mucibi ile amel oluna.*
>
> *Bu ikisinden biri olmayup mücerred şahid-i zor ikamet eylemekle hilâf-ı şer'î kavîm da'va ederlerse mademki kadılardan hüccetleri olmayup ve sicilde mukayyed bulunmaya, anın gibi tezvir ettirilmeyüp hilâf-ı şer olan da'valari istima olunmaya.*
>
> And whenever merchants and interpreters and consuls of England and the lands which are dependant upon it are engaged in the affairs of selling and buying and trade and guarantee and other matters administrated by the Holy Law in our well-protected dominions, they shall go to the cadi and have him register [the matter] in his book (*sicil*) or else they shall take a certificate (*hüccet*). Afterwards, should a dispute occur, let the certificate and cadi's book be inspected and action taken according to it.
>
> Should neither one of these two [proofs] exist and they bring an allegation, contrary to the upright Holy Law, solely by making false witnesses stand, as long as they have no certificate from the cadis or else [the matter] shall not be found registered in the cadi's book, let not such men as these be allowed to deceive and let not their allegation which is contrary to the Holy Law be heard.[49]

[49] Quoted from the English capitulations of 1580, articles 10a and 10b; Skilliter, *Harborne*, 88 (Skilliter's transliteration has been modified); Ülker, 'İzmir', 307. Because Ülker omitted article 7 of the text, in his edition these articles are erroneously numbered 8 and 9. The article first appeared in the French capitulations of 1535 (art. 3). Also see the French privileges of 1569 (art. 6), those of 1604 (art. 36 and 37), the capitulations of Genoa of 1665 (art. 18), the French *ahdname* of 1673 (art. 29), the English one of 1675 (art. 9), the Dutch ones of 1612 and 1689 (both art. 30), and the French capitulations of 1740 (art. 23). Noradounghian, *Recueil*, I, 84; 91; 100; 130; 141; 148; 176; 284 respectively.

These stipulations unambiguously recommend that the Europeans should use the notary function of the Islamic court for the registration of their business transactions. In case disputes arose later, the Europeans could then produce evidence issued by the court itself in support of their case. It was the qadi who had jurisdiction over commercial disputes between foreigners and Ottoman subjects. Furthermore, the capitulations reflected a practical development in the Islamic world that was at odds with legal theory, the ascendancy of written documents over witness statements.[50]

European records were not accepted in the Ottoman courts. The function of the ambassadorial and consular chanceries for foreigners and their protégés was similar to that of the *sicill* for Ottomans. Commercial contracts, deeds of partnership, protests, wills and all kinds of other official documents were registered in chancery for legal purposes. The form in which witness statements and claims by creditors were generally recorded was clearly inspired by Muslim practice rather than European customs, mentioning, for example, *şuhud al-hal*. Nevertheless, these documents were not acceptable evidence in the qadi courts.[51] This made obtaining *hüccet*s from these courts all the more important.

Islamic law has "no punishment for perjury, nor for giving false evidence", although "according to some authorities only, the false witness is severely beaten and imprisoned."[52] This explains why the *ahdname*s do not prescribe any punishment for false witnesses. The Porte could only attempt to reduce the risk of perjury by encouraging qadis to favour written records above the testimony of witnesses. The jurists were careful not to ban the use of witnesses in cases involving foreigners altogether, but whenever the practice is mentioned in the capitulations the courts are warned not to accept false witnesses. This is also the case with the article concerning accusations against foreigners of having insulted Islam.[53] The relevant stipulation in the English capitulations of 1675 is especially noteworthy,

[50] On this development, see Jeanette Wakin, *The Function of Documents in Islamic Law: The Chapters on Sale from Tahāwī's* Kitāb al-shurūt al-kabīr (Albany, 1972).

[51] "[Neither] Frankish laws, nor documents have any place in the law and justice of this land." D.A. de Hochepied to the States General, 30 June 1753, in *Bronnen* III, 259–260 (my translation from the Dutch).

[52] Joseph Schacht, *An Introduction to Islamic Law* (Oxford, 1964), 187.

[53] This article is quoted in Chapter Three.

because it differs from those found in other *ahdnames*. The text of 1675 not only orders the courts not to let false witnesses stand, but also that such cases should be referred to the English ambassador for adjudication.[54] This assignment of jurisdiction over such complaints to the English ambassador is unique to the capitulations of 1675. It is found in no other text, and does not appear to have had any impact in practice.

The emphasis on written records is also evident in other capitulatory articles. For example, Western merchants who had paid customs duties on their merchandize in one place, and subsequently transported it to a second location to be sold, should not be required to pay customs duties on the same goods for the second time. A common capitulatory article ordered the Ottoman customs agents to accept the certificates of payment (*tezkere*s) that the foreigners had been given after they had paid the customs duties the first time, and not to make further demands on them.[55]

Another important safeguard of Western interests was the rule that cases involving foreigners could only be tried in the presence of a dragoman. In the Dutch capitulations of 1612 we find the article formulated as follows:

> *Nederlandalunun ile bir kimesnenin nizai olsa kadıya vardıkta Nederlandalunun tercümanları hazır bulunmazsa kadı da'valarını istima etmeye eğer mühim maslahatda ise gelince tevakkuf oluna ve amma anlar dahi taallül etmeyüb tercümanımız hazır değildür diye avk etmiyeler*
>
> If, in the case of a dispute [with a Dutchman], someone goes to the cadi and the dragoman of the Dutch is not present, the cadi may not hear the case. If it is about important affairs, the case shall be adjourned till the coming [of the dragoman]. But they may not seek an excuse and try to cause delay by saying "our dragoman is not present."[56]

[54] "Si quelqu'un calomnie un Anglais, en l'accusant de lui avoir fait tort, et en produisant de faux témoins contre ledit Anglais, nos juges ne l'écouteront pas, mais la cause sera renvoyée à l'Ambassadeur, afin qu'il en décide, et ledit Anglais pourra toujours avoir recours à la protection de l'Ambassadeur." Noradounghian, *Recueil*, I, 149.

[55] See for example the French capitulations of 1535 (art. 11), of 1673 (no. 10 of the new articles), and of 1740 (art. 57). Noradoughian, *Recueil*, I, 86–87, 145, and 291–292 respectively.

[56] De Groot, *The Ottoman Empire and the Dutch Republic*, 242 (transliteration), 255 (translation). Article 36 of the Dutch capitulations of 1680 is identical to the text quoted.

The versions of this article in the French capitulation of 1569 and the English one of 1580 added that "[they] shall hold their interpreter in readiness" (*tercümanları ihzar edeler*). Again the English capitulation of 1675 deviates slightly from the other texts, article 24 stipulating that a dragoman, the consul or the ambassador should be present in court.[57]

The Imperial Council

The *divan-ı hümayun*, the Imperial Council, functioned both as the Ottoman 'cabinet' and as the supreme court of the empire. In its capacity as Supreme Court, the Imperial Council was presided over by the grand vizier, who passed sentence in lawsuits and trials on the basis of both Islamic law (*şeriat*) and state law (*kanun*). The *kadıasker* of Rumeli, who sat next to the Grand Vizier on his right, and the *kadıasker* of Anadolu, who sat to his left, were permanent members of the *divan-ı hümayun*. Occasionally they, too, passed sentence. In front of them the *çavuşbaşı* stood, whose principal officers formed two curved lines from the Grand Vizier's seat to the end of the hall, where Janissaries took over. Behind these lines of *çavuş*es were representatives of various corps of the Porte. To the Grand Vizier's left the officers of his household were lined up.

The complainants were divided in groups, the men separate from the women, the non-Muslims standing behind the Muslims. After their complaints had been read out loud by one of two *maîtres des requêtes*, the complainants personally had to explain their case further. The Grand Viziers apparently swiftly gave sentences. The *maîtres des requêtes* wrote them down on the petitions, which were subsequently signed by the Grand Vizier. He usually referred ordinary cases back to the qadi courts, as well as cases that required further examination. On certain days of the week the two *kadıaskers*, the qadi of Istanbul, and the qadis of Galata, Eyyüb and Üsküdar also attended the Imperial Council, and were allowed to discuss cases referred to

[57] Skilliter, *Harborne*, 88 (art. 16); Noradounghian, *Recueil*, I, 91–92 (French, 1569, art. 11) and 151 (English, 1675, art. 24). Cf. article 4 of the French capitulations of 1535, article 11 of that of 1569, article 16 of the English capitulations of 1580, and article 65 of the French capitulation of 1740. Noradounghian, *Recueil*, I, 84, 91–92, 294, respectively.

them there. Sessions of the *divan-ı hümayun* lasted two to three hours.[58]

In theory every subject of the sultan, whether rich or poor, Muslim or non-Muslim, and of whatever social class, could bring cases to the attention of the Imperial Council.[59] In practice, however, getting a case heard by the *divan-ı hümayun* must have required a substantial financial investment. After all, documentary evidence usually had to be procured in the form of certified deeds from qadi courts, and the complaint had to be filed with the Council, which meant that the complainant either personally had to travel to the Ottoman capital, or appoint a procurator.[60] It seems safe to assume that this limited the accessibility of the Imperial Council, but to what extent remains unknown.

According to the capitulations, certain cases could only be brought before the *divan-ı hümayun*, and not before the qadi courts. They included various types of cases involving foreigners. Article 5 of the French capitulations of 1536 assigns jurisdiction over all cases in which Frenchmen were accused of murder exclusively to the Imperial Council, where the testimony of a subject of the French king and of a non-Muslim subject of the sultan was valid, one against the other. In the absence of the *divan-ı hümayun*, the "principal lieutenant" of the sultan—probably a reference to the *kaimmakam*—should deal with such cases.[61] Although this article appears in no other capitulation, it marks the Porte's intention from an early age to retain jurisdiction over complex cases involving foreigners. Later *ahdname*s assigned jurisdiction to the *divan-ı hümayun* over all cases exceeding 4,000 *akçe*;[62] all cases involving consuls and dragomans; and all revisions of sentences passed by qadis.

The first capitulations that stipulated that claims exceeding the value of 4,000 *akçe* should only be voiced before the *divan-ı hümayun* were those awarded to the English in 1601. Article 4 of this text reads:

---

[58] Mouradgea d'Ohsson, *Tableau général de l'empire othoman* (Paris, 1788–1820), iii, 362–363.

[59] Uriel Heyd, *Studies in Old Ottoman Criminal Law*, V.L. Ménage (ed.), (Oxford, 1973), 224–226; 'Diwan-i Humayun' (B. Lewis), *EI²*, 337–339.

[60] Van den Boogert, 'Redress for Ottoman Victims of European Privateering', 94–96.

[61] Noradounghian, *Recueil*, I, 84.

[62] Invariably called *Aspers* in the Western sources.

> *İngiltere taifesi ve İngiltere bayrağı altında yürüyenlerin da'va ve husumeti vaki oldukta, tercümanları yahud vekilleri hazır olmayınca hükkâm da'valarını istima etmeyüp ve dört bin akçeden yukarıda olan da'valarî Asitane-i Saadetimde istima oluna.*[63]

An English translation of this *ahdname* is found among the papers of John Sanderson, the English traveller and treasurer of the Turkey Company. It reads:

> Item, that all Englishmen, and others under the English banner, having any difference or su*i*te, the sam*e* shall not be heard or a*d*judged [by the qadi], except [when] their drogermen or procurators be present. And also, if the sam*e* su*i*te doe amount to more then the sum of 4000 aspers, it shal*l* be h*e*ard and determined in no other place, but sent up hither to my happy throne.[64]

The words "... it shall be heard and determined in no other place ..." are not in the Ottoman text, but apart from this, it is clear from this contemporary translation that cases against the English worth more than the specified sum could not be tried by ordinary courts, but fell exclusively under the jurisdiction of the *divan-ı hümayun.* Despite serious inflation in the Ottoman Empire, the sum of 4,000 *akçe* was never adjusted to modern realities and appeared unchanged in subsequent capitulations.[65]

The second type of case that, in theory, could only be heard by the *divan-ı hümayun* consists of all claims against consuls and dragomans. The first capitulation in which this article appeared was that granted to France in 1604. Article 25 reads:

> *Ve tacirlerinin ahvalı içün nasb eyledükleri konsoloslardan bazı kimesneler da'va etdüklerinde kendülerin habs edüp evleri mühürlenüp taaddi eylemiyeler konsoloslar ile da'vası olanlarun hususlan ile Asitane-i Saadetimde istima oluna ve zikr olunan mevaddun hilâfina mukaddem ü muahhar emr-i şerif ibraz olunursa istima olunmayub ahdname-i hümayunum mucibince amel oluna.*[66]

---

[63] Ülker, 'İzmir', p. 309. Cf. Feridun Beg, *Münşeat-i Selatin*, ii, 474.

[64] William Foster (ed.), *The Travels of John Sanderson in the Levant 1584–1602* (London, 1931), 284. I have slightly modernized the spelling.

[65] The article is also found in the French capitulations of 1673 (art. 12) and 1740 (art. 41), and the English one of 1675 (art. 24 and 69). Noradounghian, *Recueil*, I, 145, 288; 151, 167, respectively. The article is not found in the Dutch capitulations of either 1612, or 1680.

[66] Cf. de Groot, *The Ottoman Empire*, 238, 251. The text of this article in the Dutch capitulation of 1612 is almost identical to that of the French of 1604.

When any persons enter upon a lawsuit against the consuls appointed for the merchants' affairs, the consuls may not suffer damage by being put under arrest or having their houses sealed. Their lawsuits involving consuls must be heard at our Threshold of Felicity. If imperial commands of prior or ulterior date contrary to the aforementioned articles be produced, they will not be heard, [but] the procedure will be according to our capitulation.[67]

This privilege was also included in several later *ahdnames*. Article 22 of the French capitulation of 1604 extended this privilege to the dragomans, too.[68] It was also reiterated in the *berats* the consuls received from the Porte to confirm their appointment.[69] Moreover, the French capitulations of 1740 added that no complainant could force a consul to appear before the court in person, dragomans being allowed to appear on his behalf.[70]

In the most extensive *ahdname* issued in the eighteenth century, granted to the French in 1740, we also find an article (no. 71) concerning revisions of cases that had already been tried by qadis.

Françe tüccârı ile âhârın beyninde vuku bulup bir defa şerile fasl ve hasm ve hüccet olunması maddelerinin vulât ve kudât ve sâir zabıtân taraflarından tekrar istimâ ve fasl olunması husûsu îrâde ve bi-d-defaat vâki olup bu takdirce o günâ fasl olunan davâdan emniyetleri olmadığından madâ bir mahalde fasl olunan davânın yine ol mahalde hilafına hükm olunur imiş deyü inhâ olunmağla ber veçhi muharrer Françe tüccârı ile âharın beyninde zuhûr edüp bir defa şerile fasl ve hükm ve hüccet olunmuş dâva ol mahalde görülmeyüp ve tekrar ruyet olunmak istidâ olunur ise Françe elçisine ihbâr olunmaksızın ve elçi-i mumâileyhin (ve) konsolosdan ve müddei aleyhden cavabı ve keyfiyyet-i ahvâlin sıhhati haberi gelmeksizin iddiâ ve müddei aleyhi ihzâr içün emri şerif virilmeyüp ve mübâşir ve çâvûş dahi gönderilmeyüp o günâ husûs(u) istifhâm ve ilâm olunmağa vefâ edecek vakit tayin olunmak câiz ola ve bu günâ davânın tekrâr istimâı fermân olunur ise Der Aliyyemde

[67] ULL, Cod. Or. 1137 (1) [Copy of the French capitulation of 1604], f. 6r. Cf. Feridun Beg, *Münşeat-i Selatin*, ii, 490–494.

[68] E.g. those of the Dutch Republic of 1612 and 1680 (both art. 6); of Genoa of 1665 (art. 13); of England of 1675 (art. 25); and of France of 1740 (art. 16). Noradounghian, *Recueil*, I, 98, 152, 173, 283, respectively. The article that extended all privileges of the "Franks" to their dragomans, as well, is found on p. 98. For this article in the Dutch capitulation of 1612, see De Groot, *The Ottoman Empire*, 238, 251.

[69] J.L. Bacqué-Grammont, "Un *berât*" (art. 8).

[70] See article 48 of the French capitulations of 1740 in Noradounghian, *Recueil*, I, 289.

> ruyet ve kat ve hasm olunmasına dikkat olunup ve bu bâbda Françelüye tâbi olanların bi-n-nefs gelmeleri ve yahut yerlerine vekili şeri nasb eylemeleri câiz ola ve Devlet-i Aliyyeme[71] tabi olanlar Françelu ile dava saddedinde olduklarında müddeilerin şeri senedât ve temessükâtları olmadukça davâları istmâ olunmaya.[72]

A contemporary French translation of this article reads

> Les affaires qui naissent entre les negocians françois et autres personnes étant vue fois jugées et terminées juridiquement par *hudjet* [*hüccet*] il arrive que les pashas, cadis et autres officiers veulent les revoir de rechef de sorte qu'il ny auroit plus de sûreté pour un procès déjà décidé et il nous auroit même été représenté que sav*oir* vu procès déjà décidé dans vu lieu il intervenoit de jugemen*ts* contradictoires aux premiers sav*oir* le cas spécifié cy dessus les procès que les François auront avec d'autres personnes ayant été vue fois vus et terminés juridiquement et par hudjet ils ne pourront plus être reçus sur led. lieux et si vu requiert de faire de nouveau revoir ces procès on ne pourra pas donner des commandemen*ts* pour faire comparaître les parties avant que d'en donner connoissance à l'ambassadeur et l'on attendra la réponse des consuls sur les informations qu'on leur demandera sur l'affaire en question on ne pourra pas non plus envoyer des chavus [*çavuş*] ny des mubachir [*mubaşir*]. Et il sera fixé un tem*ps* compétent pour prendre les informations nécessaires et s'il en expédié des commandemen*ts* pour revoir les procès ils ne pourrons être vus et décidés qu'a la Sublime Porte ou il sera apporté toute sorte d'attention pour leur décision et il sera libre a ceux qui sont dépendons de la France de comparaître en personne ou de constituer en leur place un procureur dûément autorisé dans les procès que ceux qui sont dépendant de notre Sublime Porte intenteront contre quelque François; si le demandeur n'est muny de quelque pièce juridique et de temessuk [*temessük*] billets le procès ne sera point écouté.

Only the commercial treaty signed with Russia in 1783 contains a similar article. This article, too, emphasized that retrials were only possible in exceptional cases. The ambassador had to be informed beforehand. The consul was responsible for supplying all the information he had about the case, but no *subaşı* ("*commissaire*") or other officer should be sent to force him to appear before the court. Revisions of cases that had been adjudicated before could only take place in the *divan-ı hümayun*, where the case would be reviewed on the basis of legal documents.[73]

---

[71] *Muahedât Mecmuası* i (1294), 30: "Aliyyeye".
[72] BOA, ED 29/4, 1–31, esp. 26.
[73] Noradounghian, *Recueil*, I, 370.

In theory the division of jurisdiction over cases involving Europeans thus was clear. Disputes and trials concerning only foreigners and their protégés were resolved and adjudicated by their ambassadors and consuls. In principle the qadi handled commercial disputes between Ottoman subjects and members of Western communities in the Levant, but cases involving a sum exceeding 4,000 *akçe* should be referred to the *divan-i hümayun*. Complaints against consuls and dragomans should be filed exclusively with the Imperial Council, no matter how small the sums involved.

Towards an Islamic Interpretative Framework

In the previous section we have seen that the capitulations did not grant foreigners immunity from the Ottoman legal system. The texts clearly delineated the jurisdictions of the qadi and the Imperial Council. This contradicts the common view that European communities in the Ottoman Empire enjoyed "unprecedented autonomy".[74] How should we interpret the place of foreign capitulatory communities in the Ottoman legal system? An examination of the position of indigenous non-Muslims is useful here for two reasons. Firstly, some scholars have compared the status of foreigners in the Ottoman Empire with that of *zimmis*. Secondly, the position of indigenous non-Muslims is relevant here, because it forms the background of the Ottoman protégés who were part of the Western *nations* in the Levant.

Zimmis *in the Ottoman Legal System*

A summary of the position of non-Muslim subjects according to the prescripts of Islamic law is found in the work of Shaykh al-Damanhuri (d. 1778). He emphasised the subordinate status of non-Muslims under the rule of Islam, focusing mainly on prohibitions. For example,

> They must not assist an unbeliever against a Muslim, Arab, or non-Arab; or indicate to the enemy the weak points of the Muslims, such as the Muslims' unpreparedness for battle. The *dhimmis* must not imi-

[74] Daniel Goffman, 'Ottoman *Millets* in the Early Seventeenth Century', *New Perspectives on Turkey* 11/1994, 154.

> tate the Muslims in garb, wear military attire, abuse or strike a Muslim, raise the cross in an Islamic assemblage; let pigs get out of their homes into Muslim courtyards; display banners on their own holidays; bear arms on their holidays, or carry them at all, or keep them in their homes. Should they do anything of the sort, they must be punished, and the arms seized.[75]

Moreover, all adult non-Muslim males had to pay the *cizye*, the poll tax, and other extra levies. According to the jurists, the non-Muslims were clearly second-class citizens, something scholars have tended to emphasise.[76]

The Ottomans incorporated the indigenous Christian and Jewish communities in what is known as the *millet* system, an administrative system based on religious affiliation. İnalcık has argued that four periods must be distinguished concerning the *zimma*. The first period comprised the establishment of Ottoman rule until the conquest of Constantinople in 1453, when the second period started. This classical period ended at the end of the seventeenth century, "when the first signs of decentralisation appeared." The eighteenth and nineteenth centuries until 1856 formed the third period, while the fourth and final period ended with the treaty of Lausanne in 1923.[77] Prior to the nineteenth century, when the non-Muslim communities acquired "a decidedly political function", the *millet* system does not appear to have been very systematic.[78] Daniel Goffman has shown that the Ottomans used the word *millet* referring to all kinds of groups, some religious, others occupational.[79] While *millet* seems to have covered communities as a whole, e.g. all Christians in the Ottoman Empire (or in a particular location), the word *taife* was used in reference to specific sub-groups, for instance the *taife* of the Maronites of Aleppo.[80] Only in the nineteenth century did the meaning of the term *millet* become limited to the officially recognized Christian and Jewish communities.

---

[75] Al-Damanhuri, *Iqamat al-hujja al-bahira ala hadm kana'is Misr wa'l-Qahira*; quoted in Bat Ye'or, *The Dhimmi. Jews and Christians under Islam* (Rutherford, 1985), 202–204.

[76] Ye'or particularly does this. Ibid., 52–57, 132. Also see the work of Shalit and Binswanger, referred to in the next chapter.

[77] İnalcık, 'The Status of the Greek Orthodox Patriarch under the Ottomans', 196–199.

[78] Bruce Masters, *Christians and Jews in the Ottoman Arab World. The Roots of Sectarianism* (Cambridge, 2001), 61.

[79] Goffman, 'Ottoman *Millets* in the Early Seventeenth Century', 139–141.

[80] Masters, *Christians and Jews*, 61–65.

Traditionally Metropolitans and Patriarchs headed the two established Christian communities, the Greek Orthodox and the Armenians, while the *millet* of the Jews had Chief Rabbis. These leaders of the non-Muslim communities were appointed by the Porte and received deeds of investiture (*berats*), which codified the privileges of their office. They were recognized as the spiritual leaders of their communities, as well as their chief representatives in secular matters, like taxation. The Ottoman authorities levied taxes on the non-Muslim communities in the form of a lump sum, which was subsequently divided among the tax-paying members by the leaders of these communities. In theory there were three categories of taxpayers—with low, middle and high rates—but in practice the poor paid little or nothing, while the wealthier members of the community contributed a larger share than the one formally levied on them.

The non-Muslim authorities did not operate in a legal or administrative vacuum. On the contrary, they were incorporated in the Ottoman systems. According to a sixteenth-century *berat* issued to the Greek Orthodox patriarch, he was allowed to levy taxes on the members of his community, but when they refused to pay, he had to turn to the Ottoman authorities to have his privileges enforced. An imperial order commanded the qadis to "make your investigations [into this matter] in accordance with the sharīʿa. You will let him collect in full the back payments . . . which will be established by your examination."[81]

Not only concerning tax matters did the non-Muslim communities ultimately fall under the authority of the qadi. This was also the case with their legal privileges, which seem to have been limited to matters of family law. The Ottoman *berats* of the non-Muslim clerics did not prescribe the manner of adjudication. The precise extent of their legal privileges thus is difficult to establish, but according to the Russell brothers,

> in temporal affairs, the Bishop exercises a certain degree of jurisdiction, but has no power to inflict any other punishment than ecclesiastic censure, or excommunication. In contested matters of property, when the parties are not content with his decision, the affair is carried to the Turkish tribunal.[82]

---

[81] İnalcık, 'The Status of the Greek Orthodox Patriarch under the Ottomans', 215.

[82] Alexander Russell, *The Natural History of Aleppo*, Patrick Russell (ed.) (London, 1794), ii, 39.

On the local level each community appointed its own public agent (*vekil*), who was responsible for the communal financial administration, and who acted as spokesman vis-à-vis the Ottoman authorities. The *vekil* was elected in an assembly of the notables of his community and was confirmed in office by the qadi or the governor-general. During the investiture ceremony he received a fur robe, a garment the Ottomans used in other such ceremonies, too. In areas where Turkish was not the dominant language, proficiency of it was a requisite for this salaried office. It was the *vekil* who fixed the division of communal taxes among members of his community. Although the office conferred a certain social status on its holder, as a principal representative of his community he also risked imprisonment by the Ottoman authorities in case of disputes.[83] In eighteenth century Aleppo there was also a "chief deputy of the four communities" (*tevaif-i erbaa başvekili*), who negotiated the lump sums of, for example, the *cizye* with the Ottoman authorities. He subsequently distributed the agreed sum over the communities concerned, where the communal *vekil* made the practical arrangements.[84]

At first glance there appear to be several similarities between the position of the *zimmi*s and Europeans. Both types of communities were invariably referred to with the terms *millet* and *taife*. Both systems had a chief representative in Istanbul, with subordinate representatives throughout the Ottoman Empire. Like the principal clerics, the consuls needed *berat*s from the Porte. In ceremonies of investiture the Ottomans offered fur robes to agents of *zimmi*s and foreigners alike. Furthermore, these diplomatic agents were allowed jurisdiction over the members of their communities, just like the non-Muslim clerics.

These similarities seem to have convinced Mehmet Bulut that the status of foreigners in the Ottoman Empire was comparable with that of the non-Muslim *millet*s. According to the author, "each merchant was legally attached to a *millet*, and consequently, to a covenant country's ambassador. The legal status of the *harbi* merchants could

[83] Ibid., II, 41.

[84] Masters, *Christians and Jews*, 64–65. It is not clear from Masters' account whether or not this office existed elsewhere, too. On the organisation of Jewish communities, see Cohen, Amnon, 'Communal Legal Entities in a Muslim Setting; Theory and Practice: The Jewish Community in Sixteenth-Century Jerusalem', *Islamic Law and Society* 3/1 (February 1996), 75–90.

be evaluated in this context." The text is somewhat confusing, because the author here uses the term *harbi*, someone with the legal status of enemy, where he seems to mean *müste'min*, "protected foreigner".[85] The comparison between *zimmis* and *müste'mins* is not new. The Greek legal historian N.J. Pentazopoulos, for example, had made the connection earlier. İnalcık has categorically rejected the comparison, asserting that Pentazopoulos' went "in a totally wrong direction when he compares the privileges in *berats* for Patriarchs with those given to non-Muslim rulers with extraterritorial rights."[86] İnalcık's rejection seems to be based on his perceptions of the legal position of the foreign communities, which enjoyed, in his opinion, extraterritoriality. On the basis of the texts of the capitulations alone I have argued that this characterization requires revision. Whether the similarities or the differences between the two types of communities are dominant remains open to interpretation. For the present study it is more interesting that these communities illustrate the Ottomans' ability to make special arrangements for non-Muslim and foreign communities in the first place.

Of course it was not the Ottomans who devised the *zimma*, which is rooted in much earlier times. The *ahdnames*, however, in this form were peculiar to the Ottoman era, even if they were modelled on similar practices of earlier periods.[87] The capitulations continued to develop throughout the Ottoman period, as much on the initiative of the Porte, as of the foreign *nations*. This was not the only evidence of the flexibility of the Ottoman system. Recently Svetlana Ivanova has shown that the Ottoman authorities made special arrangements for itinerant and resident Armenian and *Acem* merchant communities on the Balkans. For example, "these Armenians were subject

[85] It is possible, however, that the author actually thought that foreigners and *zimmis* had the same status, for he erroneously states that the legal status of the indigenous Ottoman *millets* were defined by the capitulations. Mehmet Bulut, *Ottoman-Dutch Economic Relations in the Early Modern Period 1571–1699* (Hilversum, 2001), 53, 55.

[86] İnalcık, 'The Status of the Greek Orthodox Patriarch under the Ottomans', 204–205. Footnote 36 has ". . . those given *by* non-Muslim rulers . . ." (my italics), but this must be an error.

[87] Theunissen has argued that the *ahdnames* were based on earlier systems. De Groot has recently argued that they were Ottoman inventions. Theunissen, *Ottoman-Venetian Diplomatics*, passim; A.H. de Groot, 'The Historical Development of the Capitulatory Regime in the Ottoman Middle East from the Fifteenth to the Nineteenth Centuries', Fleet and van den Boogert (eds), *The Ottoman Capitulations*, 1–46.

to a single tax levy paid to the state instead of their *cizye*." On the basis of decrees from the Porte and other administrative documentation Ivanova concludes that they "show indisputably the institutionalisation of the communities of such migrant Armenians as independent corporate units among the rest of the *reayya* and distinguished from the local Armenians, permanently settled in the region."[88]

Another striking example of the versatility of the Ottoman administration is found in several extraordinary documents published by Colin Heywood, which concern the status of the two chief conspirators of the betrayal of Grabusa to the Ottomans in 1691. These men, Captain Lucca della Rocca and his lieutenant Francesco Peroni, defected to the Ottomans, who rewarded them for their actions with a daily salary from the Porte. Such a reward was in accordance with Ottoman practice, but was also meant to convince others to follow the example of these two men. Della Rocca and Peroni received a *berat* from the Porte that put them in charge of such a prospective community of defectors:

> Europeans, whether on land or sea, who in emulation [of them], come over to them from enemy fortresses or ships or defeated units in the field, shall be under the command of the aforesaid, and shall be given their regulation amounts of pay and allowances and uniform, and their discipline shall be reserved to the aforementioned. Let them be punished under the authority of the aforementioned on their committing a crime, and let there be no interference on the part of any other person.[89]

The mention of a uniform and of discipline suggests that the Porte had in mind some kind of military unit composed of defectors from the West, but the way it should be organized is reminiscent of the organisation of the indigenous *millet*s and Western communities in the Ottoman Empire. This community of defectors does not seem to have materialized, but the fact that the Ottomans devised such a

---

88 Svetlana Ivanova, 'The Empire's "Own" Foreigners: Armenians and *Acem tüccar* in Rumeli in the Seventeenth and Eighteenth Centuries', van den Boogert and Fleet (eds), *The Ottoman Capitulations*, 121, 122.

89 Colin Heywood, 'All for Love?: Lucca della Rocca and the betrayal of Grabusa (1691) (Documents from the British Library *Nāme-i Hümāyūn Defteri*', Jan Schmidt (ed.), *Essays in Honour of Barbara Flemming* (Cambridge, MA, 2002) [= *Journal of Turkish Studies/Türklük Bilgisi Araştırmaları* 26/I (2002)], 353–372, esp. 366.

plan is a measure of the flexibility with which they attempted to incorporate alien elements in their administrative systems.

The Islamic Legal Triangle

In a concise article Léon Buskens has argued that students of Islamic legal systems should always keep in mind the "Islamic legal triangle", which connects Islamic law, state law and local customs. Instead of the popular binary opposition of theory and practice, the author put forward this triangular model in order to emphasize the plurality of legal norms. Buskens acknowledges that the domain of local customs is difficult to define, but that an Islamic idiom dominates all three legal spheres of the triangle. "In this model the emphasis is on the necessity of considering the different domains in relationship to each other, instead of viewing them as isolated entities." According to the author pre-modern Islamic states had only limited control over the contents of Islamic law, the *ulema* being the principal developers of legal rules. "The state could try to direct the course of legal thinking, as in the Ottoman Empire, but in general this did not lead to independent state legislation. Furthermore, the state hardly had the power to impose these official interpretations of the *sharīʿa* on the population. In practice, local customs often played an important role in the regulation of daily life. [. . .] This accommodation between the state and Islamic law, and local customs, was characterized by considerable flexibility and dynamism."[90] I propose to apply this model to the Ottoman legal system and the position of the capitulations in relation to it. The common view that the capitulations were outside it can be visualised as follows (see Fig. 1).

The only adaptation of Buskens' triangle I would suggest, is to add the *ahdname*s to the domain of legal customs, instead of giving them a place outside the Ottoman legal system. This results in an Islamic framework within which we can interpret the dynamics between the jurisdiction of consuls and ambassadors, that of the Ottoman judiciary, and the prescripts of Islamic law.

[90] Léon Buskens, 'An Islamic Triangle. Changing Relationships between *Sharīʿa*, State Law, and Local Customs', *ISIM Newsletter* 5/00, 8.

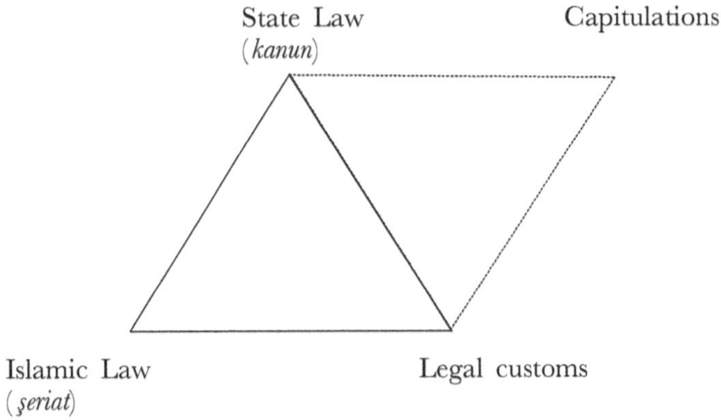

Fig. 1. *The Capitulations and Buskens' Islamic Legal Triangle.* Unbroken line: Buskens' model. Dotted Line: the traditional view on the place of the capitulations.

I also think the Ottoman state did more than direct the course of legal thinking, as Buskens argues. The Ottoman rulers incorporated the judiciary in its administrative system in an unprecedented fashion, thus controlling not only the appointments of judges at every level of society, but also their training. In the Ottoman Empire the Islamic legal component of Buskens' triangle was represented by the *Şeyhülislâm*, qadis and local muftis, who were all trained in the *medrese* system established by the state, and depended on salaried positions assigned by the Porte. Colin Imber has shown that the sixteenth-century *Şeyhülislâm* Ebu's-Suʿud systematically interpreted the prescripts of Hanafi *fikh* in such a way that they did not obstruct established practice. The eminent Ottoman jurist effectively made Islamic theory subordinate to (political) realities, transferring important legal issues from the realm of *şeriat* to that of *siyaset*.[91] This does not mean, however, that the state dictated all their decisions, or suppressed creativity and innovation. Haim Gerber has convincingly argued that local muftis were an important link in the process of mediating between the needs of a developing society, and legal prescripts that are still often considered immutable.[92]

The Ottomans also established a hierarchy of legal courts that was unknown in Islamic law. The *divan-ı hümayun* was a political

---

91 Imber, *Ebu's-suʿud.*
92 Haim Gerber, *Islamic Law and Culture* (Leiden, 1999).

council, but it functioned as a kind of Ottoman Supreme Court, as well. The Imperial Council consisted mainly of jurists, but it was presided over by the Grand Vizier, which symbolized the primacy of state interests. Anyone who felt wronged by the decisions of the Ottoman judiciary at a lower level could appeal to the *divan-ı hümayun*. This, at least, was the theory. In practice the qadis had a key position in the legal system. Judges on the basis of Islamic law on the one hand, they were state administrators on the other. In the latter capacity they were responsible for upholding state regulations, *kanun*, a responsibility they shared with the military authorities in their legal district. Although much remains unknown about the practical functioning of local courts in the Ottoman Empire, recent studies have emphasized the role of the qadi as mediator between power factions at the local level, and between the Porte and the population.[93]

The importance of local legal customs and circumstances that influenced the course of justice in the Ottoman Empire has not been studied extensively, to the best of my knowledge. The cases described in this study will shed some light on this legal domain, in which I propose to situate the capitulatory privileges that determined the legal status of foreigners and their protégés. The *ahdname*s, clearly instruments of state law, allowed the Western ambassadors and consuls to adjudicate legal matters among themselves "according to their usage" (*âdetlerince faslederler*).[94] The capitulations thus created a domain within which the Europeans could be considered autonomous, but the texts clearly delineated the boundaries of this domain. Within the framework established by the *ahdname*s the Western communities applied common legal norms that were not mentioned in the capitulations. The *forum rei* principle, and the doctrine of double jeopardy—both of which will be discussed in this study—are examples of such rules. When outsiders became involved in legal disputes of Europeans or their protégés, however, the other two legal domains could assert themselves. The model can then be visualized as follows (see Fig. 2).

[93] Ergene, *Local Court, Provincial Society and Justice in the Ottoman Empire*.

[94] Quoted above, page 35. Cf. the Dutch capitulations of 1612, article 5 of which speaks of *ayinleri*, "their customs". De Groot, *The Ottoman Empire and the Dutch Republic*, 237 (Ottoman text), 251 (translation).

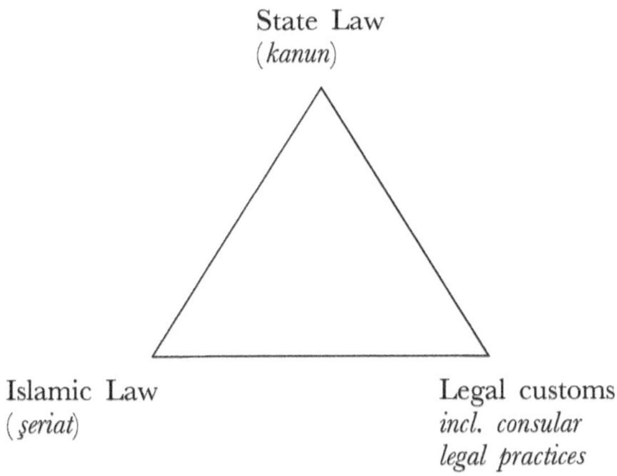

Fig. 2. The Capitulations *within* Buskens' Islamic Legal Triangle.

By interpreting the consular juridical practices as a form of legal customs, we can see them as something not in opposition to, or divorced from, the other two angles of the Ottoman legal triangle, but in constant negotiation with them. In this way Buskens' model provides an Islamic alternative for the Euro-centric discourse of antagonism that pervades the Western sources, which is characterized by an implicit, but inescapable, sense of "us" Europeans versus "them" Ottomans.

CHAPTER TWO

THE PROTECTION SYSTEM

The previous chapter has shown that the capitulations did not unequivocally delineate the boundaries of foreign communities. The Ottoman protégés of these foreign communities are easier to define with precision. This group consisted of dragomans, warehousemen, brokers and moneychangers. Ali İhsan Bağış has published a concise study that deals with the role of non-Muslim merchants in Ottoman trade between 1750 and 1839.[1] On the basis of Ottoman, British and French archival sources the book offers the best survey to date of Ottoman perceptions of the protection system, providing a number of relevant (transliterated) documents in the appendix. Bağış has made a valuable contribution to our understanding of Ottoman policies on protection, but he did not investigate the implementation of the capitulatory privileges. He thus elaborates on existing visions of the protection system, without testing them. Moreover, the author has disregarded the one source on the basis of which the protection system can be studied systematically and for an extended period: the *ecnebi devletler defterleri*, the Registers of Foreign Nations, which have proved invaluable for the present study.

The first part of this chapter is devoted to a discussion of the privileges of the Ottoman members of foreign *nations*. Again the capitulations are the principal source of privileges awarded to the foreign communities in the Ottoman Empire, but with regard to their Ottoman dragomans and protégés *berat*s and additional *ferman*s are at least as important. In the subsequent paragraphs the commercialisation of foreign protection will be examined in order to establish the extent of the system. What was the aim of the increase in number of protégés? Who determined the limits? And, finally, was this part of Western imperialist policies to weaken the Ottoman Empire? It is to these questions that we turn after a discussion of the different types of Ottoman protégés in the foreign communities in the Levant.

---

[1] Ali İhsan Bağış, *Osmanlı ticaretinde gayri müslimler. Kapitülasyonlar—beratlı tüccârlar—Avrupa ve Hayriye tüccârları (1750–1839)* (Ankara, 1983).

OTTOMAN PROTÉGÉS

The most important protégés were the dragomans, the salaried non-Muslim interpreters serving foreign ambassadors, consuls and merchants, but other kinds of Ottoman protégés were connected with foreign communities, too. They were warehousemen, brokers, or moneychangers. All were indispensable middlemen, but they did not all enjoy the same status. Another group that needs to be taken into account here consists of ambassadorial and consular personnel, who sometimes enjoyed a more privileged status than they were entitled to. Technically the Janissary guards the ambassadors and consuls employed were also protégés. They were the only Muslim protégés, who, in theory, enjoyed the same privileges as the dragomans. In practice this seems to have been a dead letter, however. For this reason they will be left out of the following discussion, although they do appear in some of the privileges quoted, particularly those shared with the dragomans.

Dragomans

The *ahdname*s contain several articles with regard to Ottoman subjects connected with foreign communities. The most fundamental privilege stated that ambassadors and consuls could employ anybody they chose as dragoman. In the Dutch capitulations of 1612 (art. 10) this is formulated as follows:

> *Ve elçileri ve konsolosları istedükleri yasakçıları ve olageldüği üzere murad edindikleri kimesneleri tercümanlıkda istihdam eyliyeler yeniçerilerden ve gayrdan istemedikleri hizmetlerine karışmıyalar*
>
> Their ambassadors and consuls may employ the consular guards they desire and those persons whom they wish to procure, following usage, as dragomans. But no one of the Janissaries, or anyone else who is not needed, may interfere with their [entrance into foreign] service.[2]

This article suggests that foreign representatives were free to employ anyone they liked as interpreters without restrictions, but in fact this

[2] De Groot, *The Ottoman Empire*, 238, 251 (1612); Cf. the Dutch capitulations of 1680 (art. 10) and the English capitulation of 1675 (art. 28) in Noradounghian, *Recueil* i, 152 (1675) and 173–174 (1680), respectively.

was not the case. First of all, the choice of dragomans was restricted to non-Muslims. Because the Europeans shared the Porte's preference in having non-Muslims function as commercial middlemen, this limitation was not problematic. The article also indicates that Ottoman subjects apparently sometimes tried to interfere with the recruitment of dragomans and Janissaries. In the English capitulations of 1675 this is emphasized in the command that no one should meddle in these affairs "by force" (*cebren*).[3] Furthermore, this capitulatory article implies that there was no limit to the number of interpreters the foreign ambassadors could employ. In practice the Ottoman government did impose such limits, which, in the second half of the eighteenth century, were also reflected in the texts of capitulations. The *ahdname* granted to Sweden in 1737 (art. 5), for example, specified that the ambassador could appoint four consuls and one dragoman.[4] The Danish representative at the Porte was allowed four dragomans, and one for each consul he appointed. The capitulation granted to Prussia in 1761 (art. 4) specified the same limitations.[5]

On the basis of article 22 of the *ahdname* granted to France in 1604 dragomans enjoyed the same privileges as their foreign employers. I will first quote the translation of Noradounghian, followed by the Ottoman text found in Feridun Beg.

> Voulons et nous plait que les interprètes et truchements [i.e. dragomans], qui seront les ambassadeurs d'icelui empereur, soient francs et exempts de payer tailles et tous autres subsides quelles qu'ils soient.

The words "soient francs" are somewhat confusing. Does this mean that all dragomans should be Europeans, i.e. that the employment of Ottoman subjects was implicitly forbidden? Or does this mean that dragomans should be considered "Franks"? These questions disappear upon examination of the Ottoman text, in which the words are absent:

---

[3] The Ottoman text of the English capitulation of 1675 reads: *ve İngiltere elçileri ve konsolosları istedikleri yasakçıları ve murad eyledikleri kimesneleri tercümanlıkdan istihdam edüb yeniçerilerden ve gayriden eğer kullanım ve eğer gayriden cebren kimesne hizmetlerine karışmaya.* Heywood, "A *Buyuruldu*", 128 n. 2.

[4] In the light of other capitulations, probably one for himself and one for each consul he appointed.

[5] Noradounghian, *Recueil* i, 241 (Sweden), 311 (Denmark, 1746, art. 8), 317 (Prussia).

> *Ve elçileri hizmetinde olan tercümanları olageldüği üzere haraçdan ve kassablıktan ve sair tekalif-i örfiyyeden muaf olalar.*[6]
>
> And let the dragomans in the service of the ambassadors be exempt from [payment of] the poll tax, the slaughter tax, and other customary levies.

The article also occurs in the French capitulations of 1673 (art. 14) and 1740 (art. 43), the latter text indicating that this privilege was universally applied, despite the fact that it does not appear in many other *ahdnames*.[7]

The article awarding dragomans equal rights is absent in the English capitulations of 1661, but another article of this text is worth quoting, because it deals specifically with the estates of dragomans:

> And the interpreters of the Embassadors of England being free by the articles, declared in the antient Capitulations, of all *Angaria*, or Taxes (*tekalif-i örfiyye*); by vertue also of this present Article, when any of the said Interpreters die (*mürde olmak*), their goods, or Estate shall not be subject to the Custom (*kassam*), but shall be divided amongst the Creditors and, Heirs.[8]

This article is important, because it is not mentioned among the privileges commonly found in dragoman's *berats*. In these warrants the tax exempt status of the beneficiaries of the documents was emphasized above all. No poll tax (*haraç*), extraordinary levies (*avarız*), butchery tax (*kassabiye* or *kassab akçesi*), or non-canonical taxes (*tekalif-i örfiyye*) should be demanded from dragomans. The *masdariye* tax levied on exported goods also did not affect dragomans. Interpreters serving the embassies in Istanbul were allowed to make wine from grapes grown in their own gardens, and neither the Superintendant of Wines nor anyone else was allowed to demand the cask tax (*fuci akçesi*).

---

[6] Feridun Beg, *Münşeat-i Selatin* ii, 490–494, esp. 492. Cf. ULL, Cod. Or. 1137, which is identical to this text except for the word *kassabiyyeden* where Feridun Beg has *kassablıktan*.

[7] Noradounghian, *Recueil* I, 139, 288.

[8] Colin Heywood, 'A *buyuruldu* of A.H. 1100/A.D. 1689 for the Dragomans of the English Embassy at Istanbul (Notes and Documents on the English Dragomanate, I)', Çiğdem Balım-Harding and Colin Imber (eds), *The Balance of Truth. Essays in Honour of Professor Geoffrey Lewis* (Istanbul, 2000), 124–144, esp. 129. The article was also included in the English capitulation of 1675 (art. 46). Noradounghian, *Recueil*, I, 157.

Another important article found in dragoman *berats* ordered that soldiers could not be billeted on the houses of dragomans.[9]

Several privileges concerned travel. Dragomans were exempt from paying customs and transit taxes on provisions, clothing and furniture. At inns and postal stations along the roads nobody should interfere with their possessions and provisions, and imperial couriers were forbidden to demand the courier tax from dragomans and their retinue. For their safety the interpreters were also allowed to wear a white turban, which was usually reserved for Muslims. Furthermore, on the basis of their *berats* dragomans could carry a sword, a bow and arrows, and other weaponry.[10] The capitulations stipulated that members of foreign nations were free to travel anywhere they liked within the Ottoman domains, and these standard articles of dragoman's *berats* suggest that interpreters also enjoyed this privilege. This is not the case, however. The capitulations notwithstanding, all foreigners and their interpreters also needed special travel permits. These permits, called *yol emri* or *yol hükmü*, mentioned the traveller's point of departure and his destination, and ordered all Ottoman authorities along the route to respect the privileges of the bearer of the document.[11]

Sons and Servants (hizmetkâr*s*)

Not only holders of *berats* benefited from them. The tax exemptions and other privileges were valid for "those serving as dragoman, as well as his sons and servants" (*tercümanlık hizmetinde olanlar ve oğulları ve hizmetkârları*).[12] The sons and servants of a dragoman thus shared his privileged status. From the Western diplomatic correspondence it is clear that this was not limited to minor sons. Adult sons of dragomans were considered protégés as much as their father, for as long as he continued to hold his *berat*. If he gave it up, was dismissed, or died, the sons instantly lost their status, too. Grandsons

---

[9] For published texts of dragoman's *berats*, see Herman Almkvist, *Ein türkisches Dragoman-Diplom aus dem vorigen Jahrhundert* (Uppsala, 1894); Bağış, *Osmanlı ticaretinde gayri müslimler*, 109; Ülker, 'İzmir', 125.

[10] Ibid.

[11] BOA, ED 51, 'Tercüman-i düvel'.

[12] DNA, LAT 1090, *berat* of Yorğakı son of Mikhali, a dragoman of the Dutch embassy, dated 2 Şevval 1149/3 February 1737.

of dragomans did not share their grandfather's privileges, despite occasional attempts by dragomans to accomplish this.[13]

The Ottomans never imposed a restriction on the number of sons to whom a dragoman's status was extended, but in the course of the eighteenth century the number of servants that could be registered as protégés was limited to two. In the Western sources these servants are often referred to as "firmanlis" (*fermanlıs*, i.e. holders of a *ferman*). This term reflects the Europeans' generally imperfect understanding of Ottoman chancery practice, for the word *ferman* simply means "order". The word was used for a wide variety of Ottoman documents, but not, it seems, to indicate the servants of *beratlıs*. For that purpose the Ottoman clerks reserved the word *hizmetkâr* (servant). The documents the Ottoman chancery issued as a record of the status of dragoman's servant were called *muaf emri* (exemption), or simply *emr-i ali* (high command). The dragomans' privilege of having two servants who shared their status was anchored in *berats* throughout the eighteenth century.

Berats thus extended the privileges of their holders to their sons and servants, but brothers were not included. For this reasons some *beratlıs* registered one or two brothers as their "servants", while nephews and sons also appear in this capacity—the latter in spite of the fact that they should benefit from their father's *berat* in any case. For example, both the *hizmetkârs* of Samuel son of David Murad Cohen, a protégé of Prussia in Aleppo, were his brothers. A *beratlı* of the Swedish consulate in Salonica had his brother and his brother's son registered as his servants.[14] The Ottoman registers show that this occurred regularly. Possibly family members jointly invested in a *berat*, registering one of the investors as its principle holder and the other(s) as his official servant(s).

European sources indicate that no master-servant relations existed whatsoever between many holders of *berats* and the persons registered as their servants. For example, in 1790 a Dutch protégé in Aleppo, Yusuf Araqtunji was dismissed from Dutch protection after

---

[13] DNA, LAT 384, Alexander Drummond [Dutch vice-consul in Aleppo] to Elbert de Hochepied [Dutch ambassador], 22 June 1752; Ibid., LAT 175, 343–244 (sic): de Hochepied to Drummond, 17 August 1752 (Both in French.)

[14] BOA, ED 51, 'Tercüman-i düvel', 117/307, 117/308, mid Şevval 1194/10–19 October 1780; Ibid., 84/169, 84/170, end Şevval 1190/3–11 December 1776. Cf. Ibid., 27/65, 27/66, mid Receb 1191/15–24 August 1777.

complaints about his drinking habits had reached the Dutch consul. His *hizmetkârs* were his own brother, Jibra'il Araqtunji, and a certain Hanna Badrus. In order to punish only the offender the Dutch consul dismissed him, but arranged for the two servants to remain under Dutch protection as titular servants of the new holder of the *berat*.[15] Another honorary dragoman of the same consulate, Mordecai David Cohen, only had one servant registered under his *berat*, because the document for the other had expired and never been renewed. The Dutch ambassador decided to fill the vacancy by applying for a travel permit in the name of one Pavlaki son of Mikhalaki, enabling him to travel in the Archipelago untroubled.[16] There is no evidence of any connection between the two men. Another example in which any employer-employee relationship was lacking again comes from the Dutch consulate in Aleppo. One of the official servants of its Greek Catholic first dragoman, Nasrallah A'ida, was a rabbi called Ifraim son of Salomon Lagniado. The rabbi had bought the office from A'ida in 1783.[17]

The Porte objected to the sale of the status of dragoman's servant, but the European ambassadors and consuls continued the practice, nevertheless. Their strategy is revealed in a letter from the Dutch ambassador, Reinier Baron Van Haeften, to the consul in Aleppo, Van Maseijk. The nobleman wrote that

> with respect to the berat, I must observe, that when one wants two 'fermans' connected with it, the names of the two persons[18] must not be mentioned in it [immediately], while in all only three and not five people can be registered. In accordance with a common abuse, [the holders of] the 'fermans' are passed off as the servants of the beratli.

The ambassador further promised to award the consulate in Aleppo more *berats* in the future, so that the number of patents in Aleppo would get back to its old level. But Van Haeften insisted that the consul act strictly in accordance with his instructions in this respect, notably

[15] DNA, LAT 774, Nicolaas van Maseijk aan Van Haeften, 26 May 1780; Ibid., 18 July 1780. BOA, ED 22/1, 430/1872, 3 Şa'ban 1194/4 August 1780; Ibid., 467/2062, mid Cemaziyelevvel 1204/27 January–5 February 1790.

[16] DNA, LAT 774, N. van Maseijk to Van Haeften, 7 November 1781.

[17] Ibid., N. van Maseijk to Van Haeften, 24 April 1783. Cf. BOA, ED 22/1, 443/1931, evahir-i Cemaziyelahir 1197/4–13 May 1783.

[18] The text has the word "Neffers", from the Turkish *nefer*, "person".

> that you make sure that you act as I have indicated, and relay the name of the 'Baratair' without mentioning the [names of the] two 'Firmans' of the berat, as we want to pass them off as the beratli's domestic servants.[19]

In the second half of the eighteenth century the status of *hizmetkâr* was thus being sold to people who were not meant to benefit from the dragomans' privileges. The patents were intended for Ottoman intermediaries who could facilitate commerce with Western Europe. The fact that dragomans enjoyed reduced customs tariffs and were exempt from other trade related taxes indicates whom the Porte intended to serve as intermediaries. Contrary to those intentions, in the second half of the eighteenth century foreign protection was increasingly sold to artisans and shopkeepers. When a proper *berat* was too expensive, they often resorted to the purchase of the status of servant of a dragoman, which gave them the same privileges at a lower price.

Warehousemen (mahzencis) *and Brokers* (simsars)

While the dragomans in the service of embassies and consulates generally performed the tasks of interpreters and councillors in all matters Ottoman, the Europeans also needed specialized guidance in the Ottoman commercial infrastructure. Many dragomans in consular service were clearly knowledgeable about (or even personally active in) international trade, but many individual merchants preferred to employ middlemen of their own. In the Western sources various names for them appear, like warehousemen (*mahzencis*)[20] and brokers (*simsars*; *sensals* in French). Like the dragomans, they were invariably Ottoman Christians and Jews. The scribes (*scrivans*) the foreign mer-

[19] DNA, LAT 752, 59–66, doc 2, Van Haeften to Van Maseijk, 18 November 1781.

[20] Although I have not come across the term *mahzenci* in many Ottoman documents, it is used in connection with Yusuf Karali, the warehouseman of the French merchant Thomas Vailhen in Aleppo, in ULL, Cod. Or. 1354, f. 6a–b. On Karali see *infra*, Chapter Four, and M.H. van den Boogert, 'Tussen consul en qâdî: De juridische positie van dragomans in theorie en praktijk', *Sharqiyyât* 9/1 (1997), 37–53, esp. 48–49.

chants commonly employed were often young Europeans learning the trade, but occasionally they, too, were Ottoman non-Muslims.

The capitulations did not award the warehousemen, brokers and scribes any privileges, but they used to acquire them nevertheless. It is not clear when this process started, but by the middle of the eighteenth century these middlemen, too, enjoyed the tax exemptions of foreigners and dragomans. A *ferman* of 1751 prohibited "the demand of money contrary to the capitulations" from *simsars* in the service of French merchants travelling between Aleppo and the coast, on the grounds that the goods they carried belonged to the French.[21] Five years later another imperial order stated that the same brokers were exempt from all non-canonical taxes, just like dragomans and foreigners were. A *ferman* from the beginning of April 1757 added the exemption from the poll tax.[22]

There is no evidence that suggests that these privileges extended to the sons and servants of warehousemen and brokers as well, as was the case with dragomans.[23] In theory their position was not hereditary, although in practice sons tended to succeed to the positions of their fathers. The families supplying the foreigners with middlemen evidently attempted to monopolize these positions, claiming the exclusive right to them (*gedik*). While many merchants probably preferred to recruit their brokers and warehousemen among the non-Muslim families they were familiar with, they objected to the monopoly these families tried to establish. This is reflected by the inclusion in the French capitulation of 1740 of a new article (no. 60) that stipulated that

> Si certains de la nation juive et autres prétendent d'hériter de l'emploi de censal, les marchands français se serviront de telles personnes qu'ils voudront; et lorsque ceux qui se trouveront à leur service seront

[21] ... *mugayir-i ahdname-i hümayun akçe talebi* ... BOA, ED 34–2/11, 57/283, end Şevval 1164/12–10 September 1751.

[22] Ibid., 112/725 end Receb 1169/21–30 April 1756: Ibid., 121/797, mid Receb 1170/11–20 April 1757.

[23] For *hüküms* about the status of *simsars* in general, see BOA, ED 34–2/11, 62/321, beginning Rebiülevvel 1165/18–27 January 1752 (Crete); Ibid., 106/680, mid Muharrem 1169/17–26 October 1755; 154/966, end Rebiülevvel 1172/22 November–1 December 1758 (Sidon); 168/1028, beginning Muharrem 1173/25 August–3 September 1759 (Izmir). For *hüküms* for individual brokers/warehousemen, see Ibid., 58/291, mid Zilka'de 1164/1–10 October 1751 (Tripoli).

> chassés, ou viendront à mourir, on ne peut rien exiger ni prétendre de ceux qui leur succéderont, sous prétexte d'un droit de retenue, nommé *ghédik*, ou d'une portion dans les censeries, et l'on châtiera ceux qui agiront contre la teneur de cette disposition.[24]

Whether or not this capitulatory article had any effect on the selection of middlemen in practice is not clear. We do know that several of these middlemen obtained dragoman's *berat*s eventually, which suggests that the status of interpreter remained more attractive.

Moneychangers (sarraf*s*)

One of the things the Porte hoped to gain from the capitulations was the import of bullion. Not without reason the privilege to import cash currency is found among the first articles of many *ahdname*s.[25] Merchants from Western Europe imported large sums of money of various types and weights into the Ottoman Empire, with which to purchase the goods they sent home. The complexity of exchange rates among foreign coinage and from Western to Ottoman currency made the services of moneychangers indispensable. Moreover, in the absence of banks the moneychangers usually acted as moneylenders as well. In the eighteenth century the trade seems to have been dominated by Jews, but Ottoman Christians, particularly Armenians, are known to have operated as *sarraf*s too.[26]

Despite their importance for the flow of international trade, moneychangers and moneylenders do not seem to have enjoyed a privileged status. They are not mentioned in the capitulations, nor have I found Ottoman documents that suggest that the *sarraf*s acquired privileges in the same gradual way as the other middlemen did. The fact that moneychangers appear among the ranks of dragomans in the eighteenth century indicates that this was the surest way for them to obtain a privileged status.[27]

---

[24] Noradounghian, *Recueil*, I, 292–293.

[25] Feridun Beg, *Münşeat-i Selatin*, ii, 492 (France/1604, art. 9); Noradounghian, *Recueil*, I, 126–127 (Genoa/1665, art. 4), 137 (France/1673, art. 4).

[26] On the importance of Jewish brokers, moneychangers and moneylenders in eighteenth-century Izmir, see Elena Frangakis-Syrett, *The Commerce of Smyrna in the Eighteenth Century (1700–1820)* (Athens, 1992), 88–89. Also see Onnik Jamgocyan, "Une famille de financiers arméniens au XVIIIe siècle: les Serpos" in Daniel Panzac (ed.), *Les villes dans l'empire ottoman: Activités et sociétés* I (Paris, 1991), 365–391.

[27] BOA, A.DVN.DVE 138, doc. 19, [1749]. Cf. BOA, ED 27/2, 96/391, 9 Şevval 1162/22 September 1749.

Haratch Papers

The final group of people that enjoyed certain capitulatory privileges consists of the servants of ambassadors and consuls. Their privileges were the most limited, but in practice the distinction between their status and that of dragomans may not always have been clear to, and thus enforced by the Ottoman authorities. This development is worth examining here, because it yields the earliest evidence of the status of dragomans being conferred on people who did not actually hold the office of interpreter.

Special arrangements existed for a number of the embassy staff with regard to the payment of the poll tax levied on all male non-Muslim subjects of the Ottoman Empire. This arrangement occurred through what are called "haratch papers" in the western sources. The procedures involved are illustrated by documents published recently by Heywood concerning the English embassy in Istanbul at the end of the seventeenth century.[28] The exemption from payment of *haraç* for a maximum of ten of the ambassador's household was anchored in the English capitulations of 1661 in the following article:

> *Ve kıral-i müşara ileyh Asitane-i Saadetimin sadakat üzere dostı olmağla, südde-i saadetime mukim olan elçisinin dahı yalniz on nefer hizmetkârı herhangi milletden olursa muaf olub rencide olunmıya*
>
> Since the aforementioned king in terms of voluntary benefactions is a friend to My Lofty Porte, of his ambassador residing at the Threshold of Felicity only ten servants of whichever community will be exempt and may not suffer damage.[29]

For this privilege to be effective, ambassadors needed to submit a petition to the *reisülküttab* listing the names of the ten men who were to be exempted from payment of the poll tax. The petition published by Heywood dates from 1689 and contains the names of six registered dragomans (*beratlıs*) and four others. In response to the ambassador's request a *buyuruldu* was issued confirming their exempt status. As far as the collectors of the poll tax were concerned, all ten men should thus be considered *tercümans*, a title also attributed to them in the Ottoman text. Despite the fact that its meaning was clearly limited to this particular context, the application of the title

[28] Heywood, 'A *buyuruldu*', 125–144.
[29] Ibid., 129 n. 4.

"dragoman" to all men on the list was misleading. Moreover, in an accompanying letter from the ambassador, Sir William Trumbull, liberally speaks of an exemption from "all the unjust taxes and imposts" for "my dragomans".[30] Deliberately or not, the ambassador failed to acknowledge the difference in status between the six actual *beratlı*s and the four *beratsız*, embracing them all as equal employees.

It may well have been this form of protection that gave rise to the first alarming accounts of the increasing number of foreign protégés, which date from the end of the seventeenth century. According to one account the Ottoman tax farmers claimed that "the suburbs of Galata and Pera had come to be peopled very largely by privileged persons." According to the same source these Ottoman officers exaggerated their complaints "in order to beat down the Farm", i.e. to reduce the price they paid for their positions. Nevertheless, the Porte took these claims seriously enough to order an investigation as early as 1677. As a result it was ordered that all dragoman's *berat*s had to be renewed, a measure that did not necessarily limit their number, but did cost the protégés extra money.[31] The suggestion that the "foreign" quarters of Istanbul were inhabited largely by protégés in this period more likely reflected common fears about the system getting out of hand, than excesses already occurring.

Like the embassies, consulates throughout the Levant also confirmed the general tax-exempt status of dragomans simultaneously with the registration of one specific tax privilege for other servants of the consulate. A list of "the names of the Persons given in, in a List to the Haratchgee[32] freed by the [English] Consul [in Izmir] from the Duty of Haratch" from 1702/3 illustrates this procedure. The first six names are those of the dragomans who were in active service, followed by four names of "sons of Druggermen". They were not, in fact, the sons of any of the former six dragomans, although two of them can be connected with a protégé mentioned in the Ottoman records of this time.[33] Subsequently, a list of twelve men is given.

---

[30] Ibid., 140.

[31] G.F. Abbott, *Under the Turk in Constantinople. A Record of Sir John Finch's Embassy 1674–1681* (Oxford, 1920), 266.

[32] *Haraççi*, the collector of the poll tax.

[33] They were Moses and Abraham Arditi, the sons of Ifrahim Arditi, whose *berat* was registered on beginning Şevval 1108/23 April–2 May 1697 (BOA, ED 35/1, 62/50). After Ifrahim's death, the patent was transferred to Moses (Ibid., 68/88,

They included the broker of one of the dragomans, the consul's butler and junior butler, his gardener, cook and assistant cooks, an assistant of the consular chaplain, a barber, and a certain "Giovanni di Crokio, fiddler". Also on the list was Nicolo di Manoli, a baker, who probably operated the consulate's own oven.[34] Finally, seven servants of the dragomans are listed as having been "freed" from the payment of the poll tax. The total number of people mentioned is 29.[35] The list was submitted to the Porte through the embassy in Istanbul.

Two groups can be distinguished on this list, the first consisting of the actual dragomans, their servants, and the dragomans' sons, the second of other consular personnel. The first group enjoyed all the privileges associated with dragomanship, while the second were "free" from payment of the poll tax only. For the first group the list confirms an existing privilege. For the second group its function is closer to that of a receipt, since the tax was in fact paid for them. Throughout the Levant, European consulates made this arrangement for their Ottoman staff. For example, every year, upon the arrival of the English ships carrying cloth to Izmir, the collector of the poll tax received fifteen pikes of cloth on behalf of the protégés, which were debited to the Levant Company's account with the consulate.[36] The Dutch in Istanbul and Aleppo did the same thing, as did the French in Salonica.[37]

The Ottoman authorities were aware of the danger that others might also claim benefit from this arrangement. This is clear from a letter the Porte sent to the cadi in Izmir in 1697, which names five servants of the British consul in the town who were exempt

mid Şa'ban 1117/28 November–7 December 1705, where the father's name is given as Ibrahim). After Moses' death, the document went to Abraham Arditi, but whether this was his brother, or even a son, is not clear (Ibid., 25 Şa'ban 1133/21 June 1721).

[34] BNA, SP 105/334: f. 101 r. [dated the end of "Gemazielula" 1087/1–10 August 1676].

[35] Ibid., f. 112r.–113v.: The names of the Persons [. . .] January 1702/3. For a similar list for the year 1735/36, see Ibid., f. 117 r.

[36] Ibid., f. 59v: 'Presents usually given in Smyrna . . .'

[37] DNA, LH 164 (i), Nota . . . hollands Consulaed in Aleppo [January to December 1738, 1739]; N.G. Svoronos, *Le commerce de Salonique au XVIIIe siècle* (Paris, 1956), 152. The English later substituted the customary presents in kind for cash payments after financial reforms in the organisation of the British Levant Trade. BNA, SP 105/217B: Peter Tooke, Treasurer at Constantinople, to the Levant Company, 25 October 1784. The Dutch did the same. DNA, LAT 1342, Folders 1772, 1776, 1778, 1784.

from payment of *haraç*. The central authorities warned that the status of these five should not prevent the judge from demanding payment of the tax from anyone else, even if they claimed also to be exempt. "Be sure not to protect anyone other than his proper servants", the command repeated.[38] Injunctions like this notwithstanding, it must have been difficult for subordinate officers in the provinces to decide which document was valid when they were confronted with contradictory evidence. Some Ottoman documents call people dragomans, who were clearly not. As a result people with legally marginal connections with a foreign embassy or consulate were implicitly presented as full protégés. The holders of mere "haratch papers" were thus sometimes awarded more comprehensive protection. While the number of people involved was limited and the effects may not have been severe, these practices were conducive to abuses of the capitulations, and may well have formed a precursor to the appointment of "honorary" dragomans.[39] The next paragraphs focus on another development with more serious consequences. It has generally been considered abusive, but was not in itself: the commercialisation of foreign protection.

COMMERCIALISATION

In the course of the eighteenth century, European protection became a commodity. Affiliation with a foreign embassy or consulate could be purchased from those institutions for large sums. The arrangement was open to non-Muslim Ottoman subjects only. To distinguish the dragomans in actual service from their nominal colleagues who had bought only the title, the Europeans generally called the latter "honorary" dragomans. Sometimes the titular interpreters were referred to as "Beratlees" (*beratlıs*), despite the fact that serving dragomans held *berat*s, too. The Ottoman sources make no distinction

[38] BNA, SP 105/334, 28: Ottoman text (12 Cemaziyelahir 1109/26 December 1697), with Italian translation.

[39] Propaganda Fide, Rome: ACTA 131 (1761) f. 400*r*.–406*r*. (in French): Report by the Vicar Apostolic in Izmir of 3 December 1760 stating that consular servants with only "haratch papers" had unjustly escaped punishment after having broken the law, because dragomans in the service of their consulates interceded with the Ottoman authorities in their defence, a form of representation to which they were not formally entitled.

between the two types of dragomans, using the word *beratlı* for both. In this study the term "dragoman(s)" will be used exclusively with reference to interpreters who actually served embassies and consulates. The term "protégé(s)" will be used as a synonym for what the Western sources call "honorary dragomans", i.e. those who were dragomans in name only. Finally, the word *beratlı*(s) will be used with reference to the entire group of active interpreters and honorary dragomans, who all enjoyed the same privileges.

Although the protection system is widely believed to have grown out of all proportion, the process has scarcely been studied. In the following paragraphs the allocation of *berat*s, the recruitment of protégés, and the price of protection in the eighteenth century will be discussed. Furthermore, the system will be quantified for the eighteenth century, and we must confront the question of whether there were Western imperialist designs behind this increase in the number of protégés.

An Ambassadorial Perquisite

The sale of *berat*s was an ambassadorial privilege with which foreign diplomats at the Porte supplemented their salaries, which were often insufficient to cover their expenses. Because the lifestyle of these diplomats was meant to reflect the splendour of the courts they represented, many lived beyond their means. They lived in palatial residences along the central street of Galata, with large households consisting of their own families, as well as housemaids, valets, gardeners, grooms, and other servants. Another member of the household was the ambassador's private minister, chaplain or priest. The Dutch ambassador, Cornelis Calkoen, for example, had a retinue of 38 people, while those of his French, British and Venetian colleagues consisted of some 78, 55, and 98, respectively.[40] The non-Ottoman members of the staff usually received housing on the embassy premises, and they would dine at the ambassador's table. Dinner parties for colleagues and other distinguished guests were recurrent events on the social calendar, as were return visits. A summerhouse in one of the villages surrounding Istanbul seems to have been an inevitable requisite. Regular trade activities could not alleviate the financial

[40] G.R. Bosscha-Erdbrink, *At the Threshold of Felicity: Ottoman-Dutch Relations during the Embassy of Cornelis Calkoen at the Sublime Porte 1726–1744* (Amsterdam, 1977), 119.

difficulties of ambassadors, as they were not allowed to engage in commercial enterprise on their own account.

In the light of these circumstances it is not surprising that the European representatives at the Ottoman Porte should have tried to make the most of their emoluments, which included the sale of dragomans' patents. It was not the European trade authorities, but the Porte that made this source of extra income available to the ambassadors. It is not clear when the first "honorary" dragoman was appointed. According to one English source the sale of titular dragomanships only started in 1737, but another states that "these Baraats are a perquisite, that has belonged to the Embassy from its first institution."[41] From the embassy registers it becomes clear that Dutch exploitation of the protection system became important only during the term of Calkoen (in office 1726–44), but for earlier periods the records are admittedly scant.[42] The same is true for the English. Although, in the words of one British ambassador, "no servants of a Crowned Head should ever be permitted to eat any bread, but that of their employers", few ambassadors could afford to stick to this rule.[43]

Since the distribution of *berat*s was a prerogative of the ambassador, he personally made decisions about the allocation of patents, and he fixed their price. He also benefited most from the sale of *berat*s. According to Calkoen, the Ottoman authorities raised the number of dragomans per ambassador on their own initiative. This measure was meant to reflect the esteem in which the ambassadors personally were held at the Porte. Although the Dutchman claims that the patents were not awarded "*nomine publici aut officii*", the number of protégés an ambassador was awarded almost certainly reflected his political importance as well. The French ambassador was thus granted more extra *berat*s than anyone else, while the British ambassador had fewer protégés than his French colleague, but more than the Dutch representative.[44]

The allocation of *berat*s was the ambassador's most important contribution to the recruitment of protégés. During most of the eight-

---

[41] BNA, SP 105/118, 98: The Levant Company to Sir James Porter, 19 January 1748; BNA, SP 110/86, doc. 12: Murray to the Earl of Shelburne, 17 August 1767.

[42] On Calkoen's embassy, see Bosscha-Erdbrink, *At the Threshold of Felicity*.

[43] BNA, SP 110/86: John Murray to the Earl of Shelburne, 17 August 1767.

[44] Bosscha Erdbrink, *At the Threshold of Felicity*, 202; Bronnen III, 82, Calkoen to the burgomasters of Amsterdam, 27 May 1736.

eenth century the demand for protection was higher than its supply. This means that for every new *berat* that was issued, or every existing one that became vacant, prospective buyers were known to exist throughout the Eastern Mediterranean. The ambassador personally decided to which consulate or vice-consulate a diploma was allocated, usually taking this decision before inquiring about specific candidates with the local (vice-) consul. Naturally, if the need suddenly arose for a dragoman in the active service of the embassy or some consulate, this was given priority. Where "honorary" dragomanships were concerned, the ambassador needed to balance the demands of the large consulates, like the one in Izmir, with the interests of the smaller ones, like those in Cyprus, and the Ionian islands. In general, the small consulates and vice-consulates were granted a maximum of one dragoman, and one or two protégés. The numbers of dragomans and *beratlı*s connected with the larger consulates varied, as will be discussed in more detail below. Most ambassadors claimed to be guided by established practice, i.e. the policies of their predecessors, but this did not prevent the price of protection from rising over the years.

The Price of Protection

Most ambassadors considered the trade in *berat*s a welcome addition to their income, and they disposed of the documents as generously as the Ottoman chancery allowed. The profits involved were substantial, for on top of the expenses incurred in the procurement of a *berat* from the Ottoman chancery the ambassadors charged hundreds of *kuruş* for their own benefit. A note in Italian about the costs of procuring a dragoman's diploma issued to the Dutch embassy in 1748 mentions the following expenses in Lion Dollars (Ld):

al Reïs Eff. (to the *reisülküttab*)	Ld 60: –
al suo Kichudáar (to his bookkeeper [*kisedar*])	Ld 40: –
alli suoi domestici (to his servants)	Ld 22: –
Per calemié (for chancery fees [*kalemiye*])	Ld 30: –
Per la Carta (for paper)	Ld 3: –
Per il Tourá (for the *tuğra*)	Ld 2: 90
al Drag.° della Porta (to the Dragoman of the Porte)	Ld 50: –
	Ld 207: 90[45]

[45] In the Dutch documents the exchange rate of the Lion Dollar to the Ottoman

The chancery expenses had risen to about 500 *kuruş* by 1766, a sum that remained stable at least until 1780.

In 1751 an English source blamed the rise of the price of dragoman's *berat*s on a French dragoman who had made the *reisülküttab* believe that the ambassadors received 1,500 *kuruş* per document. Wanting a share of this sum, the "Reis Efendi" subsequently raised the chancery costs, according to this account.[46] This suggests that the Ottoman authorities were aware of the fact that the ambassadors sold their surplus *berat*s, i.e. those documents not needed for dragomans in the service of the embassy or consulates, but did not know how much they fetched exactly. This source furthermore suggests that the alleged informer of the Porte had exaggerated greatly by mentioning an average price of 1,500 *kuruş*, but this was not in fact the case. During the second half of the eighteenth century a full *berat* with privileges for two servants sold for at least five times the sum of chancery expenses. According to the French traveller Volney, a dragoman's patent fetched as much as 5,000–6,000 *kuruş*. D'Ohsson mentions prices between 2,500 and 4,000 *kuruş*, while Dutch and English sources from the period indicate a price level of 2,500–3,000 *kuruş*.[47]

In addition to the price of the patent itself, a *beratlı* paid further charges when he needed to have it renewed at the accession to the throne of a new sultan. In 1765, Dutch protégés were each charged 300 *kuruş* for this service, but after 1780 they paid no less than 1,500 *kuruş* for renewals, which included the Ottoman chancery fees. By the beginning of the nineteenth century, around 1,000 *kuruş* had to be paid for the status of *hizmetkâr* under Dutch protection, the renewal of which generally cost 400 *kuruş*. By then a full *berat* with two *hizmetkâr*s cost as much as 4,500 *kuruş*.[48]

---

kuruş was usually 1:1. Appendix to DNA, LAT 596: Rigo to the ambassador, 16 July 1748, 'Nota delle spese alla Porta per la spedizzione d'un Beratto cons.[es] data dal med.[o] Drag.[o]' [Rudolph Bragiotti].

[46] BNA, SP 105/118, 215: The Levant Company to Sir James Porter, 15 November 1751. The Levant Company had probably received this account from Porter himself.

[47] BNA, SP 110/87: Murray to Mr. Hays [consul at Smyrna], 8 July 1766; Ibid., Murray to Henry Preston Esq. [Aleppo], 28 October 1766; DNA, LAT 752, 36–37, Ambassador Van Haeften to consul Van Maseijk, Aleppo, 7 August 1780; C.F. Volney, *Voyage en Syrie et en Egypte pendant les années 1783, 1784 & 1785*, II (Paris, 1790), 391; d'Ohsson, *Tableau général*, III, 461.

[48] Bronnen III, 9–12: N. van Maseijk to Dedel, 26 September 1765; DNA, LAT

To put the prices of *berats* into perspective, the following expenses give an indication of the purchasing power of the Ottoman *kuruş* in this period. For the price of a *berat* in 1763 (c. 2,000 *kuruş*), one could buy some 150 pikes of linen on the market in Izmir. For the same sum one could rent 111 modest storage rooms in the town for a whole year. Alternatively, the money could be invested in 16 caskets of German Moselle wine, which would yield over 3,200 bottles. For 2,000 *kuruş* one could also buy 666 tickets in the lottery run by a dragoman called Gallo, and have money left for four bottles of local wine, which went for 18–20 *akçe*, or about half a *kuruş*, each.[49] In Aleppo, for the price of a full *berat* one could purchase five Turkish riding horses of 250–300 *kuruş* each. In order to have them taken to Istanbul to be sold, another 100 *kuruş* per horse needed to be invested in grooms and fodder, for the slow caravan trip to the Ottoman capital could take up to forty days. Arabian thoroughbreds were available in Aleppo for 500–600 *kuruş*, so that two could be purchased and sent to Europe for under 2,000 *kuruş*. During the first half of the eighteenth century the total annual expenses of the Dutch consulate in the Syrian city were not much higher than the price of a single *berat*, while in the second half of the century 2,000 *kuruş* more than covered its expenses for a period of six months.[50] In other words, the purchase of a *berat* constituted a substantial investment for its holder.

Although large sums thus were paid for *berats*, their holders did not own them. Strictly speaking, it was only the usufruct of the patents that was being sold by the ambassadors. Therefore in theory the dragoman's diplomas could not be given as bond, nor could

752, 38–40: Van Haeften to Van Maseijk, 25 September 1780. DNA, LAT 975, aanwinsten 1894, no. 1bbbb; DNA, Collection 46, 109: Account between Jan van Maseijk and Van Dedem, signed Aleppo 15 September 1803. Bağış notes that the British ambassador Liston sold *berats* for 2,500–6,000 *kuruş* in 1795; Bağış, *Osmanlı ticaretinde gayri müslimler*, 29.

[49] DNA, CAS 527: Ledger of personal income and expenditures of Abraham Keun, a Dutch merchant in Izmir, 1761–1773, 2, 4, 21, 45, 47, 48; DNA, LAT 1342, File 1762, Elbert de Hochepied to Thesaurier Bongard, 3 April 1762.

[50] The price of horses is mentioned in N. van Maseijk to Dedel, 26 September 1765, in Bronnen IV/i, 9. On the costs of the consulate, see DNA, LAT 1342, Folder 1772: Account of expenses of the Aleppo consulate, 1 September 1775 [from 1 January to 30 June: 1804 *kuruş* and 74 *akçe*]; DNA, LH 247, Treasury accounts Aleppo: Expenses for 1744 (1887 *kuruş* and 64 *akçe*, 1745 (1946 *kuruş* and 13 *akçe*), and 1746 (1950 *kuruş* and 23 *akçe*).

they be sequestered or sold for the benefit of creditors against their holders' will.[51] This is also the reason why *berat*s could not formally be inherited, despite the fact that in practice they were often passed on to one of the holder's relatives. The dragoman's *berat*s were also not the property of the foreign diplomats who sold them. They were Ottoman documents of appointment, which had been issued by the imperial chancery in Istanbul, and which could thus be revoked by the Porte as well. This reality was difficult to accept for the ambassadors, and indignant protests followed the occasional suspension or revocation of the privileged status of individual dragomans by the Ottoman authorities. The same measures could be taken by the ambassadors themselves, but arbitrary dismissals were discouraged by the fact that *beratlı*s from whom protection had been withdrawn could turn to the Porte to demand redress.[52] Although Ottoman revocations and withdrawals of protection by European ambassadors were rare, their occasional occurrence underlines the precarious hold the protégés had on their privileges.

Profits

When a patent was sold to a protégé in Istanbul, almost the entire profit was for the ambassador. The sums involved should not be overestimated. The British ambassador, John Murray, stated that he made a net profit of £250 per *berat*, selling only one per year on average.[53] The diplomatic sources show that ambassadors bargained like any other merchant, initially quoting high prices, but often settling for lower sums. The highest prices paid for *berat*s in one location were cited as the standard when they were offered somewhere else. A letter from Murray to the consul in Izmir, Anthony Hayes,

[51] In practice *beratlı*s did occasionally sell their patents voluntarily to settle debts. In 1758, for example, the *berat* of an Austrian protégé in Aleppo, Naṣrallah Arkash, was sold to the highest bidder in order to pay his debt to Patrick Russell, the Levant Company physician. BNA, SP 110/62 (i): f. 4r, 11 September 1758.

[52] See for example, a complaint by a former British dragoman, Haccadur de Serpos, against his dismissal. (BOA, ED 35/1, 120/413, 10 Ramazan 1178/3 March 1765.) The Grand Vizier urged the ambassador, Murray, to reimburse the costs of his *berat*, or to reinstate the man. BNA, SP 110/86, Murray to the Earl of Shelburne, 1 June 1767; Ibid., Murray to the Earl of Shelburne, 15 September 1767.

[53] Ibid., Murray to Henry Grenville, 16 January 1766; Ibid., Murray to the Earl of Shelburne, 17 August 1767.

illustrates these points. The sale of a *berat* had been discussed in their correspondence earlier, and a bid had evidently been made for it. Murray sent the following answer.

> With regard to the price of the Berrat, they tell me here, it is too low. My Druggerman tells me, there is an expence of 500 Piastres [*kuruş*] to procure it, which I have already issued out, as the command for the 3 per cent augments the expence. The Druggerman likewise tells me, that it is usual to pay him 100 Piastres, besides the fees to the secretary. If M. Micalaki Veledi Nicolo Patrichi proposes paying all these fees exclusive, I should approve of the bargain, otherwise the Druggerman tells me 1000 Cecchins [Venetian *Cecchini* of 4 *kuruş*] is the common price; & the person may be assured that the English protection is at present in high esteem at the Porte. Notwithstanding as I am persuaded you have my interest at heart I shall leave the whole transaction to your management & the Berat shall be sent by the first opportunity, [. . .] so that I can only repeat, do your business & remit the money as soon as convenient to you.[54]

Murray's claim that the simultaneous application for another Imperial Command (a confirmation of the general customs tariff of 3% *ad valorem* for another protégé) increased the expenses of the *berat* on offer was simply false. Possibly the ambassador wanted to suggest that he was already accepting a loss on the transaction. When Patraki countered that he could buy a *berat* for a third of the quoted price elsewhere, Murray merely replied that British quality did not come cheaply. In the end Patraki bought Murray's patent for 2,600 *kuruş*, instead of the 4,000 demanded by the ambassador initially.[55] In the meantime the name of Mikhalaki son of Niqulu Patraki had already been registered in the Ottoman records as the new holder of the *berat* on 6 July 1766, despite the fact that negotiations about its price still continued at the time.[56]

This example also sheds light on the mediating role of consuls in the sale of *berats*. When the *beratlı* or *hizmetkâr* lived outside the Ottoman capital, and was under the jurisdiction of a consulate, the ambassador shared the profits with the consul. Dutch consuls received

[54] BNA, SP 110/87: Murray to Hays [consul at Smyrna], Constantinople 8 July 1766.

[55] Ibid., Murray to Henry Preston [Aleppo], 28 October 1766 mentions a price of 2,700 *kuruş*, but this is corrected in the subsequent letter, of 29 November. Patraki's bluff is mentioned in Ibid., Murray to Hayes, 6 August 1766.

[56] BOA, ED 35/1, 121/415, 28 Muharrem 1180/6 July 1766.

100 *kuruş* for every *berat* that was allocated to their consulate.[57] It seems that the English did not share in the profits of the *berat* trade of their ambassadors until the third quarter of the eighteenth century, when the Levant Company awarded the consul in Izmir a share of about 50 per cent.[58] Not only did the consuls often supply the actual protection that was sold, they were essential for the initial recruitment of most protégés. Although the ambassador made the final decision about appointments and collected most of the money paid for them, he often relied on his consuls to recommend suitable candidates.

Recruitment

Ottoman subjects who wanted to procure a *berat*, or become (nominal) *hizmetkârs*, applied for the relevant documents with the embassy or consulate of their choosing. The dragomans of those institutions played an important role in the selection of prospective protégés, since their local networks enabled them to gather information about candidates they did not already know as members of their religious community, or through commercial contact. They probably also received a part of the profit for their advice. Existing dragomans tended to favour applications by their own relatives. The Europeans were generally conservative in their choice, preferring members of families they already knew. Despite the fact that *berats* officially were not hereditary, they were thus often handed down from father to son, nevertheless.[59] In this way so-called "dragoman dynasties" came into being, the best known of which were the Testa, Chirico, Crutta, and Pisani families of Istanbul, which had western origins.[60] Outside

---

[57] Bronnen III, 9–12, N. van Maseijk to Dedel, 26 September 1765.

[58] BNA, SP 105/120, p. 173: The Levant Company, London, to Consul Hayes at Smyrna, 28 February 1777; Ibid., 181–183, esp. 182: The Levant Company, London, to Ambassador Robert Ainslie, 16 May 1777.

[59] E.g. BOA, ED 22/1, 233/923, 15 Cemaziyelevvel 1136/10 February 1724 [Aleppo]; 256/1039, beginning Şevval 1144/28 March-6 April 1732 [Izmir]; 491/2187, 8 Şevval 1211/6 April 1797 [Cyprus]; ED 96/1, 89/65, beginning Zilka'de 1166/30 August–8 September 1753 [Iskenderun]; ED 27/2, 138/623, 15 Zilka'de 1190/26 December 1776 (marginal note) [Sidon].

[60] A. Gautier, 'L'Origine des dynasties de drogmans', *BAAEDINALCO* (Oct. 1992), 3–12; A.H. de Groot, 'Dragomans' Careers: The Change of Status in some Families

the Ottoman capital the same process gave rise to smaller dynasties of dragomans and protégés. In Izmir, for example, members of the Greek Homero family enjoyed the protection of several consulates throughout the eighteenth century. The office of first dragoman of the British consulate in the town was often taken by a scion of this family, or by one of their closest rivals, the Greek Abro family. In Aleppo, members of the Maronite Karali and Sadir families, and the Greek Catholic Dallal and A'ida families were under French, British, and Dutch protection throughout the period.

The Numbers of Protégés

In the historiography of the protection system one specific passage from the twentieth-century Arabic chronicle of Aleppo by al-Ghazzi is often quoted. It concerns a report by the governor-general of the city in 1793, Süleyman Feyzi Paşa, in which he claimed that 1,500 men enjoyed foreign protection in the city, which allegedly had a negative effect on local tax revenues. The chronicle has long been considered as giving at least an approximate idea of the size of the protection system.[61] Recently Bruce Masters has cast doubt on the number mentioned by al-Ghazzi, using Ottoman reports to suggest that a much smaller group of protégés was connected with foreign consulates in Aleppo at the time.[62] Although this correction is valuable,

---

connected with the British and Dutch Embassies at Istanbul 1785–1829', Hamilton, et al. (eds), *Friends and Rivals*, 223–246.

[61] Kamil al-Ghazzi, *Nahr al-dhahab fi ta'rīkh Ḥalab* (Aleppo, 1923–1926), iii, 242. Bruce Masters, *The Origins of Western Economic Dominance in the Middle East* (New York, 1988), 97, 108; Bernard Heyberger, *Les chrétiens du Proche-Orient au temps de la réforme catholique* (Rome, 1994), 257 n. 26; Alfred Schlicht, *Frankreich und die syrische Christen 1759–1861: Minoritäten und europäischer Imperialismus im Vorderen Orient* (Berlin, 1981), 128, on the basis of Hamilton Gibb, Harold Bowen, *Islamic Society and the West. I: Islamic Society in the Eighteenth Century* ii (Oxford, 1950), 310–311. Also see Salâhi R. Sonyel, *Minorities and the Destruction of the Ottoman Empire* (Ankara, 1993), 110; İnalcık, 'Imtiyāzāt', 1187; Bağış, *Osmanlı ticaretinde gayri müslimler*, 44.

[62] Masters, *Christians and Jews*, 79. Earlier Masters called the number mentioned by al-Ghazzi "undoubtedly grossly inflated". See his 'The Sultan's Entrepreneurs: The *Avrupa Tüccaris* and the *Hayriye Tüccaris* in Syria', *IJMES* 24 (1992), 579–597, esp. 587.

Masters' statistics are limited to Aleppo only. The following systematic examination of several Ottoman registers concerns the entire Eastern Mediterranean, giving reliable numbers of Ottoman protégés throughout the eighteenth century for the first time.

A Survey

The Ottoman *ecnebi devletler defterleri* offer valuable statistical material about *beratlı*s. In these volumes the clerks of the Ottoman chancery systematically registered summaries of *berat*s and other documents that were issued to the foreign ambassadors. Separate accounts were kept for each foreign power, containing thousands of entries in more or less chronological order. Appointments of foreign consuls in the Ottoman Empire were confirmed by a deed issued by the Ottoman chancery, without which no one could actually take office. Dragomans could also only claim the privileges belonging to their station after they had received their Ottoman warrant of appointment. In principle all these documents were registered in the Ottoman chancery. In the following census three registers concerning Great Britain, France and the Dutch Republic have been consulted, all of which cover the entire eighteenth century. The volumes for Great Britain and France are so-called *nişan defterleri*, which contain almost exclusively notes about the deeds of appointment of consuls and dragomans. The ledger concerning the Dutch Republic is a so-called *ahdname defteri*, or Capitulations' Register, in which deeds of appointment are found alongside other kinds of documents issued by the central chancery, such as *hüküm*s, *buyuruldu*s, and, occasionally, *ahdname*s. For every appointment a separate document was issued, and registered. Because the Ottoman registers for foreign matters were organised chronologically, it is possible to count the numbers of dragomans in specific periods. The fact that *berat*s needed to be renewed periodically resulted in clusters of records of renewals within the registers, and it is on the basis of these groups that the following census was taken.

On his accession to the Ottoman throne a new sultan usually confirmed the appointments made by his predecessor explicitly. For foreigners this meant that all *berat*s issued to their consuls, dragomans and protégés under the previous sultan had to be re-applied for. Originally, the old documents did not need to be returned to

Istanbul, but in the course of the eighteenth century this did become necessary. Renewals were recorded both in separate entries in the *ecnebi defterleri*, and by interlinear notes over existing records. The separate entries first mentioned the reason for issuing the document, i.e. the accession to the throne of a new sultan. Subsequently the name of the person who was confirmed in office, the nature of that office, and the date of his original appointment or of the previous renewal were recorded. Finally, the entries were dated. Interlinear notes above existing records would simply state that "because of the accession to the throne the *berat* was renewed."[63] Most *berat*s were confirmed within a year of the accession of a new sultan.

The three registers studied here yield a total of 1,174 summaries and copies of *berat*s, 271 in the Dutch register, 440 in the one for Great Britain, and 463 under French protection. The sample covers the entire eighteenth century. In order to establish how many Ottoman *beratlı*s these three foreign powers had during this period, I have taken the years during which a new sultan took the throne as points of reference. Within a year of each accession most dragoman's patents were renewed, which makes it easier to count them. The data concerning the period of Mustafa II's accession to the throne, on 6 February 1695, are incomplete, so this census starts with his successor. The final probe period coincides with the beginning of the reign of Sultan Selim III, who ascended the throne on 7 April 1789. Close attention was thus given to the years immediately following the accession of the sultans Ahmed III (22 August 1703), Mahmud I (2 October 1730), Osman III (14 December 1754), Mustafa III (30 October 1757), Abdülhamid I (21 January 1774), and, finally, Selim III. A survey of these periods in which the *berat*s issued to European protégés were renewed by the Ottoman authorities yields the following statistics, in which the dragomans in active service are also included (see table 1).

[63] *Culus-i hümayun içün berat tecdid olunmuştur*; Note above ED 35/1, 118/399, *tercüman elçi*, 2 Ramazan 1174/7 April 1761; The next document, 118/400, *tercüman Mora*, 25 Ramazan [1]174/30 April 1761, has the same renewal note, but is dated 12 Rebiülevvel [1]189/12 June 1775.

Table 1. The numbers of *berats* in circulation in the entire Ottoman Empire.

	1115/1703	1143/1730	1168/1754	1171/1757	1187/1774	1203/1789
France	35	41	48	46[64]	51	46
Gr. Britain	15	34	45	43	43	43
Dutch Rep.	24	28	26[65]	30	29	34

Source: BOA, ED 27/2 (France), 35/1 (Great Britain), 22/1 (Dutch Republic).

The distribution of *berats* over the three traditionally most prominent Ottoman centres of trade with the West, Istanbul, Izmir, and Aleppo breaks down as follows (*see* tables 2a–c).

Table 2 a. The numbers of French *berats* in Istanbul, Izmir, and Aleppo.

France	1115/1703	1143/1730	1168/1754	1171/1757	1187/1774	1203/1789
Istanbul	11	17	12	15	9	14
Izmir	8	8	5	4	4	6
Aleppo	–	2	7	8	10	5[66]

Table 2 b. The numbers of British *berats* in Istanbul, Izmir, and Aleppo.

Great Britain	1115/1703	1143/1730	1168/1754	1171/1757	1187/1774	1203/1789
Istanbul	10	14	16	11	11	10
Izmir	1	6	3	5	7	6
Aleppo	2	5	11	13	10	14

Table 2 c. The numbers of Dutch *berats* in Istanbul, Izmir, and Aleppo.

Dutch Republic	1115/1703	1143/1730	1168/1754	1171/1757	1187/1774	1203/1789
Istanbul	15	16	7	3	5	5
Izmir	6	7	6	10	7	9
Aleppo	1	2	7	9	14	12

[64] Cf. BOA, ED 27/2, 202/946, undated entry, document directly above dated 7 Safer [1]172/10 October 1758, which mentions the total of 52 *beratlıs* for the French. The entry is identical to that concerning the French of BOA, A.DVN.DVE 138, doc. 19, with the exception of the name of *sarraf* Musa w. Isak, which is crossed out in the *ecnebi defteri.* The British *ecnebi defteri* notes 50 *beratlıs*; ED 35/1, 174/691, 7 Safer 1172/10 October 1758.

[65] This number is incomplete. Before the Dutch had renewed all their *berats* after the accession to the throne of Osman III, the process started over again after Mustafa III had succeeded to the throne.

[66] Cf. Heyberger, *Les chrétiens du Proche-Orient*, Annexe 5, which mentions a total of 6 *beratlıs* of the French consulate in Aleppo in 1780.

These figures show that at the beginning of the eighteenth century Istanbul was the most important centre of foreign protection. In the case of the French Izmir was a close rival, but in subsequent years the difference became more pronounced. The British ambassadors also had the most protégés in the Ottoman capital, a number that briefly reached a peak in the middle of the eighteenth century. Dutch protection was likewise concentrated in Istanbul at the beginning of the century, but the importance of the capital decreased steadily. At the end of the eighteenth century the original number of 15 had been reduced by two thirds. The importance of Aleppo as a centre of protection increased dramatically, while the role of the city in international trade declined during the same period. It is unclear whether or not any connection existed between the two developments. The ascendance of Aleppo illustrates the process of the "decentralization" of protection as a whole, for *beratlı*s were appointed not only in this Syrian city, but in the Archipelago, and Palestine as well. In places like Durazzo (Durrës), Salonica, Patras and Cyprus, dragomans began to be appointed, some of whom actively served consulates there, while others were "honorary" dragomans. In the course of the eighteenth century the number of *beratlı*s therefore increased, and the geographical scope of the protection system widened.

These statistics show that the number of *beratlı*s protected by the ambassadors of these three countries increased steadily in the course of the eighteenth century, but the actual numbers were lower than has often been assumed. D'Ohsson has claimed that the number of protégés was fixed between 30 and 40 per ambassador until the reign of Sultan Mustafa III, when "this number was doubled in favour of all embassies", but there is no sign of this in the Ottoman registers.[67] Our figures indicate that the total number of *beratlı*s probably varied between 200 and 300 for the entire Ottoman Empire at the end of the eighteenth century. This is confirmed by a series of Ottoman surveys of the *beratlı*s of nine foreign powers in 1793–1794 on the basis of which table 3 has been made.

[67] D'Ohsson, *Tableau général*, iii, 460.

Table 3. An Ottoman survey of 1793–4.

	France	Great Britain	The Dutch Republic	Venice	Prussia	Austria	Denmark	Sweden	The Kingdom of the Two Sicilies	Total
Istanbul	17	14	5	1	4	–	4	4	3	52
Izmir	6	5	9	1	1	1	1	8	4	36
Aleppo	6	12	9	6	2	1	1	5	5	47
Salonica	3	4	2	–	2	–	1	3	5	20
Morea	3	3	4	–	2	–	–	–	–	10
Sidon, Acre, Beirut	3	–	–	–	1	–	–	2	–	6
Cyprus	2	1	1	1	1	1	1	4	1	13
Chios	1	–	1	–	–	1	–	1	–	4
Tripoli (Syr.)	4	2	–	–	1	1	–	–	–	8
Yanina & Arta	2	–	–	–	–	–	1	1	1	5
Crete	2	1	–	–	1	–	–	2	2	8
Athens	–	2	–	–	1	–	–	2	2	7
Other ports	1	–	–	–	3	2	3	14	8	31
Total	50	44	31	9	17	7	12	46	31	247

Source: BOA, Hatt-ı Hümayun 9779 B, C, D, E, G, H, I, J, K.[68]

[68] Cf. BOA, A.DVN.DVE 138, doc. 19 and a similar survey in Bağış, *Osmanlı ticaretinde gayri müslimler*, 45 n. 16.

Russia is notably absent from the survey. One of the Ottoman reports in the series on which table 4 is based is devoted to the *Moskovlu tercümanları*, but it contains only three names.[69] These three dragomans were appointed after the Treaty of Jassy had been concluded with Russia on 9 January 1792. Russia had so few protégés because every time a war with the Ottoman Empire broke out the Porte revoked all Russian *berat*s. The limited number of registered Austrian *beratlı*s is probably due to the same reason.

It remains difficult to assess the actual number of people who benefited from the privileges of *berat*s, even on the basis of the previous survey. If we assume that every bearer of a dragoman's diploma had two "servants" then the multiplication factor is at least three. The number of dragoman's sons is more problematic. We cannot simply assume that every dragoman had—to mention a random number—five sons, and even if they did, they often became *beratlı*s in their own right once they reached adulthood. The safest conclusion is that every *berat* exempted an entire household, the average size of which is uncertain. Only recently some research has been published about family history in eighteenth-century Aleppo, but this deals exclusively with the Muslim elite and the applicability of its conclusions to the households of non-Muslims is unclear.[70] Reliable information about the size of households of non-Muslims in general is necessary for an accurate assessment of the impact of the protection system on the collection of taxes. Without it, we can only speculate that those who could afford to purchase a *berat* probably belonged to the social-economic elite of the non-Muslim communities, and that their contributions to communal taxes would thus have been considerable. The fact that these communities are known to have occasionally sued their own privileged members for payment seems to confirm this impression, but more detailed research is necessary for a more reliable assessment.[71] Despite these uncertainties it is useful to establish that even if every *berat* exempted ten adult men—the dragoman, his two servants and no less than seven sons—from paying taxes, the total at the end of the eighteenth century came to

[69] BOA, HH 9779-F.

[70] Margaret L. Meriwether, *The Kin Who Count. Family and Society in Ottoman Aleppo, 1770–1840* (Austin, 1999).

[71] Masters, *Origins*, 108 n. 81.

about 2,500 for the entire Eastern Mediterranean. The protection system was thus a much less widespread phenomenon than has generally been assumed.

INSTRUMENTS OF IMPERIALISM?

In his authoritative article on the capitulations in the *Encyclopaedia of Islam*, İnalcık suggests that Western powers consciously abused their privileges of protection for imperialistic aims.[72] A scholar analysing modern Turkish views and uses of the past has observed recently that a similar outlook on the decline of the empire during "the last centuries of the Ottoman period" still prevails in the modern Turkish collective memory. According to this view

> weakness at home led to the encroachment of ambitious and strong foreign powers who succeeded in infringing upon the Empire's sovereignty and territorial integrity. They took advantage of the Capitulations and the protection they had over non-Muslim communities, and interfered in the internal affairs of the state at every opportunity.[73]

On the basis of the assumption that there were many thousands of protégés, it has been suggested that the protection system was an instrument of Western imperialism. This view suggests that the Western powers considered their non-Muslim protégés a kind of fifth column within the Levant. In this chapter so far we have seen that the notion that Western ambassadors and consuls took full advantage of the protection system, and even abused it, was correct. Whenever they could, they sold *berat*s and the documents conferring the status of dragoman's servant to the highest bidder. The extent to which they abused the privilege of protection was more limited than is commonly thought, however. This conclusion in itself considerably weakens the notion of *berat*s as instruments of imperialism, but it is useful to dispel this view more comprehensively. An investigation of the political aspects of the protection system might seem out of place in this study, but the issue must be addressed here nevertheless, because

[72] İnalcık, 'Imtiyazāt', 1186–1187.

[73] David Kushner, 'Views and Uses of the Past: The Turks and Ottoman History', Çiğdem Balım-Harding and Colin Imber (eds), *The Balance of Truth. Essays in Honour of Professor Geoffrey Lewis* (Istanbul, 2000), 239–249, esp. 240.

it touches upon the legal status of Westerners and their protégés, too. At least one of the interested parties feared that growing masses of protégés might take up too much of the consuls' time, and could well clog the wheels of consular justice.

The notion that the protection system was used by Western powers as an imperialist instrument is based on several assumptions that must be made explicit here. First of all, it has often been presumed that the Western representatives controlled the issue of *berats*. Secondly, it is a common assumption that there were secret policies behind the allocation of dragoman's diplomas. Thirdly, this view presupposes that the Porte could do nothing to stop this development. In the following paragraphs the validity of these suppositions will be examined. Subsequently, the opinion of several experts of the late eighteenth century will be discussed in place of a conclusion.

Bureaucratic Procedures

Two stages can be distinguished in the bureaucratic procedures involving the application for a dragoman's *berat*, that involving the Western ambassadorial and consular chanceries, and that involving the central Ottoman chancery.

As we have seen, non-Ottomans who wanted to acquire foreign protection had to turn to either the consulate, or to the embassy of his choice. If an application was granted, negotiations about the price started. Once the prospective protégé had reached an agreement with the ambassador over the price of the *berat*, he paid the money, which, if he lived outside the Ottoman capital, was remitted to the ambassador through the nearest consulate. After the *berat* had reached the embassy, the chancellor registered the document in the embassy records. Subsequently he dispatched the *berat* to the consulate to which the new protégé formally belonged. For the dispatch of documents that needed to be delivered with urgency, the ambassadors could apply to the Porte for an Ottoman courier (*ulak*). The European representatives used this channel only when the beneficiary of the documents in question was prepared to pay the costs. In most cases the documents were dispatched along with the regular correspondence by a Janissary of the embassy, or they were entrusted to European travellers. The final destination of any *berat* was the consular chancery, as it was never actually handed over to its formal holder. Although certified copies could be obtained from the scribes of provincial courts outside the Ottoman capital, the European consulates kept the original records of the status of their protégés.[74] Whenever a dragoman or protégé ran foul of the Ottoman authorities, the Ottoman officials had to turn to the consulate for proof of the man's privileged status. If they wanted to withdraw or suspend someone's privileges, the same procedure was necessary. This may well have been the reason why the documents were kept in the chancery in the first place, for consuls occasionally reported that Ottoman governors tried to confiscate the dragomans' *berat*s in order to force them to pay taxes from which they were exempt.

Ottoman chancery procedures partly preceded those of the Europeans. The European ambassadors would not have had any *berat*s to distribute without the Porte. This point deserves extra emphasis, because is has often been claimed that the Europeans distributed patents of protection without the Porte's knowledge. Both Western and Ottoman sources contradict this view, but it continues to survive in the historiography of the Ottoman Empire's foreign relations, nevertheless. It is useful, therefore, to examine the Ottoman procedures involved in some detail.

When the Porte granted an ambassador a new *berat* for a dragoman, the news would reach the embassy through its interpreters in active service. Foreign ambassadors were commonly presented with several new patents as a gift during their first audience with the sultan, but they may well have solicited the issue of extra patents as well later.[75] The procedures described above then started. Once it had been determined who would be appointed dragoman, his name was passed on to the Ottoman chancery so that the *berat* could be issued. Patents already in circulation usually became vacant upon the death of their holders. Foreign protection could also be revoked by both the Porte and the ambassadors, but death was the most

---

[74] For such copies of *fermans* see DNA, LAT 1090 docs 26, beginning Cemaziyelevvel 1156/23 June–2 July 1743, and 53, 27 Rebiülevvel 1172/28 November 1758. The first document does not have a *tuğra*, and was authenticated by the signature and seal of the qadi of Salonica, Imad Hasan Efendi Zade. The second is a legalized copy authenticated by the qadi of Izmir, Mehmed Nurallah Sarizade. On legalization signatures, see Asparouch Velkov, 'Signatures-formules des agents judiciaries dans les documents ottomans à charactère financier et juridique', *Turcica. Revue des études turques* 24 (1992), 193–240.

[75] Bronnen IV/i, doc. 74, 92–93, Van Holst aan . . ., Directeur van de Kamer van Rotterdam, 9 April 1768.

common reason for the transfer of dragomans' *berats*. Because they were strictly personal documents, the patents could not be inherited, or sold by the heirs. When a *beratlı* died, the consulate sent the patent back to the embassy in Istanbul, where procedures were subsequently started for the re-issue of the document.

Standard procedures existed for the appointment of dragomans and for the transfer of *tercümanlık berats*. Two types of documents were involved in the process. The first were memorandums, which were composed according to a standard format. With these documents the Europeans informed the Porte of changes regarding particular *berats*, for example the death of their holder. Another memorandum of the same type subsequently announced the name of a possible new holder of the document. Finally, a petition (*arz* or *arzuhal*) requested that, in the light of the change announced in the first memorandum, the *berat* in question be transferred to the person named in the second. The memorandums were written by the Ottoman scribes whom the European embassies employed specially for the composition of these and other petitions to the Porte. Finally, the seal of the ambassador was stamped on the document (often on the back), before it was submitted to the Porte.[76]

The issue of a *berat* was often followed by a decree that confirmed it.[77] Both the *berats* and their confirmatory orders were registered in the *ecnebi defterleri*. Most entries consist of a summary of about five lines, the structure of which corresponds to that of the actual documents. First, mention is made of the petition filed on behalf of the ambassador under whose jurisdiction the appointee would come. Sometimes the name of the ambassador is included. Then the place of residence of the appointee is noted, followed by the nature of the office, i.e. consul or dragoman. When a *berat* was already in circulation, its previous holder was usually mentioned next, with some indication of the reason for his loss of office. The most frequently recurring phrase indicates that the officer in question was dismissed

[76] The documents were not signed by the ambassador, but ended with the standard signature *al-dai elçi [. . .]* ('the supplicant, the ambassador of [. . .]'). Only the French memorandums usually mentioned the name of the ambassador.

[77] The form and structure of these *fermans* from the eighteenth century were similar to the documents described by Uriel Heyd, *Ottoman Documents on Palestine 1552–1615. A Study of the Firman according to the Mühimme Defteri* (Oxford, 1960), 7–12.

without mentioning the reason.[78] Consuls usually lost their office when their term was complete, but only in the Ottoman registers for France is this reflected in the texts.[79] After the former holder of the office had been noted, the name of the new appointee was recorded. Finally, it was stated that the decree had been issued with reference to the capitulations. The entries end with the date, which was written in Arabic, and was invariably placed to the left under the text.

Most entries of this kind have marginal notes written above the text. These notes are cross-references to other entries in the register, offering information about subsequent procedures with regard to the appointment in question, such as renewals, the transfer of the office (again), or the cancellation of the document. These notes made the registers easy to consult. Once the Ottoman clerks had found one relevant entry, the marginal notes made it possible to trace subsequent developments affecting an individual *berat*. Several other elements further facilitated the use of these records. First of all, the dates of appointment of the Grand Viziers and *reisülküttab*s were noted. This made it easier to find documents that were known to have been issued during the tenure of a particular officer. In order to distinguish the *berat*s of consuls from those of dragomans, notes were often added in the margin, written in red ink. These notes also indicated the place of residence of the appointee. For example, the words *elçi tercümanlığı* introduce an entry concerning the appointment of an ambassadorial dragoman, as does the note [*elçi*] *yanında tercümanlık* ('dragomanship under [the ambassador]'). In some registers *berat*s were further marked with three dots in a triangular form, which were placed in the margin. The consistency with which these marks were used, depended on the scribes. At the beginning of the eighteenth century the registers of each foreign nation were kept by one particular Ottoman clerk.[80]

---

[78] *ref olmakla* . . ., "by being removed . . ." Cf. BOA, ED 22/1, 242/967, 18 Ramazan 1140/28 April 1728: *Konsolos teyin olan [. . .] Pilkington nam beyzade azl ve ref olunub* . . . Jean-Louis Bacqué-Grammont, 'Un *berāt* de Mahmūd Ier portant nomination du consul général de France en Égypte en 1736', *Tarih Enstitüsü Dergisi* XII (1981–1982), 259–278.

[79] The text than has the words *maddı tamam* ("his term is complete"). BOA, ED 27/2 (France), 93/375, 8 Receb 1159/27 July 1746 (Sidon); 93/376, 11 Şaban 1159/29 August 1746 (Anapoli).

[80] The accounts of the presents given during the first audiences with the sultan

Until the middle of the eighteenth century the servants of dragomans were not registered in the Registers of Foreign Matters in Istanbul. In this period records of *berat*s were usually followed by a summary of the order that confirmed its contents. If servants were mentioned at all, it was in a general fashion and not by name.[81] From about the middle of the eighteenth century records of the names of servants of *beratlı*s systematically appear in the Ottoman registers.[82]

The Ottoman registers show that the protection system was an integral part of the Porte's administration of the foreign communities in its domains. Contrary to the common view, as the number of protégés increased, so did the Porte's ability to monitor the process. Its registers were well kept and easy to consult, so that any complaints about the system could be verified efficiently. In the paragraph after the following I will examine how the Ottoman authorities made use of their records, but first we must turn to the suspected Western policies behind the increase in the number of protégés.

Western Policies

Some Western ambassadors knowingly sold *hizmetkâr*ships to people for whom the Porte had not intended them. The principal question here is whether or not they were executing secret policies of their home authorities. The documentary evidence points to a negative answer.

It has already been shown that the sale of *berat*s and the accompanying documents for dragoman's servants was a personal perquisite of the ambassadors. Just how personal this emolument was, is illustrated

---

of the British ambassador, Abraham Stanyan (1717–1730), and the French ambassador Jean-Baptiste-Louis Picon, vicomte d'Andrezel (1724–1727) both mention "the scribe who keeps the registers of the nation." DNA, LAT 1090.

[81] BOA, ED 22/1, 212/829, 23 Cemaziyelevvel 1129/5 May 1717, *nişan* recording the transfer of the *berat* of the late Musa son of Dantura in Izmir to Hovan Markar son of Ovanes; confirmed by 212/831, same date (*hüküm*). Cf. 221/881, 9 Receb 1132/17 May 1720 (*nişan*), confirmed by 221/883, mid Receb 1132/19–28 May 1720 (*hüküm*); 233/923, 15 Cemaziyelevvel 1132/25 March 1720 (*nişan*), confirmed by 233/924, same date (*hüküm*); Ibid., 210/821, 12 Rebiülahir 1129/26 March 1717.

[82] See, for example, BOA, ED 22/1, 451/1965, end Receb 1199/30 May–8 June 1785 (Aleppo); 469/2073, beginning Receb 1204/17–26 March 1790 (Istanbul); 469/2074, beginning Receb 1204/17–26 March 1790 (Patras).

by the fact that the Dutch ambassador, Colyer (in office 1684–1725), allowed his sister to coordinate the sale of the Dutch *berats*. One of his successors, Elbert de Hochepied, delegated part of the same task to his wife.[83] The ambassadors of other *nations*, too, pursued their own interests with the issue of *berats*. Only in the second half of the eighteenth century did the Levant Company unsuccessfully try to take control over the protection system—not to exploit it for imperialist aims, but, on the contrary, to curb it.

The earliest intervention I have found of the Levant Company concerning the "honorary" dragomans dates from 1746. The English consul in Aleppo and his foreign colleagues had sent a complaint to the Porte, because the governor-general of the city had extorted 3,000 *kuruş* from the "honorary" dragomans of the European nations on the grounds that they had not paid the poll tax. The Levant Company ordered that all expenses of this procedure should be paid by the protégés themselves. Moreover, the Company suggested that the best way to prevent these incidents recurring was not to issue any more *berats* in the future.[84] Two years later the Levant Company wanted to establish a limit on the number of protégés, but the ambassador, Sir James Porter, dismissed the idea out of hand. It is clear that the Company did not like this ambassadorial perquisite, which it considered a "great and new Evil".[85]

In 1760 the Levant Company again reacted to reports of Ottoman concern over the protection system. The governor and company wrote an alarmed letter to the ambassador, which is worth quoting here in full:

> May it please your Excell*ency*
> We have for some time past observed with great concern the many opportunity's taken by the Porte to express a Jealousy about the Numbers of their Christian Subjects protected by the Frank Nations, and now we beg leave to lay our fears in this respect before your Ex*cellen*cy, not doubting but that the many commands, Avanias[86] &

[83] Bronnen III, 80–84, doc. 78, Calkoen to the burgomasters of Amsterdam, 27 May 1736; Ibid., 221, A.M. de Hochepied, *née* Boelema, to Rigo, 24 May 1749; Ibid., 351–352, doc. 285, D.A. de Hochepied to Mrs De Hochepied-Boelema, 18 June 1756.

[84] BNA, SP 105/118, 32: The Levant Company to Consul Pollard at Aleppo, 14 November 1746.

[85] Ibid., 98, The Levant Company to Porter, 19 January 1748.

[86] On *avanias*, see Chapter Three.

Claims, of late proceeding from that Jealousy have rendered an object of your attention & that Our sentiments on a Point that so nearly concerns Us will be acceptable to Your Ex*cellen*cy.

The Command last year which Your Ex*cellen*cy informed Us was communicated to all the Foreign Ministers, to withdraw their protection from all Raias [*reaya*] except Drugomen & such who are conceded to them by Berrato: The opportunity taken since, in the Command sent to all the Scales to take a list of the Franks their possessions &c, to renew the many Firmans, the Consuls should protect none of the Gr*and* Sign*o*rs subjects that were not Baratlees in their Actual Service, and the exorbitant sums exacted at Tripoly & Latachia with an high hand for the Chioadar [*çuhadar*, footman] who brought that Command are alarming circumstances & seem strongly to prove what Your Ex*cellen*cy mentioned to Us in April 1759, that the Porte is displeased with the shameful abuse of Protection at the Scales.

As Your Ex*cellen*cy informs Us that this Command was inte*n*ded to check the Authority of the Consuls & that it was not very easy to get a Command to prevent the like demand for Chioadars, it much behoves Our Consuls at this time to Use their Powers with great caution in the protection of the Gr*and* Sig*no*rs subjects, a Power which at all times ought to be exercised with great discretion, but in such times as these, if it is not used very sparingly, the having so much to ask for others must be of very great prejudice to Our own affairs whenever they require any application to be made to the Porte.

What adds much to Our fears is that this enquiry about Protections was begun & carryed on by a Vezier who had been Pasha at Aleppo.

From all these circumstances we humbly apprehend that the exceeding in Protections to the Gr*and* Sig*no*rs subjects will greatly endanger Our Own Privileges.

We therefore request Your Ex*cellen*cy to Use every means in your power to prevent the growth of this evil & in particular to give orders to our consuls to be very attentive not to exceed proper limits in protecting Honorary Drugomen or their Dependants, for We apprehend that the badness of the times makes these Honorary Drug*ome*n find out new ways of using that Protection both with regard to themselves & others connected with them, which we beg leave to submit to Your Excell*ency*'s consideration.[87]

Although politely formulated, this letter did not convey requests, but orders. This time not only the ambassador was notified of the Levant Company's wishes, the English consuls throughout the Eastern Mediterranean were ordered to submit complete lists of their protégés "distinguishing the acting & the Honorary Drug*ome*n & also a

[87] BNA, SP 105/119, 64–65: The Levant Company to Porter, 12 September 1760.

List of such persons as are protected by each Drugoman distinguishing whether they are their real servants or in what other condition or circumstances they are." Furthermore, from then on the Company had to be informed whenever a dragoman died, or a new one was appointed.[88] From one of the consuls the Levant Company also demanded a translation of a dragoman's *berat*. If those of honorary dragomans were different, he was to send a translation of one of them to London, too.[89] The English authorities thus do not seem to have known which privileges the dragoman's *berat*s conferred upon their holders prior to 1760.

From that time onwards the Levant Company closely monitored the issue of *berat*s by the English ambassadors and their consuls. Its comments on the appointments of new protégés leave little doubt about the Company's opinions. In 1763 the consul in Aleppo, William Kinloch, received a letter in which the Levant Company declared: "We observe that you have got a new Honorary Druggoman, one Hanna Abdini, which we are sorry for."[90] The Company was clearly trying to wrest this emolument from its representatives in the Levant, and Kinloch may well have been a casualty of this struggle. By the end of 1765 he had been appointed chargé d'affaires in Istanbul, after the ambassador, Henry Grenville, had been recalled home. Evidently irritations had mounted over the years between Kinloch and his superiors, who acknowledged that the former "seems to think very differently from Us with regard to honorary Druggomans, we esteem their great Number to be highly detrimental to our Affairs & expect that there will be no increase of them in your time."[91] It is not clear how Kinloch responded to this implicit order not to exploit his ambassadorial prerogative, but it seems unlikely that he was compliant. Six months later he was suddenly dismissed from his post, because he had greatly offended the Levant Company somehow.[92] In the end the Levant Company never succeeded in wresting the appointment of protégés from their ambassadors, despite its

[88] Ibid., 66: The Levant Company to Consul Crawley, Smirna & to Consul Kinloch, Aleppo, 12 September 1760. The same letter was sent to Consul Turner in Cyprus, and Consul John Abbott in Tripoli (Syria).

[89] Ibid., 67: The Levant Company to Edward Purnell, vice-consul in Latakia (Syria), 12 September 1760.

[90] Ibid., 126: The Levant Company to Kinloch, 25 March 1763.

[91] Ibid., 177–178: The Levant Company to Kinloch, Agent at Constantinople, 10 December 1765.

[92] Ibid., 197–198: The Levant Company to Kinloch, 1 July 1766.

repeated attempts. Kinloch's successor was initially more reluctant to sell *berats*, but he, too, eventually sold each extra dragoman's diploma he was granted by the Porte.

The French claim to be the champion of Catholicism in the Levant has been much studied, and some scholars have suggested that the issue of *berats* was an aspect of this policy. In my opinion there is insufficient evidence for this claim. Like their colleagues, the French ambassadors, too, were motivated by financial considerations where the protection of Ottoman non-Muslim subjects was concerned. The instructions they received from the French government clearly ordered them to continue the role of France as the protector of the Catholicism, but they do not mention as an instrument the issue of *berats*, which was a personal privilege of the ambassadors. The only difference from most other embassies was that candidates for French protection were occasionally suggested by the Propaganda Fide in Rome.[93] Even then, French commercial interests always came first, and recommendations that might jeopardize them were politely rejected.[94]

Most French ambassadors and consuls doubtless preferred to have Catholic protégés, and those with good credentials probably had an advantage over other candidates, but this did not mean that France protected Catholics exclusively. In Istanbul, in particular, a considerable number of *berats* connected with the French embassy was held by Jews.[95] There is insufficient evidence to conclude that France systematically used the protection system as an instrument of proselytisation.[96] In principle the recommendations from Rome were obviously inspired by the claim of the French kings to be the protectors of all Catholics in the whole Ottoman Empire, but in practice this was a different matter altogether.

---

[93] Propaganda Fide, Rome, SC Maroniti 4 (1728–1736), f. 374r. mentions the recommendation of a Maronite from Aleppo for the post of dragoman of the French consul in Sidon on 20 December 1732. Other cases are mentioned in SC Maroniti 6 (1741–1752), f. 144 ff. and SC Maroniti 8 (1761–1772) f. 905r.

[94] Ibid., SC Maroniti 7 (1753–1760), fos 128–129, Copie de la lettre de Mr. Rouillé, Ministre et Secretaire d'Etat au Cardinal De Tencin (?) du 29 Avril 1754.

[95] BOA, A.DVN.DVE 138, doc. 19; However, Heyberger, *Les chrétiens du Proche-Orient*, annexe 5, shows that the vast majority of the protégés of the French consulate in Aleppo in the years 1769, 1771, 1772, 1775, 1776, and 1780 were Roman-Catholics.

[96] Robert Haddad, *Syrian Christians in Muslim Society. An Interpretation* (Princeton, 1970); Schlicht, *Frankreich und die syrische Christen*, 128.

The claim to a kind of protectorate over all Catholic communities in the Levant was a central component of French policy in the Ottoman Empire, and it appears prominently in the instructions given to French ambassadors in Istanbul.[97] The idea, which can be traced back to the times of the crusades, was first reflected in the capitulations awarded to France in 1604, the fifth article of which granted free movement to priests, monks, and pilgrims in the Holy Places in Jerusalem. The capitulations of 1673 extended this privilege to pilgrims from countries that did not have formal relations with the Ottoman Empire. Moreover, France was recognized as the guarantor of the safety of all Catholic clergy in the Levant. At the same time the Porte retained for itself the right to decide who should have custody of the Holy Places.[98] One of the greatest French successes in this respect was the transfer of custody from the Greek Orthodox to the Greek Catholic clergy in Jerusalem in 1690. The French interest in the situation of Maronite churches elsewhere in the eastern Mediterranean is well documented, too, but the grant of dragoman's *berats* was not an instrument used to help them.[99]

France claimed to represent the interests of all Catholics, which was a much larger group than the French community alone, and even less defined. It included foreign missionaries, priests and pilgrims, but also the clergy and members of the Catholic factions of Christian communities throughout the Ottoman Empire. In theory, the magnitude of the French claim grew in direct proportion to the number of Catholic converts in the Levant. The notion that the French ambassadors considered themselves entitled to intercede with the Porte in connection with any issue touching Catholic interests undermined Ottoman sovereignty to an extent that the protection system never did. However, in reality the French were unable to effectuate its protection on such a large scale. In the end it was not France, but Russia that took the concept of communal protection a significant step further.

---

[97] Pierre Duparc, *Recueil des instructions données aux ambassadeurs et ministres de France depuis les traités de Westphale jusqu'à la Révolution Française* (Paris, 1969).

[98] Feridun Beg, *Münşeat-i Selatin*, II, 491; Noradoughian, *Recueil*, I, 136–145, esp. 137 (art. 2), 143–144 (new articles no. 1).

[99] Jan Schmidt, "French-Ottoman Relations in the Early Modern Period and the John Rylands Library MSS Turkish 45 & 46", *Turcica*, 31 (1999), 375–436, esp. 393–398, 401–402.

In the second half of the eighteenth century the religious policies of France in the Levant weakened as those of Russia became stronger. While the French kings claimed a protectorate over the Catholics, the rulers of Russia were the champions of the Greek Orthodox Church. The general importance of the treaty of Küçük Kaynarca of 1774 in this matter is undisputed. As it was concluded after a Russian victory over the Ottoman armies, it marked a momentous shift in the international balance of power. The treaty gave Russia direct access to the Black Sea, and by its acknowledgment of the independence of the Tartars it cleared the way for Russia's annexation of the Crimea. The principalities of Wallachia and Moldavia remained under Ottoman suzerainty, but Russia was given a special position there. Russian merchants gained free passage to the Mediterranean, and could travel there by land and over sea as a result of the treaty. The Russian right to permanent representation at the Porte, and to the establishment of consulates throughout the Ottoman Empire was also reaffirmed. The treaty, therefore, definitively established Russia as an international power to be reckoned with in the East, and it seriously weakened the position of the Ottoman Empire. The treaty has also long been thought to have granted Russia the right to protect the interests of the Greek church in the Ottoman Empire, which was not actually the case.

The significance of the treaty was not lost on contemporary observers, one of whom thought that the total dominance of Russia in Asia Minor was imminent and inevitable, and that the Greek Orthodox subjects of the sultan would support this development. The observer in question was an Austrian diplomat, Franz Thugut, who has been revealed by Davison as the source of the interpretation of the treaty that has dominated the debate about it for two centuries.[100] Davison has authoritatively rejected the idea that the treaty gave Russia any kind of protectorate over Ottoman Christians. Contrary to popular opinion, the relevant articles were precise and clear. Moreover, Davison has shown that these articles were not of great importance to Russia when the treaty was negotiated, and that they were inserted on the initiative of the chief Russian negotiator. Once

[100] Roderic H. Davison, "'Russian Skill and Turkish Imbecility': The Treaty of Kuchuk Kainardji Reconsidered", Roderic H. Davison, *Essays in Ottoman and Turkish History, 1774–1923. The Impact of the West* (London, 1990), 29–50.

the treaty had been concluded, however, Empress Catherine II issued a manifesto emphasizing the guardianship over Christians in the Ottoman Empire that Russia had secured. The Russian government also published a French translation of the treaty which stretched its meaning subtly but significantly. This hoax—as Davison calls it—was extremely successful, because the Russian translation into French became the working text of the treaty throughout Europe. The fact that there was no legal basis for the Russian claim to guardianship over Ottoman Christians did not prevent Russia stating it. By this time the treaty of Küçük Kaynarca had become a pretext for Russian imperialism. It culminated in the Crimean War (1854–1856), for which Russia's assertion of a right to protect the Orthodox Christians was a *casus belli.*

An important conclusion from Davison's analysis of the treaty of Küçük Kaynarca and its various interpretations is that the treaty was not the result of Russian policy, but was one of its sources instead. The article thus traces the transformation of the treaty from the actual text to being a mere pretext for imperialist aims.

The Interpretative Agreement of 10 March 1779 granted the Russians additional commercial privileges. In the present context the most important one implied that Greeks could sail the Black Sea under the Russian flag. This clause was also included in the Treaty of Jassy of 1792. Moreover, the Greeks were allowed to remain in previously Ottoman territories that had come under Russian rule. Thus Greek vessels, with Greek captains and crews, were sailing under the Russian flag, claiming the privileges that Russian ships were entitled to on the basis of the Russo-Ottoman treaties. During the first half of the nineteenth century the Russians were reported to encourage Ottoman Greeks conducting business with the northern shores of the Black Sea to call themselves Russians. British reports from Trabzon noted that Russia was appointing Ottoman subjects as agents everywhere along the coast and in the interior, and that interpreters and other Ottoman employees of Russian consulates were receiving medals, money and jewelry from Russia. The British representatives estimated that thousands of Ottoman Christians were under this new type of Russian protection by the middle of the nineteenth century. In the second half of the century Great Britain and France adopted the same policy.[101]

[101] Salâhi R. Sonyel, 'The *Protégé* System in the Ottoman Empire and its Abuses', *Belleten* LV/214 (December, 1991), 676–868, esp. 678 ff.

While the tenor of foreign dispatches from the Ottoman Empire accurately chronicled the development of western imperialism there, the numbers they mention should not be accepted at face value. Many questions about the logistics and practical implementation of these imperialist policies in the nineteenth century remain unanswered, but it is clear that we are dealing with a kind of protection different from that of the eighteenth century. Contrary to widely held views about the protection system the sale of *berat*s was not an instrument of Western imperialism in this period. It started as an ambassadorial perquisite, a financial emolument granted them by the Porte as a token of its appreciation. The numbers of protégés gradually rose in the course of the eighteenth century, but there is no evidence that this was part of secret expansionist designs on the part of the Western Levant trade organisations. On the contrary, one of these home authorities, the Levant Company in London, repeatedly attempted to put a stop to the increase of British protégés, whom it clearly considered a liability, rather than an asset.

Ottoman Policies

The central Ottoman authorities were aware of the possible dangers of the protection system even before the eighteenth century. As early as 1677 Grand Vizier Merzifonlu Kara Mustafa Paşa issued a *ferman* against the excessive sale of titular dragomanships by European ambassadors and consuls after an official inquiry into the practice.[102] The Porte took similar steps throughout the eighteenth century. As we have seen earlier the suspension of all *berat*s of both consuls and protégés in times of war was an effective instrument, but it did little to stem the structural growth of the number of *beratlı*s in the second half of the eighteenth century. Other measures clearly did have an effect on this development, albeit a limited one.

The Ottoman authorities are known to have investigated and taken measures against the excessive proliferation of dragoman's *berat*s throughout the second half of the eighteenth century. In 1758, for example, the Ottoman authorities conducted a survey of the numbers of protégés of all foreign embassies and consulates in the Ottoman Empire. It was not the numbers of protégés the Porte objected to,

---

[102] Abbott, *Under the Turk in Constantinople*, 266–267.

but their concentration in certain cities. For example, Austria was considered to have ventured beyond "the point of moderation" (*hadd-i i'tidal*), because the Austrian vice-consulate in Aleppo had nine *beratlıs*, where the Porte regarded two as enough. In Salonica the Austrian vice-consulate had three dragomans, one too many in the eyes of the Porte.[103] It was details like this that the Porte took measures against at this point, not the numbers of protégés. On 10 October 1758 a decree was issued, ordering that the officers of the Ottoman chancery should henceforth check the registers each time an application was submitted by a foreign embassy for the issue of a dragoman's *berat*. Patents that became vacant after their holders had died or retired should not be re-issued until the numbers of protégés of all nations were reduced to their appropriate levels.[104] The new system (*nizam-i cedid*) affected seven *berat*s held by Swedish protégés, eight by Austrian protégés, and eight by Sicilian *beratlıs*, in all, 42 out of the 218 patents that were in circulation. The chancery officials eagerly complied with the order, even blocking the re-issue of nine *berat*s held by French protégés, nine by British *beratlıs* and one by a Dutch protégé, despite the fact that the order did not concern these nations.[105]

In 1766 another investigation into the number of protégés was reported, but its only result seems to have been the issue of a decree forbidding the protection of people without *berat*s.[106] It is clear from the Western correspondence that it became more difficult for the ambassadors to obtain *berat*s. Dragoman's diplomas with two exemptions for *hizmetkâr*s were especially difficult to get. In 1767 Murray wrote that, "with regard to the Command for two servants, the Reis Effendi is determined to abolish them, as he says it is making three

[103] BOA, A.DVN.DVE 138/19.

[104] BOA, A.DVN.DVE 81/40 (= BOA, ED 35/1, 174/691) refers to the decree issued 7 Safer 1172/10 October 1758. The document is undated.

[105] For example, on 7 Safer 1172/10 October 1758 a marginal note was written above the record of the *berat* of a British protégé, Kazar son of Arutin, which stated that the document should not be re-issued (BOA, ED 35/1, 108/339). It had been issued originally after 1730/1. After the *berat* had become vacant, it was kept in the Ottoman chancery, which was noted on 24 Rebiülevvel 1189/24 June 1775 (Ibid., 108/339). The entry in the register was crossed out, and the word *terkin* (cancellation) written across it.

[106] BNA, SP 105/119, 219: The Levant Company to Hayes [Izmir], 15 May 1767.

Drugomen instead of one."[107] Although it did not come to such drastic measures, the central Ottoman authorities continued to attempt to prevent the number of *hizmetkârs* getting out of control. At the end of 1781 the Porte sent a decree to all foreign embassies making it clear that *beratlıs* were only entitled to two "servants". It was also announced that new *berats* would only be issued after the old documents had been handed in. It was difficult to miss the central issue of the document, as the text repeats the message no less than six times. On the same day another decree stated that the applications for travel permits (*yol emris*) would henceforth be checked more closely to ensure that only registered *hizmetkârs* could obtain them.[108] For a number of years the Ottoman chancery had been keeping a separate register for travel permits, but the problem was that the legitimate *hizmetkârs* used travel permits to disguise the fact that they actually lived in a different location from the *beratlıs* they nominally served.[109]

Five years later, on 12 May 1786, the Porte dispatched a memorandum to all foreign diplomatic representatives in Istanbul about the abuse of the protection system. According to the document, many honorary dragomans only had a vague idea of what the office they formally held entailed. The system was not meant for people like them, artisans, cloth salesmen, shopkeepers, and gold and silver smiths who carried out minor trade in the khans. They had obtained *berats* in large numbers, while they had no connection whatsoever with foreign consulates. Only when they were in trouble did they turn to their consul. As *beratlıs* were entitled to two servants, so these artisans and shopkeepers also duly registered their *hizmetkârs*, whose connections with the consulates were likewise theoretical. The Porte was determined to put an end to this practice. For this reason it had issued an order that all those who had *berats* should wear the uniform of dragomans and that they should be put to work in that capacity under the supervision of their consuls. They were forbidden

---

[107] BNA, SP 110/87, Murray to Hayes, 25 May 1768. Cf. DNA, LAT 664: Nicolaas van Maseijk to Dedel, 10 October 1766; Ibid., same to same, 15 January 1767.

[108] BOA, ED 22/1, 2/5, 13 Muharrem 1196/29 December 1781; Ibid., 2/6, same date.

[109] Bağış, *Osmanlı ticaretinde gayri müslimler*, 31–32. The register referred to is BOA, ED 51.

to interfere in the business of the guilds, to be active locally as *ihtiyarlar* (*pir* or *şeyh* of a guild), and to become tax farmers. Moreover, they were not to disgrace the foreign nations to which they belonged in any way. The *hizmetkârs*, many of whom were abroad on the pretext of consular business, were to return to the location where they were registered. The ambassadors were pressed not to apply for *berats* for such people any more. The protégés were given two months to comply with the order. The status of any *beratlı* or *hizmetkâr* who failed to report to his consul for active duty as dragoman would be revoked. Protégés who were caught acting as *ihtiyar*, or tax farmer, or meddling in local matters in another way would have to face the same consequences. Judging from a reference to "labourers from Chios" the memorandum was probably inspired by the situation in Izmir, but an inquiry into the protection system in Aleppo a few years later would reveal the same problems.[110]

The measure clearly had an effect on the protection system. Three years after the issue of the memorandum, the Dutch ambassador, Van Dedem, complained to his consul in Aleppo that not a single *berat* had been sold to an inhabitant of the city for some time, urging the consul to try harder. The consul explained that the Porte's stricter policies deterred the Ottoman merchants of Aleppo from acquiring foreign protection. Since 1786 no "Dutch" *berats* under the new system had been assigned to the city, and the consul suggested that the ambassador send him "an example of such a document, which can be shown to those people who have negative ideas about them." He also hinted that the ambassador might want to consider a change—i.e. decrease—in the price of *berats* in order to make them more attractive to prospective protégés.[111] In other words, a drop in the supply of patents did not lead to an increase in prices, since demand apparently also slackened, at least in Aleppo.

Despite other inquiries into the number of protégés in the final quarter of the eighteenth century, between 1758 and 1806 the Porte cancelled less than a dozen *berats* as a result of its measures to curb the growth of the protection system.[112] While this is an insignificant

---

[110] DNA, CAS 127: Traduction de l'extrait d'un exposé que la Sublime Porte vient de communiquer ministeriellement à tous les Ministres Etrangers ce 12 Mai 1786.

[111] DNA, LAT 1266: Jan van Maseijk to Van Dedem, 4 February 1789 (in French).

[112] E.g. BOA, ED 35/1, 108/339, cancellation after death 24 Rebiülevvel 1189/24

number, it shows that the Porte was aware of the development of the protection system, and attempted to redress imbalances. Moreover, the Ottoman authorities managed to slow down the increase of the protection system, and the ambassadors were finding it increasingly difficult to make money from the sale of *berats*. The Porte's most effective operation to curb the excessive increase of the number of Western protégés occurred at the beginning of the nineteenth century, the period during which the Ottomans are generally thought to have lost their grip on the protection system altogether.

A *hatt-ı şerif* issued at the beginning of 1806 repeated the policy set forth in the decree of 1786, and now the Porte actually began to enforce it. According to the Dutch consul in Izmir the *beratlıs* and *hizmetkârs* in the city had continued to pursue their small arts and trades in the local markets, maintaining the shops and warehouses the Porte had ordered them to give up if they wanted to keep their privileged status. *Hizmetkârs* who officially resided elsewhere had also remained in Izmir, ignoring the order to go to the place of residence of the *beratlıs* whose servants they were supposed to be. In Istanbul, also, the authorities endeavoured to determine who were ordinary subjects of the sultan, who were actually foreigners, and who belonged to the European communities as protégés.[113] It was probably the most successful measure the Porte had ever undertaken to curtail the protection system, but it marked the changing relations between the Ottoman authorities and the western ambassadors in Istanbul at the same time.

The sultanic writ of 1806 ordered all *beratlıs* and *hizmetkârs* of France, Great Britain, Austria, Russia and Prussia who did not reside in the same place as the consulates they nominally served to return to their stations. If they disobeyed the order, they would lose their privileges and again become ordinary Ottoman subjects. The Porte asked the ambassadors of these five countries to call upon their protégés to comply with the order, but they protested, saying they needed

---

June 1775 (crossed out); 131/485, cancelled 25 Rebiülahir 1198/18 March 1784 (crossed out); 133/504, cancelled after death end Şaban 1213/28 January–5 February 1799 (crossed out); ED 27/2, 117/500, cancelled 21 Şaban 1217/17 December 1802; 117/501, cancelled 21 Şaban 1217/17 December 1802 (crossed out); 135/600, cancelled 22 Şaban 1217/18 December 1802; 135/601, cancelled 29 Zilhicce 1217/22 April 1803.

[113] Bronnen IV/i, 724: Jacques de Hochepied to the Directors, 2 July 1806.

to consult with their governments. The Ottoman authorities then had the decree announced publicly in Istanbul, Edirne, and Salonica, ordering all concerned to comply with it before 3 May, or else lose their privileges. This measure was primarily directed against Russia, which was widely believed to have recruited 200,000 protégés.[114] These numbers remain unsubstantiated, and are probably an indication of the concerns of the Ottoman authorities, not of the actual situation, but the Russians got the message. The British ambassador, Charles Arbutnoth, attempted to mediate between the Porte and his Russian colleague, in order to prevent a rupture between the two states. Despite all foreign protests, the Porte persisted in its implementation of the sultanic writ, ordering the offices and warehouses of all protégés sealed. As a result of this measure many *beratlı*s and *hizmetkâr*s returned to their official stations, while others relinquished their privileged status. The Registers of Foreign Matters, in which dozens of *berat*s were struck off the record, bear witness to this. In July 1806 the English, for example, lost fourteen of their *beratlı*s in Aleppo in a single day. Around the same time *beratlı*s of Great Britain in Istanbul, Izmir, Crete, Salonica and Morea lost their status.[115] The French lost more protégés than anyone else in the Ottoman capital, where at least eight *berat*s were cancelled, but numerous patents of French protégés were also revoked or handed in in Izmir, Yanina and Arta, Salonica, and Aleppo.[116]

The Porte's increased vigilance with regard to the protection offered by foreign embassies and consulates coincided with the emergence

---

[114] Johann Wilhelm Zinkeisen, *Geschichte des osmanischen Reiches in Europa* VII (Gotha, 1863), 396–398.

[115] BOA, ED 35/1, 139/572, 5 Cemaziyelahir 1221/20 August 1806 (Izmir); 140/583, Muharrem 1222/11 March–9 April 1807 (Morea); 140/588, end Cemaziyelevvel 1221/6–15 August 1806 (Izmir); 140/590, Şa'ban 1221/14 October–11 November 1806 (Salonica); 141/594, 5 Cemaziyelevvel 1221/21 July 1806 (Istanbul); 141/595, end Cemaziyelevvel 1221/6–15 August 1806 (Crete); 141/596, Muharrem 1222/11 March–9 April 1807 (Morea). The following *berat*s were all revoked on 5 Cemaziyelevvel 1221/21 July 1806, all in Aleppo: ED 35/1, 138/561, 138/562, 138/563, 138/564, 138/565, 139/569, 139/570, 139/574, 140/581, 142/598, 142/603, 143/604. The dates mentioned are those of their cancellation. Most entries were crossed out in the register, but they are still legible.

[116] BOA, ED 27/2, 169/806, beginning Şaban 1221/14–23 October 1806 (Salonica); 169/807, 3 Cemaziyelevvel 1221/19 July 1806 (Yanina and Narda); 169/809, end Cemaziyelevvel 1221/6–15 August 1806 (Izmir); Eleven other entries were crossed out in these pages of the register, some with reference to the *nizam-i cedid* (e.g. 169/807, 169/808), but the notes of their cancellation are undated.

of a competing system of patents and privileges by the Ottoman state. While the system of the so-called "Europe merchants" (*Avrupa tüccarı*) had been initiated in August 1802, the issue of this new type of *berat* seems actually to have begun only in 1806, the year the Porte revoked so many dragoman's patents. It offered a limited number of non-Muslim merchants a status similar to that enjoyed by the protégés of foreign embassies and consulates. The Porte thus effectively created its own parallel protection system, which was extended to Muslim merchants a few years later with the organisation of the *Hayriye tüccarı*. A notable difference between the *beratlıs* of the embassies and consulates and the protégés of the Porte was that the latter were liable to the payment of *haraç*, but the low sums involved suggest that the tax was predominantly symbolic. It is an indication that, as Masters has concluded, one of the principal aims of the establishment of the *Avrupa tüccarı* was to regain Ottoman sovereignty over those non-Muslim merchants who had previously sought foreign protection. Although the success of this measure varied from place to place, for a short period the Porte succeeded in creating a system that was attractive enough for members of Aleppine families formerly under foreign protection to enrol in it themselves.[117]

Throughout the eighteenth century, the Ottoman state kept a close eye on the numbers of protégés connected with foreign embassies and consulates. The modest effect of the Porte's policies must be attributed to several factors. First of all, the buyers of *berats* were willing and able to exploit the system to their own advantage by selling nominal *hizmetkâr*ships, whereby they quickly recouped part of the sum they had invested in their patents. This went against the spirit of the protection system, but that was probably none of their concern. The ability of the protégés to abuse the system was linked to the inability of the Ottoman authorities to enforce new policies and to prevent *hizmetkârs* living in different locations from the *beratlıs* they nominally served. The fact that the offices of Grand Vizier and *reisülküttab* tended to rotate rapidly, sometimes changing twice in one year, may have had a negative effect on the implementation of Ottoman policy. Finally, the resistance of foreign ambassadors and consuls to reforms of the protection system also thwarted the Porte's

[117] Masters, 'The Sultan's Entrepreneurs'.

policies. Despite the limited effect of many of the measures taken by the Ottoman authorities, it must be remembered that the number of *berats* in circulation at the end of the eighteenth century did not exceed 250, a total that was much lower than has generally been thought heretofore. The Porte was certainly aware of the gradual growth of the number of foreign protégés, but its own inquiries showed that the system had not got out of hand, despite reports to the contrary.

The Legal Status of Beratlıs: *Expert Opinions*

The following discussion of a document from 1797 serves as a conclusion to this chapter. It concerns a questionnaire about the legal status of the Ottoman protégés of foreign communities sent to chancellors of the embassies and legations in Istanbul of Prussia, Venice, Sweden, Spain, Austria, Russia and the Kingdom of the Two Sicilies. Although the document is found in the family archives of the Dutch ambassador Van Dedem van de Gelder, it is not exactly clear who formulated the questions posed to these officials, or why.[118] Six questions touching upon several fundamental aspects of the protection system, including the legal status of Ottoman protégés, were put before the chancellors. The first to answer them was Michel Bosgiovič, the chancellor of the Prussian legation, with whose opinions three of his colleagues agreed completely. Here the questions and answers will be presented together.

> Q: If a *berat* or a *ferman* [i.e. an order exempting a dragoman's servant] becomes available in Izmir, or in another port of the Levant, is it the ambassador resident at the Porte who may dispose of it as he sees fit in favour of someone else, or is it the consul of the same nation or someone else [who can dispose of it]?
>
> A: The *berats* and *fermans* belonging to them [i.e. the protégés] were a privilege the Sublime Porte accords directly and personally to the ambassadors of the respective nations residing at [the Porte]. Nobody else has the right nor the ability to dispose of the said diplomas when they are available, or when they have to be assigned for the first time.

[118] DNA, DGC, 23. The answer of Bosgiovič is undated, but that of Francesco Alberti, the secretary of the Venetian embassy was dated 11 March 1797. The others followed in subsequent weeks, Giacomo de Marini Reggio of the Sicilian legation being the last on 17 April 1797.

Bosgiovič and his colleagues thus confirmed the notion that the *berat*s formed a personal emolument of the ambassadors, and nobody else—not even the home authorities of the ambassadors—had the right or the ability to appropriate this privilege.

> **Q**: If a *beratlı* or servant ["*firmanli*"] established in Izmir or elsewhere is involved in a legal suit with a European ["*Frank*"] or a *beratlı* or servant of another nation are they to be tried in the first instance by his consul in the same way as a national?
>
> **A**: Every holder of a *berat* or *ferman* immediately comes under the protection of the ambassador who has granted him his diploma. Consequently, he is admitted to the enjoyment of the *nation*'s prerogatives, right and privileges, and therefore in all cases of disputes and discussion with a European or with a protégé of another *nation*, he must be judged and sentenced according to the laws of that *nation*.

In other words, the *beratlı*s fell under consular jurisdiction in the same way as foreigners, and any disputes between them and foreigners or protégés of other foreign communities fell under consular jurisdiction. The emphasis on the limitation of the consul's jurisdiction to disputes among foreigners and/or protégés is clear. By implication in all disputes involving common Ottoman subjects, the consul did not automatically have (sole) jurisdiction.

The vice-chancellor of the Spanish embassy, Comidas de Carbognairs, objected to Bosgiovič' answer because it suggested an "undefined nationality" and "equality of privileges" which the Spanish officer considered principally incorrect. He stated that only because they were protégés, did the *beratlı*s and their servants fall under consular jurisdiction. Two of his colleagues who were sent the questionnaire after De Carbognairs, agreed with his comments. This alternative opinion did not drastically differ from the view of Bosgiovič in practical terms, but the Spaniard correctly insisted that the protégés only enjoyed the same privileges as foreigners as long as they were protected.

> **Q**: If a consul established in Izmir or elsewhere has passed a sentence against a *beratlı* or servant of his own nation, and the latter procrastinates or disobeys the execution [of the sentence] within the prescribed term, is it not absolutely necessary for the aforementioned consul, should he not have the power to constrain him, to employ force to have his sentence executed; or should he ask, and wait for the permission and a special order of the ambassador of his nation to the Ottoman Porte to be able to have his sentence executed?

> **A**: The consuls established in the ports of the Levant represent their ambassadors in the consular duties of their jurisdiction, therefore they have absolute power to pass sentence against *beratlı*s and other protégés of their community who are established within [the area of] their jurisdiction; [they also have the power] to enforce the execution of the said sentence[s], even by way of force, without being obliged to ask for an order and permission from the ambassador, unless it is preceded by an appeal concerning the rules.

This view of the jurisdiction of foreign consuls is consistent with their consular *berat*s, as well as the regulations and laws of their own governments. Again the vice-chancellor of the Spanish embassy disagreed with his Prussian colleague, arguing that on no condition was appeal to the ambassador possible before a sentence was passed. On the remaining points, all seven chancellors were in agreement.

> **Q**: If a *beratlı* or servant considers himself aggrieved and offended by the sentence of his consul, can he appeal against it; and in such a case, which is the tribunal of the competent judge at which he must [file] appeal in the second instance [against] the sentence of his consul?

> **A**: The *beratlı*s and servants have the right to appeal against the sentence of a consul to the superior tribunal of the ambassador in Istanbul, observing the usual formalities of appeal.

Again we see that the arrangements codified in the capitulations with regard to adjudication in the first and second instance were still in force at the end of the eighteenth century.

> **Q**: Should a *beratlı* or servant be considered the absolute owner of his diploma, or rather an insecure possessor and usufructuary of the privileges attached to it?

> **A**: The *beratlı*s and servant are not, and should not be considered the absolute owners of the documents granted to them, so they cannot estrange [them], nor dispose of them in any way imaginable; but [they can only] simply, by virtue of the same [documents], enjoy during their entire life, and depending on the circumstances, the privileges and immunities expressed and contained in them.

The answer to the final question confirms that to the first, emphasizing that the holders of *berat*s did not own them and only enjoyed the concomitant benefits.

> **Q**: If someone is the creditor of a *beratlı* or servant, can he sequester, seize, and take hostage his diploma as security for the debt, and can such a diploma be mortgaged for a debt or for any other reason?

> **A**: The aforementioned *beratlı*s and their servants, as usufructuaries of their diplomas, and consequently being temporary holders, cannot mortgage for any reason their diploma; and similarly it is not possible to sequester [the diplomas] because of a [contractual] commitment or private debts of the usufructuary holder of the diploma, which as *fidei-commis* belongs incontestably to the ambassador in question.

Of these six questions the third was the most fundamental, and the comments of the Spanish vice-chancellor are especially important. Ottoman protégés were not naturalized foreigners, and therefore only enjoyed their privileges as long as they had got a *berat*. The answers to questions 5 and 6 confirm this further. This conclusion corresponds with the view of the English ambassador, Sir Robert Ainslie, who lectured his Prussian colleague about the status of protégés in the course of a dispute between two British merchants in Istanbul and a Prussian protégé as follows:

> You say, Sir, that Mr. Figa is a *naturalized Prussian*, because he has a *berat*, and because he is a dragoman. Well, a European ["*Franc*"] does not need a *berat*, and all *beratlı*s are honorary dragomans. It's the title that the Porte grants to subjects of the Grand Signor, who obtain, either by payment, or by other means, the protection of foreign ambassadors. These *berat*s are sometimes revoked, when they conduct themselves indignantly; in other words, they never cease to be subjects of the sultan ["*Rajas*"].[119]

This point cannot be overemphasized. The Ottoman protégés of foreign embassies and consulates may have enjoyed the same privileges as foreigners, but they always remained Ottoman subjects at the same time. This had a profound influence on the way in which disputes involving protégés were resolved, as the case studies of the following chapters show in more detail.

---

[119] BNA, SP 105/186, 207–209: Sir Robert Ainslie to De Gaffron, 30 March 1777 (in French). The underscoring appears in the original document.

CHAPTER THREE

AVANIAS: MISREPRESENTATIONS OF THE OTTOMAN LEGAL SYSTEM

When the British ambassador, Heneage Finch, was about to leave Istanbul for home in January, 1669, after a stay of eight years in the Ottoman capital, he wrote: "I thank God, that I am going, and soon shall be far away from the thousand dangers which here trouble mind and body: plague, earthquakes, loneliness, fire, *avanias*."[1] The last of these perils forms the subject of this chapter.

The word *avania* occurs frequently in the Western diplomatic correspondence and travelogues of the seventeenth and eighteenth centuries, and it has found its way into modern historiography, too. No standard definition of the word exists, but it is commonly understood as a synonym for "extortion", which is probably also what Finch meant. In Western sources, and even in some modern secondary literature, the word has become synonymous with the capriciousness of the Ottoman administration and legal system. For this reason alone the phenomenon of *avanias* deserves a place in this book, but there is even more to learn from it. An examination of some incidents labelled *avanias* in the Dutch and English sources reveals that several of them are easily recognizable as legal disputes. The fact that the foreigners involved at the time considered the outcome of these cases unjust should not prevent us from re-examining them with specific attention for the procedures followed and the Ottoman officers who implemented them.

An obvious starting point is the examination of the definitions of *avania* found in the relevant literature. Subsequently an analysis of the Western terminology and procedures of *avanias* is necessary. What do the regulations of the English Levant Company say about them, for example? Who decided what constituted an *avania*, and how was

[1] HMC, *Report on the Manuscripts of Allen George Finch, Esq. Of Burley-On-The-Hill, Rutland* i (London, 1913) (hereafter: *Finch*), 518, The Earl of Winchilsea to Sir John Finch, 20–30 January 1668–9. Finch was in office from 1660 to 1669.

the decision taken? In order to answer these questions a number of case studies will be presented, followed by an analysis. The sums of money the Westerners paid to resolve *avanias* will also be taken into account, because they shed further light on the Ottoman officers and the procedures involved. But first, I will discuss the relevant literature.

Historiography

Not a great deal has been written about *avanias*. Countless travelogues and diplomatic reports from the Ottoman Empire mention them, but scholarly analyses of them are rare. In the seventeenth-century volume of his classic *Histoire du commerce français dans le Levant*, Paul Masson opens with the period of what he calls "commercial anarchy" between 1610 and 1661. The first chapter deals exclusively with *avanias*. He defines them as "sums of money the pashas claimed from the merchants in the ports under the most diverse pretexts, pretexts that were unjust most of the time, and sometimes extremely bizarre."[2] Masson's definition speaks volumes. It identifies the culprits as "the pashas" and denies their claims against the French any possible legitimacy. The generic term "pashas" is not explained further. In subsequent pages the Ottomans officers' venality and hostility towards foreigners are given as explanations for their behaviour. Protesting on the grounds that certain actions were violations of the capitulations was often futile, Masson suggests, and could only be effective in combination with the threat of a complaint to the Porte. Even then the Westerners had to be lucky, according to the French author. If the "pasha" had friends at court, official complaints usually backfired. A protracted procedure before the *divan-ı hümayun* would then ensue, which was better avoided.[3] Masson's approach to the subject is unquestionably outdated, but his definition of *avanias* was shared by most of his contemporaries.[4]

---

[2] Paul Masson, *Histoire du commerce français dans le Levant au XVII*[e] *siècle* (Paris, 1896), 1.

[3] Ibid., 2–23.

[4] Cf. W.E. van Dam van Isselt, 'Avaniën in de Levant (1662–1688)', *De Navorscher* 56 (1906), 525–577. Also see Gérard Tongas, *Les relations de la France avec l'empire ottoma durant la première moitié du XVII*[e] *siècle. l'ambassade a Constantinople de Philippe de Harlay, Comte de Césy (1619–1640)* (Toulouse, 1942), 144: "La cupidité des pachas était la principale cause des avanies."

In his *History of the Levant Company* Alfred Wood calls *avania*s "a regular source of income to the local officials." He continues that

> in theory the merchants were adequately protected against such injustice by their capitulations, which, on paper, combined guarantees for security with an unusual degree of independence. But they rested only on the generosity of the sultan, and, in practice, their observation was governed by the discretion, and even more by the weakness of the Turkish government.[5]

According to Wood, the capitulations were tenuous agreements, the observation of which was always uncertain. The basic premise is that the Ottoman government was either unable or unwilling to enforce properly the privileges it had awarded foreigners. This pessimistic view of the capitulatory system is often found in the Western correspondence with the Levant and both Masson and Wood seem to have accepted it at face value. In the eyes of these authors *avania*s occurred because of the weakness of the central authorities and their inability to enforce theirs commands in the provinces. In other words, these authors considered *avanias* a symptom of the decline of Ottoman state authority and the centre's loss of control over provincial rulers.

The German scholar Karl Binswanger had a similar view on what he called *invania*s, but his approach is different from other scholars. In an attempt to formulate a new definition of the term *zimmet* (Ar: *dhimma*),[6] Binswanger investigated the status of non-Muslims in general in the Ottoman Empire of the sixteenth century. His research thus focused primarily on the legal status of the Jewish and Christian subjects of the sultan, not on foreigners from the West. Binswanger was chiefly preoccupied with proving that the *zimmet* was an agreement the Muslims did everything in their power to thwart. The author considered *avania*s proof of the Muslims' unwillingness to honour the arrangement.[7] The fact that Binswanger's book is seldom referred to in modern studies on the status of non-Muslims in the Ottoman Empire implies that it is either not widely known, or its radical views are not taken seriously.[8] There is, in any case, reason

[5] Alfred C. Wood, *A History of the Levant Company* (Oxford, 1935), 232–233.
[6] 'Dhimma' (Cl. Cahen), *EI*², 227–231.
[7] Karl Binswanger, *Untersuchungen zum Status der Nichtmuslime im osmanischen Reich des 16. Jahrhunderts mit einer Neudefinition des Begriffes "Ḏimma"* (Munich, 1977), 37–39; 321–322.
[8] For an indication of how Binswanger's book was received, see Hans-Jörgen Kornrumpf's review in *Südost-forschungen* 39 (1980), 492–495.

to question the solidity of Binswanger's methodology. For example, his analysis of the term *avania* relied exclusively on definitions found in sixteenth-century Western travelogues. The author made no attempt to assess the anti-Islamic biases frequently encountered in these works, nor does he seem to have examined individual cases of *avania*s mentioned in them. Furthermore, Binswanger's argumentation is weak at some points. For example, out of the nine reasons for revoking the *zimmet* that he identified in the Islamic law books, only three seemed to be relevant for *avania*s: the "seduction" of Muslims to apostasy; insults to God, the Koran or Islam; and adultery with Muslim women. The six other grounds for annulment of the *zimmet* were not, as far as Binswanger was able to establish, common pretexts for *avania*s. The author did not come across *avania*s caused by non-Muslims taking up arms against the Muslims; refusing to subject to the Muslim authorities; refusing to pay the poll-tax, committing highway-robbery; or collaborating with the enemy. Interestingly, Binswanger also did not find *avania*s in connection with the murder of Muslims. The author clearly felt he had to explain why only three out of nine "pretexts" appeared relevant for *avania*s. The reason, he argued, was simple: the other six accusations were too difficult for the Muslims to prove, and, more importantly, non-Muslims could less easily be tricked into these compromising situations![9]

The open fashion with which Binswanger discards data that might contradict his theories disqualifies the book's principal conclusions. The study is useful, nevertheless, because of its legal perspective and some of its results. It is interesting, for instance, that the author identifies the conditions under which Hanafi legal scholars considered the annulment of the *zimmet* legitimate. This means that individual non-Muslims could lose their *zimmi* status if they violated the pact in the eyes of the jurists. From a strictly legalistic point of view some procedures labelled *avania*s in Western sources might, then, have been unjust according to their reporters, unlawful these procedures were not as far as Islamic law was concerned. This fundamentally changes the perspective on at least some so-called *avania*s.

[9] Binswanger, *Untersuchungen zum Status der Nichtmuslime*, 321: "Waarum kommen die Punkte 1, 2, 3, 5, 6, und 9 nicht in Invania-Muster vor? Die Antwort liegt in diesem Muster selbst begründet: es ist klar, dass diese Punkte als Gegenstand einer Anklage schwieriger zu beweisen sind, aber vor allem kann eine solche Handlung dem Ḏimmī nicht untergeschoben, bzw. er kann dazu schwerlich verleitet werden!"

Olnon has recently challenged the common notion that *avanias* were illegitimate procedures by definition. His analysis of two *avanias* from mid-seventeenth-century Izmir shows that neither incident should be considered examples of Ottoman injustice, as Western sources suggest. The stereotype of the Ottoman legal system as arbitrary does not do justice to the complexity of most cases labelled *avanias*. European merchants, consuls and ambassadors reporting *avanias* to their home authorities were more concerned with justifying their conduct than with the accuracy of their accounts. Olnon rightly warns us not to rely exclusively on these European accounts, and to interpret *avanias* within their context.[10] He emphasizes that negotiations often took place during which incidents could still take a relatively positive turn, and if they did not, the Europeans themselves were sometimes clearly to blame. Olnon's argument that *avanias* were not necessarily arbitrary violations of the capitulations is convincing, and is supported by the distinction the Western authorities of Levant trade made between "national" and "personal" *avanias*. The Ottomans were blamed for incidents of the first category, while for incidents of the second kind the individual victims were held responsible.[11] Unfortunately Olnon does not offer further classifications of, or approaches to the phenomenon of *avanias* as a whole. His principal contribution lies in the introduction of case studies, the analysis of which sheds light on procedures of dispute resolution that were often omitted from official accounts.

Our survey of literature dealing with *avanias* has shown, then, that Masson considered them influential enough to characterize the earliest period of French contacts with the Levant as one of anarchy. Wood suggests that, in the face of rapacious *avanias* by Ottoman officials, the capitulations were little more than a paper tiger. Binswanger's argument that *avanias* were proof of the Muslims' universal malevolence vis-à-vis non-Muslims can confidently be rejected. Interestingly, however, from his material we can draw the conclusion that many procedures called *avanias* by Western observers were

---

[10] Merlijn Olnon, "Towards Classifying *Avanias*: A Study of Two Cases involving the English and Dutch Nations in Seventeenth-Century Izmir", in Alastair Hamilton et al. (eds), *Friends and Rivals in the East*, 159–186.

[11] This distinction is also noted by Daniel Goffman, *Britons in the Ottoman Empire, 1642–1660* (Seattle/London, 1998), 130, 208.

firmly rooted in Islamic law and thus perfectly legal from the Ottoman point of view. Olnon has taken a valuable step towards a new interpretation of *avanias* by focusing on the procedures involved, and by adopting an Ottoman perspective to analyse them. Now it is time to turn our attention to the primary sources and take a fresh look at the terminology of *avanias*.

Avania: *Definitions and Origins*

According to Alexander and Patrick Russell, the British physicians in Aleppo around the middle of the eighteenth century, "the word [*avania*] is Italian, meaning literally an undeserved injury. It is universally used in the Levant, and applied to all oppressive, or unjust exactions under false pretences." Its purported Italian origins notwithstanding, the Russell brothers also give an Arabic spelling for the word: اوانى.[12] The most important aspect of *avanias* that this definition conveys is the perception of injustice. The Russells use no less than four adjectives to emphasize this: "undeserved", "oppressive", "unjust" and "false". The Scotsmen's work is widely considered one of the most reliable Western accounts of Ottoman society in the pre-modern age, because of its scholarly detachment and unbiased approach. The Russells' definition of *avania* represents a rare lapse in judgement, which has probably gone unnoticed until now, because modern definitions tend to agree with it.

İnalcık asserts that the word *avania* was derived from the Arabic *ʿawān*, "anything extorted", and that "the attitude of the central government to the extortion of *avanias* by pashas varied according to the circumstances and the prevailing climate of relations with the 'nation' involved."[13] Like Masson, İnalcık thus suggests that governor-generals—the *beylerbeyis*, whose office was marked by the title "pasha"—were responsible for *avanias* and that the central Ottoman

[12] Russell, *The Natural History of Aleppo*—Patrick Russell ed., i, 316. In volume ii of this edition (p. 41), the communal taxes levied on the Ottoman *millets* are called *avanias*, as well.

[13] 'Imtiyāzāt' (Halil İnalcık), *EI*², 1181. Also see his contribution to Halil İnalcık with Donald Quataert (eds), *An Economic and Social History of the Ottoman Empire 1300–1914* (Cambridge, 1994), 9–409, esp. 191 (in the section "International Trade: General Conditions").

authorities did not necessarily disapprove of their actions. Sharing this view, Abraham Marcus notes that "the officials had a familiar repertoire of income extension devices to serve their ends: subjecting groups to exactions on contrived pretexts, a practice commonly known as *ʿawān* (or *avania*, as the Europeans in the region called it); issuing intolerable orders with the purpose of obtaining payments for rescinding them; and making various services and benefits dependent on bribes and exorbitant fees."[14] Goffman has recently defined the word *avania* as "an irregular and possibly crippling levy" and "an extraordinary demand for monies".[15] Finally, François Charles-Roux has characterised *avanias* as a form of "blackmail—a sum of money extorted from the nation [community] under the threat of persecution".[16] These definitions reflect the majority opinion, but alternative views have also been put forward. De Groot, for example, speaks of "so-called *avania* (financial retribution of an incidental nature, *vulgo* extortion)".[17] This definition suggests that *avanias* were not a structural phenomenon but had an "incidental nature". Moreover, by calling them a form of retribution, De Groot implies that the Europeans brought such incidents upon themselves somehow. Despite this and other alternative definitions, the majority of historians today still interpret *avanias* in the same way as Westerners did in the eighteenth century, as proof of the unreliability of the Ottoman administrative and legal system.

The notion that the etymology of word *avania* must lie somewhere in the Eastern Mediterranean is still current, although its exact origins remain unclear.[18] Neither Western nor Middle Eastern languages offer obvious possibilities for the word's etymology, but modern scholars tend to assume that it was derived from an Arabic term. In itself

[14] Abraham Marcus, *The Middle East on the Eve of Modernity. Aleppo in the Eighteenth Century* (New York, 1989), 95.

[15] Goffman, *Britons in the Ottoman Empire*, 56, 141.

[16] F. Charles-Roux, *Les Echelles de Syrie et de Palestine au 18ème siècle* (Paris, 1928), 86–87; quoted in Ye'or, *The Dhimmi*, 55, where *avanias* are discussed in a section on *avanz*.

[17] Alexander H. de Groot, 'The Dragomans of the Embassies in Istanbul, 1785–1834', Geert Jan van Gelder and Ed. de Moor (eds), *Eastward Bound. Dutch Ventures and Adventures in the Middle East.* (Amsterdam/Atlanta GA, 1994), 130–158, esp. 154.

[18] Aldo Gallotta, Alessio Bombaci, "The History of *avania*" in Barbera Kellner-Heinkele and Peter Zieme (eds), *Studia Ottomanica. Festgabe für György Hazai zum 65. Geburtstag* (Wiesbaden, 1997), 53–73.

the idea that Europeans might have borrowed an Ottoman term—be it Turkish, Arabic, Persian,[19] or otherwise—is plausible. Plenty of names of Ottoman offices, textiles, taxes and legal terms are found in the Western correspondence from the Levant. The orthography generally reflects how the Ottomans words sounded to the foreign ear. Common examples are "haratz" or "garatz" (*haraç*, poll-tax), "hattesherif" (*hatt-ı şerif*, handwritten order of the sultan), "illam" (*i'lâm*, report) and "hoggiet" (*hüccet*, legal deed). These words were so much part of the vocabulary of every-day life of Westerners in the Ottoman Empire that they also found their way into the letters and reports they sent home.[20] It is important to note that the actual Ottoman terms were indeed universally used throughout the seventeenth and eighteenth centuries, so there is no reason to doubt the correspondence between the Ottoman originals and the European loans. This is not the case with *avania* and *ʿawān*, however. Nor do the Ottoman documents appear to contain any similar words, which might correspond with *avania*.

An Ottoman document in which one might expect to find the Turkish equivalent for *avania* concerns the unwarranted demands made on behalf of the admiral of the Ottoman navy on British ships at the end of the seventeenth century, a clear violation of the capitulations. The soliciting of presents seems just the sort of thing that merited the label of *avania*, but the Turkish text of the *ferman* addressing the issue simply states that

> *Kapudanım . . . İbrahim Paşa . . . tarafindan İngiliz gemilerinden hilâf-ı ahdname-i hümayun pişkeş ve hedaya talebiyle rencide olunduğun bildirüb . . .*
>
> Having been informed that English ships were bothered by my admiral . . . İbrahim Paşa with demands for gifts and presents contrary to the capitulations . . .

---

[19] Edhem Eldem states that *avania*, "probably derived from the Persian *avan* (bully, brute), was one of the most frequently used terms to describe the abuses and extortions experienced by European merchants at the hands of Ottoman officials." Edhem Eldem, "Istanbul: from Imperial to Peripheralized Capital", in Edhem Eldem, Daniel Goffman, and Bruce Masters, *The Ottoman City between East and West. Aleppo, Izmir, and Istanbul* (Cambridge, 1999), 160.

[20] For a list of Ottoman terms that often appear in Western sources, as well as a list of Turkish expressions that occur specifically in Dutch sources from seventeenth- and eighteenth-century Ankara, see the final pages of Jan Schmidt, "Dutch Merchants in 18th-Century Ankara", *Anatolica* XXII (1996), 237–260.

The English ambassador had demanded that a *ferman* be issued forbidding this practice, which was granted by the Porte. Further on in the document the Ottoman navy was told in no uncertain terms that such practices were forbidden, but none of the words used even resemble *avania*.[21] The same is true for other Ottoman documents concerning the harassment or molestation of foreigners.[22]

Documents concerning the execution of a Maronite dragoman in the service of the Dutch consulate in Aleppo for killing a shepherd illustrate how the word *avania* crept in during the translation process. This *avania* will be discussed in more detail below, but the documents involved must be mentioned already at this point. They include the Ottoman translation of a petition to the Porte by the Dutch ambassador, a report by the qadi of Aleppo sent to Istanbul to explain the incident, and the Ottoman government's response to the ambassador's petition. A letter about the issue from the *nekibüleşraf* in Istanbul to his substitute in Aleppo has also survived. None of these texts in Ottoman Turkish contains the word *avania*, but one of the Western documents does. It is interesting therefore to compare this document with the Turkish translation, paying particular attention to the use of the word *avania*. The Dutch ambassador's petition first recounts his version of events, pointing out that the affair was a violation of European privileges. The Italian original of the petition states that:

> *Ora dunque facendosi dell'avanie al Dragomano del Nostro Console di Nederlanda, dimorante nella Città d'Aleppo dicendoglisi voi avete fatto moriri una Persona, che di ciò il passato Governatore di Aleppo, Eccellissimo Mustaffa Pascia, senza far ragvoglio [sic] alla Fulgida Porta, fecè contra l'Imperiali Capitulazioni impicare il nostro Draghomano . . .*[23]

Avanias were thus committed against the dragoman of our consul of the Netherlands, residing in the city of Aleppo, saying "you have killed

[21] Necmi Ülker, *XVII. ve XVIII. Yüzyıllarda İzmir şehri tarihi I: ticaret tarihi araştırmaları* (Izmir, 1994), 92–93.

[22] See, for example, two *hüküms* from Murad II ordering Ottoman officials not to molest three Englishmen (Skilliter, *Harborne*, 214–217, 241), and several safe-conducts (Ibid., 240, 242, 234). None of these documents contain the words *avania*, *ʿawān*, or any similar term. Also see ENA, SP 110/88: 193r–192r (Ottoman), 192v–191v (Italian): Ferman, dated beginning Safer 1100/25 November–4 December 1688, chastising the dragoman of the *mahkema* in Aleppo, Arslan Çelebi, for meddling in the affairs of the English community and extorting money from the English. Neither text contains the word *avania* or anything similar to it.

[23] DNA, LAT 1095, 62–63: Suplica [1731].

a man", on which [accusation] the former governor of Aleppo, his Excellency Mustafa Paşa, without having recourse to the Sublime Porte, had our dragoman hanged . . .

The Ottoman translation of the petition reads:

> *Medinet-i Haleb'te mukim Nederlanda konsolosumuzun tercümanın itham ve katl-i nefs eyledün diye iftira ve musabiqan Haleb valisi saadetlu Mustafa Paşa hazretli Asitane-i Saadete arz ve havala etmedi hilâf-ı ahdname-i hümayun tercümanımızı salb etmekle* . . .[24]
>
> Mustafa Paşa, the former governor of Aleppo, accused a dragoman of our Dutch consul residing in the city of Aleppo and slanderously suggested that "you have killed [a man]", but he did not [write] a petition and send it to the Porte, but by hanging our dragoman contrary to the Imperial Capitulations . . .

The Italian *avanie*, the plural of *avania*, was translated into Ottoman with the words *diye iftira*, "slanderously suggested", which appear in a similar context in other documents.[25]

These examples suggest that the word *avania* was, or had become, an exclusively Western term by the beginning of the eighteenth century. If the word was derived from the Arabic *ʿawān* (or a similar word) to begin with, it was not, or no longer, the term used by the Ottomans to describe the incidents it covered in the eyes of the Europeans in this period.

Avanists

The previous section has shown that the occurrence of the word *avania* in Western translations of Ottoman documents should clearly be treated with suspicion, but some are worth quoting here, nevertheless. Consider, for example, the translation of article 72 of the French capitulations of 1740, published in the memoirs of the French ambassador, the Count de Saint-Priest:

---

[24] Ibid., Ottoman text between pages 63 and 64 on folios without pagination.

[25] Susan Skilliter translated the phrase *diye iftira* in the English capitulation of 1580 (art. 11) as "[to] calumniate". Skilliter, *Harborne*, 88. The same words are used in the English capitulation of 1601 in Feridun Beg, *Münşeat-i Selatin*, 476. This early eighteenth-century translation of *diye iftara* for *avania* is also consistent with the *Regola del parlare Turcho* referred to by Bombaci. Gallotta and Bombaci, 'The History of *Avania*', 72. The authors do not mention the date and place of publication of this *Regola* and I have been unable to identify it.

> On nous aurait aussi représenté que, dans les procès qui surviennent, les dépenses qui se font pour faire comparaître les parties, et pour les épices ordinaires, étant supportées par lui qui a le bon droit, et les *avanistes* qui intentent des procès, n'étant soumis à aucun frais, ils sont invités par là à faire toujours de nouvelles avanies; sur quoi, nous voulons qu'à l'avenir, il soit permis de faire supporter les susdits dépens et frais par ceux qui oseront intenter contre la justice un procès dans lequel ils n'auront aucun droit: [. . .][26]

In the Ottoman legal system the party most favoured by the outcome of the trial (*lui qui a le bon droit*) paid the court fees and other expenses. This made the filing of frivolous claims an attractive form of harassment, because even if the case was decided in favour of the accused, he still had to foot the bill. At the request of the French, this article was therefore introduced in the French capitulations of 1740, stating that when people brought suits "contrary to justice", the qadi should demand payment of the court's expenses from them, instead of the party who had been wrongly accused.

This article is interesting for several reasons. Firstly, it illustrates the dynamics of the capitulatory system, since the addition of the article clearly aims to prevent from recurring certain negative effects of Ottoman legal procedures the French had experienced in the past. Secondly, the article shows how the system could be abused to create an *avania*. Finally, and most importantly, it shows that anyone could be responsible for an *avania*. All one had to do was file an unfounded complaint at the courthouse. The words *les avanistes* clearly refers to anyone who did this.

A letter written by the Dutch consul in Aleppo in 1767 indicates that the problem addressed by this article in the French capitulations of 1740 still existed almost two decades later. In the document the consul identified two officers of the city's central Islamic court as *avanist*s. They were Mustafa Efendi, the chief clerk of the court, and Bekir Ağa, the *çavuşlar ağası*, or leader of the court's ushers. These officers, who were reportedly in league with the city's governor-general, were held responsible for several unspecified *avanias*.[27] Relatively little is known about the role of officers of this level in

---

[26] M. le Comte de Saint-Priest, *Mémoires sur l'ambassade de France en Turquie et sur le commerce des Français dans le Levant*, (Paris, 1877), 512–513. My italics.

[27] DNA, LAT 664: Nicolaas van Maseijk to Willem Gerrit Dedel, 24 November 1767.

the court procedures, but as chief clerk the former was probably responsible for the registration of complaints. The capitulations contained explicit orders not to accept claims without proper documentation, which implies that a check took place before cases actually came to court. In practice this check was probably the responsibility of the court's chief clerk. Therefore it seems likely that the Dutch consul's complaint concerned Mustafa Efendi's acceptance as legitimate of complaints that, in the eyes of the Dutchman, should have been rejected out of hand on the basis of a lack of documentary evidence. The leader of the court's ushers was probably responsible for the delivery of the summons to appear before the qadi, which might explain his role in the "scheme" the consul complained about. With the support of the governor-general these men thus seem to have facilitated *avania*s, rather than personally causing them.

The word *avanist* was not only used in connection with Ottoman officers. The seventeenth-century French traveller and diplomat Laurent Chevalier d'Arvieux mentions an incident in 1683 in which the Armenian cook of a French merchant had accidentally burned himself. After seeing the wounds, the cook's brother threatened to go to the qadi to demand compensation from the French. D'Arvieux refers to this man as an *avaniste*, despite the fact that no actual *avania* seems to have occurred.[28] Another example of this wider meaning of the word *avanist* is found in a letter written by the English ambassador, John Murray, of 1769. He wrote that "I am sorry to say [it], but the Turk is not the only Avanist in the Country."[29] Here the word *avanist* does not refer to anyone involved in *avania*s, but has a more general meaning. In fact, this statement refers to the unreliability of the ambassador's own interpreters. Murray seems to have thought that their conduct made him more vulnerable to Ottoman pressure, instead of shielding him from it. *Avanist* here clearly meant (potential) "troublemaker" of any kind.

The word *avania* itself thus also spawned a new "technical" term, *avanist*. The use of this term in our sources shows that it was applied to various Ottoman officers, and sometimes also to common non-Muslim subjects of the sultan. Anyone who might cause an *avania*

[28] Laurent Chevalier d'Arvieux, *Mémoires du Chevalier d'Arvieux* (Paris, 1735), V, 404–405.

[29] BNA, SP 110/86: John Murray to Lord Stormont, 3 January 1769.

risked being branded an *avanist*. The most important conclusion we can draw from this is that not only senior Ottoman officials were responsible for the instigation or execution of *avanias*, as most modern definitions of the word maintain.

The Making of Avanias

Who decided what constituted an *avania*? What were the procedures involved? Because the term *avania* does not seem to occur in the Ottoman sources of this period, it is only logical that we turn to the European records for answers.

The Europeans in the Ottoman Empire distinguished "personal" from "national" *avanias*. The Levant Company regulations of 1679 concerning *avanias* show the difference between the two categories. The first sentences read:

> That no Avania or pretence whatsoever happening in Turk*ey* be adjudged National, where the same ariseth by the default or misdemeanour of any particular person or persons, in w*hi*ch case the person or persons so offending shall bear his or their own Avania at his or their own cost, and Expence;[30]

According to the Levant Company an *avania* was a "pretence" by definition, but Englishmen could clearly be held responsible for them nevertheless. Only when no individual member was to blame for the occurrence of an *avania*, should the English communities in the Levant consider it a "national" affair. *Avanias* that were considered "national" were paid from the treasury of the community. The money was paid from the revenues of the consular duties paid by the merchants on imported and exported goods. As the English ambassador wrote in relation to an *avania* in Izmir in the year 1663, "what indeed doe they pay their consulage for, but to be protected?"[31] The Dutch and French communities in the Ottoman Empire had similar arrangements, also distinguishing "personal" from "national" *avanias*.

---

[30] BNA, SP 105/178, 262–263, "An order of the Levant Company concerning Avanias, Made the 19th of May 1679."

[31] HMC, *Finch*, 379–382, esp. 380: The Earl of Winchilsea to Sir Heneage Finch, 5 June 1665. The *avania* concerned one Weymouth Carew, an English merchant in Izmir, but the circumstances of the case are unclear.

Whether a certain incident was a "personal" or a "national" *avania* was usually determined by the consul and the assembly of the merchants on the basis of the home authorities' regulations. For example, the Dutch governing body, the States General,

> have on 7 October 1675 adopted in their own statute the rule that the consul, deputies, and the entire nation should judge any extraordinary cases that may occur, which, respecting this resolution, was also done in this case by the Gentlemen Directors.[32]

The Directors of the Levant Trade, whose headquarters were in Amsterdam, thus had the authority to review the decisions made by the ambassador or consul and the local community of Dutch merchants. In the end the States General retained the right definitively to determine which incidents were paid from communal funds. The Dutch authorities did not prescribe decision-making procedures, contrary to their English counterparts.

The English regulations were more detailed than those of the Dutch:

> And if it shall happen to be doubtful whither an Avania be personal or National, The L*or*d Embassadour or respective Consuls in the Factories of the Company & such as have license to Trade, and the sons & servants of Freemen/Excepting those who are particularly concerned in such Avania/& shall offer a voluntary Oath to be taken by them & shall take the judgements & opinions of all those who do take the said Oath and according to the plurality of such votes the case shall be accounted to be either Personal or National; but still with ref*e*rence to the Comp*any* at home to be finally determined as the Comp*any* themselves shall judge.[33]

The differences between the English and Dutch regulations were largely due to the different forms of their trade organisations. Until the middle of the eighteenth century the Levant Company had a monopoly it was anxious to protect. Hence the precise rules about who was entitled to vote in this procedure. Those who could vote first had to take an oath, probably swearing that they did not have any personal interests in the matter under consideration. Although this vote is called voluntary, the opinion of anyone who refused to

[32] DNA, LH 239: Document concerning the discharge of extr*aordinary* avanias, 1708.

[33] See footnote 30.

take it was not to be taken into consideration. Decisions were based on a simple majority of those who had taken the oath.

The possibility to have an incident declared a "national" *avania* was only meant to function as a safety net, and a system of checks and balances existed to prevent its abuse. On the local level this was the responsibility of the consul. If an individual member of the nation was confronted with a claim he considered unjust, he could report it to the consul as an *avania*. It was thus the "victim" of the *avania* who usually asked for it to be declared a matter of national concern. If the consul thought the individual himself was to blame for what had happened, he could dismiss the request and refuse to call an assembly. The applicant could appeal against this decision to the ambassador. Similarly, when the consul considered the incident clearly unjust, he could apparently declare it a national *avania* without consulting the community of merchants first. In most cases, however, the consul called an assembly of the nation to discuss the matter. The minutes of such meetings show that each participant was asked for his opinion. When the discussions had ended, the consul formulated the decision on the basis of the majority opinion.

In the Dutch consular system the impartiality of the consul was ensured further by the election of several deputies (*assessoren*) by the assembly of the nation. The deputies assisted the consul, while supervising his office at the same time. With all foreign communities in the Levant, appeals to decisions of the consul and nation could be filed with the ambassador, who would either review the matter personally, or delegate the task to one of his officers. The ambassador, in his turn, answered to the home organisation for the Levant trade, which reviewed all *avania*s declared "national". In case of a disagreement between the community in the Ottoman Empire and the organisation of the Levant trade over such a declaration, the sovereign had the final word.[34]

---

[34] In 1665 the English ambassador, Finch, refused to accept the decision of the Levant Company that an *avania* that occurred in Izmir in 1663 had been declared national without good reason. He wrote that he would disregard the Company's orders, unless the King confirmed them. In this case it seems the victim had offered to pay the *avanias* himself and leave the Levant, but the community decided otherwise regarding the case as a violation of the capitulations. It was thought that the Ottomans would construe the innocent Englishman's departure as an admission of his guilt, which would create a dangerous precedent. HMC, *Finch*, 381.

Since every reported *avania* was judged on its own particular circumstances, it is difficult to determine which criteria the members of foreign assemblies in the Ottoman Empire who had to classify such incidents used. Everyone was supposed to put the national interest before any other considerations, but in practice personal sympathies must have played a role that is impossible to measure. Cases were invariably declared "national" when what had happened was considered a violation of the capitulations. This remains a vague criterion, because the texts of the *ahdname*s generally allowed various interpretations. In the same way *avania*s were considered "personal" if the "victim" could not reasonably be held accountable for the incident. When reported *avania*s were not clear-cut, it came down to the personal opinions of the members of the assembly. In those cases it seems that, if an incident was considered random, and it could have happened to anyone, it was declared "national".[35]

The procedures by which incidents were labelled *avania*s were exclusively European. Any member of a foreign community could present a case as an *avania* to his consul or ambassador asking to have it declared "national", which meant that he was compensated for the expenses from the treasury. The consul or ambassador decided if the case needed to be voted on or not. If he considered it clear-cut, his decision was enough to settle the issue until the assembly confirmed it at a later date. Once a "victim" had presented an incident as an *avania*, the label stuck. The only distinction made was between "personal" and "national" *avania*s, the former being payable by the "victims" themselves, the latter being recognized as unavoidable examples of Ottoman injustice for which the payment of consular duties formed a kind of insurance. It would be preferable not to consider cases declared "personal *avania*s" *avania*s at all, but we cannot for the sake of analytical convenience ignore the fact that the Europeans in the Levant applied the term to both categories. In the remainder of this chapter I propose to examine examples of both types of *avania*s.

[35] Ibid., 300: The Factory of Smyrna to the Earl of Winchilsea, 31 December 1663.

Case Studies

Despite the frequency with which *avania*s occur in Western sources, few case studies have been published. Two examples are discussed in Olnon's article, and in a Dutch publication of 1906 several more are described, but not analysed.[36] Shalit briefly mentions three *avania*s as proof of the systematic suppression of foreigners by the Ottoman authorities.[37] Our investigation of this phenomenon requires qualitatively and quantitatively more substantial data. This section offers only nine examples of *avania*s found in Dutch and English archives. Naturally this is still too small a sample to serve as a basis for solid conclusions. Their presentation has two aims. First, to identify the variables, that, added up by the victims and the assembly of the *nation*, resulted in the application of the label *avania*. Second, I will apply the Islamic legal approach proposed in Chapter One to test whether it furthers our understanding of Ottoman mechanisms of justice.

The European Perspective: Summaries of Nine Avanias

An inventory of the resolutions of the Dutch States-General in the seventeenth and eighteenth centuries yields the first four references to *avania*s, the others were reconstructed from English sources, as well.[38]

Case 1. On 1 December 1663 the States General allowed the Directors of the Levant Trade to levy the sum of 200,000 Guilders from the Dutch mercantile communities throughout the Levant to pay the *avania* of the ship *Keizer Octavianus.* This first example of an *avania* concerns the surrender of his ship and cargo by a Dutch captain who was caught unaware by several Maltese corsairs, while he was

[36] Van Dam van Isselt, 'Avaniën in de Levant (1662–1688)', 525–577. The author approached the subject in much the same way as Masson. Cf. supra, 1–2.

[37] Shalit at one point inexplicably equates *avania* with *kasabiyye*, but elsewhere he calls *avanias* "erpresserischen Forderungen". Shalit, *Nicht-Muslime und Fremde in Aleppo und Damaskus*, 19, 278. The cases are found on pages 279–280.

[38] DNA, LH 235. This volume has neither page nor folio numbers. Since matters were registered chronologically, the references to the following examples are traceable by their dates.

lying at anchor off the Egyptian coast. Not a single shot was fired during the surprise attack, during which only the ship's cargo was taken. These goods were destined for Istanbul and partly belonged to a number of high-ranking Ottoman officers in Egypt. The captain of the *Keizer Octavianus* did not report the incident to the Egyptian authorities, but quickly lifted anchor and sailed off instead. The owners of the robbed goods held the Dutchman responsible, suspecting him of being in league with the corsairs. In his absence they laid their claim before the *divan-i hümayun* in Istanbul, where the Dutch resident in the Ottoman capital represented the Dutch captain. Assigning responsibility for the loss of the cargo to the Dutch government, the Imperial Council sentenced the Dutch resident to pay an enormous sum to reimburse the Ottoman victims. In order to raise this sum a tax was levied on all Dutch communities in the Levant. The Dutch considered the whole affair highly unjust, claiming that the Ottoman government had been misled by the Egyptian victims of the corsairs. The Dutch in the Levant clearly thought that the Egyptians had instigated this *avania*.[39] The scale of this event and the fact that it affected all Dutch merchants throughout the Eastern Mediterranean makes this the "national *avania*" *par excellence.*

Case 2. On 18 December 1698 the ruling body of the Dutch Republic made arrangements for the payment of an *avania* levied on account of a soldier on the ship *Admiraal Tromp* who had done something to "a Turkish woman". Little is known about this *avania,* but it was evidently an incident on a much smaller scale than the previous one. It seems that a Dutch soldier had arrived by ship in İskenderun (Alexandretta), Acre or Cyprus and had given offence to a "Turkish" woman, which probably means that she was a Muslim. What he did exactly is not mentioned in the sources, but the considerable fine or bribe of 7,000 Dutch Guilders is. This was four times the annual expenses of the Dutch consulate in Aleppo around this time.[40] Since the States General paid the sum, it was evidently declared a "national" *avania.*

---

[39] Several documents about this case were published in Bronnen II, 444–459.

[40] DNA, LH 235; Expenses of the Dutch consulate in Aleppo in 1697 amounted to 1,748 Guilders. DNA, LH 162 (1), "Nota der onkosten..." (Account of the expenses of the consulate).

Case 3. Our third brief example of an *avania* was registered on 24 October 1709, when the Dutch government ordered their consul in Livorno to reach an agreement with an Ottoman emissary, allowing him to draw the funds required to pay this *avania* from the treasury of the States-General. The reference concerns a case similar to that of the *Keizer Octavianus*, but this time the corsairs in question were Dutch. They had raided a number of French ships, capturing both cargo and Ottoman passengers. In contravention of Dutch agreements with the Ottomans, the corsair captains sold the passengers as slaves. The victims, the owners of the goods captured as well as some of the slaves who survived, eventually complained to the *divan-i hümayun*. The Ottoman government sent an emissary to Livorno, where some passengers were still held prisoner, in order to demand their release from the Dutch consul there. Although the Dutch government did not think the Ottoman authorities had a case, they decided to order the consul in Livorno to negotiate a compromise to prevent further escalation of the dispute.[41] The Dutch ambassador in Istanbul eventually settled the case several years later and the expenses were paid from the national treasury.

Case 4. The fourth summary of an *avania* from the Dutch States-General's registers is dated 1 October 1753, when a letter from the ambassador in Istanbul to the Dutch rulers was read in an assembly. It concerned the *avanias* against the Dutch consul in Aleppo caused by his English colleague. The context of this case is different again. For several years the Dutch consulate in the Syrian city of Aleppo had been in the care of the English consul there. In 1753 the States-General appointed an arrogant, young Dutchman to the post. He travelled to Syria to take over the consulate from his English colleague, instantly demanding to be recognized as consul. This was counterproductive, because he had not yet received his Ottoman deed of appointment (*berat*). The English consul refused to relinquish the post until had he received official confirmation of his dismissal, raising the Dutchman's anger. When the new consul subsequently applied for his official audience with the Ottoman authorities despite the fact that he had not received his *berat* yet, the governor-general

[41] For a more extensive discussion of this and other such cases, see van den Boogert, "Redress for Ottoman Victims of European Privateering', 91–118.

of Aleppo admonished him for his impatience. The English consul reported that the Ottoman authorities had forced the Dutchman to pay a fine, which would constitute an *avania*, but the alleged victim denied this. If it had been true, the Dutch ambassador would have withdrawn his support of the consul, which indicated it would undoubtedly have been considered a "personal" *avania*.[42]

Case 5. In 1693 an *avania* occurred in Aleppo "due to a pair of green slippers belonging to the wife of one Richard Verschuer". According to an account by Verschuer, his wife had gone to the bazaar to have her worn slippers mended when he was out of town. Mrs Verschuer approached a shoemaker and showed him her slippers, asking him to mend them. The man instantly became enraged at the request. The shoemaker turned out to be a *şerif*, a descendent of the prophet Muhammad, who allegedly removed the Dutchwoman from his shop, taking her to the *nekibüleşraf*, the leader of the *eşraf* in Aleppo. The *nekibüleşraf* turned to the qadi, filing a complaint about the foreign woman's conduct. In the meantime a crowd had formed, which threatened to stone Mrs Verschuer. Eventually the interpreter of the Dutch consul, Jacob Cohen, intervened on her behalf. He agreed to the payment of some 519 Lion Dollars, bringing the incident to an end. The Dutch merchant had to pay this "severe *avania*", as he labelled it, from his own purse.[43] This case will be analysed in more detail below, as will the following three.

Case 6. A case involving the British community in Istanbul is also worth mentioning here. In May 1714 the British merchant Edward Stafford reported that about a month earlier one of his servants, an Armenian man called Zacharia, "being under distracted thoughts" had—in a suspected suicide—drowned in Stafford's cistern. The Englishman had instantly paid the qadi, his *naib* and other officers of the local court to prevent an *avania*. He also paid several witnesses "to prove him [Zacharia] non compos mentis". Others who

[42] This case is discussed in M.H. van den Boogert, "European Patronage in the Ottoman Empire: Anglo-Dutch Conflicts of Interest in Aleppo (1703–1755)" in A. Hamilton et al. (eds), *Friends and Rivals in the East*, 187–221, esp. 203–205.

[43] DNA, LH 161 (2); Notulen van de vergadering... (Minutes of the assembly...), 6 October 1693; Ibid., Richard Verschuer to the consul and nation, 7 October 1693.

received money included the "Imam of the Parish" and the witnesses whose names were mentioned in the *hüccet* that was drawn up in court about the incident. Stafford also rewarded the widow and her children for confirming "that he [Zacharia] had before attempted to make away with himself." Moreover, he spent money on the funeral and additional legal deeds to prevent future lawsuits. Several years earlier Stafford had had to pay twenty *kuruş* to prevent an *avania* when an irregular Ottoman soldier (*levend*) had been murdered near his house, but in 1714 he claimed to have spent 137 *kuruş*. This was still a small sum compared with the 2,500 *kuruş* that one Alexander Jacob had reportedly paid for a similar *avania* in the past, but Stafford applied for reimbursement from the community's treasury nevertheless.

In a general court of the British nation in Istanbul the chancellor read Stafford's petition out loud, as well as the Levant Company order of 19 May 1679 about *avanias* quoted above. Stafford claimed that he had incurred these preventive expenses on the advice of Giorgio Timoni and Luca Chirico, the ambassador's first and second dragomans. At the request of the council the claimant and Timoni publicly swore that their version of events was true. According to the regulations the council had to decide whether the *avania* was a communal ("national") burden or an individual one. The merchants unanimously declared it a national *avania*. Moreover, the council awarded him another 20 *kuruş* as compensation for the earlier incident. Formally the Levant Company still had to confirm these decisions, but Stafford received the money without delay.[44]

Case 7. Less than two years after Stafford's request, three British merchants in Istanbul submitted a similar petition to the ambassador. Robert Constantine, Robert Stamper and Dudley Foley reported that a corpse had been found in the vicinity of their houses. In order to "clear" the *avania* with the local authorities, the sum of 608 *kuruş* had been spent. This sum was split into eleven shares. The houses of Stamper, Constantine and two Italian merchants contributed two shares each, paying a total of 442 *kuruş* and 24 *akçe*.[45] The share of

[44] The council consisted of ten British merchants and was presided over by the ambassador, Sir Robert Sutton. BNA, SP 105/179, 565–6, Petition by Edward Stafford to Sutton, 11 May 1714; Ibid., 566, A general court held in Pera of Constantinople, 11 May 1714.

[45] The houses involved were those of Bernardo di Negri and another, probably

the three Britons came to 221 *kuruş* and 8 *akçe*, for which they demanded compensation from the community's treasury. The merchants knew that they could probably not have been forced to play blood money on the basis of Islamic law, but they feared that their refusal to cooperate might lead to public unrest in the neighbourhood. Moreover, the claimants feared that the matter would come to the attention of the Grand Vizier "who is a declared enemy of all Franks & Christians, would immediately upon his first notice of the matter of fact turn them all out of their houses & very probably cast some infamy upon them, no body knowing what mischief his humour might suggest to him." The three merchants had thus clearly incurred the expenses in the interest of the entire British community, they argued. One of their colleagues countered that the men would never have been involved in the first place if the dragoman had not meddled in the affair, but he failed to convince the rest of the council. The case was declared a "national" *avania* with a majority of votes.[46]

Case 8. Twelve years after the *avania*s in Istanbul another case involving the death of an Ottoman subject occurred in Aleppo. The Dutch consul in Aleppo, Daniël Boumeester, reports that he was on a leisure trip in the countryside with a group of English merchants. Hanna Jarah, a Maronite dragoman of the Dutch consulate, accompanied the party. According to Boumeester lightning struck an Ottoman shepherd pasturing his herd, killing the man. The Europeans simply happened to be around, but had nothing to do with the shepherd's death. Nevertheless, Jarah was arrested and imprisoned soon afterwards for murdering the man. A concerted effort by all European consuls residing in the city soon led to Jarah's release, but later the Dutch dragoman was taken into custody once again. The consuls were reportedly told that this was necessary to prevent the populace of Aleppo turning against the Maronite interpreter. The European representatives agreed to this form of protective custody after reassurances from the governor-general about the prisoner's safety. Despite

---

Italian, merchant, called Carli. The two houses contributing smaller shares (the reason for which is not explained) were those of Francesco Bragiotti, and someone called Pagano.

[46] Account of expenses in clearing an avania [1 Marzo 1715/6]; BNA, SP105/179, 783. For the full text, see below, 23.

the *beylerbeyi*'s guarantees, however, Jarah was subsequently taken to the citadel of Aleppo and strangled to death. His corpse was hung up for everybody to see "wearing the full dress of a dragoman, to the shame and ridicule of all Frankish nations." Adding even more insult to injury the qadi furthermore sequestered 180 *kuruş* from Boumeester himself, and 150 *kuruş* from Jarah's widow.[47]

Case 9. The final summary of an *avania* also concerns a dragoman in Aleppo, this time of the English consulate. In the first half of May 1767, Jirjis Aida, the First Dragoman of the English consulate in Aleppo was arrested and incarcerated in the citadel of Aleppo for the second time in his life. He was officially accused of "having assisted the Chelebi Effendi, or Chief of the Green Heads,[48] now exiled to Prusa [Bursa], in oppressing the Mahometan subjects, but it is generally imagined, that his offence is his riches, as he is a man that has carried on a very large trade for many years & is supposed to be the richest man in the place." Çelebi Efendi was the name by which Muhammad Tahazade, several times the *nekibüleşraf* of Aleppo and probably the most powerful man in Aleppo of this period, was commonly known. His close business connections with Aida, undoubtedly the most powerful non-Muslim in the city, will be discussed in some detail below. Although there were rumours that the dragoman would be sent to Istanbul to stand trial, this does not seem to have happened.[49] Aida remained imprisoned in the Aleppo citadel for a period of some sixteen months before he was released at the end of July, 1768. During that period the ambassador repeatedly pleaded his case with the Ottoman authorities, while Aida had also employed his personal network to affect his release.[50] The fact that no trial ever took place strengthened the English' conviction that the dragoman had been arrested on trumped-up charges. In a

[47] The Dutch version of events is mentioned O. Schutte, *Repertorium der Nederlandse vertegenwoordigers residerende in het buitenland 1584–1810* (The Hague, 1979), 358, and in Bronnen III, 30 n. 3, 31.

[48] The "Green Heads" were the *eşraf*, on account of their green turbans.

[49] DNA, LAT 664: N. van Maseijk to Dedel, 15 May 1767 (in Dutch). On "Çelebi Efendi" Muhammad Tahazade, see Margaret L. Meriwether, *The Notable Families of Aleppo, 1770–1830: Networks and Social Structure.* Unpublished PhD dissertation, University of Pennsylvania, 1981, 25, 238, 249.

[50] "The Aga of the Janisaries is Aide's friend & he has many that are ready to do him justice . . ."; BNA, SP 110/87: Murray to Preston, 11 July 1767.

letter to Aida the ambassador wrote: "your Capacity & your Industry have brought upon you the Envy of your idle Neighbours."[51] In the eyes of the directors of the Levant Company Aida's case was "from his] supposed great riches easy to be accounted for by any person that has had the word *Avania* explained to him."[52]

Some preliminary conclusions can be drawn from these summaries, despite their limited number. They show, for example, that the label *avania* was applied to a wide variety of cases spread over the entire Eastern Mediterranean. The scale of the incidents varied. The first and third cases are large incidents that involved the Dutch community in the Levant in general. The cases of the *Keizer Octavianus* (no. 1) and the Ottoman slaves in Livorno (no. 3) display a combination of aspects of international trade, law, and politics. Both cases eventually reached the *divan-ı hümayun*, where a mix of legal and political considerations determined their resolution. Interestingly, neither case constituted a violation of the capitulations by the Ottoman authorities.[53] The second and fourth cases had a more limited scope, involving, it seems, only a few people. About incident number 2 too little information has survived to allow firm conclusions from it, but it is clear that the incident involved only two people, one Dutch mariner and one, probably Muslim, woman. Moreover, it must have been considered a "national" *avanias*, because the States-General bore the financial consequences. None of the first three accounts of *avania*s thus unequivocally confirms the common notions about *avania*s. The fourth incident may not actually have been much of an incident at all. Even reports of *avania*s were potentially harmful to a consul's reputation, so this might have been little more than a malicious rumour. Regardless of whether it really was, or not, the report conforms with the stereotype of the *beylerbeyi* initiating an *avania*. The final five cases summarized above cast more doubt on the validity of received wisdom about *avania*s. They will be analysed in more detail in the next section.

[51] ENA, SP 110/87: Murray to Mr. George Aidé, 27 May 1767. Like other letters from the ambassador to A'ida this one was "sent in Italian, he not understanding English". Cf. ENA, SP 110/87: Murray to M. Aide, 11 July 1767.

[52] ENA, SP 105/119, 247: The Levant Company to the Pro-Consul & Factory at Aleppo, 5 February 1768.

[53] van den Boogert, 'Redress for Ottoman Victims of European Privateering', passim.

Analysis: The Ottoman Legal Perspective

In Chapter One I have argued, after Buskens, that state law (*kanun*) was the dominant element in the Ottoman legal system. In theory even the sultans were subject to the prescripts of *şeriat*, but in practice the Ottoman authorities had no qualms about adjusting theory to legitimise practice. The Europeans' legal regulations and consular practices of dispute resolution were un-Islamic and thus had no obvious place in the Ottoman legal system. I have argued that the Ottomans used *kanun* (in the form of the capitulations) to incorporate the European juridical customs in the Ottoman legal system. Under certain circumstances the Europeans were allowed to settle disputes among themselves. The most important condition was that these practices not be contrary to *şeriat*, an ill-defined criterion, the significance of which escaped most Europeans. In this section I will analyse five of the *avania*s summarized above by applying an Ottoman legal perspective as an alternative to the Euro-centric approach of many of the available sources.

In this section each individual case will be examined on the basis of the following questions. What is the legal issue involved? Do the capitulations apply to this problem, and, if so, what do they say? Finally, what was the role of the chief representatives of the Ottoman legal system, the qadi and the *beylerbeyi*?

The first case—number 5 of the previous section—involved a Dutchwoman and a shoemaker in Aleppo. The problem was the colour of her slippers, which were green. Green was the colour of Islam, which adorned the turbans of the descendants of the prophet Mohammad (*eşraf*), who for this reason are often referred to in the English sources as "Greenheads". Non-Muslims were not allowed to wear green, because it was considered an insult to Islam. The Ottoman authorities generally do not seem to have enforced this rule. Foreigners in Istanbul and Izmir never had any problems of this kind, the Dutchwoman's husband pointed out in vain.[54] Insulting Islam or the prophet Muhammad was a violation of the *zimmet*, as Binswanger has shown. The Dutchwoman was not a *zimmi*, but a *müste'mine*, so what do the capitulations say about this issue?

---

[54] DNA, LH 161 (2); Richard Verschuer at Larnaca, Cyprus, to the Dutch *nation* at Aleppo, 16 April 1694.

Neither the Dutch capitulation of 1612, nor that of 1680, contains an article about this type of incident, but article 11 of the English capitulation of 1580 is of interest here:

> *Ve bazı kimesneler "bize şetmeyledünüz" diye iftira idüp şahid-i zor ikamet eyleyüp mücerred celb ve ahz içün hilâf-ı şer-i kavim rencide ve remide eylemek istediklerinde men olunalar*
>
> And when people calumniate, saying: "You have insulted us", (and) make false witnesses stand, wishing to afflict and affright, contrary to the upright Holy Law, solely for the sake of extortion, let them be prevented.[55]

On the basis of the most-favoured nation clause, found in article 40 of the Dutch capitulations, the Dutch "victims" of this particular *avania* could have invoked the English article. However, this meant that the couple would have had to appear before the qadi in a formal suit brought against them by a *şerif*, who could probably have produced the two reliable Muslim witnesses needed for a conviction. Moreover, the non-Muslim foreign woman involved did not deny the charges, but argued only that this particular rule of Islamic law was hardly ever enforced.

Whether or not insulting Islam was a legitimate reason for revoking *aman* according to *şeriat* in this case, it is significant that the Dutch consulate and the assembly of the *nation* do not appear even to have considered invoking the capitulations in this case. The Dutch in Aleppo clearly blamed the couple itself for what had happened. This suggests that the Dutch community knew and accepted this basic prescript of Islamic law, expecting all its members to honour it, or bear the financial consequences of giving offence. This was therefore a "personal" affair, for which the Dutch community did not hold the "pasha" responsible.

Although the Dutchwoman was reportedly dragged before the qadi, the incident did not go to trial. A dragoman of the Dutch consulate quickly negotiated a settlement, agreeing that the couple paid a considerable fine to end the matter. How large a sum was 519 Lion Dollars in 1694? Changed into Ottoman currency the

[55] Transliteration by Ülker, *İzmir*, 307; Translation by Skilliter, *Harborne*, 88, 235. The words "solely for the sake of extortion" is a translation of... *rencide ve remide eylemek istediklerinde*, literally "wanting to cause damage and hurt."

amount stayed the same, so it is useful to know that "a sum of 500 *kuruş* represented a small fortune for Ottoman Aleppines."[56] This is illustrated by the fact that with this amount one could buy almost 35 standard camel loads (*kantars*) of grain in Aleppo around this time, which came close to 7,000 kilos.[57] The sum paid by Verschuer to put an end to the controversy over his wife's slippers thus was indeed considerable. To whom did the money go?

From the summary of the case above we have seen that the Ottoman parties involved in this incident were a *şerif*, the *nekibüleşraf*, and the qadi. The fact that a crowd had formed which threatened to stone the Dutchwoman also made it a matter of public order, which fell under the authority of the *beylerbeyi*. The following account of the expenses of this incident (table 4) shows which of these officers were included in the settlement.

The qadi received 150 Lion Dollars/*kuruş*. His subordinates, his lieutenant, deputy, servants, and Janissary as well as the doormen of the courthouse, were paid a total of almost 48 *kuruş*. In all, the qadi and his men received 40 per cent of the total sum. The *nekibüleşraf* received the same sum as the qadi, with an additional 17 *kuruş* for expenses, in all 32 per cent of the total. The interim governor-general of Aleppo (*müsellim*) and his officers received a total of 100 *kuruş*, c. 20 per cent. *Seyyid* Ahmad, *şeyh-i hare*, was probably the leader of the neighbourhood where the incident happened. I have been unable to establish who Esad Çelebi was, but he may have mediated in the matter. Since he had a scribe and two dragomans, he must have been a senior official whose office brought him into contact with the foreign communities in Aleppo. Hüseyin *Çavuş* was mostly likely a messenger in the service of the interim governor-general. The remaining name, *Seyyid* Ya'qub, was probably that of the shoemaker whose confrontation with Mrs Verschuer set this incident in motion.

[56] Masters, *Origins*, 61.

[57] Calculations based on Masters, *Origins*, 'Note on Weight and Currency Terms' (no page number) and page 113, where the average price of one *kantar* of grain is said to be between 10 and 20 *kuruş* in the period 1600–1750. For this calculation I have fixed the average price at 15 *kuruş* per *kantar*.

Table 4. Expenses incurred in the avania of Si[gn]ore Verschuer on account of the green slippers of his wife.

To the qadi Uzun İsmail Efendi	150
To his *kahya*	30
To the *naib*	15
To the servants of the qadi	5
To Es'ad Çelebi	10
To Ahmed Çelebi, his scribe	10
To his two dragomans	3
To the principal Janissary of the qadi	7: 40
To the *yasakçı* (? "Jessakie")	7
For two 'medini' per 'p.rae'[58]	7: 40
To the doormen of the [Court of] Justice	–: 40
To the leader of the *eşraf*	150
To *Seyyid* Yaqub	10
In the hands of the leader of the *eşraf* for expenses of his office	17: 40
To the *şeyh-i hare* called *Seyyid* Ahmad	5
To the *müsellim*	50
To his *kahya*	15
To Husayn *Çavuş*	10
To the 'shahnader'[59] of the *müsellim*	5
To his other servants	10
Lion Dollars	518
For the exchange of seven sequins	1: 60
In all	519: 60

Source: DNA, LH 161 (2): Onkosten gedaen voor de avanie van Si*gn*ore Verschuer wegens de groene muylen van synes vrouw.

The sums paid by Verschuer in 1694 to conclude the *avania* on account of his wife's green slippers afford a glance at the mechanisms of dispute settlement that were used. More than 90 per cent of the money went to the three branches of local government whose support for the settlement had to be secured. Because the case con-

[58] I have been unable to determine the meaning of these words. The abbreviation might mean Piasters, but even then it is not clear to me what justified this charge.

[59] The spelling is clearly *shahnadar*, but elsewhere the similar word *chasnadar* appears, which is almost certainly an abbreviation of *hazinedar*, treasurer. According to Redhouse's *Turkish and English Lexicon*, 845, the word *hazne* was short for *hazine*.

cerned a descendant of the Prophet Muhammad the support of the *nekibüleşraf* for the settlement was indispensable. The *eşraf* formed a large and influential group in Aleppo and their leader was undoubtedly asked to ensure that no further claims against the Dutch community arose from this incident after the settlement. The *müsellim* and his men were responsible for enforcing the arrangement among the rest of the inhabitants of Aleppo and they received 100 *kuruş* for their cooperation. Finally, the largest share went to the qadi and his subordinates, whose involvement was evidently the most important legitimisation of the settlement.

This affair may have been unjust in the eyes of the self-proclaimed victims, but it was neither a violation of the capitulations, nor a shining example of the injustice of the Ottoman legal system. Even the Dutch community in Aleppo blamed the couple involved themselves. A dragoman of the consulate prevented a trial by negotiating a settlement. The sum the couple had to pay did not constitute extortion, and although the "pasha" was included in the settlement, he had nothing to do with the original course of events.

Our second case did go to trial. It is interesting because it sheds light on Ottoman criminal procedures involving members of foreign communities, about which I have found relatively little material. It concerns case number 5 of the previous section, where a dragoman of the Dutch consulate in Aleppo was executed for the death of a shepherd, who died after having reportedly been struck by lightning. The case was not as simple as the Dutch consul represented it, however.

The Ottoman documents present a different version of events. According to a report by the qadi of Aleppo the incident happened on 7 Rebiyülahir 1143/20 October 1730, when the Dutch consul, his dragoman and a number of Englishmen were in the countryside. At the same time *Seyyid* Mehmed ibn *seyyid* Ali was pasturing his herd in the area, when he was hit in the head by a stray bullet fired from the harquebus of one of the Europeans. The wound was not instantly fatal. The dragoman, Hanna Jarah, reportedly reached the shepherd when he was still alive, because the man begged him for his life. Nevertheless, Jarah was said to have pushed the wounded man into the river, whereupon he drowned. Two Muslim witnesses confirmed the account, which was related to the court two days after the event by Husayn ibn *seyyid* Ali, a cousin of the victim. The authorities subsequently specially obtained a fatwa, which recommended that the dragoman be sentenced to death in retaliation for what he had done. The dragoman was subsequently sentenced to death by hanging.[60]

Jarah was probably arrested soon after the incident had been reported to the authorities. A concerted effort by the Dutch consul and his colleagues resulted in the dragoman's temporary release, but he was soon arrested once again. The Dutch consul was told that this done to protect the dragoman against the rage of the populace. Another Ottoman document records the extent of this civil unrest. It is a petition to the Porte signed by fourteen notables of Aleppo, all descendants of the Prophet Muhammad. This document reported that the popular unrest as a result of the case had been orchestrated by the *nekibüleşraf*, *Seyyid* Umar Efendi. According to this document, Umar Efendi had called upon everyone to follow the standard of the Prophet Muhammad and join him *en masse* to the courthouse in order to get the Dutch dragoman sentenced to death. The petitioners had refused to join the crowd, stating that the matter was the qadi's business. Nevertheless, *Seyyid* Umar had raised the standard of the prophet and continued his quest, inciting serious popular unrest. He directed the crowd to the governor-general's palace. The mob reportedly wrecked several markets and khans, even killing several Muslims, *eşraf* as well as others. There is no corroborating evidence for this final claim, which seems to have been intended to spice up the complaint. It seems that these *eşraf* seized the opportunity of the Dutch complaint to the Porte to try to get rid of the leader of their faction, but without success.[61]

The capitulations did not apply in this case, because acts of vio-

[60] ... *hususiyyen sadır olan fetva-yi şeriyye mucibinci mestur Hanna yerine kısasan katluhu hüküm etmeleriyle mastur Hanna şeran katl olunmağın* ... DNA, LAT 1095, The Ottoman text of this *hüccet-i şeriyye* is found on the folios between pages 55–56 and 57–58. For the Italian translation, see Ibid., 56–58, "un scritto p. Giustitia fatto circa il soprad.[to] affare, venuto da Aleppo [dated] nel giorno decima della Luna di Rebiulsani 1143 di nostra salute, circa li 22 Ott.[re] 1730." The names of the witnesses were Sulayman ibn Halil and Hasan ibn "Janiyula".

[61] DNA, LAT 1095, *Haleb'ten gelen mahzarın surettir*, on folio between pages 55–56. The Italian translation is found on 55–56. The *nekibüleşraf*'s superiors clearly did not take the account seriously, because the *Şeyhülislâm* and the *nekibüleşraf* of Istanbul merely warned him not to violate the privileges of the Dutch community. DNA, LAT 1095, Ottoman texts on unnumbered pages between 77–78 and 78–79: The *Şeyhülislâm*, Mehmed [Efendi], to the *nekibüleşraf* in Aleppo, undated; Ibid., same pages: The *nekibüleşraf* in Istanbul to his deputy in Aleppo, undated.

lence cancelled all privileges guaranteed by the *ahdnames*. The promise of friendship and peace on the part of the beneficiaries of capitulations was a fundamental condition for the grant of privileges on the part of the sultan. It was this promise that made the extension of *aman* permissible according to Islamic law. Naturally the killing by a non-Muslim of a Muslim constituted a violation of the condition and promise of peaceful conduct. Moreover, the capitulations only awarded jurisdiction to consuls and ambassadors in criminal matters exclusively involving members of their own community. In this case a *şerif* was killed, who was connected neither with the Dutch *nation*, nor the English. Even according to the capitulations, therefore, the Ottoman authorities had jurisdiction over this case.

From the Islamic legal point of view, the case was clear-cut. A cousin of the victim brought the case before the qadi. It was thus the next-of-kin of the victim who filed suit against the alleged killer, which is in accordance with Hanafi legal theory and Ottoman legal practice, where homicide is categorized as private prosecution. The next-of-kin of the murdered man was entitled to demand that his killer's life be taken in compensation for their loss. If the family forgave the killer, or agreed to an alternative punishment, the killer could not be sentenced to death.[62] In this case the cousin of the victim demanded Jarah's blood. The confirmation of this version of events by two reliable Muslim witnesses, also *eşraf*, was sufficient to establish guilt. Whether or not Jarah had been offered the possibility to speak is not clear from the documents, but in any case it would have been the word of one non-Muslim against that of three *eşraf*. The authorities subsequently specially obtained a fatwa, which recommended that the dragoman be sentenced to death in retaliation for what he had done.

The Jarah case appears largely to have conformed to Hanafi prescripts.[63] Only the fines imposed on the Dutch consul and the convicted dragoman's widow after the execution do not seem justifiable by law. These fines cannot be considered blood money (*diyet*), because the payment of compensation could be an alternative for capital punishment, not an addition to it. With some imagination it may argued

---

[62] Ibidem.

[63] Imber, *Ebu's-su'ud*, 236 ff.; also see his "Why You Should Poison Your Husband. A Note on Liability in *Hanafi* Law in the Ottoman Period", in Colin Imber, *Studies in Ottoman History and Law* (Istanbul, 1996), 253–261.

that the qadi used his discretionary powers to make the consul liable for corrective punishment (*ta'zir*), substituting a flogging with the payment of a fine. Similarly, it is possible that the money demanded from Jarah's widow was meant to cover legal fees. In the absence of more sources these explanations necessarily remain conjectural. If there was any truth to the report about the *nekibüleşraf*'s actions, concerns about public order may well have become mixed with strictly legal considerations, but the case against Jarah was legally solid and procedurally correct. The foreign communities in Aleppo at the time considered the punishments in this case excessive, but there is no reason to regard the Jarah case as an Ottoman infringement of the capitulations—unless it really was lightning that killed the shepherd.

The two similar *avania*s involving British merchants in Istanbul (summaries 6 and 7 of the previous section) revolved around the legal issue of communal liability. If a corpse was discovered murdered somewhere and the person had apparently died under extraordinary circumstances, it was Ottoman policy to hold the entire neighbourhood collectively responsible. If no culprits were found, the neighbourhood as a whole had to pay the blood money.[64]

The two cases in Istanbul occurred several decades after an article addressing this issue appeared for the first time in the French capitulations of 1673. It stipulated that

> Et s'il arrive qu'on tüe quelqu'un dans des quartiers ou sont les François, Nous deffendons qu'ils soient molestez en leur demandant le prix de sang [*diyet*], si ce n'est qu'on prouve en justice que ce sont eux qui ont fait le mal.[65]

On the basis of the most-favoured nation clause in their own capitulation of 1675 (art. 18), the English merchants could have invoked the article in the French capitulations. One of the dragomans of the embassy went to the Porte on a daily basis, and, in theory, he could have applied for a *ferman* exempting the English from the payment of *diyet* under these circumstances. If they had done this immediately after the first incident, the *ferman* could also have been used the sec-

[64] See Heyd, *Studies in Old Ottoman Criminal Law*, 106 and 115. These mechanisms of justice have been described in some detail for Aleppo in Marcus, *The Middle East on the Eve of Modernity*, 322 ff. Cf. Bianchi's notes about this in Noradounghian, *Receuil*, I, 304.

[65] Ibid., 145. It was the thirteenth of the new articles included in this capitulation. Noradounghian has numbered them separately.

ond time. This is not what happened, however, because the English nation chose to pay 745 *kuruş*, instead.

In the first case the largest share was clearly spent on legal procedures (see table 5). The qadi, his substitute (*naib*) and other officers of the *mahkema* are mentioned, as well as witnesses to the *hüccet* by which the drowned servant was declared *non compos mentis*. Unfortunately the sum paid to these officers is not further specified for the individual officers, but it constituted 68 per cent of the total. Moreover, legal deeds were also drawn up to ensure that no future claims would result from the incident. Court fees accounted for another 16 per cent of the total.

Table 5. Account of the charges of which Mr [Edward] Stafford disbursed to prevent greater mischief about the death of his servant, [Constantinople] April 1714.

Accompt of expenses made on occasion of my servant Zacharya drowning himself in my cistern.	
To the molah [qadi], Naip [*naib*] & other officers of the Mechemee [*mahkema*], witnesses to prove him non compos mentis, the Imam of the Parish & other witnesses to the Hoggiet	P. 93:60
To the widowe, guardian of his children to persuade them to confesse him distracted & that he had before attempted to make away with himself & other collateral circumstances	P. 12:00
More to them charges of his funeral	P. 10:00
For several Hogiets made with them to release me from all future demands	P. 22:00
[total:]	P. 137:60

Source: BNA, SP 105/179, p. 565.

For both cases it is useful to put the sums mentioned into perspective. What was the purchasing power of 137 *kuruş* in Istanbul in 1714? It was the price of some 78 Istanbul pikes (c. 53 meters) of Florentine satin of prime quality, or almost 40 pikes of fine Dutch broadcloth in white or red. The same sum purchased 17.25 *okka* (48.3 lb.) of cinnamon, nutmeg, or cloves. The sum of 137 *kuruş* was more than two years' salary of the "Turkish scribe" in the service of the Dutch embassy. The dragomans of the embassy received roughly this sum to cover their ferry expenses for the trip between Galata and Istanbul proper for a period of two years and eight months.[66] In other words, 137 *kuruş* was no fortune, but by local standards certainly a considerable sum. By the time Constantine, Stamper and Foley spent 608 *kuruş* in the Ottoman capital two years later in order to avert an *avania*, these prices do not seem to have changed significantly.

For the case involving the three English merchants in Istanbul in 1715/16 an "account of expenses in clearing an *avania*" has survived, which is reproduced in table 6.

Table 6. Account of expenses in clearing an *avania* [1 Marzo 1715/6].[67]

To the *voyvoda* of Galata	300
To 'Turks' of three neighbourhoods, Imams, and others	115
To the *mumçi*[68] officer of the *topçu* from Stamper & Foley	
4 pikes of cloth and one Sequin	23
To another neighbour one *çarşılık* [?]of cloth and a "good cut"[69]	11
To the officers of the *voyvoda* in all	15
To Abdullah, the *kahya* of the *voyvoda*	16
To the *voyvoda* of the Four Streets	16
To the *subaşı* and his officers	10
To the scribe of the *i'lâm* and others	10
To the sons of Hüseyin Ağa 8.5 pikes of Mahud cloth @ 4 Piasters	34
To their cousin 4 pikes of cloth	12
To the aforementioned sons of Hüseyin Ağa in cash in new *zolota*[70]	40
Added to a sample[71] and a pair of spectacles	6
	608

Source: BNA, SP105/179, p. 783.

[66] The Istanbul pike (*çarşu arşını*) measured 0.68 meters. See Eldem, *French Trade*, 35 n. 5. These prices were taken from DNA, LH 240, Account book of the Dutch embassy treasury in Istanbul, 1710–1724. The cloth prices concern the expensive quality that the Dutch presented in gifts to senior Ottoman officials.

[67] My translation from the Italian.

[68] Redhouse, *A Turkish and English Lexicon*, 2037 mentions *mumcu*, 'a matchlock-man; especially when employed as a body-guard'.

[69] The text has *ciaescirlik*, which might mean *çarşılık*, '(standard) market measure'. In Turkish the Italian word *mano* was gambler's slang for 'money' or a 'share' (of money). *Redhouse Turkish-English Dictionary* (Istanbul, 1997), 730. I gratefully acknowledge the help of Jan Schmidt and Elena Frangakis-Syrett with these terms.

[70] 1 *zolota* = 30 *Para*; 40 *Para* = 1 *kuruş*. Since 40 *kuruş* are mentioned here, the actual sum paid was 53 *zolota* and 10 Para.

[71] *mostra*; probably of cloth.

More than half of the sum paid by the English merchants went to the office of the *voyvoda* of Galata (54.44 per cent). He personally received 300 *kuruş* (39.34 per cent) while his lieutenant, Abdullah, was paid the relatively small sum of 16 *kuruş* (2.63 per cent). Other unnamed officers of the *voyvoda* received 15 *kuruş*. The *voyvoda* of the Four Streets, the Western nickname for the Beyoğlu quarter of Galata, also received a modest sum. The *subaşı* and his men, who were part of the executive branch of the Ottoman administrative and justice system, probably had to see to it that the settlement was enforced, which explains why they, too, received money. The payment made to an officer of the Master General of the Artillery (*topçu*) may indicate that he was somehow personally involved, but it is also possible that the proximity of the Imperial Canon Foundry (*tophane-i amire*) made it expedient to include a representative of the military in the settlement. The list of official charges ends with the entry of 10 *kuruş* paid to the scribe who wrote the official report about the matter and unspecified "others". The other expenses all concerned the family of one Hüseyin Ağa, presumably the man whose corpse was found in the vicinity of the English merchants' residences. They make up 15.13 per cent of the sum paid by Constantine, Stamper and Foley. At the top of the list of expenses the sum of 115 *kuruş* (18.91 per cent of the total) appears. The money was paid to unidentified Muslim inhabitants of three neighbourhoods, imams and others. The reason for their payment is not mentioned, but the entry is similar to one in the financial account of the Stafford case, in which witnesses, imams and neighbours were compensated for their testimony.

The British merchants involved in these cases admitted that they probably would not have had to pay any blood money, but they did so, nevertheless. In the first case the English merchant, Edward Stafford, had had negative experiences with this kind of cases before, and wanted to prevent matters from getting out of hand once more. This implies that the capitulations had not worked before, and Stafford had little faith in a positive outcome this time. This was the reason for paying the money he presented before the British assembly, at least. Moreover, he had incurred the expenses at the advice of Georgio Timoni and Luca Chirico, the First and Second Dragomans, respectively, of the British Embassy.[72] Although the majority of the

[72] BNA, SP 105/179, 566, A general court held in Pera of Constantinople May 11 1714 presiding his Excellency Sir Robert Sutton.

assembly declared the affair a "national" burden, there was one dissenter. This merchant, Ralph Pemberton, claimed that the corpse had been found in the grounds of the residence of one Bernardo di Negri, who would have been the only one to suffer from it, if Chirico had not "stirred in this business" without instructions from the ambassador. Pemberton claimed that the dragoman had attempted to settle the matter quietly with the neighbourhood and the *voyvoda* of Galata. The first secret meeting about the matter had taken place in the house of Francesco Bragiotti, Pemberton's own scribe. Chirico decided it would be wise not to take any chances of popular unrest and the Grand Vizier hearing about the case, and advised the Englishmen to pay the "blood money", despite the fact there was no legal obligation for them to do so.[73]

In the second instance the three merchants argued that the Grand Vizier was so much inclined against the English that he might seize any opportunity to ruin them. The principal consideration in this case seems to have been that under normal circumstances the Englishmen could have obtained an exemption from payment, but the animosity of the Grand Vizier made it inadvisable to apply for such a document at that particular time. The British *nation* in Istanbul evidently blamed the Grand Vizier for this, declaring the affair a "national" *avanias*, despite the fact that no officers of the Porte were even involved in the matter. Essentially, the English in Istanbul in these years did not trust the Ottoman authorities to honour the capitulations.

Distrust of the Ottoman legal system was at the centre of the final case study (summary no. 9), too. The First Dragoman of the English consulate in Aleppo was apparently arrested on corruption charges, but no trial ever took place. The suggestion that this was yet another example of Ottoman injustice does not hold up under scrutiny, however. There was nothing illegitimate or unpredictable about the conduct of the Ottoman authorities in this case. The English ambassador was even told about it in advance. Some two weeks before the arrest the ambassador, John Murray, was discretely advised to withdraw

[73] Ibid., 776–779, A Court about the avania made on Messrs Constantine & Stamper [18 February 1715/6]. For a fictionalised account of a similar intervention by a dragoman, see Edhem Eldem, "Istanbul: from Imperial to Peripheralized Capital", 135–206, esp. 142–147.

his protection from Jirjis A'ida, because he was about to be arrested. The warning came from the Chief Dragoman of the Porte, İskarlat Karaca, a former dragoman of the Dutch ambassador.[74] Murray surmised that Karaca's message had been sent with the acquiescence of both the Grand Vizier and the *reisülküttab*, so he sent a petition to the latter

> to beg, that the Porte would not proceed to any act of violence against an English Drugoman without first permitting him to answer the accusation against him; that if the Porte would permit me, I would send for him to Constantinople, or that I would submit, that his process should be made at Aleppo in presence of the Factory & that in case it was proved that he had been guilty of any crime against the State, I should immediately withdraw my protection; but that I hoped that the Porte would not in the meantime do any act to offend the Law of Nations, more especially against so good a friend as the King of England: to which the Reis Effendi answered, "very well, very well, I intended to do the Amb*assado*r a favour, but if he is not sensible of it, I can't help it." What the Porte will do in consequence of this, I know not, as their proceedings are incomprehensible. One day they say one thing & the next another.[75]

Naturally the direct speech in Murray's letter cannot be accepted at face value, and sufficient proof has already been given of the Western notion that the Ottomans were unreliable, but several other aspects of this fragment make it worth citing. Firstly, this is one of the earliest references to "the law of nations" I have found in Western diplomatic correspondence from the Levant in the eighteenth century, a period when the phrase was apparently seldom used. Secondly, the ambassador's presentation of the problem as an international incident is a strategy that was frequently used by Western diplomats in Istanbul. It stems from the notion that the king was represented by the ambassador, the ambassador by the consul, and the consul by the dragoman—so that in the end the arrest of an Ottoman subject in English service was considered an affront to the King of England. Finally, Murray's proposal about legal procedures is noteworthy. The ambassador's suggestion that the English community in

[74] Schutte, *Repertorium*, 322.

[75] ENA, SP 110/86: No. 8: Murray to the Earl of Shelburne, Constantinople, 2 May 1767; Cf. ENA, SP 110/87: Murray to Mr Preston, Constantinople, 20 April 1767.

Aleppo should first be allowed to assess the strength of the case against A'ida implies that he did not trust the Ottoman judiciary to have good reasons for the arrest. He also claimed a degree of legal autonomy far beyond the privileges of the capitulations. Murray's account thus misrepresents both the Ottoman legal procedures and the juridical status the English enjoyed on the basis of the capitulations.

The *ahdnames* stipulated that lawsuits against consuls and dragomans could only be heard by the Imperial Council in Istanbul, but in this case the Porte soon revoked Jirjis A'ida's dragoman status. Within a month of his arrest, A'ida's *berat* was cancelled and literally struck from the record at the end of June 1767.[76] This process began in Aleppo directly after the arrest, around the middle of May. Dragomans' *berats* were commonly kept in the consular chancery, so the *beylerbeyi* demanded that the English consul hand it over. The consul, William Preston, initially refused to surrender his dragoman's *berat*, but he gave in after both his Dutch and French colleagues had advised him to cooperate. They feared that a refusal might endanger A'ida's family, while cooperation might gain him some credit. In any case, the governor-general was much too powerful for the English consul to defy. A'ida's *berat* was thus surrendered by a deputation of dragomans from the English, Dutch and French consulates.[77] From that moment onwards Aida ceased to be a British protégé. The cancellation of his *berat* officially reduced him to a common subject of the sultan, which unequivocally gave the Ottoman authorities full jurisdiction over A'ida.

Not only did the English ambassador misrepresent the Ottoman procedures, he ignored them, too. Murray continued to represent A'ida's interests regardless of the fact he was no longer the First Dragoman of the English consulate in Aleppo. Murray continued to use his office to defend someone whose ties with the English community had officially been severed. There was nothing in the capitulations that justified this, but the Porte apparently condoned it. In the eyes of the English ambassador his conduct was proved right by the official re-instatement of A'ida as dragoman in Aleppo on 20

[76] BOA, ED 35/1, 109/347, *tecdid culus* 1 Safer 1171/15 October 1757, see the marginal note saying that, on the basis of an imperial order of 24 Muharrem 1181/22 June 1767, Aida's *berat* was cancelled (*battaldi*).

[77] DNA, LAT 664, Nicolaas van Maseijk to Dedel, 15 May 1767.

July 1768, but he had in effect stretched his jurisdiction beyond its official limitations.[78] This is precisely what the Europeans frequently accused Ottoman officers of doing.

Conclusion

There were undoubtedly Ottoman officers of all levels who abused their office to extract money from the people under their jurisdiction. Their victims were not only common Ottoman subjects, for occasionally the Europeans suffered such unjust demands, too. It has become received wisdom that *avania* was the common technical term for these extortionate demands, particularly at the hands of senior Ottoman officials, the "pashas". The term *avania* is widely believed to stem from an Arabic, Persian, or Turkish word with connotations of injustice. This chapter has challenged these common notions.

The European sources from the eighteenth century proclaim most *avania*s violations of the capitulations. Contemporary consular regulations were conducive to this form of one-sided, often distorted, accounts of encounters with the Ottoman judiciary. It literally paid to paint a grim picture of the unreliability and injustice of the Ottoman administrative and legal system. If a majority of one's *nation* accepted this version of events, the expenses were reimbursed from the Company coffers. I aimed to balance this Euro-centric, antagonistic view on *avania*s with an Islamic legal approach, based on the notion that the capitulations were part of the Ottoman legal system, not a separate system divorced from it. This chapter thus attempted to reinterpret *avania*s in terms of legal jurisdictions by identifying Western perceptions of Ottoman injustice, and testing them on the basis of the capitulations, Islamic legal theory and Ottoman *kanun*, and legal practice.

The two central questions in the analysis of incidents labelled *avania*s by the Europeans above were, first, was a certain case a vio-

[78] BOA, ED 35/1, 109/347, *tecdid culus* 1 Safer 1171/15 October 1757, see the second marginal note to this document, which mentions that A'ida had been forgiven and re-instated on 5 Rebiyülahir 1182/19 August 1768. Cf. Ibid.: 123/423: 5 Rebiyülevvel 1182/20 July 1768.

lation of the capitulations? And, second, what was the role of the two most important representatives of the Ottoman legal system on the local level, the qadi and the *beylerbeyi*? The number of cases presented in this chapter is admittedly small and limited to a few locations. Egypt, for example, where Westerners reported many *avanias* throughout the period, does not appear in this discussion.[79] Nevertheless, I believe that one fundamental conclusion can be drawn from them: *Avanias* first and foremost reflect the Europeans' perceptions of the Ottoman justice system based on their preconceptions about their own legal privileges. Many foreigners, including ambassadors and consul, had inflated ideas about the degree of legal autonomy they enjoyed within the Ottoman Empire. Few of them were sufficiently familiar with Islamic legal prescripts and indigenous mechanisms of justice to understand the Ottoman legal system in general, or their own place within it in particular. Miscommunication and misunderstanding were a common result, sometimes leading to serious incidents. These incidents were not necessarily violations of the capitulations. In the Aida case we have seen that the English ambassador claimed legal privileges he was not entitled to according to the capitulations, while the English *nation* in Istanbul preferred a financial settlement with the authorities in Galata to petitioning the Porte for the *ahdnames* to be enforced to the letter.

Most European diplomats and merchants systematically interpreted the capitulations in their own favour, regarding them as the sole basis for their legal status. Different interpretations, like those of the Ottoman authorities, were rejected out of hand. This dogmatic approach to the capitulations created a tension between theory and practice, often making them difficult to reconcile. The common Ottoman solution of settlements was equally difficult to explain, because concessions might be considered confessions. Moreover, negotiations might erode the privileges of the capitulations, many Europeans seem to have feared. In practice, however, this method of dispute resolution facilitated the implementation of the capitulations. In most of the cases discussed above some sort of arrangement was eventu-

[79] Masson, *Histoire du commerce . . . au XVIIe siècle*, 7, 11–12. On page 19 Masson states that "l'Egypte fut la terre classique des avanies." This was echoed by Tongas, *Les relations*, 152: "L'Échelle du Caire fut par excellence la terre des avanies."

ally mutually agreed upon. The fact that Westerners tended to label these arrangements *avania*s should not prevent us from identifying settlements as a pragmatic method of dispute resolution between Ottomans and Europeans that was more common in this period than many Europeans cared to admit.

CHAPTER FOUR

THE DIVISION OF ESTATES

The first chapter of this study offered a brief outline of the relevant legal theory concerning the estates of foreigners and *beratlı*s on the basis of the capitulatory privileges and other Ottoman prescripts. Together with additional imperial decrees the *ahdname*s formed the corpus of normative texts in accordance with which the Ottoman judges and other officers should treat members of Western communities. The present chapter will focus on the practical implementation on these regulations with regard to estates.

Even within individual foreign *nation*s in the Ottoman Empire we should distinguish three types of estate. The first was the estate belonging to a proper member of a certain community, i.e. a French member of the French *nation*, or an Englishman of the English *nation*. In that case the consul was generally familiar with the relevant procedures, as well as with the person who had died. Wills were often registered in the consular chancery, which made it easier to establish whether it existed and what its terms were. There were several possible complications, like the status of Ottoman wives, but in general procedures were fairly straightforward. Matters were often more difficult when "merchant strangers" died. These foreigners did not conduct trade under the flag of their own country, but joined other *nations* in the Levant. For example, many Dutch communities in the Ottoman Empire also had German members. The Dutch also protected Portuguese Jews in this way. They were considered Dutchmen to all intends and purposes, but, when they died, their estates had to be divided according to the customs of their real place of origin. The third type of estate belonged to the dragomans and protégés of foreign embassies and consulates. Their estates fell under consular jurisdiction, too.

This chapter will argue that the basic procedures were the same for all three types of estate, but their implementation was often more complicated in the case of *beratlı*s than of Europeans. For this reason the chapter is divided in two sections. The first section offers a concise analysis of the procedures and problems of each type of estate. Brief practical examples from the eighteenth century will illustrate this first section. The second part of the chapter consists of a case study of the division of the inheritance of one particular dragoman. This case will be discussed and analysed in detail, with the aim of offering rare insights into the dynamics between consul and qadi concerning the estate of a non-Muslim Ottoman dragoman.

The Capitulations

Guarantees that the Muslim authorities would not confiscate the estates of deceased foreigners predate the Ottoman period. A treaty between the Mamluk Sultan al-Mansur Qalawun and King Leon III of Lesser Armenia of 1285, for example, arranged for the estates of Muslim merchants who had died in King Leon's territory to be delivered to the representatives of the Mamluk sultan, and vice versa.[1] The Ottoman capitulations also offered guarantees of this kind. Article 9 of the English capitulation of 1580 conveys a fundamental privilege enjoyed by foreigners in the Ottoman Empire:

> *Ve eğer biri mürde olsa, esbab ve emvalin kime vasiyet ederse ana verile, vasiyetsiz mürde olsa konsoloslan marifeti ile ol yerle yoldaşına verile, kimesne dahl eylemeye, araya girmeye.*
>
> And if one of them [i.e. the English] should die let his goods and properties be given to whomsoever he has bequeathed them;[2] should he die intestate let [the effects] be given to that person's compatriot,[3] with the cognisance of their consul: let no one interfere.[4]

---

[1] P.M. Holt, *Early Mamluk Diplomacy (1260–1290): Treaties of Baybars and Qalāwūn with Christian Rulers* (Leiden, 1995), 93–105, esp. p. 101 (art. 11).

[2] The translations of some *ahdname*s state that the goods should be handed over to the executors of the estate, but this is an incorrect translation of the words *kime vasiyet ederse*. See, for example, Noradounghian's translation of the French capitulations of 1740, art. 22 (*Recueil*, i, 284), and M. Bianchi's correction in note VIII on page 302.

[3] Literally: "fellow-traveler".

[4] Ülker, 'İzmir', 307; Skilliter, *Harborne*, 88. Not only foreigners from Western Europe enjoyed this privilege, so did itinerant merchants from Persia conducting trade in the Ottoman Empire. See Ivanova, 'The Empire's "Own" Foreigners: 118, 122–123.

Over the years this article was elaborated several times. Two articles from the English capitulation of 1601 (articles 6 and 7), quoted here from a modern edition, illustrate this process:

> *İngiltere ve İngiltere bayrağı altında yürüyenlerden biri mürde olsa ahdnameye muhalif emval ve erzakına beytülmalciler mal-ı gaibtir diye dahl etmeyeler.*
> *Ve kassamlar ve kadılar tarafından resm-i kısmet talep olunmaya*[5]

Sanderson's contemporary translation of the second of these two articles shows that even modern editions of capitulations cannot always be accepted at face value. The article is significantly longer in Sanderson's version:

> Item, that if any Englishman or other under the*ir* banner, havinge any goods or faculty, shall dye within my dominions, the Petimaghae [*beytülmalcı*], or others of my officers, shall not meddle there*w*with, sayinge they are the goods of the dead (or absent).
>
> Item, that all such commandments that are heretofore, or shall be hereafter, granted to the English nation, or any other under the*ir* banner, which are for the*ir* good and benefit, it shal*l* be of effect and for*ce*, [and] that it may not seeme to infringe this our capitulations; and that the Casamees and Cadies shall not demand the tenth, called Cismett.[6]

It is not the seventeenth-century translation, but the modern edition of this text that is unreliable here, from which several lines have been omitted, which, as Sanderson's translation indicates, precede the injunction to the qadis and *kassam*s not to demand taxes.[7]

These extended articles from the English capitulation of 1601 make it clear that anyone conducting trade under the English flag was also covered by the capitulations. Furthermore, they specifically state that qadis, *kassam*s (the dividers of inheritances), and *beytülmalcı*s (officers of the fisc) should not interfere with the estates of foreign merchants who had died. The tax on the partition of estates (*resm-i kısmet*) should not be demanded in these cases. This order was reiterated in a separate article (no. 27) when the English capitulation was renewed in 1675.[8]

---

[5] Ülker, 'İzmir', 310, articles 6 and 7.

[6] Foster (ed.), *Sanderson*, 284. In a footnote Foster explains "faculty" as "pecuniary means".

[7] These lines read: *ve İngiltere taifesine verilen evamir-i şerifi ve şimden sonra verilecek ahkâm-i munifi muhakkem ve-muakked olup taife-i mezbureye ve sancakları altında yürüyenlere daima nefli ve faidalu ola.* See Feridun Beg, *Münşeat-i Selatin* ii, 474.

[8] Noradounghian, *Recueil*, i, 152.

In the course of the eighteenth century the Porte granted capitulations to several smaller powers, the scale of whose commercial relations with the Ottoman Empire was too modest to justify the establishment of a large number of consulates. Denmark, for example, received its own *ahdname* in 1756, but there were few Danish consuls in the Levant. The diplomats of both sides must have foreseen this, for the capitulation of 1756 specifically addresses the possibility that a Danish merchant might die in an area without Danish representatives. In that case the nearest qadi was ordered to collect the effects of the deceased, seal and guard them, and send them to the Danish ambassador in Istanbul. The qadi was not allowed to levy any taxes on the estate or demand fees for his services.[9] The Prussian capitulation of 1761 (art. 6) furthermore ordered the qadi to draw up an inventory of the estate before sending it to the ambassador.[10]

These privileges were in conformity with the principles of Hanafi theory. One of the Ottoman Empire's most popular reference books of Islamic law, Ibrahim al-Halabi's *Multaqa al-abhur*, offers a concise discussion of testaments by non-Muslim subjects. The rules were basically the same for Muslims and non-Muslims. The most important principle was that only one-third of the estate could be bequeathed. The remainder should be divided among the heirs on the basis of the laws of succession in which fixed shares are allotted to strictly circumscribed categories of heirs. This rule also applied if a Christian or Jew had converted his house into a church or synagogue, and the value of the house represented more than one third of his possessions. Regardless of the testator's wishes, the converted house remained part of his estate. Anyone could benefit from bequests, provided they lived in the Ottoman Empire. It was therefore not possible for non-Muslim Ottoman subjects to legate parts of their possessions to family members living abroad. The sole exception to these rules concerned the estates of foreigners (*müste'mins*). They were allowed to leave a will and testament benefiting anyone, regardless of whether they resided in the Ottoman Empire, or elsewhere.[11]

---

[9] Ibid., I, 313 (art. 13). Polish merchants in the Ottoman Empire enjoyed exactly the same privileges. See Panaite, "The Status of Trade and Merchants in the Ottoman-Polish *'Ahdnāmes* (1607–1699), 275–298, esp. 285–286.

[10] Noradounghian, *Recueil*, i, 318.

[11] Ibrahim al-Halabi (d. 1549), *Multaqa al-abhur* (s.l. [Istanbul], s.d.), 205. For a translation into French of this section and the important glosses, see D'Ohsson, *Tableau général*, iii, 129.

The articles in the capitulations concerning the estates of deceased foreigners unambiguously assign jurisdiction over them to the consul, or, in his absence, to the ambassador of the *nation* in question. According to the *ahdnames* these diplomats then had to hand over the estate to the rightful heirs. There was an intermediate stage in this procedure that is not mentioned in the capitulations, however. The estate of merchants who had been active in trade right until the time of their death tended to be burdened with financial obligations. Loans contracted by the deceased had to be paid off before the estate could be sent to the heirs. Naturally it was also in their interest that debts due to the estate were collected. More often than not the debtors and creditors of the estates of foreign merchants included Muslim and non-Muslim Ottoman subjects, with whom it was not always possible to negotiate amicable arrangements. It is at this point that the jurisdiction of the qadi prevailed in his capacity as adjudicator of commercial affairs.

Standard Procedures

When a Western resident in the Ottoman Empire died, in principle the embassy or consulate concerned made the arrangements concerning his or her estate. The procedures were the same for everyone, regardless of social or diplomatic status. The estates of ambassadors, consuls, and merchants('s widows) thus were all handled in the same way. With regard to succession the following questions were important: Had a will been drawn up? Had the deceased had been married? If so, to another foreigner, or to an Ottoman subject? Were there any surviving children or grandchildren? These questions were preceded by issues of procedure. First it had to be established whether the estate had debts in excess of its assets. If this were the case, it would probably complicate consular procedures. The origins of the creditors were also significant. If the deceased had a large number of Ottoman creditors, whether Muslims or non-Muslims, there was a greater chance that they might seek the help of the Islamic court.

According to the capitulations estates had to be handed over to the heirs, but in practice the consulate or embassy concerned made the necessary administrative financial arrangements first. Creditors of the estate had to be paid, and debts owed to it collected. The costs of the funeral were also deducted from the balance of the estate, as were the chancery fees for these services. Sometimes parts of the estate, most notably real estate, were sold by the consulate or embassy on behalf of the heirs. This could be done to raise the necessary capital to pay the debts of the estate, or to prevent disputes among the heirs over the division of ownership.[12] Only after these procedures had been concluded, was the balance of the estate handed over to the heirs.

An important step in this process was making an inventory of the estate. After a foreigner had died, his or her possessions were sealed on the authority of the consul or ambassador in question as soon as possible. The chancellor of the consulate or embassy usually performed this task, accompanied by one or two dragomans, and a Janissary guard. Subsequently he made an inventory of all the possessions of the deceased, or appointed someone else to do this. Making an inventory was generally a time-consuming process. Every single item of clothing had to be recorded, as well as furniture and unsold merchandise. Moreover, every title of every book was usually catalogued. The lists of possessions were subsequently registered in the records of the chancery. One example of a typical inventory should suffice to illustrate the procedure. It concerns the estate of David Francis De Bezancenet, the British vice-consul in the Syrian port of Latakia, who died in 1778. The ten-page inventory was introduced in the chancery of the British consulate in Aleppo as follows:

> 1778 Register'd p*er* order & on act of D.A. Sciperas, assign to the estate of D.F. De Bezancenet late Consul [sic] of Latachia deceased. *Latachia the 9th September 1778.*
>
> Inventory of Household Furniture, wearing apparel, Goods & Merchandize found in the house, apartments & warehouses of David Francis De Bezancenet Esq.[r] late British consul at Latachia deceased on the 30.th August 1778, and made over to Mr Dominick Anthony Sciperas by order of the Consul & British Factory of Aleppo as p. their Letter to us dated the 4 September 1778.[13]

---

[12] See, for example, DNA, CC, 556 for an Italian translation of a *hüccet* from the Islamic court of Galata, dated 27 fievval 1154/5 January 1742. It recorded the sale of a house in the village of Belgrade that belonged to Dionis Houset, a Dutch merchant who had died in his house in Hüseyn Ağa mahallesi, just outside Galata, in the spring of 1742. The house was sold on behalf of Houset's heirs to the Dutch ambassador for 1,000 *kuruş*.

[13] BNA, SP 110/62 (ii), fos 270v–275r.

This entry is followed by a brief note on the vice-consul's furniture. Three subsections are marked in the document under the headings "Wearing Apparell", "Catalogue of Books" and "Temezooks". The list of *temessüks* (written acknowledgements of debt) is followed by a list of "effects supposed to be Pawns found without any notes or Temezooks". The catalogue of books is followed without pause by a list of kitchen apparel and other domestic articles of limited monetary value, such as "One Tin Watering Pot without a Nozle" and "One Shelf Pidgeon Hole". On behalf of De Bezancenet's assign, Sciperas, two British merchants, John Boddington and Henry Shaw,[14] made the inventory over a period of six days with the help of the vice-consul's local broker.[15]

After an inventory had been made of the estate, the next stage consisted of paying the creditors of the estate, and collecting debts owed to it. Creditors tended to come forward to state their claims on their own initiative as soon as someone's death became public knowledge. They had to visit the chancery of the consulate or embassy concerned, where their claims were registered usually in the original language in which they stated them. For this reason the Western chancery records often contain entries in Turkish, Arabic, Armenian, Greek and Hebrew, accompanied by full translations or summaries of their contents. Examples of this part of the consular procedures abound in the case study of this chapter and those of the following two chapters.

The collection of money owed to estates tended to be more difficult than paying its debts. If the debtors were Europeans, or *beratlı*s under European protection, the foreign representatives had several instruments at their disposal to collect debts. If the debtor belonged to the same community as the person to whom he owed the money,

[14] The names are abbreviated "Bod." And "Sh.", but this seems the most likely identification.

[15] Cf. BNA, SP 105/179, 92–102: An inventory of what found in the Magazines of the deceased Mr Thomas Savage in Galata of Constant*ino*ple on the 9th of February 1708/9; Ibid., 759–765: Inventory of all the Goods, Effects, Wearing Apparell, Books, Letters & Writings found in M.r Robert Glover's Chamber [in Istanbul] after his death, which happened on the 12 December 1715; DNA, LAT 1063, 129–143: [Estate of Jan David Reuter, minister of ambassador Calkoen, who died at Pera on 29 December 1724]; DNA, LAT 1064, 70–72 [Estate of Daniel van der Sanden, Dutch merchant in Ankara, dated 1/12 October 1731.

the assigns or the consul (or ambassador) first called upon the debtor to repay the debt. If he refused, or denied owing anything, the consul or ambassador could have goods belonging to the debtor of a proportional value sequestered, provided there was sufficient written proof against him. If the debtor belonged to another foreign community, the consul or ambassador could request his counterpart to do the same. Ottoman merchants without connections with foreign embassies or consulates fell outside consular jurisdiction, so they could not be forced to pay their debts in this way. Some pressure could be applied by pronouncing a boycott (*battelation*). This meant that it was forbidden for merchants of the community proclaiming the boycott to have any commercial dealings with the person boycotted. In theory Ottoman merchants who conducted international trade were sensitive to this measure, but actual success depended on the support it received from the other foreign communities as well. The most effective way to force these debtors to pay was to sue them before the Islamic court, but it is not clear if this was a common course of action for assigns or heirs of European residents in the Ottoman Empire.

Estates of Europeans were often sold, either partly or completely, in the place where they had died, instead of being divided among, or sent to, the heirs. Sometimes real estate or furniture was sold to generate cash currency, with which debts and expenses could be paid, but often the entire estate was sold by public auction. These sales were generally organized by the embassy or consulate involved. They were announced beforehand "in all public quarters", and prospective buyers could undoubtedly inspect the articles on offer before bidding started.[16] The auctioneer, an officer of the consulate or embassy, or someone appointed by the heirs, had a list of all the goods, and recorded the prices they fetched in the margin. After the sale this list was copied in the chancery registers. The proceeds of the auction were recorded too, before they were added to the balance of the estate. Transparency was a major advantage of this procedure. While it was possible to have furniture, merchandize and jewelry valued by experts, the value of many other effects, like cloth-

[16] ". . . l'ha fatta metter al Incanto Publico facendola p. qualche tempo proclamare p. tutte le Publiche Contrade . . ." DNA, CC, 556, translation of a *hüccet* from Istanbul dated 5 Ramazan 1143/14 March 1731.

ing, was more difficult to estimate. Moreover, creditors or heirs disappointed with the estimates might voice suspicions of fraud, which could attract the attention of the Ottoman judiciary. Although the valuation of unsold goods remained problematic, the proceeds of public auctions were more difficult to manipulate, because all interested parties could witness the procedures. It was probably for this reason that the creditors of an estate themselves sometimes insisted that all goods be auctioned publicly.[17]

Some people had the opportunity to arrange their own affairs and draw up a will before they died. Then the officers of the embassy or consulate only had to ensure that the conditions of the will were honoured, and offer the heirs assistance whenever possible. This was the case, for example, with Simon van Breen, a Dutch merchant who had resided at Edirne for several years. He drew up his last will and testament in his house in Pera on 11 August 1727 in the presence of two witnesses. Van Breen was bed ridden, but *compos mentis*. He first revoked his previous will, which he had drawn up on 20 March of the same year in the presence of the former French consul in Edirne. Van Breen's second wife, the daughter of a French merchant, would get her dowry of 536 *kuruş* back, as had been agreed upon in the marriage contract registered in the chancery of the French embassy on 19 July 1718. She also received the 233 *kuruş* the couple had inherited from her father, in accordance with the division of the estate registered in the French chancery in Pera on 4 July 1720. Finally, she inherited 500 *kuruş* for her maintenance, also as stipulated in the marriage contract. Van Breen also left his widow everything he had given her during his life, "sans que ses Enfants puissant s'y opposer, ni les rechercher". Van Breen had been married before, to Eva Chavan, who had died. Their son, Justinus van Breen, inherited 800 *kuruş*. Forty *kuruş* went to the fund in Istanbul for the deliverance of Dutch slaves, and Van Breen left small sums to his servants. The remainder of his possessions the Dutchman left to his three children by his second wife, Abraham,

[17] This is what happened, for example, after the death of the widow of the late Dutch ambassador Colyer, on 12 March 1730. Her debts exceeded the estimated value of her estate, so the creditors secured a public auction through the intervention of the *kahya* of the qadi of Galata. The auction was still organized by the embassy. DNA, LAT 1063, 232–234: "Nota delli Mo[b]ili et altri Effetti della def*un*ta Madama Vedova Colyer . . ." [16 March 1730].

Angelique and Marie Elisabeth van Breen. Angelique also inherited the small golden bracelets she always wore, without her brother and sister being able to claim them. The Dutch merchant died the same evening he had changed his will. The chancellor of the embassy made an inventory of the estate, which was sold by public auction at the request of the widow over several days within three weeks of Van Breen's death.[18]

Possible Complications: Ottoman Wives

Matters of inheritance were often more complicated when a European merchant had married an Ottoman wife, and had children by her. In many ways, the legal position of Europeans in this situation seems to have been better than in their home countries. Divorce, for example, was much easier in the Ottoman legal system than it was anywhere in Europe. According to D'Ohsson, the European husbands could simply repudiate their Ottoman wives, or abandon them by leaving sultan's territory. Europeans did not need permission for leaving, but their Ottoman wives did.[19] When foreign merchants died, however, the arrangements concerning their estate were often less advantageous, for they could not simply be sent home without further trouble to the diplomatic representatives in the Levant. From the European point of view the estate itself unquestionably remained under consular jurisdiction, but the fate of the indigenous widow and her children was less certain. The continuation of their privileged status seems to have depended chiefly on the willingness of the ambassador or consul to protect them for the time being. From the perspective of the Ottoman authorities there was no question about the status of the widow and children. They remained Ottoman subjects as a matter of course, while the status of the inheritance was more likely to be a bone of contention. Merlijn Olnon has

---

[18] DNA, LAT 1063, 9–11, 12–22, 32–38, 188–190.

[19] D'Ohsson, *Tableau général*, iii, part 2 (Paris, 1820), 17. It must be noted here that d'Ohsson seems to have clung to the theory of Islamic law, even when established practice was different. For example, he states that safe-conduct (*aman*) could not legally exceed a one-year period, after which the beneficiary would automatically become a subject of the sultan. In practice, however, the *musta'men* status of foreigners was generally valid indefinitely. Only in rare cases was this challenged by the Ottoman judges, as in the case of Samuel Pentlow, described below.

recently described a fascinating example of a conflict that arose out of this conflict of interpretations. The case concerns the estate of Samuel Pentlow, a British merchant in Izmir, who died in 1678.

Pentlow died one year after the Ottoman authorities had issued a *ferman*, which effectively stated that European men who married Ottoman women thereby lost their status as protected foreigners, and became ordinary subjects of the sultan for all practical purposes. In a period in which English relations with the Porte were generally troublesome, Pentlow's death resulted in a dramatic conflict. It is clear from Olnon's reconstruction of events that the English themselves were largely to blame for the clash of Ottoman and European jurisdictions in the settlement of Pentlow's estate. Problems arose when the English arranged to send the widow and children to England, where Pentlow had also left an estate. Clumsiness on the part of the Englishmen entrusted with these arrangements led the Ottoman authorities to obstruct the departure of Pentlow's family. From the Ottoman perspective it was perfectly reasonable to object to the unauthorized departure of the Ottoman widow, but the status of the children had long been less clear. However, the *ferman* of 1677 even declared Pentlow himself an Ottoman subject, automatically solving the problem concerning his children. In Pentlow's case the Grand Vizier even applied for a fatwa from the *Şeyhülislâm*, who advised that the penalty for unauthorized departure from the sultan's dominions was the confiscation of all their possessions. The Grand Vizier thus made an effort to prove the legitimacy of his own conduct. In the end, from the point of view of Ottoman law, the seizure of Pentlow's estate by the Ottoman authorities was perfectly legitimate, but at the same time it went against everything the English thought the capitulations guaranteed. Ironically, the affair only came to an end after Pentlow's Ottoman widow had strategically used her status as an Ottoman subject. When she announced her intention personally to apply to the sultan for justice, the Grand Vizier reportedly became milder. The prospect of a mother with children decrying the consequences of his actions to the sultan appears to have made him lower his financial demands on the English. This enabled the English *nation* in Izmir collectively to meet the Grand Vizier's demands, which ended the affair.[20]

---

[20] Olnon, 'Towards Classifying *Avanias*', 159–186, esp. 174–185. Additional details from Abbott, *Under the Turk in Constantinople*, 266–277.

Several decades later another dispute brought back memories of these problems. When the Ottoman wife of a foreign merchant had died, custody over the children could lead to problems as well. This is illustrated by a custody battle before the *divan-i hümayun* between another member of the Van Breen family, Anthony, and his mother-in-law from his first marriage, which took place in 1710. Anthony van Breen had conducted trade in Ankara for some time before settling in Istanbul. His first wife was his cousin, Clara de Brosses, the daughter of François de Brosses. Anthony van Breen and Clara de Brosses had two daughters, who remained with their grandmother after their mother had died. Van Breen apparently refused to provide for his daughters and mother-in-law, who was also his maternal aunt. The old woman was reportedly destitute, something for which De Brosses had already been reprimanded by the Dutch ambassador. The scandal became worse when van Breen remarried, to the daughter of a Dutch colleague. He subsequently forcibly removed his two daughters from the custody of their grandmother, evicting her from the lodgings in which she was staying in Istanbul. Moreover, he did not allow her to see the children anymore. When the younger child subsequently died, the widow De Brosses submitted an "arsuhal, or petition" to the Grand Vizier in a plenary meeting of the *divan-ı hümayun*, begging to be awarded custody of her daughter's daughter until she reached the age of seven, correctly claiming that this was "in accordance with the laws of the land".[21] The Grand Vizier issued a *buyuruldu* ordering the parties to appear before his tribunal. A *çavuş* appeared in the Dutch embassy to demand cooperation with the procedure. He was accompanied by the widow De Brosses who renounced Dutch protection, proclaiming herself a subject of the sultan. She also made veiled threats that she might convert to Islam, which would considerably complicate matters for the ambassador. The case would be heard by the *divan-ı hümayun* on the next day and the ambassador ordered one of his dragomans to attend the hearing. After having questioned a number of witnesses, the qadi of Galata, who adjudicated the matter, subsequently awarded the custody of the girl to her grandmother, ordering van Breen to

[21] In matters of child custody Islamic law favours the maternal line. In the absence of both parents, custody first transfers to the maternal grandmother. D'Ohsson, *Tableau général* iii, 104.

hand over his daughter in the presence of witnesses. Furthermore, the widow De Brosses demanded restitution of her daughter's dowry, as well as alimony for the maintenance of her granddaughter. She also demanded ownership of the slave girls her daughter had had. I have not found any traces of later developments concerning these later claims, but it is clear that they embarrassed the Dutch embassy profoundly.

The widow De Brosses's actions may have gone against all unwritten rules among Europeans, she merely used her dual status, like the widow Pentlow. The widow De Brosses had been born in the Ottoman Empire, the daughter of immigrants from Geneva. On religious grounds many Protestant Swiss joined the Dutch nation in this period, for lack of capitulations of their own. The parents of the widow De Brosses may well have done the same, but by renouncing Dutch protection in the presence of the Grand Vizier's *çavuş* she reduced her own status to that of common Ottoman subject. Her strategy was successful, as that of Pentlow's widow had been earlier. Within the Ottoman legal system the procedures were perfectly legitimate, but this did not prevent the Dutch blaming the Grand Vizier for everything. The Dutch interpreted the incident as evidence of "the evil intention of the present Grand Vizier to bring the European merchants who are married to women of this country under the law of the land as much as possible on every occasion." This policy reminded them of the "dangerous government" of Grand Vizier Kara Mustafa Paşa—an indication that the Pentlow case may have lingered in the collective memory of foreign communities for several decades.

The imperial command of 1677 did not establish a lasting practice. The Pentlow case notwithstanding, European merchants continued to marry women from the Ottoman Christian and Jewish communities. This is illustrated by an Ottoman survey of the French community in Istanbul in the autumn of 1759. It shows that thirteen out of the nineteen Frenchmen listed had married local women, despite objections against this practice from both the Ottoman and the French authorities.[22] In general this seems to have affected neither

---

[22] BOA, A.DVN.DVE 101/48, Ottoman survey dated 11 Safer 1173/4 October 1759. The document is divided in three columns, the first for married Frenchmen owning real estate, the second for bachelors owning real estate. The third column was for *müsta'men tercümanlar* owning real estate and married Frenchmen without real

their status, nor that of their children, although the Ottoman authorities did periodically issue orders similar to that of 1677. At the end of 1791, for example, a *ferman* was issued which declared that Europeans were not allowed to own real estate in the Ottoman domains; that Europeans who had married Ottoman wives before the order was issued remained European, but that henceforth Europeans marrying local women would be considered as Ottoman subjects by the Ottoman authorities; and, finally, that all dragomans' *berat*s issued after 1781/82 were revoked collectively.[23] None of these measures were put into practice universally and consistently, but their recurrence illustrates the on-going concern of the Ottoman administration with these matters.

Merchant Strangers

The term "merchant strangers" originally referred to traders from Western powers that did not have diplomatic relations with the Porte, who joined another foreign *nation* in the Levant. In the course of the eighteenth century more and more European countries established formal relations with the Ottoman Empire, reducing the number of unaffiliated merchants in the Levant. In the eighteenth century traders belonging to one *nation* occasionally switched to another. While they were not called "merchant strangers" anymore, the problems that could occur in connection with their estates were the same.

A document concerning the physician Andrea Freudenreich sheds light on the difficulties sometimes encountered with the estates of Western protégés who had died. This doctor seems to have arrived in Istanbul in the second quarter of the eighteenth century and became the personal physician of the Dutch ambassador, Calkoen. Later he served high Ottoman officials in the same capacity. He

estate. For the French authorities' injunctions against marriages with Ottoman women, see Masson, *Histoire de commerce . . . au XVIIIe siècle,* 156–157. It was also forbidden by the French authorities for Frenchmen to own real estate in the Levant.

[23] *Ferman* of 7 Rebiyülahir 1206/4 December 1791. The French translation of this text was published in Bronnen IV/i, 480–482.

married a local, probably Greek, lady named Balazitsa, with whom he had several children. Freudenreich seems to have died on or just before 23 March 1779. His will, dated 28 November 1760, was found among his possessions. Freudenreich and his family had always been considered Dutch, but after the physician's death questions about his nationality arose that affected the division of his estate. Unsure of how to proceed, the embassy solicited legal advice from the home authorities. The answer offers valuable insights in the relevant procedures.

According to the authorities the first step was to determine on what grounds the deceased and his widow were considered Dutch. Was this because they had been part of Calkoen's retinue, or for some other reason? If the Freudenreich family was rightfully considered Dutch, it was crucial to establish where the doctor, or his wife, had resided in the Dutch Republic before they settled in the Ottoman Empire, because the estates of Dutch subjects abroad should officially be arranged according to the local customs of their original place of residence. These customs varied from province to province, and even within each province different rules were often observed from one city to another. Moreover, Freudenreich and his wife might have chosen their own method of succession, which could be recorded in a prenuptial agreement, or in their will. If they had, this affected not only their own estate, but also those of any of children who died *ab intestat*. Having listed these difficulties, the home authorities suggested a simple solution. The estate amounted to 3,000 *Pezos* (probably Spanish Reals-of-Eight) of which the mother should receive half. The remaining half should be divided among the children, sons and daughters receiving equal shares. The authorities acknowledged the fact that some local customs excluded the widow from the arrangement altogether, but they considered the proposed solution more equitable. "A mutual consent will end all questionable procedures, and therefore it is advisable to settle all affairs."[24]

---

[24] DNA, LAT 1084, doc. 47, undated [probably 1779/1780].

Possible Complications: Witnesses

We have already seen that the Ottoman legal authorities could become involved with the estates of foreigners who had died in the sultan's domains. When this happened, problems could arise when the only witnesses were non-Muslims. This problem was already addressed in the *Kitab al-Siyar* of Shaybani (d. 189/804). This authoritative treatise on international law stated that the property of *müste'mins* who had died in the lands of Islam, leaving behind property there, while their heirs were outside the areas ruled by Muslims, should be held in custody until the heirs arrived to claim it. The estate should not be handed over without evidence to prove their claim to the inheritance, however. This provokes the question

> If the evidence were provided by the Dhimmīs, should their testimony be accepted?
>
> He replied: I should say no on the basis of analogy, but on the basis of juristic preference [*istihsan*] their testimony should be accepted and property that has been left should be handed over to the heirs, if they attest that they do not know of any other heirs of his.

The *Siyar* makes it clear that "a letter from the ruler of the territory from which they came" identifying the heirs would not suffice. If the ruler stated that witnesses had confirmed the claim of the heirs, this did not make the letter any more acceptable, even if the witnesses had been Muslims. The evidence had to be produced in the lands of Islam.[25]

A ruling by Ebu's-su'ud's suggests that these rules also applied in the Ottoman Empire. A case brought to the attention of the Porte in 1543 complicated the matter, however. It concerned the estate of a merchant from Ragusa (Dubrovnik) who had evidently died in the Ottoman Empire. In response to a petition the Porte ordered that it should be investigated if Muslim witnesses could be found. Some interpreted the decree as a rejection of equity, but others were not sure what it meant. Had the decree been intended as a precedent for all similar cases or was its application limited to the one particular case? Because an earlier fatwa by Ebu's-su'ud had not sufficiently clarified the matter, the *Şeyhülislâm* turned to the sultan.

---

[25] Majid Khadduri, *The Islamic Law of Nations. Shaybānī's Siyar* (Baltimore, 1966), 167–168.

> When the petition was presented, [the Sultan] decreed: "They should act according to equity." The phrase: "Let Muslim witnesses be found" was specific to the Ragusan because, in this claim, there was understood to be fraud.[26]

The most significant conclusion that we can draw from this is that, with regard to estates of foreign non-Muslims, Ottoman judges should generally accept the testimony of other non-Muslims on the basis of *istihsan*. Only when there were suspicions of fraud did the Porte insist on Muslim witnesses. This was important not only for the estates of Westerners, but also for those of their dragomans and Ottoman protégés.

The Estates of Dragomans

What were the procedures when dragomans or *beratlı*s died? According to the capitulations did their estates fall under the foreigners' privileges, or not? And if so, according to whose principles was the estate divided? The answers to these questions must be sought in the capitulations, as well as supplementary *ferman*s.

Few formal arrangements concerning the status of dragomans existed before 1661. In that year Sultan Mehmet IV granted the English ambassador, Finch, several new privileges. Article 65 of the renewed capitulations stipulated that when a dragoman died his estate was exempt from the division tax (*resm-i kismet*) and that it should be divided among his creditors and heirs.[27] The English capitulations of 1675 contained a significant amendment to this article. In case a dragoman died article 66 stipulated that

> should he be a subject of our Dominions, they [all his effects] shall be delivered up to his next heir; and having no heir, they shall be confiscated by our fiscal officers.[28]

It seems more likely that this extra clause reflected established practice, rather than forming a departure from it. It may well have been added in response to a specific conflict over the estate of a dragoman who had died without heirs, but it may just have easily have

[26] Imber, *Ebu's-su'ud*, 108–109.
[27] This article has been quoted in full in Chapter One.
[28] Hurewitz, *Diplomacy in the Near and Middle East* I, 28.

had an exclusively symbolic function. In any case, this extended article explicitly reaffirms the status of Ottoman dragomans in European service as subjects of the sultan.

The French capitulations did not have any articles that explicitly addressed the problem of the estates of dragomans who had died, but in 1673 they were firmly placed under consular jurisdiction nevertheless. This occurred on the basis of one of the new privileges secured for France by its ambassador to the Porte, de Nointel. The final article of the extended capitulations of 1673 stated that all the privileges enjoyed by the French were now also valid for their dragomans (art. 53). Neither the Dutch capitulations of 1612, nor those of 1680 included any articles about the status of dragomans' estates after their death. Only in 1702 did the Dutch embassy obtain a *ferman* from the Porte that addressed the issue, after problems had arisen in the wake of the death of Dutch dragomans in Chios and Izmir. In an order addressed to the qadi of Chios and the deputy qadi of Izmir, the Porte stated that France and England had long enjoyed the privilege that the Dutch formally lacked, but which had always been applied to them too. This imperial order now made this official. Referring to the English capitulations of 1675 the *ferman* repeated that when a dragoman of English origin died, his estate fell under the authority of the English ambassador or consul. When the dragoman in question was an Ottoman subject, the estate should be handed over to his heirs. Only if there were no heirs, were the officers of the *beytülmal* allowed to claim the estate for the Ottoman treasury.[29] The *ferman* was based on the most-favoured nation clause, which stipulated that when any nation was granted a privilege that was more advantageous than that enjoyed by others, the new, more favourable text was valid for all capitulatory nations. On this basis France had evidently long ago been acknowledged by the Ottoman authorities as a beneficiary of article 66 of the English capitulations of 1675, and now so was the Dutch Republic.

[29] DNA, CC, 555, Italian translation of a *ferman* dated 15 Şevval 1113/15 March 1702.

Possible Complications: Heirs Who Converted to Islam

The division of estates of Ottoman dragomans and protégés could get complicated when one of the heirs converted to Islam and attempted to renegotiate on the basis of this new legal status. This is illustrated by the inheritance of one Aci Hizr son of Yusuf, an inhabitant of Izmir, who died around 1756–57 (1170 A.H.). He left one adult son, Yusuf, and two adult daughters, Sophia and Marya. Before the inheritance was divided, Sophia also died, leaving a husband, three adult sons and an adult daughter. It was Sophia's eldest son, Kiriaco, who contested the division of the inheritance of his grandfather in court, accusing his uncle of having appropriated part of the estate illegally. Eventually the two parties reached an amicable settlement (*sulh*), which was recorded in a deed of partition (*hüccet tereki*). Twenty-seven years after his grandfather's death, however, Kiriaco again sued his uncle over the inheritance. The qadi of Izmir, Mustafa Paşazade Mir Mehmed, rejected Kiriaco's claims out of hand, considering the earlier settlement definitive. According to a letter to the Dutch ambassador, the judge described Kiriaco as someone who caused *avania*s in this *hüccet*. A *ferman* from the Porte reportedly confirmed this assessment. Kiriaco subsequently converted to Islam, and attempted to have the case re-opened at the orders of the Porte. In an attempt to thwart these designs, Yusuf, who had become a Dutch protégé in the meantime, subsequently asked the ambassador to obtain another *ferman* confirming the earlier procedures.

Several documents about this case have survived. Apart from a letter in French by Yusuf's procurator to the Dutch ambassador, Van Dedem van de Gelder, I have found authenticated copies of the *hüccet*, of a *buyuruldu*, and two *ferman*s. The *hüccet* shows that the qadi based his decision on the existence of a deed of partition, which had been registered in the court. The *buyuruldu* confirmed this *hüccet*, repeating its entire text almost verbatim. The two *ferman*s also reiterate the text of the legal deed, with slight additions. None of the four Ottoman documents about this case contain the word *avania* or any similar Ottoman term. The *hüccet* merely states that the qadi granted Yusuf's request that it be recorded that Kiriaco had no case against him. Nothing further is said about Kiriaco, or his behaviour. The first *ferman* called his actions "in violation of the Holy

Law and contrary to a legal deed forbidding his unjust harassment".[30] The second *ferman* summarized the preceding procedures, mentioning all three previous texts. Moreover, this final *ferman* mentioned a search among the fatwas of the *Şeyhülislâm* about this case.[31] Finally, the case was even discussed in the *divan-i hümayun*. There all the documents were reviewed once again, and a final verdict was passed against the claimant. Interestingly, only the final *ferman* acknowledges the special status of the accused. The first section, which reiterates the contents of the *hüccet* and subsequent developments, merely calls him "the aforementioned Yusuf", but in the second half of the document this changes into "the aforementioned dragoman". This is the only indication that the Dutch ambassador, Van Dedem van de Gelder, may have interceded with the Porte on his protégé's behalf, despite the fact that there is no word about this in the text.[32]

Several aspects of this case are interesting, apart from its confirmation of a central argument of the previous chapter. First of all, this non-Muslim family evidently made use of the Islamic court to register the initial partition of the estate. Unfortunately this document does not seem to have survived, but it was essential for the lawsuits that ensued later. Partly on the basis of this document the qadi in Izmir rejected the claims against Yusuf in the first instance. The fact that the claimant had converted to Islam and the accused had become a protégé of the Dutch embassy in the meantime probably explains why this case concerning the estate of a non-Muslim was even eventually discussed in the *divan-ı hümayun*. All the deliberations of the Ottoman authorities were clearly based on Islamic legal principles, as the consultation of the fatwas of the *Şeyhülislâm* illustrates. Nevertheless, the final judgement was not in favour of the convert to Islam. These legal procedures, which ended in the Ottoman "Supreme

---

[30] . . . *hilâf-i şar şerif ve mugayir hüccet şariyye zahir olan müdahila ve taaddi men ve ref edersin.*

[31] . . . *davasına muvafik fieyhülislâmdan fetava-ı şerifi verildiğen buldurub.*

[32] DNA, LAT 1321: 1803: Pièces relative aux prétensions malfondées de Kiriaco di Arpadi contre son Cousin Joseph Tor Chudir Barattaire à Smirne. The file consists of a cover letter by Giuseppe Dissindiri to [ambassador] Van Dedem van de Gelder, 28 February 1803 (in French), with authenticated copies of a) a *hüccet* dated 21 Rebiyülevvel 1217/22 July 1802; b) a *ferman* dated end Rebiyülahir 1217/21–29 August 1802; c) another *ferman* dated end Zilkade 1217/15–24 March 1803; and d) a *buyuruldu* dated 17 Receb 1218/2 November 1803.

Court", thus confirmed the capitulatory principle that legal disputes should be adjudicated on the basis of written evidence. Having authenticated documents issued by a qadi court in support of one's case clearly strengthened it. In the case of the estate of Aci Hizr justice seems to have prevailed in the end, but for Yusuf it probably meant that part of his capital was sequestered for a long period of time. Moreover, in the Ottoman legal system the party that won usually had to pay the court fees. If this was also the case here, the suits against him may well have cost Yusuf a considerable part of his inheritance.

The first part of this chapter necessarily remains impressionistic, because it is impossible here to discuss all possible courses of events concerning the estates of members of foreign *nations* in the Ottoman Empire in the period under study. Still this section has shown that even when the capitulations seemed unequivocally to assign exclusive jurisdiction over foreign estates to the consul or ambassador in question, in practice the Ottoman judiciary could become involved, nevertheless. Only when all parties involved belonged to foreign *nations* could European diplomats expect to be able to handle the case as they saw fit. When any of the parties petitioned the Porte in their capacity as subjects of the sultan, asking the Ottoman authorities to intervene, consuls and ambassadors could no longer take their own privileges for granted. The following case study supports this conclusion.

A CASE STUDY: THE ESTATE OF DIMITRI DALLAL

This case concerns the estate of a dragoman, a non-Muslim subject of the sultan under foreign protection. The principle question concerns jurisdiction. Did the estate continue to fall under the jurisdiction of the consulate in question, or did it fall under Ottoman jurisdiction because the family of the deceased dragoman was no longer considered privileged? Did the authorities of the dragoman's own *taife* have any authority concerning the division of the estate? Which procedures were followed in such cases?

Some 25 years passed before the definitive arrangements concerning the estate of Dimitri Dallal, a dragoman of the Dutch consulate in Aleppo, had finally been made. The remainder of this chapter will primarily focus on three aspects of this complex case.

First, the settlement of the estate, which included the collection of debts owed to it, and the payment of its creditors. Secondly, a number of ensuing disputes among the heirs will be examined. These concern claims of ownership of parts of the estate by individual heirs and others. Finally, the actual division of part of the estate will be analysed.

Actors

Dimitri son of Jirjis Dallal lived in the Sisi neighbourhood of the predominantly non-Muslim quarter of Jdayda in Aleppo. He seems to have been a member of the Catholic faction of the Greek Church in the Syrian city, which used Arabic as a liturgical language. The date of Dallal's birth is unknown, but he was probably at least 60 years old when he died. Dallal became an honorary dragoman of the Dutch consulate in Aleppo at the end of June 1735.[33] Being an honorary dragoman must have been profitable for Dallal, for in the 1740s he contributed considerable sums in order to keep afloat the Dutch consulate in Aleppo. The aim of this arrangement, by which several Ottoman protégés funded the consulate for several years, was clearly to prevent the loss of their fiscal privileges, such as the reduced customs tariffs codified in the capitulations.[34] What little additional evidence we have about him, suggests that Dimitri Dallal was an astute businessman with a thorough knowledge of Islamic law and the intricacies of the local marketplace.[35] Using these skills Dimitri Dallal seems to have amassed considerable wealth, which was inherited by his family when he died on 16 December 1755.

During the final years of his life Dimitri Dallal does not seem to have been active in trade himself. Instead, he probably only invested in the trade conducted by his sons. Father and sons kept separate

[33] BOA, ED 22/1, 272/1110: 28 Muharrem 1148/20 June 1735, transfer of *berat* from Ilyas Tawtel w. Jurji to Dimitri w. Jirjis [Dallal]; Ibid., 348/1511: 11 Rebiyülevvel 1171/23 November 1757, transfer of *berat* from Dimitri w. Jirjis to [his son] Zakhariyya [Dallal]. Also see DNA, LAT 1091/47: Firman pour le drogman du consulat d'Aleb année de l'Hegire 1168/1754–55 [Dimitri w. Jirjis.]

[34] I have described these developments in my article on 'European Patronage in the Ottoman Empire' in Hamilton ed al. (eds) *Friends and Rivals in the East.*

[35] For an indication of Dimitri Dallal's skills in the Islamic court, see M.H. van den Boogert, 'Consular Jurisdiction in the Ottoman Legal System in the Eighteenth Century', Van den Boogert and Fleet (eds), *The Ottoman Capitulations*, 60–71.

accounts of these transactions. After Dallal's death only his son, Yusuf, had access to his father's business records, which he took with him to Istanbul. Neither the other heirs, nor the consulates involved appear to have been able to examine these records, which seriously complicated the division of the estate.

Dallal's heirs were his widow Qudsiyya; his three daughters, Maria, Cicilia and Irina; and his three sons, Yusuf, Zakhariyya, and Abdullah. Qudsiyya was Dimitri's second wife, and she was probably not the mother of his sons. Dimitri's first wife, Elena, had presumably died before him. At the moment of Dimitri's death, his sons had long reached adulthood, as had at least one of his grandsons. None of his sons had *berat*s of their own when Dallal died, but afterwards all three acquired one. Dimitri Dallal's own *berat* as Dutch protégé in Aleppo was transferred to his second son, Zakhariyya, while Abdullah, the youngest, obtained a patent from the vice-consulate of Ragusa in Aleppo in 1756. In 1757 Yusuf Dallal became a protégé of the envoy of the Kingdom of the Two Sicilies in Istanbul.[36]

It is useful also to introduce the European consuls involved in this case. Dimitri Dallal had been a protégé of the Dutch consulate, and his second son, Zakhariyya, was subsequently awarded his father's *berat*. For these reasons the consuls of the Dutch *nation* were important throughout. Because the case dragged on for a long period, no less than four Dutch consuls must be mentioned here. The first was Matthias van Asten, Second Secretary to the Dutch ambassador in Istanbul, Elbert de Hochepied. The ambassador sent Van Asten to Aleppo in 1755 to take over the consulate from Hendrik Haanwinckel, who fled to Lebanon in a vain attempt to escape his creditors. Van Asten was acting consul in Aleppo until 1756, when he returned to Istanbul, where he became chargé d'affaires of the embassy at the beginning of 1763. After Van Asten's return to the Ottoman capital in 1756 the Dutch consulate in Aleppo was taken over by Jan van Kerchem, who held the post until his death in July 1760. Van Kerchem's business partner, Jan Heemskerk jr., succeeded him to the consulate in 1760. Heemskerk's fate will be discussed in detail in the next chapter. Suffice it to say here that he retired in 1763.

---

36 BOA, ED 96/1, 92/91: Appointment of Halebh Yusuf w. Dimitri [Dallal], 29 fiaban 1170/19 May 1757; Ibid., 98/130: transfer of *berat* in Istanbul to Mikhail w. Yusuf [Dallal], 5 Muharrem 1189/8 March 1775.

His successor was Nicolaas van Maseijk, under whose consulate the Dallal case was finally closed. Besides these consuls, the First Dragoman of the Dutch consulate, Antun Bitar, was also important. Bitar functioned as interpreter to the consulate for most of the period of the disputes over Dallal's estate, and as agent for some of the heirs for a short time.

Because Dimitri Dallal's two other sons also became *beratlıs*, the consulates to which they were nominally connected should be mentioned here, as well. Abdullah Dallal, the youngest son, became a protégé of the vice-consulate of Ragusa (Dubrovnik) in Aleppo in the autumn of 1756. Since Ragusa did not maintain an independent consulate of its own in Syria, the Venetian consul, Gerolamo Brigadi, also acted as Ragusan vice-consul in this period. The chancellor of the combined Venetian-Ragusan consulate, Pietro Corella, and one of the consulate's dragomans, Hanna Dib, also had a role in the Dallal case. In 1757 Yusuf Dallal became a protégé of the envoy of the Kingdom of the Two Sicilies in Istanbul. Sicily did not have a consulate of its own in Aleppo, either. During this period the French consul, Pierre Thomas, also acted as Sicilian vice-consul in Aleppo. He reported directly to the Sicilian Minister in Istanbul, the Count of Ludolf, whom we will encounter towards the end of the case.

Legal Issues

After 1757 all Dimitri Dallal's heirs were under European protection, so in theory it was clear that consular jurisdiction should apply. Because Dimitri Dallal had been a dragoman of the Dutch, and his second son became the next holder of the *berat* his father had held, the Dutch consulate could claim jurisdiction in this matter. The capitulations assigned jurisdiction over the estates of members of a foreign community to the consul concerned. Only the English capitulations of 1675 (art. 66) explicitly confirmed that this privilege included the estates of dragomans, but this was generally considered to be the case anyway. Thus it was the Dutch consulate to which creditors of Dimitri Dallal should address their demands. Dragomans in Dutch service in their turn would demand that debtors pay what they owed, threatening them with litigation in the qadi court, or in Istanbul, if necessary. The capitulatory privilege stipulating that cases concerning consuls and dragomans involving more than 4,000 *akçe* should only be heard by the *divan-ı hümayun* was generally considered favourable for the Europeans in cases like this. After all, on the initiative of the consul lawsuits could be moved to Istanbul, where the embassy would simply take over the monitoring of the proceedings. For the accused, however, this meant having personally to travel to Istanbul, or to appoint someone as agent—all of which cost time and money. It was generally in the best interest of all parties that the case be concluded locally.

If jurisdiction was so clearly defined, then why did it take 25 years to settle Dallal's estate? The principle reason was that two of Dallal's sons each claimed to own goods that the other heirs and the Dutch consulate considered part of the estate. At this point it is useful briefly to discuss what happened in the first year after Dimitri Dallal's death.

Initially the Dutch consulate agreed with the heirs that the latter would make all arrangements themselves without help from the consulate. The eldest son, Yusuf, went to Istanbul soon after his father's death, to attend to business matters there. He took his own business administration, which included the accounts of his father, with him. He gave his two brothers power of attorney, authorizing them to make an inventory of their father's estate in Aleppo. In the following year several disputes arose among the heirs. This discord among the heirs made a consular intervention necessary in the interest of the creditors of the estate. The Dutch consulate therefore ordered the sequestration of Dimitri Dallal's possessions. This meant that warehouses and rooms in private residences, which contained goods belonging to Dallal, were sealed on the authority of the Dutch consul. Parts of the family home were also closed as a result of this procedure, while the relatives continued to live in the house. Subsequently, the creditors and debtors of the estate were called upon to present themselves in the chancery of the Dutch consulate, so that their claims and debts could be registered. Creditors tended to be more inclined to cooperate than debtors. For this reason consuls could ask their colleagues to sequester goods belonging to the estate in the hands of members of their *nations*. The chancery fees charged for these measures were paid from the balance of the estate (see Table 7).

The first claim that obstructed a swift division of Dimitri Dallal's estate was voiced by his youngest son, Abdullah. Just before his father had died Abdullah had returned from Basra with textiles of various kinds and qualities, and of an unspecified quantity of pearls. The value of the textiles is not mentioned, but the pearls alone were worth some 14,000 *kuruş*. The capital Abdullah had needed to buy this merchandize had been supplied by his brother, Yusuf, and by his father. After his return from Basra, he had therefore handed over the cloth and the pearls to Yusuf. When the Dutch consulate sequestered all Dimitri Dallal's possessions after his death, this measure included the goods from Basra, which were stored in Khan al-Wazir. After his father's death Abdullah was reluctant to admit that his father and brother actually owned the goods, but he did eventually after repeated summons from the Dutch consul.[37] After Abdullah Dallal had become a *berath* of the vice-consulate of Ragusa in the autumn of 1756, however, he changed his mind and claimed that the goods from Basra belonged to him, and were not part of his father's estate.[38]

Already before Abdullah's claim had surfaced, the heirs in Aleppo started to suspect that Yusuf might have an agenda of his own. This began when more than a year had passed since Yusuf's departure to Istanbul, and he refused to return to Aleppo. Soon afterwards Yusuf Dallal openly claimed that the goods kept in Khan al-Wazir were his alone, and did not belong to his father's inheritance. He claimed that his father had retired from the business fifteen years prior to his death, leaving him, Yusuf, in charge of his affairs. According to Yusuf, his father had already given all his sons their part of the inheritance during his lifetime, which amounted to 25,000 *kuruş* each. While his brother Zakhariyya had gone bankrupt twice already by the time his father died, Yusuf boasted more success. He claimed that all goods that were sequestered by the Dutch after his father's death (the value of which he estimated at 100,000 *kuruş*) actually belonged to him. He was willing to return the original sum of 25,000 *kuruş* to the estate, but only on the condition that his brothers do the same.[39] Although the sequence of events is not clear, Yusuf prob-

---

[37] DNA, CAS 320, f. 2–3, Lett. B, 'Enregistrement du compte des marchandises qu'Abdulla Dallal à apporté avec luy de Bassora', especially the 'Fattura delle mercanzie venuta di Bassora con Sig.[r] Abdulla figlio del defunto Dimitrius Dallal e consignato in mano del suo fratello Sig.[re] Giuseppe Dimitrius Dallal.'

[38] A comprehensive account of Abdullahs claim is found in DNA, CAS 320, 'Memoire instructif de ce qu'il est passé au sujet de l'uzurpation qu'Abdullah Dallal drogman barrattaire de Raguze voulloit faire de rien par luy apporté de Bassora en 1755 au prejudice des heritiers de Dimitry Dallal decedé au barrat de drogman de Leur Hautes Puissances . . .', 20 Janvier 1758.

[39] DNA, LAT 1118: 'Informatiën'.

ably stated these claims after he had obtained a *berat* from the Sicilian embassy.

Both claims concerned ownership, for which proof was obviously required. When unequivocal proof was produced, claims could be dealt with swiftly. This is illustrated by the claim by a certain Şukri Şamuni, concerning a number of precious stones and other goods that Abdullah Dallal had brought from Basra to Aleppo for him. After Dimitri Dallal's death, these goods had been sequestered along with everything else, but Şamuni had failed to come forward directly. Only some eight years later did the claim come to light. Dimitri's widow and three daughters appointed Hanna al-Antaki, a *beratlı* of the British consulate, to settle the Şamuni claim. The ownership of the stones in question was relatively well documented. A letter written by Abdullah Dallal in which he acknowledged Şamuni's ownership was found in the records of the Dutch consular chancery. Moreover, another local merchant, Yusuf A'ida, testified that Abdullah Dallal had personally told him in Basra that the stones belonged to the claimant. Thus, Hanna al-Antaki decided that the stones should be handed over forthwith, despite Yusuf's absence and Abdullah's objections. Al-Antaki personally accepted full responsibility for the decision. As a result on the morning of 29 December 1763 the precious stones and other goods were handed over to Şamuni or his heirs, eight years and two weeks after Dimitri Dallal's death.[40] Despite the fact that this claim surfaced years after the Dutch consulate's appeal to creditors to come forward, the matter was arranged without delay, because it was well documented and there was additional testimony by a witness. I have not found any evidence that the arrangement was challenged by anyone later.

Strategies

Which options did the parties involved have to pursue their individual claims? We should distinguish four separate parties here. There was Abdullah Dallal, the first son to state claims on the estate to

[40] BNA, SP 110/62 (1), fo 79r.: 'Questo giorno 28 Decembre 1763 . . .; Ibid., f. 159r, 'Register'd at the request of Sciochri Sciamuni 29 Dec. 1763' [Act of procuration of Hanna b. Abdallah al-Antaki, in Arabic], and a short note in Italian concerning the testimony of Yusuf A'ida; BNA, SP 110/62 (i), f. 81r.: 'Il giorno 29 Decembre 1763 [. . .]'

the disadvantage of the other heirs. Then Yusuf did the same, claiming ownership of the bulk of what the others considered his father's estate. The rest of the heirs—Dallal's widow, daughters, and second son, Zakhariyya—formed the third interested party. The fourth party was the Dutch consulate. In theory the consulate acted on behalf of all the heirs and the creditors of the estate, but it also had an agenda of its own, which influenced its actions.

From a strictly legal point of view the best strategy for both Abdullah and Yusuf was to present unequivocal proof of their claims in the form of written evidence, or witness testimonies. Abdullah presumably had his own business administration, excerpts from which were acceptable as evidence in consular procedures. Yusuf had taken the administration of both his own commercial activities, and those of his father, with him, so he, too, should have been able to produce written evidence of some kind. Neither did so. Instead, they resorted to the other means at their disposal to pursue their claims. I can think of two possible reasons for this, but they necessarily remain speculative. It is possible that neither party actually had the proof needed to substantiate their claims, since many transactions between father and sons were not formally recorded. It is equally possible that an inspection of the business records could bring to light dealings or funds they preferred to keep quiet. Whatever their motives, the pursuit of their claims was not based on the presentation of evidence, or on a strategic use of their privileged status as *beratlı*s. The fact that the estate remained sequestered in the meantime had financial consequences for all heirs, but this possibly made protracted litigation a viable strategy for those who could afford to wait for their inheritance. If they waited long enough, the others might have to make concessions, because they simply needed the money.

On the basis of his *berat* Abdullah was entitled to legal aid from the Ragusan vice-consul, Brigadi. This considerably strengthened his case, because it potentially elevated his claims to a diplomatic dispute. Much depended on the experience and common sense of the consul involved in these matters, and Abdullah Dallal seems to have benefited from the fact that Brigadi had only been consul for a year or two when this matter arose. A more experienced consul would probably have been more reluctant to get involved in Abdullah's battles with his relatives. In any case all correspondence between Abdullah and the other heirs now had to go through their respective consulates. This considerably delayed procedures, putting pressure on those parties who wanted the disputes resolved quickly, either for personal reasons, or because they needed their share of the inheritance. At the same time Abdullah remained a subject of the sultan. He could therefore still take cases to the qadi court, or apply for them to be heard by the *divan-ı hümayun*. The Europeans expected him to respect the, often unwritten, rules of dispute resolution among foreigners in the Ottoman Empire, which meant keeping the Ottoman judiciary out of the matter, but they could not actually stop him turning to the qadi, or other Ottoman officers.

Yusuf's position was similar to that of his brother, Abdullah, in the sense that his Sicilian *berat* entitled him to assistance from the Sicilian embassy. A significant difference was that he was connected to the embassy, and not to the vice-consulate in Aleppo, because this made Istanbul his official place of residence. This is important, because the *forum rei* principle provided that the ambassador or consul of the accused rule on the case. The Sicilian envoy in the Ottoman capital should therefore adjudicate cases filed against Yusuf Dallal. In other words, it could be in Yusuf's interest to become the accused in disputes with his relatives over the inheritance, because it would transfer jurisdiction from the Dutch consul in Aleppo to the Sicilian envoy in Istanbul.

Dimitri Dallal's female heirs acted in concert with his second son, Zakhariyya. In principle the Dutch consulate guarded their interests, but the consulate was also responsible for those of the creditors of the estate. The heirs therefore also appointed agents who acted exclusively on their behalf and in their interest. Initially they chose Jirjis A'ida, the First Dragoman of the British consulate in Aleppo, as their agent. A'ida was one of the most powerful non-Muslims in Aleppo, but in this case he only acted as agent for the heirs for a short period. When the claims of Abdullah and Yusuf surfaced, this group of heirs transferred their power of attorney to Antun Bitar, the First Dragoman of the Dutch consulate. Like Abdullah and Yusuf Dallal, in principle these heirs were expected to play by the European rules and keep the Ottoman authorities out of the matter as such as possible.

The Dutch consulate's task was to look after the interests of Dallal's heirs, as well as those of his creditors. This was not only important for these two groups, but also for the reputation of the consulate itself. It was essential for the Dutch to keep developments firmly under control, and vigorously to guard their own consular jurisdiction. From the perspective of the Dutch consul the only acceptable reason for applying to the Ottoman authorities was to obtain confirmation of his own jurisdiction over the case. This could lead to conflicts of interest, if their protégés considered involving the Ottoman authorities as potentially beneficial to their case.

Mediation was always a possible method of dispute resolution, and in this case, too, it was attempted several times. The critical condition for success was the sincere promise of all parties beforehand to accept the outcome of the mediation, because forcing the parties to keep their word was often difficult. In this case that would require either the cooperation of all consulates and embassies involved, or enforcement of the agreement by the Ottoman authorities, an unattractive option for most European representatives.

Outcome: Abdullah's Claim

The Dutch consul, Van Kerchem, denied Abdullah's request to be assigned the goods he claimed as his personal property. To end the matter, the Dutchman proposed to divide the inheritance himself. For this reason he applied to his French colleague, Thomas, to send someone to assist him with the task. Thomas also acted as vice-consul for the Kingdom of the Two Sicilies, and in that capacity had jurisdiction over the Sicilian *beratlı*, Yusuf Dallal. The Frenchman refused to cooperate with Van Kerchem's plan, however. Instead, he sent a petition to the Sicilian ambassador at the Porte asking for either a representative, or for Yusuf personally, to be sent to Aleppo to see to his father's affairs.[41]

Around 20 December 1757, Abdullah appeared in the local qadi's court. According to the Ragusan vice-consul, Abdullah had been summoned to court by his creditors, and thus had not taken the initiative to turn to the qadi himself. This implies that the Ragusan protégé, who had been active in trade independently from his father and brothers, had difficulty repaying his own creditors. Hanna Dib,

[41] DNA, CAS 320, fos 6–7, Lett. F, 'Supplica delli eredi di Dimitry Dallal dragomano barratario d'olanda . . . 10 Decembre 1757'; fos 7–8, Lett. G, 'Messa delli siggilli secondo la domanda qui sopra'; f. 8, Lett. H, 'Significazione della supplica qui dietro all'Illmo Sig.[re] Console di francia.'

the first dragoman of the Venetian and Ragusan consulates, represented Abdullah in the *mahkame*. Dib argued that Abdullah was able to satisfy all of his creditors, but that the Dutch unjustly denied him access to his possessions. However, according to an account of Antun Bitar, the Dutch dragoman, Abdullah had turned to the court to claim ownership of the cloth and pearls that were kept under the Dutch consular seal. After his appearance in court, Abdullah went to the house of his father and brother in the company of Pietro Corella, the vice-chancellor of the Venetian-Ragusan consulate, and some of his creditors. He was met there by Bitar, who was acting both in his capacity as the procurator of the other heirs, and that of First Dragoman of the Dutch consulate. According to Bitar, he prevailed upon Corella to keep the qadi out of the matter. He convinced the Venetian by pointing to the articles in the capitulations concerning consular jurisdiction, which explicitly stated that the Ottoman authorities should not meddle in conflicts like these. Informal discussions about an amicable settlement of the dispute between representatives of the Dutch consulate and Corella did not lead to a solution, however.[42]

In the final days of December 1757 a correspondence ensued between Van Asten and Brigadi about the validity of the capitulations in this matter. The debate clearly shows the Venetian's inexperience. According to Brigadi, who should represent the interests of Abdullah Dallal, the Dutch consul was extending his protection to the widow and daughters of Dimitri Dallal, who were *reaya*, ordinary subjects of the sultan not entitled to capitulatory privileges. While it was in Abdullah's interests to have the sequestration of the estate by the Dutch consulate lifted, Brigadi's argument that protégés lost their privileges upon death undermined a fundamental privilege codified in the capitulations. The Dutchman denied these claims by pointing to the capitulatory article that gave ambassadors and consuls jurisdiction over the estate of deceased members of their *nation*. Van Asten maintained that he did have authority over the goods in question until the estate had been settled and the inheritance was finally divided. Although the text of the capitulations is

[42] Ibid., fos. 11–13, Lett. L, 'Fatti successi colla giustizia turca nella casa di Dimitry Dallal . . . 22 Decembre 1757.' At these informal discussions, which took place in Dimitri Dallal's house, Antun Bitar was accompanied by Butrus Tarablusi, the second dragoman of the Dutch consulate, and Jacobus Zijen, its chiaux.

not very explicit about these matters, Van Asten's case seems to be stronger, since among Europeans the estate commonly remained under consular jurisdiction until its division.[43] Not much later Dimitri Dallal's *berat* was transferred to his son, Zakhariyya, which made him a Dutch protégé. This appointment unequivocally justified Van Asten's involvement, but the argument with Brigadi over jurisdictions continued unabated.[44]

To prevent Brigadi challenging Dutch jurisdiction before the local authorities, Van Kerchem applied to them first, on 22 December 1757. During this time a new governor-general was due to arrive in the city, so the Dutchman applied to the *müsellim*, requesting that the local court be ordered to stay out of the matter. Although Van Asten's request was granted, it had the opposite effect, because the *kahya* of the qadi had his own seal placed on Dallal's storage rooms next to that of the Dutch consul. On 24 December, the day after the new governor-general had arrived, this error was redressed, and the Dutch were issued a *buyuruldu* stating that this was a conflict among Europeans and should remain so.[45]

The vice-chancellor of the Venetian and Ragusan consulates again tried to conclude an amicable settlement, but this time he negotiated directly with the other heirs in Aleppo. They were inclined to allow Abdullah an advanced payment on his share of inheritance, on the condition that someone stood surety for him. Hanna Dib offered his services, but the majority of the heirs rejected him, preferring a fully independent guarantor. When no one else could be agreed upon, the whole arrangement was cancelled, despite the need of the other heirs for advanced payments for themselves as well.

In the first week of January 1758 another change in the local Ottoman administration led to the conclusion of the dispute. The governor-general had dismissed his *kahya* and appointed someone else to the office. This time Brigadi was the first to turn to the Ottoman

[43] Ibid., f. 11 [sic; actually 9], Lett. I, Protesto fatto dall'Ill.mo Sig.re Console d'olanda all'Ill.mo sig.re vice-console di ragusi', 22 Decembre 1757; fos 11–10, Lett. K, 'Risposto del protesto qui sopra', 22 Decembre 1757.

[44] BOA, ED 22/1: 348/1511, The transfer is dated 11 Rebiyülahir 1171/23 December 1757; DNA, CAS 320, f. 14, Lett. N, 'responsa [by Van Kerchem] al protesto qui dietro', 11 January 1758; fos 14–16, Lett. O, 'Signifficazione fatta dall'Ill.mo Sig.re Brigadi . . .', 12 January 1758; fos 16–17, Lett. P, 'Risposta [by Van Kerchem] della signifficazione qui sopra', 12 January 1758.

[45] DNA, CAS 320, 'Memoire instructif' [f. 5].

authorities. On 8 January his dragomans presented Abdullah's case before the new *kahya*, who was ignorant of its history. He therefore summoned the dragomans of the Dutch consulate to appear before him on the next day, but they turned to the *beylerbeyi* himself instead, who decided to rule on the case personally. In the following days both parties presented their cases, after which the governor-general passed sentence on 12 January 1758. The *beylerbeyi* ruled that the disputed goods were part of the estate. Because the estate fell under Dutch consular jurisdiction, he allowed Van Kerchem to sell the goods in his care.[46]

In principle the claim of Abdullah Dallal may have been a matter between the Dutch and the Ragusan consuls, but the Ottoman authorities in Aleppo had a decisive role in the conclusion of the conflict. The Dutch denunciation of Abdullah's submission of his case to the qadi as a violation of the capitulations is a misrepresentation of the facts. Abdullah was fully entitled to turn to the Ottoman authorities, because he remained an Ottoman subject, even after having acquired a *berat*. The fact that the Dutch consul thought this undermined his own authority did not make Abdullah's forum shopping illegal, or even irregular. Regardless of whether the Ragusan vice-consul's accusation that his Dutch colleague had bribed the Ottoman authorities is true, or not, the decision of the governor-general of Aleppo to uphold Dutch consular authority over the estate of its dragoman was in line with the tenor of the capitulations, as well as with European custom in the Levant.

Outcome: Yusuf's Claim

At the beginning of 1758 the female heirs of Dimitri Dallal and his second son, Zakhariyya, sent a petition to the central Ottoman authorities. They stated that Yusuf had fled from Aleppo after his father's death, and requested that he be sent back to Aleppo against

---

[46] An undated document from the English chancery records (BNA SP 110/62 (1), 3), which states that Zakhariyya Dallal was accused in court of fraud by his brother, Abdullah, probably refers to this trial. It mentions Bakir b. Abdurrahman, *hacc* Yahya b. Qurna, *hacc* Muḥammad b. Qurna, *hacc* Ahmad b. Qurna, and a 'Mulla Ibrahim Cateb' [*Katib*] as witnesses, as well as Butrus Tarablusi, Jirjis w. Hanna Qirmiz, and Antun w. Nimatallah Ghadban. Ghadban was a Swedish *beratlı*. BOA, Cevdet Hariciye 6002, undated.

his will if necessary. The petition was reportedly supported by letters from the governor-general of Aleppo, and from the city's *muhassıl* and *nekibüleşraf*.[47] Probably in response to this petition, the Porte sent a *çavuş* named Abdalhalim al-Ghannam al-Askerî to Aleppo to gather information about the inheritance of Dimitri Dallal.[48] By this time Yusuf had acquired the status of dragoman of the ambassador of the Kingdom of the Two Sicilies in Istanbul, which enabled him to refer to the capitulatory article stating that lawsuits against dragomans could only be tried in the *divan-ı hümayun* in Istanbul when more than 4,000 *akçe* were at stake. Using the privileges of his newly acquired status, Yusuf Dallal not only denied the charges brought against him, but he also voiced counter claims.

Yusuf's principle claim was that his father had consigned all his business to him fifteen years prior to his death, and that all the goods found in his father's house, where he and his wife also lived, actually belonged to him. He estimated the value of these goods at 200 purses, or 100,000 *kuruş*. In Yusuf's eyes the sale of the goods by the Dutch consul in Aleppo had been illegitimate. He blamed his brother, Zakhariyya, a Dutch protégé, and the first dragoman of the Dutch consulate, Antun Bitar, for the loss he had suffered from it. Yusuf demanded that both be summoned to Istanbul to appear in the *divan-ı hümayun*. This defence and counter-suit, which was sent to the Porte through the offices of the Sicilian envoy, resulted in the issue of a *ferman* ordering the case to be tried in Istanbul. Instead of Yusuf being forced to return to Aleppo, Zakhariyya Dallal and Antun Bitar were now summoned to the Ottoman capital. A *kapıcıbaşı*, Osman Ağa, was sent to Aleppo to deliver the *ferman*, which was issued before May 1758. Since virtually the entire Ottoman administration of Aleppo had supported the petition of his adversaries, Yusuf Dallal must have had powerful patrons at the Porte who secured the *ferman* in his favour.

---

[47] The response to the petition in Istanbul (BOA, CH 8594, Cemaziyelahir 1171/10 February–10 March 1758) is too damaged for consultation. However, the document's contents, and the response to it are mentioned in a draft version of a Dutch petition to the Porte, which probably dates from the first half of 1758; DNA, LAT 784 (in French).

[48] Cf. Antonis Anastasopoulos, "Building Alliances: a Christian Merchant in Eighteenth-Century Karaferya" (Forthcoming), where an officer is sent out from Istanbul to Karaferya to investigate the complaints of a *beratlı* of the British consulate in Salonica in 1765.

The arrival of Osman Ağa and the *ferman* he delivered, seem to have been an unpleasant surprise for the *çavuş* who had investigated the matter during the first months of 1758. He disagreed with the central authorities' decision adamantly. In a lengthy and detailed report, Abdalhalim Çavuş advised the Porte to reverse its recent decision, and to delegate jurisdiction to the local court in Aleppo.[49] The report systematically addressed the claims of Yusuf Dallal. The imperial agent rejected Yusuf's claim that he alone was the rightful owner of everything that had been seized from his father's residence. According to the investigator this was well known in Aleppo to be untrue. The estimated value of 100,000 *kuruş* for the capital in question was a gross exaggeration, according to Abdalhalim Çavuş, who had investigated the matter personally. He also reported that there was no reason to question the legitimacy of the sale of the goods. The procedures followed by the local authorities in this matter had been a model of cooperation between the heirs, the Ottoman administrators, and, at the insistence of the former, the Dutch consulate. Yusuf Dallal's wife had been given the goods she had claimed, or a part of them, before the rest of the confiscated properties had been sold. Even the consuls of Ragusa and the Kingdom of the Two Sicilies had been invited to attend the sale on behalf of their protégés, said Abdalhalim Çavuş. Finally, he contradicted Yusuf Dallal's accusations against Antun Bitar. The Dutch dragoman had not been in office yet when Dimitri Dallal died, so he could not have had a hand in any of the consular measures to which Yusuf Dallal objected. Bitar had not even been in Aleppo in this period, but in Latakia, where he spent some two years.[50] Moreover, Bitar enjoyed an excellent reputation in Aleppo, and in the experience of Abdalhalim Çavuş he had always fulfilled his duties as dragoman conscientiously. This in contrast with Yusuf Dallal, who was generally known in Aleppo as unreliable and whom the author of the report calls a liar and a troublemaker.[51]

---

[49] DNA, LAT 596, folder D, 'Espiegazione d'un memoriale del cadij [sic] per la Seneriss:[ma] Porte in Constantinopoli' [25 Şaban 1171/4 May 1758] (without Ottoman text).

[50] This is confirmed by a declaration in Italian registered by the heirs of Dimitri Dallal in Aleppo on 19 April 1758: BNA, SP 110/62 (1): 2r.

[51] The text has *buggiardo* (liar) and *avanista*, a word denoting someone who causes *avanias*. The term *avania* is used rather indiscriminately in the Western sources, and

Abdalhalim Çavuş recommended that the qadi in Aleppo adjudicate the disputes over Dimitri Dallal's estate. The envoy noted that numerous reliable and knowledgeable witnesses were available there. Furthermore he argued that it would be prejudicial to many if the case were moved to Istanbul, while its adjudication in Aleppo only inconvenienced Yusuf Dallal. Apart from the legal arguments the report offered in favour of the court in Aleppo, its contents in general were clearly detrimental for Yusuf Dallal. Further pressure on the Porte to delegate authority in this matter to the local qadi came from the Dutch ambassador.[52] Possibly as a result of mounting opposition, Yusuf Dallal decided to accept mediation.

Few details about the actual mediation process are known, which took place in Istanbul. It is not clear, for example, who took the initiative, and whether or not the Ottoman authorities were involved in any way. We do know that Yusuf Dallal had apparently dropped his complaints against his brother, Zakhariyya, for only Antun Bitar took part in the settlement. Bitar was represented in Istanbul by his servant, Nimatallah son of Jirjis. The accusations levelled against the Dutch dragoman were the following. Yusuf Dallal accused him of illegitimately seizing pearls, textiles and precious stones from his room in Khan al-Wazir in Aleppo, and from his house in the Sisi quarter after Yusuf had gone to Istanbul. According to Dallal, the value of these goods amounted to 22,802.5 *kuruş*. He also demanded payment of 4,500 *kuruş* for two letters of credit, which Bitar had allegedly removed along with the other goods. In the Ottoman capital it was agreed that Bitar would pay 2,500 *kuruş* to Dallal to settle the demand of the letters of credit. Nimatallah reportedly stood surety for this sum in case Bitar refused to pay. About the claim concerning the pearls, textiles and precious stones, it was agreed that Dallal would file suit before the qadi in Aleppo.

Thus, the local court in Aleppo was again asked to rule on a dispute relating to the estate of Dimitri Dallal. The case came to court on 17 December 1763, almost eight years after the dragoman's death. The judge was confronted with two contradictory, but unsubstantiated, versions of events. Dallal referred to the terms agreed after

here the general translation of 'troublemaker' seems most appropriate. Cf. above, Chapter Three.

[52] DNA, LAT 784, Draft version of petition, undated (in French).

mediation in Istanbul, but could not produce any documents in support of his claim. Bitar maintained that all disputes between the claimant and himself had already been settled at the beginning of 1762. This had allegedly taken place around the beginning of March of that year, when Yusuf Dallal arrived in Aleppo as a member of the retinue of the new governor-general, Bekir Emin Paşa al-Mutabbakh.[53] The mediation was said to have taken place in the house of Bekir Paşa's personal physician. The Dutch dragoman was given two days to produce written evidence of his claim, but could not do so. It was the word of one man against another, and the qadi decided not to rule on the case. At the insistence of Nimatallah and Bitar an account of it was drawn up nevertheless. Aleppo's *muhassıl* and interim governor-general, *nekibüleşraf* Çelebi Efendi, and several others of the city's officers and notables acted as the court's witnesses, which suggests that this was a high-profile case.[54]

In the wake of this undecided court session, the Dutch consul, Nicolaas van Maseijk, appealed to the city's governor-general, Bekir Paşa's successor, Mustafa b. Ahmad Damad Paşa.[55] According to Van Maseijk, Yusuf Dallal had tried to recruit false witnesses in support of his case, and had bribed officers of the Islamic court to declare them reliable. Two of the witnesses allegedly turned out to have been in Diyarbakır at the time of the events about which they were supposed to testify. When he had applied to the mufti for a fatwa, Dallal was reportedly turned away. In the meantime he had had Bitar's servant arrested and imprisoned by the *tufenkçibaşı*, the head of the governor-general's personal guard, a treatment usually reserved for defaulting creditors. On the basis of Bitar's *berat*, however, this treatment of his servant was not allowed. The consul considered these actions harassment, and argued that his own reputation suffered from them. For this reason he requested that the governor-general put an end to Dallal's campaign against the first dragoman of the Dutch consulate.[56] In response to the Dutchman's petition,

[53] al-Ghazzi, *Nahr al-dhahab* iii, 236.

[54] DNA, LAT 1124: Translation of an *i'lâm* by the qadi of Aleppo, dated 13 Cemaziyelevvel 1177/19 November 1763.

[55] al-Ghazzi, *Nahr al-dhahab* iii, 237.

[56] DNA, LAT 1124, Traduction d'un memoire presenté par Mr le Consul Heemskerk à Mustapha Pacha Gouverneur d'Alep. Although this document is undated it refers to events, which happened in Aleppo at the end of December 1763. Heemskerk left the Levant on 26 December 1763 on a ship from Istanbul,

Mustafa Paşa ordered the release of Bitar's servant. He also made it clear to Yusuf Dallal that he did not want to hear of the case again.[57]

Yusuf Dallal had exhausted all possibilities for demanding justice within the Ottoman administration, both in Istanbul and in Aleppo. This left him only one option, that of turning to the Sicilian minister in Istanbul. In his first letter to the count of Ludolf, of 19 June 1764, Dallal briefly explained his situation. He omitted most of his failed attempts to obtain satisfaction by way of the Ottoman justice system, and emphasized the injustice of Aleppo's governor-general. A second letter quickly followed, on 9 July, in which Dallal requested that Ludolf demand payment of 27,302.5 *kuruş* directly from Van Maseijk, who was now briefly in Istanbul.[58] The Sicilian minister did not turn straight to the Porte to obtain its support, as Dallal may have wanted. Instead, Ludolf, who had been in contact with the Dutch ambassador about the case since 1763,[59] gave Van Maseijk the opportunity to respond to Dallal's letters.

Dallal was evidently less comfortable with foreign diplomatic rules of engagement than he was with the Ottoman legal system, for his own petitions offered arguments against his case. According to the unwritten rules of the European communities in the Levant, Dallal should have turned to the Dutch consul in Aleppo with his claims against the consulate's first dragoman. Appeal against the consul's verdict would have taken the case to Istanbul, where the Dutch ambassador should rule on it. Only then would the Sicilian minister formally be entitled to become involved in the matter. Yusuf Dallal had not followed these procedures. The course he had taken instead now became a liability, the evidence of which can be read in his own letters. First, Dallal had admitted having engineered the arrest and imprisonment by the Ottoman authorities of the servant

where he had travelled from Aleppo before June of the same year. O. Schutte, *Repertorium der Nederlandse vertegenwoordigers in het buitenland 1584–1810* ('s-Gravenhage, 1979), 353. It must therefore have been his successor, Van Maseijk, who presented the petition.

[57] DNA, LAT 1124, Copia [N.1], 'Hazi Jusuf dragomano onorario di Napoli', in Istanbul, to Ludolf, envoy of the Kingdom of the Two Sicilies, 19 June 1764 [in Italian].

[58] Ibid., Copia N.2: Hazi Jusuf to Ludolf, 9 July 1764 [in Italian].

[59] DNA, LAT 602, [The Dutch ambassador] to Heemskerk, 26 March 1763 [in Dutch].

of a fellow dragoman in European service. In the eyes of most Europeans in the Levant this was an unforgivable violation of the capitulations. The Dutch consul's request to the governor-general to have the man released must have seemed more than reasonable to the Sicilian envoy, but Dallal had decried the act as unjust. On top of this, Dallal had asked the envoy to demand payment from a consul of another *nation* of a sum owed by one of the consul's dragomans. This meant that one man was held responsible for another man's debts, something the capitulations expressly forbade. Finally, the tone with which Yusuf Dallal had proposed the Sicilian envoy breach all diplomatic protocol must have seemed insolent to Ludolf. Fully observing diplomatic protocol, Van Maseijk pointed out all these things except the last in his carefully worded response.[60]

Dallal composed another letter in which he countered several of Van Maseijk's arguments. For example, he explained that the servant whom he had had arrested had stood surety for Bitar's debt to him. Since imprisonment of defaulting debtors or their guarantors was a common instrument in the collection of debts in the Ottoman system, Dallal's initiative was not as outrageous as it seemed in European eyes.[61] Although this was true, the argument could hardly have won the Sicilian envoy's sympathy. The case subsequently disappears from the Dutch records for a number of years, which probably means that Ludolf took no official action in the matter.

Only briefly did the conflict between Yusuf Dallal and Antun Bitar resurface at the end of 1779, some 24 years after Dimitri Dallal's death. By October of that year a final agreement between the two *beratlıs* had been reached. Neither the official correspondence, nor the chancery records of the Dutch consulate mention the circumstances of the arrangement, about which nothing is known, apart from the fact that an official deed of quittance was exchanged between Dallal and Bitar.[62]

---

[60] DNA, LAT 1124, Van Maseijk, in Istanbul, to Ludolf [undated, in Italian].

[61] Ibid., Copia N.3: Hazi Jusuf to Ludolf [undated, in French].

[62] DNA, LAT 774, Van Maseijk to Van Haeften, 13 October and 1 December 1779; LAT 752, Van Haeften to Van Maseijk, 10 November 1779.

The Division of Part of the Estate

Before all the disputes arose among the heirs of Dimitri Dallal, part of his estate was divided seemingly without incident. This procedure is worth describing briefly here, because it sheds further light on the flexibility of legal practices in this period.

A year after the initial procedures by the Dutch consulate described above, the English consul in Aleppo sequestered the sum of 11,303 *kuruş* and 55 *akçe* from a member of his *nation*, Thomas Vernon. The Englishman had owed this sum to Yusuf Dallal for unspecified goods he had bought from him. By that time Yusuf was still in Istanbul, and refused to return to Aleppo to attend to his father's affairs. Despite the fact that Vernon had stated that he owed the money to Yusuf Dallal, the other heirs considered it part of Dimitri's estate. There is no evidence that Yusuf ever complained about this, so the sum might indeed have belonged to Dimitri's estate. It was deposited in the British chancery on 11 January 1757.[63] While most of the estate remained sequestered pending disputes among the heirs, this sum was unencumbered by claims by others. For this reason, it was divided separately from the rest of the estate. The procedures followed by the Dutch consulate and the heirs can be considered a model for the manner in which the entire estate might have been divided. In the absence of information about the final partition, we should analyse the procedures surrounding this small share in more detail.

The British consulate first paid the British creditors of both Yusuf and Dimitri Dallal, including Alexander Drummond, the English consul, himself. Most of these debts resulted from delayed payments of commercial transactions, or from loans extended by British merchants at interest. What money remained the English consulate handed over to the Dutch, who continued the process of repaying father and son's creditors. The Dutch chancery had also incurred several expenses after Dimitri's death, the total of which, 127:40 *kuruş*, was also deducted from Vernon's sum. Finally, the payment of 52 *kuruş* made for two months rent of two rooms in Khan al-

[63] The reason for the delay is not mentioned, but it is possible that payment only became due a year after the call for sequestration. Yusuf never contested the sequestration of this sum as part of his father's estate.

Wazir in which Dimitri's estate was kept, was deducted. From the original sum of 11,303:55 *kuruş* which Thomas Vernon had handed over to the British consulate, only 2,089:60 *kuruş* remained.[64] This sum was considered part of Dimitri Dallal's estate.

Dallal does not seem to have left a will, so his heirs and the Dutch consulate had to come to an agreement themselves. One might expect the heirs, all members of (probably the Catholic faction of) the Greek community of Aleppo, to apply to their church to help divide the inheritance in accordance with its prescripts, but this was not the case. No clerics of the Greek *taife* were involved at all. As Table 8 shows, the 2,089 *kuruş* and 60 *akçe* were divided "*secondo l'uso*". Dimitri's widow, Qudsiyya, received 261:17 *kuruş*, which equalled "one-eighth [share], according to custom". His three daughters each received a ninth share of the remaining sum, which came to 203:13 *kuruş* each. The three brothers inherited double the amount their sisters had received. Zakhariyya and Abdullah personally collected their shares of 406 *kuruş* and 27 *akçe* each, while that of Yusuf was kept on deposit in the Dutch chancery until he returned to Aleppo to collect it. Thus, the division of the money among the heirs, which was said to have been in accordance with custom, in fact conformed to the shares prescribed by Islamic law. Because children had survived, the widow received one-eighth of the total net sum. The remainder was divided among the children, whereby the men were allotted double the share of the women.

In the absence of information about the final partition of the inheritance, that of the sum Vernon had owed must be considered indicative of the usual procedures. It is not surprising that a number of creditors were paid first, or that the British and Dutch consulates deducted their own expenses before releasing the remainder of the sum to the heirs. More remarkable is the allotment of Islamic shares of the inheritance among Greek Catholic heirs under consular supervision. Other examples of divisions of the estates of dragomans indicate that this was not an uncommon procedure.[65]

---

[64] The receipt was written in Ottoman Turkish by Mehmed Ağa, and is dated 1 M 1170/26 Sept. 1756. See DNA, LAT 664 'Extract du Registre de la Chancellerie Neederlandoise de cette Ville d'Alep sous Lettre C a F:° 106', 15 February 1757 [p. 5].

[65] See documents concerning the division of the inheritance of Haccadur Hadid in Aleppo in 1782; BNA, SP 110/65, fos 69–70; and those with regard to the inheritance of Antun Balit in 1793; SP 105/189, 596–597, 604–605, 614–615.

Conclusion

Several legal mechanisms contributed to the division of Dimitri Dallal's estate and the settlement of disputes over it. These incidents shed light on the practical limitations to consular jurisdiction, the possibility of *beratlıs* to practice "forum shopping" *avant-la-lettre*, the role of the central Ottoman authorities in legal disputes of this kind, and customary procedures for dividing estates among non-Muslims.

The concept of exclusive European jurisdiction over matters involving Europeans or their protégés depended to a large extent on the consuls and ambassadors involved working in concert. For example, the Dutch managed to keep the settlement of Abdullah's claims under consular jurisdiction, despite an attempt to involve the qadi court in Aleppo, but only because the Ragusan vice-consulate eventually decided to compel its protégé, Abdullah, to cooperate. Dutch attempts to force Yusuf Dallal to do the same failed, because solidarity between consuls was impossible in this case; the vice-consul of Sicily claimed to lack the authority to put pressure on Yusuf Dallal, whose *berat* was directly connected to the Sicilian embassy. In the quarrel between the two consulates over who had jurisdiction, both turned to the Ottoman authorities in Aleppo, but their aim was clearly to obtain confirmation of their own authority.

It is not clear whether Abdullah was summoned to court by his creditors, or if went to the Islamic court to claim ownership of the goods of his own accord. Abdullah stuck to the former version of events, the Dutch suspected the latter was true. In the case of Yusuf Dallal there can be no doubt that he continuously preferred to pursue his claims through the Ottoman legal system, instead of the consular courts. Only when his options in the Ottoman system had been exhausted did Yusuf try to involve the Sicilian embassy. This could be considered a form of forum shopping, in which a party determined which legal forum was most likely to grant his claim and subsequently attempted to have jurisdiction over the dispute moved there. In the eyes of most European representatives this was unacceptable behaviour from any member of their community, be they Europeans or *beratlıs*, but from a strictly legal point of view there was nothing illegitimate about it. Apparently unable to win his case on the basis of solid proof, Yusuf Dallal simply used all the instruments at his disposal on the basis of his double status as *beratlı* and Ottoman subject.

The Ottoman authorities had an important role in the settlement of Yusuf's claims. In response to a petition from the heirs in Aleppo, the Porte sent an agent to the city to investigate the matter. Even before this agent had submitted his report, which favoured adjudication by the qadi in Aleppo, the Porte subsequently decided to have the case adjudicated in Istanbul. After the Dutch ambassador had petitioned the Ottoman authorities to reconsider, and further pressure had been put on Yusuf Dallal, the latter finally accepted mediation. This resulted in a partial settlement, with the agreement to lay the remaining disputes before the qadi in Aleppo. Due to a lack of proof the ensuing court session ended undecided, but it does seem to have put an end to Yusuf's options to pursue the matter further through the Ottoman legal system.

Finally, it is interesting to consider the actual division of Dimitri Dallal's estate. Despite several disputes over the inheritance, the heirs were able to divide part of the estate without the involvement of the Ottoman or European authorities. In many ways, the Dutch consulate had a role similar to the one the qadi usually had in such matters. Foreign supervision gave the heirs the freedom to decide among themselves how they wanted to divide the estate. Paradoxically, they chose to follow the same rules the qadi would have applied, allotting each non-Muslim heir Islamic shares of inheritance.

APPENDIX

Table 7. Enregistrement du Compte du Chancellier d'Hollande L'hoirie de Dimitry Dallal Drogman Barattaire d'Hollande. Doit pour fraix de Chancellerie scavoir.

Pour l'Acte de Comparution des heritiers de Dimitry & Copie	P	5:–
pour idem concernant la demande des papiers d'y celluy & Copie		5:–
pour avoir levé le sceau a l'appartement ou Etoient les papiers rescellé l'Acte sur ce fait & Copie		10:–
pour avoir scellé un mouchoir ou les papiers ont resté en Depot avec l'Acte & sa Copie		7:40
pour l'Acte de procuration faite par divers heritiers en faveur du S.r Giorgios Aide & sa Copie		7:40
pour l'Acte d'Interpretation faitte a Youssef sur la redition de Compte, sa responce & Copie		5:–
pour avoir scellé les magazins au Camp Vezir & divers appartemens a la Maison de Dimitry, l'Acte & Copie		7:40
pour l'Acte Interpellation & fixation de terme faite a Youssef pour donner le compte de son Pere avec la Copie		5:–
pour l'Acte de manquement de comparution de Youssef & Copie		5:–
pour l'Acte de requisition aux Sieurs Consuls pour faire sequestrer entre les mains de leur nation aux ce [?] qu'il pouroient devoir a Jusef avec la Copie		5:–
pour l'Acte d'Interpellation faite a divers marchands armeniens pour la sequestration comme dessus & Copie		5:–
pour l'Acte de comparution d'y eux [?] avec la Copie		5:–
pour l'Acte de recherche dela personne de Usuf & Copie		5:–
pour l'Acte de comparution de Zacharia, demendant sequestre de 2. Balles soyes avec la Copie		5:–
pour le sequestre fait a l'Aga du Kantabrak		2:40
pour l'Acte de Protestation & Copie fait par Monsieur Van Asten contre le manquement d'obeissance de Youssef		5:–
pour avoir mis le sceau a un appartement de Youssef & l'Acte sur ce passé		5:–
pour avoir levé le sceau a un appartement ou Etoient des Arbres d'orange	2:40	
pour avoir rescellé le dit appartem:t & l'Acte sur ce passé	5:–	7:40
pour l'Acte de comparution d'Abdulla fils de Dimitry		2:40
pour l'Enregistrement du Compte des merchandises qu'il avoit apporté avec luy de Bassora		2:40

pour avoir descellé une chambre ou etoit du tabaq & rescellé	5:–
pour avoir descellé 3 Chambres pour transporter d'une a l'autre de meubles & les avoir Rescellés & passé la dessus un Acte	7:40
pour l'Acte d'approbation du S:[r] Georges Ayde n'ayant peu Etre present a l'ouverture des dittes Chambres	2:40
pour l'Acte de comparution du S:[r] Ayde, Zacharie & Abdalla demandant le sequestre de Michael	2:40
pour celluy des dits demendant sequestre E[ntre] mains de Seid Abdul Kader	2:40
	P 127:40

J'ay recu payement du Compte cy dessus Jusques au dit Jour de la comparution du Turk Seid Abdelkader, a Alep, le 16 fevrier 1757. Signé a l'original Longis Chancellier

Source: DNA, LAT 664.

Table 8. Account of the [division of part of] estate of Dimitri Dallal.[66]

Dare	Sig:[r] Usef Dimitry Dall		Havere	
1757 Gen.[o] 21	pagato al Sig:[r] David Haijs in pieno	P 1791:44	1757 Genn.[o] Ricevuto dall Sig:[r] Thomaso Vernon	P 11303:55
23	d:[o] all'Illmo Sig:[r] Console Drumond in pieno	1292:–		
Febraro 15	d:[o] al Sig:[r] Shaw in pieno	4025:50		
	d:[o] al Hovanes servit:[e] di Sr Aide in pieno	470:–		
	Trattenuto da mè p. Conto dell Sig:[r] Antonio Bittar, essendo Io il suo Procuratore	599:14		
	p. 2 p.cento sulla somma di P. 11303:55 essendo il mio Dritto di Cancelliere p. il ricevere in Deposito, è li pagamenti a me fatto della d:[a] somma	226:–		
		P 8404:28		
	Per saldo	2899:27		
		P 11303:55		P 11303:55

Enregistrement du Comte fait du liquide de P. 2899:27 mentiones cy contre scav.[r]

Saldo ricevuto della Cancellaria Brittanica	P 2899:27 }	
	}	2870:27
Aggio a 1 p. % p. la Buona Moneta	29:– }	

Pagato a Mons:r Bernard Mercante francese p. Capitale	P 550:– }	
Interessi al detto p. 9 Mesi 1/3 a 1 p. Cento	51:27 }	
Per il Conto del Cancelliere Olanda	127:40 }	
Affitto di due Magazini in Campo Vezir come pare	}	
p. il ricevuto in Turco cui avanti	52:– }	780:67
	Resta liquida	P 2089:60
Per la Parte, è porzione della moglie del Defunto		
Dimitry p. un ottavo secondo l'Uso		P 261:17
		P 1828:43
Per la Parte, è porzione delli 3. figlie del medesmo		
ogn'una p. una nova parte		609:41
Dovendo questa somma spartirsi in 3. porzione eguale		P 1219:.2
p. li figlioli del medemo cioè		
per il terzo competente a Juseff figlio maggiore		
la qualle resta in Deposito in questa Cancellaria		
fin alla deffinizione dell'heridita del suo Padre		P 406:27 1/3
per il Terzo di Zaccaria il 2:do figlio che ha ricevuto		
sopra la sua quittanza		406:27 1/3
per il Terzo di Abdulla		406:27 1/3
		P 1219:2

Source: DNA, LAT 664.

[66] This account was drawn up by Louis Longis, the chancellor of the Dutch consulate in Aleppo. Schutte, *Repertorium*, 349 does not mention this phase in his career.

CHAPTER FIVE

BANKRUPTCY

At the beginning of 1713 the English firm of Woolley & Cope went bankrupt in Istanbul. The French house of Le Roy & Gasan, also established in the Ottoman capital, suffered this fate in 1740. In the same year Boisson & Co., a French firm in Salonica, declared bankruptcy. The English vice-consul in the Syrian port of Latakia, a Dutchman called Daniel Boumeester, was forced to do the same in 1758. About ten years later Richard Usgate, the English consul in the Palestinian town of Acre, went bankrupt.[1] This list is by no means complete. Bankruptcies were as common a phenomenon in the Levant as everywhere else where trade was conducted. Merchants from all foreign communities in the Ottoman Empire were confronted with them in all periods. Bankruptcy was an occupational hazard that could be caused as much by personal mismanagement on the part of the bankrupt, as by external factors beyond his control.

In a region where cash money was invariably scarce credit was an inevitable instrument of trade, but it could complicate the balancing of accounts. A merchant's ability to pay his debts often depended on the ability of his own debtors to do the same. A combination of defaulting debtors and creditors demanding instant payment thus could easily ruin a trader. Insolvency, the inability to meet the demands of creditors, did not necessarily lead to bankruptcy, because creditors could allow insolvents to continue in business with the aim of paying their debts. If the creditors were divided, however, and the debtor was unable to negotiate an arrangement with them, he was generally forced to declare bankruptcy.

Despite the fact that bankruptcies were an integral part of the

[1] ENA, SP 105/179, 495, 9 April 1713 (Woolley & Cope); Ibid., SP 110/72 (iii), f. 589: Daniel Boumeester, Latachia, to Alexander Drummond, Colvill Bridger, Nathaniel Free, Jasper Shaw, Thomas Vernon, David Hays and George Aidy [i.e. Jirjis A'ida], Aleppo, 3 November 1758; Ibid., SP 110/29, f. 242, Richard Usgate, Acri, to Consul & Factory at Aleppo, 21 August 1778; Bronnen III, 140 n. 2; Ibid., 125–26, 131–32, 154–55.

conditions of trade in the Ottoman Empire, the legal procedures involved have received little scholarly attention. Economic historians tend to focus on larger developments, rather than individual incidents. From that perspective references to bankruptcies often merely illustrate a noticeable decline in the fortunes of a particular nation.[2] In the case of bankruptcies, the historian of the legal status of foreigners and their protégés in the Ottoman Empire is invariably faced with the problem that most records have been lost. Only the cases that required the involvement of the consul or ambassador appear in our sources, and they tend to be the complicated ones. While it is thus relatively easy to find bankruptcies that sent shockwaves through the foreign communities, it is more difficult to reconstruct the procedures followed in less conspicuous cases. This chapter first offers a tentative survey of the procedures and possible complications of bankruptcies occurring in foreign communities in the Levant. This survey is followed by the detailed description and analysis of four connected bankruptcies that took place in Aleppo from 1763.

The Capitulations

Cash currency was often in short supply in the Ottoman Empire and transactions on credit were the rule, so it is only logical that the capitulations should address the issue of debts incurred by foreigners. The most important principle was that no one should be forced to pay the debts of another, unless he had agreed to stand surety beforehand. To turn again to the English capitulations of 1580, articles 8 and 12 stipulate that

> *Eğer İngilterelünün birisi medyun olsa, deyni borçludan taleb oluna, kefil olmıyacak ahar kimesne tutulup taleb olunmaya.*
>
> *Ve bunlardan biri medyun olsa veya bir veçhile müttehim olup gaybubet eyeleye anun için kefaletsiz ahar kimesne tutulmaya.*

---

[2] I am aware of only two exceptions: Bosscha-Erdbrink, *At the Threshold of Felicity*, 187–193 mentions several bankruptcies. Jan Schmidt, "Dutch Merchants in 18th-Century Ankara", 237–60 [reprinted in his *The Joys of Philology* 1, 301–328, to which I refer here] discusses one of the cases mentioned by Bosscha-Erdbrink in more detail. Neither focuses specifically on the legal procedures, however.

> If one of the English should fall into debt, let the debt be claimed and taken from the debtor; no other person, as long as he is not standing bail, shall be arrested and sued.
>
> And should one of these people fall into debt or be suspected [of a crime] in some way and abscond, let no other person, who is not standing bail, be arrested on his behalf.[3]

Articles of this tenor appear in all the capitulations, from those of the sixteenth to the end of the eighteenth century.[4] Some of these later texts repeat the emphasis on the importance of written evidence to prove that someone had stood surety for someone else.[5] The capitulation granted to Genoa in 1665 was the first to mention explicitly that this clause also applied in cases of bankruptcy.[6] In a similar fashion the French capitulations of 1740 (art. 53) stipulated that that the debts of a bankrupt should be paid from the balance of his estate. It also declares that ambassadors, consuls and others who have not stood surety cannot be held responsible. It is a reiteration in a more specific context of article 22, which stresses the personal responsibility of debtors and their guarantors.[7]

Letters of credit were an instrument of trade and finance that became so widespread in the Ottoman Empire that inevitably articles concerning their non-payment eventually appeared in the *ahdnames*. Article 66 of the French capitulations of 1740 reads

> Lorsque notre *miri* ou quelqu'un de nos sujets, marchand ou autre, sera porteur de lettres de change sur les Français, si ceux sur qui elles sont tirées ou les personnes qui en dépendent ne les acceptant pas, on ne pourra sans cause légitime les contraindre au payement de ces lettres, et l'on en exigera seulement une lettre de refus, pour agir en conséquence contre le tireur, et l'ambassadeur de même que les consuls

[3] Skilliter, *Harborne*, 88; Ülker, 'İzmir', 307.

[4] See, for example, the French capitulations of 1535 (art. 6), 1569 (art. 4), 1604 (art. 34 and 39), 1673 (art. 27 and 32), and 1740 (art. 22). Noradounghian, *Recueil*, i, 85, 90, 100–101, 141, and 284.

[5] E.g. the French capitulation of 1604, art. 39. Feridun Bey, *Münşeat-i Selatin*, ii, 490–494.

[6] Noradounghian, *Recueil*, i, 130. The clause is also found in the English capitulations of 1675 (art. 58), the Dutch ones of 1612 and 1680 (art. 28 in both texts), the French capitulation of 1740 (art. 53) and the treaty with Russia of 1783 (art. 69).

[7] Belin, *Des capitulations*, 101. Article 22 of the capitulations of 1740 is the same as article 34 of the French capitulations of 1604 and article 23 of those of 1673. Cf. the corresponding article 28 in the Dutch capitulations of 1612 in De Groot, *The Ottoman Empire and the Dutch Republic*, 254.

> se donneront tous les mouvements possibles pour en procurer le remboursement.[8]

This article was obviously introduced to prevent foreign merchants being forced to pay letters of credit drawn on them without prior notice, or by people they did not know or trust. Like the articles concerning debt, this new article aimed to regulate the payment of money owed, directly or indirectly, by Westerners to Ottoman subjects.

The imprisonment of foreigners is an issue closely connected with their contracting debts, because defaulting on a debt was a common reason for imprisonment in this period both in the Ottoman Empire and in Western Europe. We have already seen that the capitulations prohibited the arrest of consuls and dragomans, claims against whom could—in theory—only be tried before the *divan-ı hümayun*. This privilege was included in a capitulation for the first time in 1604.[9] For more than 130 years it remained unchanged, but then the scope of the article was somewhat extended. Only two capitulations document this development, the French of 1740 and the Spanish of 1782. Article 70 of the former text states that

> Les gens de justice et les officiers de ma Sublime Porte, de même que les gens d'épée, ne pourront sans nécessité entrer par force dans une maison habitée par un Français; et lorsque le cas requerra d'y entrer, on en avertira l'ambassadeur ou le consul, dans les endroits où il y en aurait, et l'on se transportera dans l'endroit en question, avec les personnes qui auront été commises de leur part; et si quelqu'un contrevient à cette disposition, il sera châtié.[10]

The *ahdname* granted to Spain in 1782 contains an abbreviated version of the same privilege, which forbids Ottoman officers from imprisoning any subject of the Spanish crown unnecessarily.[11] It should be noted that these articles did not extend the protection enjoyed by consuls and dragomans to all foreign merchants and their protégés. In theory the fact that ambassadors now had to be informed beforehand when provincial authorities intended forcibly to enter a foreigner's residence seriously limited these authorities' jurisdiction.

---

[8] Noradounghian, *Recueil*, i, 294.

[9] See above, page 21; Cf. The English capitulations of 1675 (art. 25) in Noradounghian, *Recueil*, i, 152.

[10] Ibid., 295.

[11] Ibid., 346.

In practice, however, the article was probably vague enough to keep local balances of power intact.

Imprisoning a debtor in order to force him to pay was a common procedure in Islamic law. The qadi did not take the initiative to imprison defaulting debtors, acting always at the request of the creditor, instead. According to the jurists, if the debtor had remained in prison for two or three months and he could prove that he had no property, the qadi should release him. After the bankrupt's release his creditors could immediately pursue him for payment again, but they could not prevent him travelling or conducting trade. The qadi could also grant the bankrupt respite until he could pay his debts, in which case his creditors had to wait. Colin Imber states that upon his release from prison, the debtor was issued a certificate of bankruptcy (*hüccet-i iflâs*), which indicated whether or not the qadi had granted him respite.[12] While Imber's view may be an accurate reflection of Islamic legal theory, it seems that in practice the Porte could issue a declaration of insolvency (*müflis fermanı*) that released the bankrupt from the obligation to pay his creditors and took away their ability to sue him further. This practice, which is mentioned in a document from the Dutch embassy in Istanbul of 1740, is confirmed by D'Ohsson, who states that "les créanciers perdent le droit de surveillance (*mulâzemet*), lorsque le débiteur obtient son élargissement à titre de faille."[13]

Unlike elsewhere in Europe, in the Ottoman Empire there were separate prisons for the detainment of defaulting debtors. In this respect the late eighteenth-century English traveller and prison reformer, John Howard, considered the Ottoman Empire an example for his native country. He wrote: "In those cities which I have seen in Turkey, the debtors have a prison separate and distinct from those of felons. Without such a separation in England, a thorough reformation of the gaols can never be effected." In Scotland and the Dutch Republic the imprisonment of debtors was also common practice, but there they were not separated from the prisons' general population, either.[14]

---

[12] Colin Imber, "Four Documents From John Ryland's Turkish MS No. 145", *Tarih Dergisi*, XXXII (1979), 173–186; reprinted in Colin Imber, *Studies in Ottoman History and Law* (Istanbul: The Isis Press, 1996), 161–174.

[13] Bosscha-Erdbrink, *At the Threshold of Felicity*, 189 n. 110. D'Ohsson, *Tableau général*, iii, 177–179.

[14] John Howard (1726–1790), *An Account of the Principal Lazarettos in Europe with*

It seems that for a long time conversion to Islam was a way by which Westerners could clear all their debts. Conversion was, most capitulations stipulated, only legal when the convert acted voluntarily and while fully *compos mentis*. Furthermore, the conversion to Islam had to take place, or be confirmed, in the presence of the consul, or a dragoman in the service of the convert's (former) community. Article 48 of the Dutch capitulation of 1612 stated that the convert should hand over to the consul those goods belonging to others, so that they could be returned to their owners.[15] In subsequent *ahdnames* nothing is said about debts, until the Kingdom of the Two Sicilies obtained its own capitulation in 1740. Article 12 of the text stipulated that the convert was obliged to pay his debts from his possessions, and in case he held goods belonging to others, they should be consigned to the Sicilian ambassador so that they could be returned to their rightful owners. The same article is found in the French capitulation of 1740, and those awarded Denmark in 1746 and Spain in 1782.[16] Only in the second half of the eighteenth century did the *ahdnames* thus state explicitly that converting to Islam would not solve a foreign merchant's financial problems.

The capitulations are noticeably silent about the role of the Islamic courts in the bankruptcies of Western merchants. I have found only one relevant capitulatory article, number 73 of the English capitulations of 1675. It states that

> *İngiltere tüccarlarının bir kimesne üzerinde olan hakkı da'va ve şerle mübaşir marifetiyle tahsir olundukda tahsil olunan akçeden mahkemelerde verildiği üzere yüzde iki akçe mübaşire ve çavuşa resm ziyade bir akça ve bir habbe taleb olunmaya.*[17]

> If there is a legal case against an English merchant and he has been declared bankrupt with the agreement of the court usher, the usher is entitled to two percent of the recovered money, and the *çavuş* to no more than the established rate and not one kernel more.[18]

---

various papers relative to the Plague; together with further observations on some foreign prisons and hospitals; and additional remarks on the present state of those in Great Britain and Ireland (2nd edition with additions, London, 1791), 62, 72, 76, 125.

[15] De Groot, *The Ottoman Empire*, 244, 257; Cf. article 61 of the English capitulations of 1673 in Noradounghian, *Recueil*, i, 165.

[16] Ibid., 273 (Sicilian/1740); 295 (French/1740), 313 (Danish/1746), and 347 (Spanish/1782).

[17] Ülker, 'İzmir', 313.

[18] According to Noradounghian's translation it was the court's *çavuş* that performed this service, not the *mübaşir: Recueil*, i, 168.

This article suggests that English consuls occasionally cooperated with Islamic courts in order to settle the affairs of bankrupt Englishmen. The arrangement must have been common enough to have it included in the capitulations, and to fix the fee (*resm*) of the Ottoman court officials. The texts indicates that the *mübaşir* (court usher) was in charge of the administration of bankruptcies. The role of the *çavuş* is not clear, but he may have announced bankruptcies publicly, calling on all interested parties to come forward. Interestingly, the article recurs neither in any of the subsequent English capitulations, nor in those of other nations.

The *ahdnames* protected Western merchants and their protégés from unexpected financial demands as a result of debts incurred by others. Only those who had stood surety for a debtor could be held liable for payment of a debt. The capitulations were clear in this respect. The imprisonment of debtors was a common method to force them to pay what they owed, and foreigners in the Ottoman Empire were not exempt from this practice, which was equally common in their home countries. For a long time conversion to Islam seems to have offered an escape route for desperate debtors, but eventually this loophole was closed, too. Foreigners in dire straits could always turn to their consuls and ambassadors for help, but when they owed money to Muslims or to non-Muslim subjects unconnected to any foreign community, there was always the chance of a lawsuit in the qadi's court.

"An Unhappy Affair": The Ideal Bankruptcy

On 25 January 1763 Thomas Lansdown, an English merchant in Aleppo, wrote to one of his patrons and creditors in London that "for my own part, I am quite ruined & undone & shall not have an Asper [*akçe*] in the World remaining as the Effects I have in England must be appropriated to the payment of my creditors & even with those I much doubt if there will be more than 50 p*ercent* for them."[19] Lansdown wrote this latter two days after he had declared bankruptcy. His downfall was caused by the bankruptcy of his two

[19] ENA, SP 110/37, f. 154v: Thomas Lansdown to Mr Jonathan Brideoake, London, 25 January 1763.

Maronite warehousemen, the brothers Yusuf and Antun Sadir, which will be analysed in detail later in this chapter. As we will see the bankruptcy of the Sadir brothers turned into a nightmare for the consulates involved, but that of Lansdown, by contrast, was probably how the European representatives in the Ottoman Empire wished all bankruptcies would be. It is useful therefore here to examine the procedures involved, which also shed light on the personal side of bankruptcies that seldom finds its way into scholarly studies.

Davis' classic study of English trade with Aleppo is partly based on Lansdown's correspondence, so there is no need to discuss his career here.[20] The most important aspect of his business is that he worked both as a factor (agent) for merchants in England, and as an individual merchant on his own account. Negative economic developments and the bankruptcy of several of his patrons weakened Lansdown's position considerably, but until the beginning of the 1760s he still thought his luck would change. At the beginning of 1763, however, his two warehousemen, Yusuf and Antun Sadir, went bankrupt. At an earlier stage the Englishman had agreed to stand surety for the sum of 40,000 *kuruş* to enable them to continue in trade, but this eventually worked against him.[21] Due to the close business connections with them, the bankruptcy of the Sadir brothers also ended their employer's career.

Lansdown's correspondence shows that the Englishman was uncertain about his ability to pay his creditors. This was the result of a method of conducting trade that was typical of foreign merchants in Aleppo, and probably the rest of the Levant, too.[22] The foreigners needed locally recruited warehousemen and brokers, who spoke the language(s) of the marketplace and were familiar with its mech-

[20] Lansdown's career is described extensively in Ralph Davis, *Aleppo and Devonshire Square: English Merchants in the Levant in the Eighteenth Century* (London, 1967), 94–95. Davis incorrectly dates the bankruptcy in 1765 and does not mention the Sadir connection.

[21] ENA, SP 110/37, f. 162v–163r: Lansdown to Samuel Touchet, London, 14 February 1763.

[22] Elena Frangakis-Syrett, "Networks of Friendship, Networks of Kinship: Eighteenth-Century Levant Merchants", *Eurasian Studies* I/2 (2002), 183–205, esp. 187–88, indicates that the trading method described was common practice throughout the Levant. The Dutch consul, Heemskerk, employed the same method in his dealings with his own warehousemen, as we will see below.

anisms. Most European merchants personally kept the records of their transactions with other Europeans and their business contacts abroad, or they employed a European scribe for this part of their commercial administration. It seems that separate accounts were held by the Ottoman warehousemen, who were responsible for all dealings with local Muslim and non-Muslim merchants. The foreign merchants tended to settle their accounts with their own employees regularly, but in the meantime the warehousemen and brokers seem to have enjoyed a great deal of autonomy. Lansdown's business administration consisted of two sections, the one he kept himself, and the one held by his warehousemen. This initially complicated matters somewhat when Lansdown was forced to declare bankruptcy, because Yusuf and Antun Sadir went into hiding, taking their business accounts with them. Luckily for the Englishman they were soon arrested, so that he would at least be able to calculate the negative balance with some accuracy.

Another common practice among foreign merchants in Aleppo saved Lansdown the disgraces of imprisonment and lawsuits before the consular tribunal, and possibly the Islamic court. Foreign merchants created a legal barrier between themselves and their warehousemen by forcing them to conclude most transactions in their own name. For example, if an English merchant wanted to buy silk, he ordered his warehouseman to purchase the desired quantity for a certain price. In this transaction it was not the Englishman, but his warehouseman who was legally the buyer. If the contract was registered in the local court it did not mention the foreign merchant's name, despite the fact that the transaction occurred at his orders. Once the warehouseman had bought the silk, he instantly sold it to his employer. This constituted a separate transaction, which was generally not recorded in the local court.[23]

Lansdown's business methods ensured that he had no Ottoman creditors, other than his own warehousemen. All his creditors were English or French colleagues, the First Dragoman of the English consulate the only exception. Moreover, there were no suspicions of fraud or embezzlement on the part of the Englishman, who was fully

---

[23] Davis, *Aleppo and Devonshire Square*, 243, 245. On the role of non-Muslim intermediaries in sales and barter transactions of Europeans in Izmir, see Frangakis-Syrett, *The Commerce of Smyrna*, 87–90.

prepared to cooperate with his creditors to pay them as much as possible. In fact he was considered as much a victim of his warehousemen's bankruptcy as their other creditors. The combination of these factors made Lansdown's bankruptcy a model procedure in the eyes of the Europeans. There was no risk of any interference by the Ottoman authorities, the bankrupt was not to blame for his predicament, and he was willing to cooperate. Lansdown was spared the disgrace of imprisonment in the consular gaol, and did not have to witness all his possessions being seized by the consulate's officers and sold by public auction. Instead, he was allowed personally to make all the necessary arrangements. There was only one restriction. Until he had reached an agreement with his creditors, all his merchandize and everything sent to him on arriving ships was detained on the orders of the consul. This meant that Lansdown was unable to continue in trade without the consent of all his creditors, whom he was allowed personally to inform about his bankruptcy. Nevertheless, what Lansdown repeatedly characterized as "an unhappy affair" did not have a happy ending for him.[24] Almost eleven months after he had declared bankruptcy a dispute arose among Lansdown's creditors in London over the ownership of unsold merchandize found in his warehouse in Aleppo. Estimating that the resolution of this dispute would probably take several months, Lansdown handed over all his possessions and accounts to the chancellor of the British consulate, and returned to England.[25]

The bankruptcy of Thomas Lansdown was a personal tragedy, and the losses suffered by his creditors were significant. Nevertheless, from the point of view of the English consulate, the affair could not have been more pleasant. There were no high-profile lawsuits that might be detrimental to the reputation of English trade in general and no confrontations with the Ottoman authorities over who had jurisdiction. The case was arranged by the bankrupt himself, who personally informed, and negotiated with his creditors. When a dispute eventually erupted among the creditors, this happened in London. The consul in Aleppo could simply await its outcome. This is how

---

[24] ENA, SP 110/37, f. 183: Lansdown to Benjamin Barker, Galata, 14 June 1763.

[25] Ibid., f. 193r–194r: Lansdown to Isaac & John Hughes, London, 10 December 1763.

foreign consuls preferred such incidents, but more often than not it was necessary to follow procedures more stringently.

Standard Procedures

The consular administrative procedures concerning bankruptcies resembled those concerning estates of members of foreign communities in the Levant. In both cases officers of the consulate sequestered the financial administration of the person(s) involved. With estates this was in the interest of the heirs (who did not always appreciate such measures, as the Dallal case has shown), while with bankruptcies the procedure aimed to guarantee the interests of the creditors. Just like with estates, the ambassador or consul usually appointed two or three trustworthy members of the nation who were not involved in the case to investigate the books of account and calculate the exact extent of the debts accumulated by, and the assets due to, the bankrupt. Naturally they could call on the dragomans to assist them with financial papers in Arabic, Ottoman Turkish, Armenian, or Hebrew. We have already seen that (parts of) estates were often sold by public auction, either to generate cash to repay debts, or to facilitate the division of the estate among the heirs. With bankruptcies, too, the possessions of the bankrupt were commonly sold publicly. The funds raised in this manner were used to pay the creditors. Both with estates and bankruptcies the chancery fees of the embassy or consulate involved were subtracted from the balance first. The kinds of documents found in the registers of consular chanceries concerning bankruptcies were also similar to those concerning estates: inventories of possessions, *temessüks*, claims by creditors, lists of chancery fees, witness statements, deeds of sequestration, etc.

Most European embassies and consulates in the Ottoman Empire had a fortified room on the premises that could be used as a prison. Bankrupts were often incarcerated there, when they were suspected of wanting to escape their creditors by fleeing. It was probably the dragomans and the Janissary guards who made the arrests ordered by the consul.

The registration in the consular chancery of claims by creditors started as soon as bankruptcy was declared publicly. Although they varied in length and detail, claims always mentioned the name of the creditor, the sum or goods he or she was owed, and the existence of either written or oral evidence of the claim. Every claim was recorded in the chancery along with a translation or a brief summary. When a bankruptcy was not controversial and the creditors did not challenge consular authority, every creditor was offered a dividend upon registration. This was a down payment, which might later be supplemented after the final balance of the estate had been calculated. To accept the dividend was effectively to acknowledge a substantial loss on the original debt. As long as there were no suspicions of foul play, most creditors accepted the dividend offered, knowing that the chances of fully recouping money owed by a bankrupt were small. When creditors were unable to collect their dividend, or to have it collected for them by a formally appointed agent, the money was kept in the chancery on deposit. The share of those who rejected the dividend was sometimes also kept on deposit until it was accepted, but the consul could rule that whoever rejected the settlement was not be entitled to anything at all. When the consular procedures could continue unchallenged by creditors, and without the involvement of the Ottoman authorities, the concluding step in the process was the calculation of the final balance of the estate. Sometimes a final dividend was paid to the creditors, after which the case was closed. Thomas Lansdown's hopes of being able to pay his creditors half of what he owed them were optimistic. In general it seems that creditors of bankrupts had to accept repayment of only a quarter of the sum they were owed, or even less. The creditors of Yusuf and Antun Sadir, for example, were eventually paid a total dividend of 10% in three instalments.[26]

Possible Complications: Fugitive Bankrupts

Originally the consul not only had the function of chief representative of a community of foreign merchants, his presence was also meant as a guarantee. Prior to the Ottoman era the consul was thus considered to stand surety for the actions of all merchants under his authority. This meant that the consul could be held personally liable for the payment of debts left by traders of his community who had fled their creditors. The Ottoman capitulations of the sixteenth cen-

[26] ENA, SP 110/62 (ii), 234.

tury onwards only reflect this in articles that emphasized that the rule no longer applied. No one should be held liable for the payment of another's debts, unless he had stood surety out of his own free will, the *ahdnames* stipulated. While the consuls and ambassadors were thus no longer financially liable for fugitive countrymen who were trying to escape their creditors, few things were more embarrassing for them. The European sources show that the ambassadors and consuls clearly felt more vulnerable to Ottoman interventions ("interference") under such circumstances. Moreover, their concern about the reputation of the *nation* suggests that the marketplace continued to hold the diplomats partly responsible for the conduct of the merchants under their authority.

Few fugitive bankrupts seem to have successfully escaped their creditors. Pietro Leystar, a bankrupt Dutch merchant in Ankara, for example, attempted to flee in 1739. His horses were saddled and packed, and his valet was awaiting their departure, when Leytstar's Armenian broker appeared and prevented the escape. The broker had been informed about the bankrupt's intentions by vigilant creditors. The Dutchman was arrested, as was his Dutch associate.[27] In October 1755 the Dutch consul in Aleppo, Haanwinckel, was initially luckier. He was almost caught in the act by his dragoman, but the consul convinced him that he was riding out to meet his successor halfway on the journey from the coast. Haanwinckel succeeded in fleeing to Mount Lebanon in the company of a consular Janissary, his falconer and his servant, taking with him his most important account books "to copy them for his own information and justification". The Dutchman evaded arrest for several months, but was eventually caught on board a ship that had sailed from Palestine for Malta, but had made a detour to İskenderun first. From the port Haanwinckel assisted the Dutch consulate in Aleppo with the necessary arrangements, and died soon afterwards.[28]

European consuls had the authority to arrest and imprison members of their own communities, but occasionally they requested the assistance of the Ottoman authorities too. Only the disputed French capitulations of 1536 contained an article that explicitly gave the ambassador and consuls the right to apply to the *subaşı* for help in

---

[27] Schmidt, "Dutch Merchants in 18th-Century Ankara", 314.
[28] Bronnen III, 340–41, 342.

these matters. The fact that it did not reappear in any subsequent capitulation did not prevent the Europeans turning to the Porte for an arrest warrant if necessary. This was the case in the Leytstar bankruptcy in 1740, for example, when the Dutch ambassador applied for a *ferman* ordering the arrest of Leytstar, his associate, and their three Armenian brokers. The order was delivered in Ankara by a *çavuş* of the Porte, who also escorted the prisoners back to Istanbul. Interestingly, they were not handed over to the Dutch ambassador, but were incarcerated in an Ottoman prison.[29] In 1754 the Dutch embassy again applied to the Porte for an arrest warrant. This time the fugitive was Jan Hendrik Meijer, the bankrupt former treasurer of the Dutch nation in Istanbul, who is mentioned in the Introduction. The warrant ordered the Ottoman authorities along the Dardanelles (Meijer's most likely escape route) to arrest the fugitive and hand him over to the Dutch ambassador, in order to be, as the contemporary translation reads, "expédié à la Sublime Porte, à fin qu'il répond à ses créanciers et satisfit ses correspondents". Meijer would thus eventually have been brought before the *divan-ı hümayun* if he had been found, but he got away.[30]

Possible Complications: Ownership of Consignments

One of the most common complications of bankruptcies in the Ottoman Empire concerned the ownership of goods consigned to a bankrupt merchant by his principals. Unless it could be determined exactly who owned which unsold merchandize in the bankrupt's warehouse, it was considered part of the bankrupt estate, which was divided among all creditors. This often led to conflicts of interest between local creditors and those overseas.

---

[29] Bosscha-Erdbrink, *At the Threshold of Felicity*, 188; Schmidt, "Dutch Merchants in 18th-Century Ankara", 314.

[30] DNA, LAT 1160, "Commandement addressé à tous les Juges qui se trouvent vers les Dardanelles, et à l'entour des mêmes dans toutes les Isles et Jurisdictions, comme aussi à tous les officiers de Police; et autres qui se trouvent à l'entour de ces endroits par mer et par terre." [Translation of the arrest warrant for Meijer, issued the end of Rebiyülahir 1167/c. 15 February 1754]. Meijer fled to Rome, where he was eventually arrested for tax evasion and identified as the fugitive from Istanbul. He was convicted on appeal, but this verdict was later overturned. By this time Meijer had died in prison and his estate was confiscated by the Papal authorities. DNA, LAT 453.

Most European merchants in the Levant conducted trade both on their own accounts, and, as agents, on those of principals abroad. These principals sent merchandize to their agent to be sold in the Levant. Bills of lading specified the nature and quantity of the goods, which bore ownership marks identifying the principals. When the ship carrying the cargo arrived at its destination, the agent collected his consignments from customs, paying the necessary duties on them. The transfer of the merchandize from the principal to the agent did not entail a transfer of ownership. The agent merely sold it on his principal's behalf in the same way a broker or auctioneer can sell goods without personally owning them. Legally, therefore, the consignments remained the property of the principal, also after the agent had taken possession of them. This is where the problem started, nevertheless.

Upon receiving the merchandize the agent had to ascertain that it was undamaged. This meant removing the packaging, which also bore the marks of ownership. This procedure probably happened immediately after the goods had been unloaded from the ship and before they were declared to customs. Therefore, by the time the merchandize reached the customs agents it was already difficult to determine precisely which bales and packets had been sent by which principal. Bills of lading could easily solve this problem at this stage, but for the payment of customs duties it was not important. Once the goods had arrived in the agent's warehouse, however, they were stored together with all his other stock. Considering the fact that prospective buyers had to be able to inspect the goods, most of the original packaging was probably removed. After this final stage of the transfer of the merchandize it was very difficult to determine which individual bales of cloth belonged to which principal—which was precisely what was needed when the agent had gone bankrupt.

In cases of bankruptcy Western ambassadors and consuls tended to appoint commissioners who had to draw up an inventory of all assets. Unsold merchandize commonly formed one of the most important assets of a bankrupt estate. Goods that were immediately recognizable as the property of principals overseas were kept aside, but when there was doubt about the ownership of certain goods, they were counted as assets. Naturally the owners abroad often protested against this, but their claims inevitably only arrived several months after the declaration of bankruptcy. By this time most local creditors had already collected the first down payment, which was fixed on the basis of the balance of the bankrupt estate calculated by the commissioners. Claims from overseas could therefore have a negative effect on the final percentage of reimbursement of all other creditors, who had relinquished their rights to pursue the bankrupt further when they accepted the first down payment. The prospect of loosing the remainder of the reimbursement often led to protests by local creditors.

Sequestration was a common instrument with which creditors could attempt to secure maximum repayment. There were two stages in this procedure. First the creditor had to state his claim on part of the property of the insolvent or bankrupt to the ambassador or consul concerned, who had the authority to act on it. Consuls and ambassadors could also sequester goods pre-emptively, if they expected members of their community to benefit from this measure. They did this by issuing a writ of sequestration, ordering the actual sequestrators to separate the goods in question from the rest of the estate. If bankruptcy had already been declared, this meant that the goods were already under a general sequestration, and a specific sequestration was added. In case of insolvent estates, the sequestrators probably removed the goods and stored them in the embassy or consular house pending further procedures. The sequestrators generally included the chancellor of the embassy or consulate, a dragoman, and a Janissary guard. Protocol dictated that sequestrations of goods belonging to members of other foreign communities were filed with their ambassador or consul. If multiple sequestrations were issued on the same goods, the determination of ownership could seriously delay the rest of the bankruptcy procedures. In that case the ambassador or consul could order that the goods in question should be sold, and the revenue of the auction kept in the chancery.[31]

In the case of Thomas Lansdown all the quarrelling creditors were English, so the disputes among them were eventually resolved in London. Lansdown's most important principals, the company of Isaac & John Hughes, claimed to own a quantity of unpacked woollen cloth found in the bankrupt's warehouse, and they had obtained a statement from the Attorney General in support of their claim. The other English creditors in London disagreed, arguing that the tex-

[31] See, for example, the bankruptcy of the Greek firm of Gio. Avierino & Co. in Izmir in 1786. Bronnen IV/I, 391–92.

tiles should be sold for the benefit of all creditors. The dispute arose about ten months after Lansdown had declared bankruptcy. It took another seven years to settle it. At the end of 1770 an arbitration committee of five members of the Levant Company eventually assigned ownership of the disputed bales of cloth, which had been kept in Aleppo all these years, to the Hughes brothers. There were two conditions. Firstly, they had to withdraw the bill they had filed in the king's High Court of Chancery. Secondly, the Hughes brothers had to pay all their own expenses of the legal procedures. The other creditors also had to pay their own expenses.[32] Even when controversies arose among creditors of the same "nationality" protracted procedures could thus ensue.

Bankruptcies were especially difficult to manage for the ambassador or consul responsible when creditors belonging to more than one foreign community in the Levant were involved, or creditors residing abroad. Because merchants involved tended to voice their claims through their own representatives, the bankruptcy of an individual merchant could easily turn into a diplomatic conflict between various consuls or ambassadors. This is what happened, for example, in Istanbul in 1740 with the bankruptcy of the Venetian firm of Gad Conegliano, Treves & Co., which conducted a great deal of trade with the Dutch Republic. When the firm went bankrupt, some of the unsold merchandize found among its stock belonged to Dutch principals. Despite the fact that these goods were allegedly recognizable as the property of Dutchmen, the Venetian ambassador declared them part of the assets of the bankrupts. Moreover, the Venetian ambassador had reportedly assigned ownership of the goods the firm had recently dispatched to the Dutch Republic to Ottoman creditors. Furthermore, the ambassador had told these creditors that the Dutch in Istanbul were responsible for retrieving these goods. Both measures favoured the local creditors at the cost of the Dutch. The Dutch ambassador, whose accounts are the only sources I have been able to consult, was outraged by his Venetian colleague's conduct.[33] Not only did the decisions harm Dutch interests, the Venetian

[32] ENA, SP 110/37, f. 193 r–194 r: Lansdown to Isaac & John Hughes, London, 10 December 1763; Ibid., SP 110/72 (iii), fos 504–505, [Sentence of arbitration dated 15 December 1770].

[33] Calkoen to Fagel, 26 November 1740 and 9 December 1740, in Bronnen III, 140–42, 142–43, respectively.

diplomat had taken them without consulting with his Dutch counterpart. The correspondence of the Dutch ambassador is full of Latin legal terminology in support of his argument that the entire bankruptcy was fraudulent and all subsequent procedures should consequently be considered invalid. The Dutch ambassador probably aimed to impress his superiors with his knowledge of the law, but his arguments were irrelevant in the Ottoman context. Instead of referring to concepts of Roman and canonical law, the Dutch diplomat should have reasoned on the basis of Islamic law. The Venetian ambassador's proclamations may have led some creditors of the bankrupt firm to attempt to pressure Dutch merchants in Istanbul to reimburse their losses. It was unlikely, however, that the Islamic courts would have supported them solely on the basis of the Venetian diplomat's statements. The Dutchman may not have been familiar enough with Ottoman legal procedures to know this, or, if he was, he may not have trusted the Ottoman courts. In any case this incident illustrates one of the difficulties that could ensue over the ownership of consignments to bankrupts, while it again brings to light the difficulties many Western diplomats had with the Ottoman legal system at the same time.

Bankrupt Merchant Strangers and Ottoman Protégés

Bankruptcy procedures for merchant strangers and protégés were the same as those for other members of the same community. The ambassador or consul had full authority in these matters. This is illustrated by the verdict of the English consul in Aleppo, Alexander Drummond, concerning the bankruptcy of Mikhail Shidyaq, a Maronite *berath*, which provides valuable information about the personal circumstances of the event at the same time.

> Whereas Michael Shudiac was on or about the 15th day of September 1755 declared Bankrupt, he was incarcerated the 16th day of the said month where he remained till the 30th day of January 1756 that his creditors might have sufficient time to enquire into his affairs, and to bring proofs of their several allegations, but no sufficient evidence of any crime cognoscible by us being adduced, on the said 30th day of January public notice was given to the several consuls, for the behoof of their national subjects or protected, likewise to the natural subjects of the Grand Sig:[r] that the friends and relations of the said Michael Shudiac [*Shidyaq*], out of compassion to his wife and tender infants,

were willing to contribute, such a certain sum as shou'd amount to 25 p.Cent of his debts, providing the said creditors wou'd grant a full acquittance to the said Michael Shudiac, so as he might be unmolested, at liberty to labour in an honest way for the bread of himself and family. Till the 20th of last month was given for further inquisition, and determination, several persons not having accepted of the above generously compassionate offers, they cannot be entitled to them. These are therefore decreeing and ordaining the said Michael Shudiac to be liberated, or released from Prison on the 9th day of this month having made oath before the Reverend Father Giovanni son of Curi Nameh [Yusuf w. *khuri* Nimatallah] that all he has declared to his several creditors is true, and that he has not directly nor indirectly secreted any part of his effects. But shou'd any person be unsatisfyed with the legal requisites which have been perform'd & require his confinement being continued, he shall be obliged /he shall be obliged/ to grant the said Michael Shudiac such a daily allowance, to be paid p. advance, as shall be sufficient for the nourishment of himself and family, in a proportional way to his former condition, according to Law. Given at Aleppo 6 day of April 1756.
Alexander Drummond, Consul[34]

This verdict sheds valuable light on the consular procedures of imprisonment of bankrupts. Shidyaq was imprisoned to allow his creditors to investigate his bankruptcy and establish whether or not it was fraudulent. When nothing untoward appeared to have happened, the English consul announced his intention to release him. Shidyaq had already spent three and a half months in the consular gaol. The creditors were subsequently given another six weeks for further enquiries. No complaints were filed against the bankrupt, who still had to swear an oath before a local priest declaring that his had not defrauded his creditors. Only then was Shidyaq released, three days after the consul's verdict. The Maronite *berath* was saved by his friends and relatives, who paid a quarter of his debts in return for a full quittance from his creditors.

In the first part of this chapter I have discussed several aspects of bankruptcies that had not been sufficiently studied hitherto. The most common complication concerned the ownership of consignments to merchants who had gone bankrupt by the time the goods arrived in the Ottoman Empire. This often resulted in disputes between consuls and ambassadors of different European *nations*, in which the

[34] ENA, SP 110/72 (iii), f. 548.

Ottoman authorities sometimes became involved, too. The problem of fleeing bankrupts was also significant. Communal liability was normal in Ottoman society, and the fact that Western *nations* were exempt from this on the basis of the capitulations must occasionally have frustrated Ottoman creditors and the Ottoman authorities. Nevertheless, many bankruptcies of foreign firms and factors in the Levant appear to have been settled without noteworthy problems. The case of Thomas Lansdown is an example of smooth procedures, but the bankruptcy of his warehousemen and their brothers show just how different a turn these events could take.

A Case Study: The Bankruptcies of Four Ottoman Warehousemen (1763)

On 22 January 1763 Jarmanos Sadir, a Maronite warehouseman employed by the Dutch consul in Aleppo for his private business, declared bankruptcy. This set in motion three other accounts of bankruptcy, those of his brothers, Yusuf and Antun Sadir' and his own business partner, Antun Diyab. The settlement of these cases offers valuable information about the interaction between Ottoman and consular jurisdictions, and about the effective status of the capitulations in matters of considerable complexity. Important questions concerned the management of the bankrupt estate (who had jurisdiction?), the legal limitations imposed on the bankrupt, and the position of the consul. The remainder of this chapter will focus on the parties involved in these bankruptcies, the legal issues, the various strategies the parties could adopt, and the outcome of the numerous legal procedures.

Legal Issues

A brief summary of the basic procedures and principles of jurisdiction is useful at this point. When Europeans or their protégés went bankrupt, in principle the consul concerned had jurisdiction. It thus was the consul who appointed someone curator of the bankrupt estate, in many cases the chancellor of the consulate. This curator (sometimes more than one was appointed) was responsible for the maintenance and administration of the bankrupt estate, and eventually for the organisation of its settlement. In the Ottoman legal system the settlement of bankrupt estates was performed by the qadi, or someone appointed by him, but the capitulations granted foreigners the privilege of making arrangement according to their own laws and customs—provided, as always, that only foreigners and their protégés were involved. When Muslim or other Ottoman creditors were involved who rejected the consul's jurisdiction, the qadi could take over jurisdiction at their request. If this resulted in disputes between the consul and the qadi, the governor-general determined who had jurisdiction.

In cases of bankruptcy the repayment of as large a share of the bankrupt's debts as possible was the principal aim of both the consular and Ottoman authorities. For this reason they tried to secure payment of any debts owed to the bankrupt, and to verify claims by creditors. In both cases proof was needed in the form of written documents—preferably drawn up in a qadi court—testimony of reliable witnesses, or a combination of both.

For the consular authorities the enforcement of their authority was often difficult when debtors or creditors from other foreign *nations* were involved. Success then depended on the cooperation of their fellow consuls. The leaders of foreign communities could force neither Ottoman debtors to pay, neither creditors to accept a settlement, without help from the Ottoman authorities. Moreover, Ottoman creditors could not be prevented from appealing to the local authorities, which the Europeans tended to want to keep out of such matters.

Sadir and Diyab were under Dutch protection, so in theory their bankruptcy fell under the jurisdiction of the Dutch consul, Heemskerk. The Dutchman was also their employer, however, and one of their principal creditors. In the eyes of most of the other creditors this created a conflict of interests, but Heemskerk disagreed. His jurisdiction was further threatened when rumours of fraud started to circulate in connection with this bankruptcy, and open accusations were levelled against the Dutch consul. Because the consul had a central role in the settlement of bankruptcies among Europeans and their protégés, it is useful first to examine here the legal position of foreign consuls in the Ottoman Empire.

The Legal Position of the Consul

In the eighteenth century the concept of diplomatic immunity had yet to develop fully and was neither accepted nor implemented universally. Nevertheless, European consuls in the Ottoman Empire did enjoy more privileges than their countrymen there. These privileges were codified in the capitulations and the consular *berats*.

As early as 1604 the French capitulations stipulated

> Que les consuls français qui sont établis par les lieux de notre empire pour prendre soin et sûreté d'iceux trafiquants, ne puissant pour quelque cause que ce soit être constitués prisonniers, ni leurs maisons scellées et bullées; mais, commandes que ceux qui auront prétention contre eux seraient renvoyés à notre Porte, où il leur sera fair justice.[35]

As we have seen, the capitulations granted to Genoa in 1665 (art. 13) almost literally echoed the French article of 1604, and furthermore elaborated on it by adding that in lawsuits against consuls before the Porte the ambassador concerned should represent his consul. The Italian text reveals that this privilege was granted to prevent ambassadors and consuls being held liable for debts incurred by their countrymen.[36] Articles of this nature occur in many capitulations issued throughout the eighteenth century.[37]

As we have seen, the capitulations awarded to France in 1740 also stipulated that officers of the Ottoman judiciary should notify the ambassador or consul beforehand when they intended forcibly to enter the residence of one of their subjects. The Spanish capitulations of 1782 appear to take this privilege one step further. The text ordered that the Ottoman judiciary should not imprison any subject of Spain. If this occurred, nevertheless, the prisoner should be handed over to the consul of ambassador upon his request without delay. From the context of the article it is clear this only applied to cases which exclusively involved Spaniards or their protégés, and does not give this entire group—and by extension, all foreigners under the capitulatory system—immunity of arrest by the Ottoman authorities. The articles' implications thus were not as wide as it might seem at first glance.[38]

The French capitulations of 1740 (art. 48) also stipulated that no consul could be forced to appear personally before the qadi. In cases

---

[35] Noradounghian, *Recueil*, 98 (art. 25).

[36] Ibid., 129.

[37] E.g. the Dutch capitulations of 1612 (art. 6); the French of 1673 (art. 17); the English of 1675 (art. 25); the Dutch of 1680 (art. 6); the French of 1740 (art. 16); and the Russian of 1783 (art. 57). De Groot, *The Ottoman Empire and the Dutch Republic*, 251; Noradounghian, *Recueil*, 139, 152, 173, 283, 368, respectively.

[38] Ibid., 283, 347.

brought before the qadi against the consul, his dragoman was allowed to appear on his behalf.[39] Interestingly, this article allows the possibility that consuls be summoned to the qadi court, and that cases against them be heard there. This contradicted, and undermined, the article quoted from the French capitulations of 1604, which ordered that all cases against consuls should be moved to the Porte. The possibility to turn to the Ottoman authorities in disputes involving consuls is further strengthened by another article in the French capitulations of 1740 (art. 52), which formalized the custom among Europeans to put disputes between (the representatives of) different Western *nations* before their ambassadors. It added that

> tant que le demandeur et le défendeur ne consentiront pas à porter ces sortes de process par-devant les pacha, cadi, officiers ou douaniers, ceux-ci ne pourront pas les y forcer ni pretender en prendre connaissance.[40]

Does this mean that only when *both* parties refused to accept the involvement of the Ottoman authorities, the governor-general and all other Ottoman officers were not allowed to interfere? The text certainly allows this interpretation, and in practice the invitation by one of the parties was often justification enough for the Ottoman authorities to get involved.

While the capitulatory articles concerning the inviolability of Western consuls increasingly left room for conflicting interpretations as the eighteenth century progressed, consular *berat*s were unambiguous throughout the period. They reiterated explicitly that no consul should be arrested by the Ottoman police, and that the Ottoman authorities were not allowed forcibly to enter a consul's residence.[41]

---

[39] Ibid., 289.

[40] Ibid., 290.

[41] DNA, Family archives De Hochepied, 86: Contemporary "traduction du Bérat du Consul de Smyrne et ses dépendences pour le Citoyen Lanmond, Consul de la Répub.e F.se", dated 25 Rebiyülahir 1210/8 November 1795. These articles already appeared in earlier consular *berats*: see Bacqué-Grammont, 'Un *berāt* de Mahmūd Ier", 259–278, articles 3 and 5, respectively. At the end of the seventeenth century one of these articles already appeared in a *berat* issued to the English consul in Izmir, William Raye: "... ve konsolos elçilerinin vekilleri olmagla asla habs olunmayub ve evleri mühürlenmeyüb ve kendüleri aranmayub ...", the contemporary translation of which reads: "And the Consuls being Vekils of the Ambassadours shall upon no account be put in Prison, neither shall their Houses be sealed up, neither shall their Persons be Sought after", ENA, SP 105/334, fol. 1v—dated

Neither the capitulations nor the consular *berat*s contained any rules or guidelines that were aimed to prevent conflicts of interest between the consul's capacity as judge and his private interests. For the consuls of most Western countries this was not necessary, because the trade authorities forbade them to conduct trade on their own account, to engage in money-lending or to participate in other risky activities. In theory this should prevent them having to adjudge disputes in which they had a financial interest. The French and English trade authorities issued several regulations of this kind, but the evidence suggests that many Western representatives in the Ottoman Empire ignored or circumvented these rules. The Dutch system was different, because Dutch consuls (but not the ambassadors!) were allowed to engage in commercial activities. It is surprising that the situation did not lead to conflicts of interest more often, but the fact that it did not explains why there were neither precedents nor guidelines when the problem arose during the consulate of Jan Heemskerk junior at Aleppo.

Interested Parties

This chapter focuses on the connected bankruptcies of four warehousemen in European service in Aleppo in 1763. They were the three brothers Yusuf, Antun, and Jarmanos Sadir, and Antun Diyab, all members of the Maronite *taife*. All four were active in trade both on their own, individual accounts, and in association with one another. Legally they constituted four separate accounts of bankruptcy, but here they will be discussed as two couples. Due to the closeness of their business connections and the fact they were both under British protection, the cases of Yusuf and Antun Sadir will be dealt with together. The same is true of Sadir and Diyab. Although Jarmanos Sadir, a Dutch *beratlı*, had strong connections with his two brothers, his principal business associate was Diyab, who was also under Dutch protection.

Little is known about the warehousemen themselves, apart from the dates of their appointment as honorary dragomans. A *berat* for

beginning Rebiyülevvel 1089/beginning April 1678. For Merlijn Olnon's edition of this document, from which I have quoted, see http://members.chello.nl/m.olnon/archive/berat_raye.htm.

Antun w. Hanna Sadir was issued on 13 January 1755 in the Ottoman chancery and registered in the British embassy records on 5 March.[42] Yusuf Sadir's *berat* was issued on 7 March 1756, and registered in the British chancery on 31 March.[43] Their brother Jarmanos came under Dutch protection on 3 March 1761, but he entered the service of Heemskerk at least a year earlier. Antun w. Jirjis Diyab followed five weeks later, on 10 April 1761.[44]

Yusuf and Antun Sadir were employed as warehousemen by the English factor and merchant Thomas Lansdown, whom we have already encountered. Jarmanos Sadir and Antun Diyab were the warehousemen of the Dutch house of Heemskerk, Van Maseijk & Company, whose first partner was the Dutch consul, Jan Heemskerk junior. At the age of twenty-two, this son of a merchant from Rotterdam arrived in Aleppo on 1 March 1757 as the new associate of Jan van Kerchem, who was Dutch consul at the time. After Van Kerchem's death, the States General appointed Heemskerk Dutch consul in 1761.[45] Not much is known about Heemskerk's mercantile career, since his capacity as a merchant is eclipsed in the available sources by his role as consul. At an uncertain date he formed a new partnership with his countryman Nicolaas van Maseijk, who had arrived in Aleppo in the spring of 1755.[46] During this period the Dutch *nation* in Aleppo, which had languished some two decades before, was still small with its four or five merchants, but it was no longer threatened with abandonment by the Dutch authorities. In contrast to the preceding decade, Anglo-Dutch relations in Aleppo were good in the 1760s.[47] The complicated scandal that

---

[42] BOA, ED 35/1, 95/274: 29 Rebiyülevvel 1168/13 January 1755; ENA, SP 105/183, [no page number], 5 March 1755: 'Granted honorary Druggerman to Sig:r Antonio Sader at Aleppo.'

[43] BOA, ED 35/1, 104/320: 5 Cemaziyelahir 1169/7 March 1756; ENA, SP 105/183, 31 March 1756: 'Granted [. . .] to Useph Figlio di Hannah Sader at Aleppo.'

[44] Two Ottoman documents mention the period of three years in which Jarmanos Sadir worked for Heemskerk. BOA, A.DVN.DVE 138, doc. 18, undated petition by Mustafa Paşa, the *beylerbeyi* of Aleppo; Ibid., doc. 20, end Şevval 1176/5–13 March 1763. For his *berat*, see BOA, ED 22/1, 370/1611, 26 Receb 1174. For that of Diyab, see Ibid., 408/1768, 5 Ramazan 1174.

[45] Schutte, *Repertorium*, 353.

[46] Schutte seems to have been unaware of Nicolaas van Maseijk's first term in Aleppo, since his biography of him only starts after his return from the Dutch Republic, in 1763. Ibid., 354.

[47] On Anglo-Dutch relations in the 1750s, see Van den Boogert, 'European Patronage in the Ottoman Empire', 196–202.

ensued after Heemskerk's warehousemen did not result in the consul's own bankruptcy, but it did end his Levantine career.

Within a year and a half of their appointment, Jarmanos Sadir and Antun Diyab had accumulated considerable debts. At the beginning of August 1762, they made a list of their creditors, whom they owed a total of 215,602 *kuruş*.[48] The immediate cause of this calculation is not clear. Since only debts are listed, and nothing is said about assets, it is impossible to calculate the balance of the partnership, which also included Jibrail Sadir. Within six months of composing the list of creditors, Jarmanos Sadir came to the conclusion that he could not meet his financial obligations any longer. On 22 January 1763 he declared himself bankrupt. The bankruptcy of his brother Jibrail probably followed immediately, or very soon after, but none of our sources provide any details. Yusuf and Antun Sadir had stood surety for their brothers for some 85,000 *kuruş*, a guarantee they could not make good when Jarmanos' business collapsed. Yusuf and Antun Sadir therefore also declared bankruptcy, dragging their employer, Lansdown, down with them.

Very little is known about the creditors of Yusuf and Antun Sadir, except for *el-hacc* Abdalqadir Amiri, a prominent member of a notable Muslim family of Aleppo.[49] The sources do not specify how much the Sadir brothers owed him, but Amiri seems to have claimed ownership of their houses, which were eventually sold for some 2,500 *kuruş*.

For the partnership of Jarmanos Sadir and Antun Diyab a list of creditors dated August 1762 has survived, which lists 35 names (see Table 9). The smallest debt mentioned amounted to 39 *kuruş*, while only six other creditors were owed less than 1,000 *kuruş*. Here only some of the largest creditors will be mentioned by name, because of their role in the settlement of the bankrupt estates. *Hacı* Musa b. Hasan Amiri was owed 35,000 *kuruş*, making him the largest of the sixteen Muslim creditors. The largest non-Muslim creditor was Jirjis A'ida, the First Dragoman of the English consulate, whom Sadir and Diyab owed 48,000 *kuruş*, part of which on account of debts of Yusuf and Antun Sadir. Thomas Lansdown was a creditor of Sadir and

---

[48] DNA, LAT 624, Nota delli debiti di Germanos & Jibrail Sader & Anton Diab [8 agosta 1762]. See the Appendix, doc. 9.

[49] On the Amiri family, see Meriwether, *The Notable Families*, 133–134.

Diyab for some 17,600 *kuruş*, a sum owed by Yusuf and Antun Sadir for which Jarmanos had stood surety. The largest European creditor after Lansdown was a Frenchman, Jean-François Pons, who was owed almost 11,500 *kuruş*.[50] It is also interesting that both the English consul, William Kinloch, and his Dutch colleague, Heemskerk, are found on the list. Six months before the bankruptcy of Jarmanos Sadir the Englishman was owed over 3,000 *kuruş*, while the debt to the Dutchman amounted to some 7,500 *kuruş*.

After Jarmanos Sadir had gone bankrupt, his principal associate, Antun Diyab, attempted to remain in business. With the help of the Dutch consul and chancellor, Diyab drew up a document which stated that his partnership with Jarmanos Sadir had been dissolved six months earlier. Sadir was apparently forced by his consul and employer to sign the statement, on the basis of which the Dutch claimed that Diyab was unaffected by the bankruptcy. Not surprisingly, none of the creditors accepted the obviously fraudulent deed. Heemskerk and Diyab even seem to have attempted to bribe the principal creditors, but this ploy also failed. When the pressure rose on Diyab to pay his debts, he, too, declared bankruptcy.[51]

Soon after the bankruptcies became public Jarmanos Sadir was arrested on the authority of the Dutch consul and imprisoned in the consular jail to prevent him escaping his creditors. His two brothers, Yusuf and Antun, instantly "both absconded & have taken away all their Books & Outstanding Notes Cash &ca." Fleeing was seldom a successful strategy for bankrupts, and the Sadirs under British protection, too, were soon found and arrested.[52] They were incarcerated in the pavilion of the English consular house in Khan al-Jumruk, where they remained for at least four months.[53] Their business administration was also seized. The books of Jarmanos were likewise

---

[50] For Pons' career, see Katsumi Fukasawa, *Toilerie et commerce du levant au XVIIIe siècle d'Alep à Marseille* (Paris, 1987), 84–85.

[51] DNA, LH 165, folder 1763, Heemskerk to the Directors, 29 April 1763; DNA, LAT 1118, Petitions by François Pons to Heemskerk, 4 March and 21 March 1763.

[52] ENA, SP 110/37, f. 154v.: Thomas Lansdown to Mr Jonathan Brideoake, London, 25 January 1763.

[53] Ibidem, f. 183, Lansdown to Benjamin Barker, Galata, 14 June 1763; ENA, SP 110/62 (i), [no page number] Chancery note, 27 January 1763; ENA, SP 110/62 (i), page 131, Chancery note, 6 June 1763. Jarmanos Sadir and Antun Diyab were secured in the Dutch consular khan. It is not clear how long they remained in prison.

recovered within days of his arrest, and were put in a bag which was secured with seals of wax imprinted with the consular signet.[54]

The sequestration of written evidence went hand in hand with that of the bankrupt's possessions. In the case of Jarmanos Sadir and Antun Diyab, the khan in which Heemskerk lived and conducted his business had to be searched and an inventory made of all goods that might belong to them. The same procedures were applied to the private residences of the bankrupts in the Jdayda quarter of Aleppo. Within days of their bankruptcies, several rooms in the houses of Sadir and Diyab were sealed off.[55] Moreover, the French consul was asked to sequester cloth that was stored in the warehouse of a French merchant, but which belonged to Heemskerk or his warehousemen.[56] The English chancellor, Eleazar Edwards, followed similar procedures, sending an order to Baghdad on 25 February 1763 to have goods belonging to Yusuf Sadir sequestered. Together with one of the dragomans, Edwards also sealed off parts of the houses of Yusuf and Antun Sadir and their families. On the order of Consul William Kinloch even the apparel and jewelry of Yusuf's wife were sequestered. Her protest was duly recorded.[57]

The fate of the family of bankrupts is seldom explicitly referred to in the sources. Presumably the wife and children of a bankrupt *berath* were granted a modest allowance for their livelihood, but there is no evidence of such arrangements. It is clear that they were allowed to continue to live in their house, provided they did not enter the parts that were sealed off unless they were specifically ordered to do so. Antun Sadir's wife, for example, received orders from the British consulate "to continue in the house and be responsible if the seals were broke open and to water the orange trees." Such maintenance activities were actually the responsibility of the consulate, since it was as much in the interest of the consulate as in that of the creditors involved that the value of the estate be as high as possi-

---

[54] Jarmanos' French creditors claimed that the individual books should also have been bound with rope before being put in the bag. Distrusting the Dutch consul, they insisted on putting a French seal next to his. DNA, LAT 1118.

[55] DNA, LAT 1118, Extrait des Minutes de la Chancellerie du Consulat d'hollande de cette ville d'Alepo & ces dépendances . . . 1 June 1763.

[56] DNA, LH 165, folder 1763, Memorie van d'H^{r} Heemskerk van Aleppo 1765, page 17.

[57] ENA, SP 110/62 (i): p. 124 [?]/f. 63r, Charges attending the Affairs of Juseph & Anton Sader, British Honorary Drugomen & Bankrupts.

ble. Thus, on 23 March 1763, a room in Yusuf Sadir's house was opened to inspect the damage rain had done to the *divan*. On the same day Antun Sadir's orange trees were moved outside, while on 19 May, the British chancellor and dragoman "by order of the consul went to air Joseph's furs." The estate was charged a total of 45 *kuruş* for these services.[58]

Legal Strategies

The interested parties have been introduced in the previous section. In the following pages the legal strategies they adopted will be analysed. The individual claims will not be discussed separately, but in sections based on the way they pursued their claims, i.e. by negotiating with the consulate concerned, by turning to the local Ottoman authorities, by turning to the Porte in Istanbul—or by trying several of these strategies. This allows us to assess which legal strategies were the most successful under the circumstances.

a. *Dealing with the Consulate*

The bankruptcy of Yusuf and Antun Sadir had been caused by that of their brother, Jarmanos Sadir. The fact that Jarmanos' bankruptcy was possibly fraudulent did not make that of his brothers under British protection suspect. There were no legal grounds for complaints against the British consulate, or the bankrupts themselves, so there was nothing else that most creditors could do but to accept the consular settlement. The creditors of Yusuf and Antun Sadir who registered their claims in the British chancery included family members, fellow *beratlı*s of the same consulate, protégés of others, and non-Muslims without any connection to Western consulates. For example, Zakur w. Abdullah Sadir and Antun w. Mikhail Sadir—cousins once removed of the bankrupts—came forward with a claim of 146 *kuruş* which had never been put on paper. Since two witnesses confirmed it, the chancellor accepted and registered their claim.[59] Two other creditors, the Venetian protégé Azar Qatarmiz and his daughter, Miriam, were able to show *temessük*s that proved

[58] Ibid.

[59] ENA, SP 110/62 (1), p. 231/f. 115r, Arabic text with Italian translation, dated 14 November 1764.

their claims. The former was owed 869 *kuruş*, the latter 2,120 *kuruş*, the remaining half of the original debt.[60] Our final example concerns Yusuf, heir to his father Hanna Qirmiz, who claimed a debt of 849 *kuruş* owed to his late father, for which no *temessük* was ever drawn up. Again the claim was only registered after two witnesses had confirmed it.[61]

All these creditors accepted the consular arrangements, receiving a first down payment upon registration of their claims. They seem to have had few alternatives. Many of the creditors registered in the British chancery probably had more to lose than to win by challenging the consular arrangements. The British consul could threaten to revoke the *berat*s of protégés who undermined consular jurisdiction, while the consuls of other *nation*s could do the same with their own *beratlı*s who disregarded the unwritten rules among Western communities in the Ottoman Empire. Even those creditors who lacked direct connections with foreign consulates were not necessarily impervious to the pressure they could exert. After all, if the British consulate announced a boycott (*battelation*) against them, this would make it very difficult to continue doing business with European merchants in the city and their middlemen. Considerations like these—on top of the fact that in itself the bankruptcy of Yusuf and Antun Sadir was not controversial—probably encouraged most creditors to accept the consular settlement.

The bankruptcy of Jarmanos Sadir and Antun Diyab was different, because it was suspect from the beginning. For this reason there appear to have been no creditors who simply turned to the Dutch consulate and accepted a preliminary down payment. As we will see below most creditors in this case turned to the qadi in Aleppo with their claims. Nevertheless, in the case of Sadir and Diyab, too, there were creditors who preferred to deal directly with the consulate, without involving the Ottoman authorities. They were not only Europeans, but also powerful Ottoman creditors. The sources reveal that only the Ottomans, three tax collectors and Çelebi Effendi, managed to come to an agreement with Heemskerk.

---

[60] Ibid., illegible page number, two Arabic *temessük*s dated 3 Adar 1762 and mid Şaban 1175. Although the documents were clearly private, and not registered in court, both mention several *şuhud al-hal*, who are also referred as such.

[61] Ibid., p. 221/f. 110r., Arabic text with Italian translation, dated 23 October 1764. One of the witnesses, Antun w. Nimat Hasruni, also confirmed the claim by the bankrupts' distant cousins.

Just three days after Jarmanos Sadir had declared bankruptcy, the French merchant Jean-François Pons, together with his colleagues, Jean-Paul Magy, Jean-Pierre Augier, and Michel Gilly, already accused Heemskerk of treachery (*fourberie*). In their opinion Heemskerk had contributed to the bankruptcy in two ways, by embezzling goods belonging to his warehouseman, and by paying him less than current market prices for silk Sadir had purchased for him. The Dutchman always insisted that his warehousemen bought the goods on their own account first and subsequently sold it to him in a separate transaction, a method to which we will return below. The Frenchmen now accused Heemskerk of paying 17 or 18 *kuruş* for silk Sadir had purchased for 22 *akçe* per unit. Not only did they level these accusations directly to Heemskerk in the Dutch consular residence, they also formalized them by starting a correspondence with the Dutchman via the French consulate.[62]

In response to these claims Heemskerk offered to have these matters resolved by arbitration, but the Frenchmen rejected this out of hand. The reasons for this rejection are easy to reconstruct. Their acceptance of arbitration automatically meant that they would have to accept its outcome, which was uncertain. The merchants' accusations were based on the testimony of the bankrupts themselves, and they must have felt that their case was strong enough to take to any court. There thus was no reason for them to place the matter into the hands of arbiters. It was probably considerations like these that led the Frenchmen to reject Heemskerk's arbitration proposal.

The French merchants actively cooperated with other creditors, including both foreigners and notable Ottomans. For example, Muhammad Ağa, a scion of the notable family of Kabkaboğlu, acted in concert with the foreign creditors. The bankrupts owed him over 4,200 *kuruş*, as the list of their debts drawn up in 1762 shows. The same is true for *el-hacc* Yahya Usays al-Mausuli, who was owed 8,500 *kuruş* in payment for a quantity of white silk he had sold the bankrupts. These creditors did not immediately turn to the Ottoman authorities, but tried to find alternative solutions. At the end of February 1763, for example, a general assembly of Sadir and Diyab's

[62] DNA, LAT 1118, Answer by Pons (via the French consulate), dated 5 March 1763, to a letter by Heemskerk of 25 February.

creditors met twice in the British consulate. No results seem to have come from these meetings, apart from protests against Heemskerk's attendance at them in the capacity of a creditor rather than in that of the competent consul, but the concerted efforts to come to some agreement with the Dutchman are worth mentioning in themselves.[63]

The Western creditors of Jarmanos Sadir and Antun Diyab initially followed consular procedures, demanding that Heemskerk compensate their losses. They were supported by their own consul, Pierre Thomas, but there was little he could do to change his Dutch colleague's mind. Their attempts to deal directly with the Dutch consulate had failed, but others were more successful.

In 1762 three tax collectors, Ismail b. Ahmad, the collector of the annual tax revue (*saliyaneci*) of the Crimea and a *çavuş* of the Porte, Ali Çavuş b. Süleyman, the *saliyaneci* of Nafplion, and Hasan Çavuş b. Ali, who was a *cebeci saliyaneci*, had made use of the financial services of Jarmanos Sadir.[64] Ismail Çavuş consigned 4,000 *kuruş* to the warehouseman, the sum of 2,120 *kuruş* was deposited by Ali Çavuş, while Hasan Çavuş entrusted Sadir with 2,500 *kuruş*. Jarmanos thus received a total of 8,620 *kuruş*, for three specific purposes. First, an unspecified part of this sum should be changed into gold coins.[65] The second part was meant to allow the officers to draw bills of exchange on Sadir.[66] The third part of the entrusted sum would remain on deposit with the warehouseman, who was probably paid commission for its safekeeping.

When Jarmanos Sadir went bankrupt at the beginning of 1763 the three Ottoman officers could easily have turned to the authorities in Aleppo, or to the Porte, in order to reclaim their deposits. This is not what they did, however; they turned directly to the Dutch

---

[63] DNA, LAT 1118, Extrait des Minutes de la Chancellerie du Consulat de France à Alep [30 May 1763]. This file also contains two petitions by Pons, dated 4 March and 21 March 1763, along with Heemskerk's replies of 8 March and 28 March 1763, all in French.

[64] DNA, LAT 1118, 'No. 4', Ottoman text dated 1 Şevvel 1176/15 April 1763, with an Italian translation which mentions 'Ismail Ciaus Saliangi Cherem [a misreading of *Krim saliyaneci*] figlio di Ahmad, è Ali Ciaus Saliangi Anapoli figlio di Soliman, è Hassan Ciaus Saliangi Giabagian [i.e. tax collector of the armourers of the Janissary corps] figlio di Ali'.

[65] The Italian translation has 'parte per scambiarli in Zecchini', suggesting Venetian sequins (in Ottoman *yaldız altunu*) are meant.

[66] The Italian translation has 'per fare Polizze'.

consulate, instead. To facilitate procedures they appointed an agent to make the necessary arrangements on their behalf. This agent was not a local Janissary, nor even a Muslim, but the chancellor of the Dutch consulate, Jean Gollmart.[67] Six weeks after they had registered their claim, the three Ottoman officers were given 8,620 *kuruş* worth of cloth from Sadir's estate. The payment was duly registered in the qadi court. The *hüccet* that was drawn up of this consignment states that the arrangement was made "to avoid a deficiency in the salaries" (*emval-i mevacibe keser ve nuksan terettüb olmamak*). This suggests that the third aim of the funds placed in Jarmanos' care was the payment of the Janissaries' salaries, which would certainly explain the extraordinary swiftness with which the consignment was arranged, since it was in the interest of everybody concerned to avoid riots by underpaid Janissaries in Aleppo. It also explains why the name of Ahmad Ağa, Aleppo's *muhassıl* and *mütasellim*, appears on the *hüccet* as one of the court's witnesses.[68]

These tax collectors were extraordinary creditors, for whom the Dutch consulate quickly made an extraordinary arrangement. The settlement with the tax collectors was controversial, because the French creditors considered it prejudicial to their own interests, but it had the support of the Ottoman administration. If the Dutch home authorities should disapprove of this preferential payment, the consulate could easily argue that preventing Janissary unrest was for the common good.

In contrast to the first arrangement between an Ottoman creditor of Jarmanos Sadir and the Dutch consul, the second benefited the other creditors, because it was paid by Heemskerk himself. It was a settlement between the Dutchman and Çelebi Effendi, which was brokered by Jirjis A'ida, the First Dragoman of the British consulate in Aleppo.

---

[67] This procuration took place between 22 January 1763, the date of Jarmanos' bankruptcy, and 26 January, when Gollmart declared that he was busy with matters 'qui m'ont procuré les Chious du GG: SS:' [i.e. the Grand Signior, the sultan]. DNA, LAT 1118, Extrait des Minutes de la Chancellerie . . . 1 Juin 1763 [statement by Gollmart].

[68] Other witnesses mentioned on the *hüccet* were Çelebi Effendi, the *serdar*, and members of the Kawakibi and Trabulsi families. The three Ottoman officers collected the cloth assigned to them in the afternoon of 3 March 1763 in order to have it sold by public auction. DNA, LAT 1118, Extrait des Minutes de la Chancellerie du Consulat de France à Alep [30 May 1763].

At the end of 1762 Heemskerk agreed to three barter transactions brokered by his warehouseman, Jarmanos Sadir, and his brother, Jibrail.[69] The other party was Çelebi Effendi, who used Jirjis A'ida as his broker. In return for broadcloth and iron, Heemskerk would receive cotton from Çelebi Effendi. The Dutchman was interested in the deals, but insisted that his warehouseman should not broker the deal, but actually be the seller himself. This meant that Jarmanos Sadir first had to buy the cotton from Çelebi Effendi on credit, and then resell it on his own account to Heemskerk. This method was also commonly used by British merchants in Aleppo, who nominally sold the cloth they received from England on credit to their warehousemen, while buying silk on credit through them at the same time.[70] In this way, the amount of cash needed remained limited. More importantly, the arrangements created a juridical buffer between the original seller, in this case the powerful Çelebi Effendi, and the eventual buyer, Heemskerk. Sadir agreed to the conditions of the Dutch consul, so the deals, only the first of which was recorded, were confirmed. Before all the transactions could actually take place, however, Jarmanos Sadir went bankrupt.

Muhammad b. Ahmad Tahazade, who was generally known as Çelebi Effendi, was probably Aleppo's most prominent *nekibüleşraf* of the period. Not only did he lead the political faction of the *eşraf* several times, he was also active in international trade.[71] Jirjis A'ida was a Greek Catholic merchant, who had inherited considerable real estate in the city from his father. He was also active in international trade on his own account, serving as First Dragoman to the British consulate at the same time. A'ida's ties with the British consulate did not prevent him acting independently in this matter, for the dragoman was simply too powerful for the British consul to control. The connection between A'ida and Çelebi Effendi contributed to this. Heemskerk characterized Çelebi Effendi as A'ida's "great pro-

[69] The principal source for this settlement is DNA, LH 165, folder 1763, Heemskerk to the Directors, 29 April 1763.

[70] Lansdown had used the same method with more success, as we have seen above. Davis, *Aleppo and Devonshire Square,* 243, 245. On the role of non-Muslim intermediaries in sales and barter transactions of Europeans in Izmir, see Frangakis-Syrett, *The Commerce of Smyrna*, 87–90.

[71] On Çelebi Effendi, see Meriwether, *The Notable Families,* 78–79, 192193, 248, 249, 250; Marcus, *The Middle East,* 83–84, 87, 133.

tector".[72] When Çelebi Effendi was exiled to Bursa a few years later, A'ida was also arrested on the charge of "having assisted the Chelebi Effendi in oppressing the Mahometan subjects".[73] The two power-brokers thus appear to have operated together more often.

Soon after the bankruptcy of Jarmanos Sadir had become public, Çelebi Effendi and A'ida put pressure on the Dutch consul to pay off the cotton he had agreed to barter with them via his warehousemen, the details of which are irrelevant here. Heemskerk referred to the conditions of the transaction, claiming that his warehouseman should be held responsible, since he had concluded the transaction with A'ida. The British dragoman disagreed, saying that doing business with a warehouseman was the same the thing as dealing with his principal. During a heated argument between the British dragoman and the Dutch consul in the latter's residence, Antun Diyab intervened and prevailed upon his employer to give in to A'ida's demands, since he and Çelebi Effendi formed too powerful a couple to resist successfully. Subsequently, Heemskerk grudgingly agreed to fulfil the terms of the unwritten agreements between Jarmanos Sadir and A'ida, in which the Dutchman had not legally been a party.

Heemskerk's strategy to distance himself from the deals had failed. Çelebi Effendi and Jirjis A'ida may not have had any legal basis for their claims, but they threatened to obtain a fatwa "sentencing" Heemskerk personally to pay the debts of his warehousemen, nevertheless.[74] The Dutch consul took this threat seriously and was eventually convinced that these men were simply too powerful for him to oppose. For the other creditors of Jarmanos Sadir this arrangement was beneficial, because the bankrupt's obligations to Çelebi Effendi were now taken over by Heemskerk.

In the case of Sadir and Diyab the only creditors who dealt directly with the Dutch consulate were those powerful enough to circumvent consular procedures altogether: three tax collectors whose deposits with Jarmanos Sadir included the Janissaries' salary, and Çelebi Effendi, the powerful *nekibüleşraf* of Aleppo. Heemskerk was unable

[72] DNA, LH 165, file 1763, Heemskerk to the Directors, 3 March 1763.

[73] ENA, SP 110/86: No. 9: Murray to the Earl of Shelburne, Constantinople 1 June 1767.

[74] DNA, LH 165, file 1763, Heemskerk to the Directors, 3 March 1763.

simply to reject their claims and was forced to deal with them. The Porte in Istanbul offered the rest of the creditors another way to pursue their claims on the estate of Sadir and Diyab, because it soon revoked the Dutch consul's jurisdiction in this case.

b. *The Porte*

In connection with the Sadir bankruptcies six separate petitions were sent to the Porte, one by Abdalqadir Amiri, a creditor of Yusuf and Antun Sadir; one by the qadi of Aleppo; one by its governor-general; one by the Dutch consul; and one by *el-hacc* Sulayman b. Muhammad Shaykh, a creditor of Sadir and Diyab. The aims of the first five petitions to the Porte will be discussed in this section, the last will follow in a later section.

Most creditors of Yusuf and Antun Sadir accepted the British consular settlement of their bankrupt estate, but *el-hacc* Abdalqadir Amiri did not. The other creditors consented to being repaid no more than 10% of what the bankrupts owed them, but Amiri refused to accept this situation. In order to raise the money for the dividend, the English consulate had had the bankrupts' houses sold, among other things. Amiri claimed these houses, and although the legal basis of his claims is not specified in the sources, we know that he attempted to have all sales of the Sadir brothers' possessions reversed. He did this by sending a petition to the Porte, contesting English consular jurisdiction over the bankrupt estate of the Sadir brothers altogether.

Amiri's letter was not the first report about this matter that reached Istanbul. Already in the second week of March 1763 the qadi of Aleppo had sent a report to the Porte about the bankruptcy of the four Sadir brothers, asking that jurisdiction in this matter be assigned to him.[75] At the same time the governor-general of Aleppo sent a petition of his own to Istanbul, proposing that neither the consuls nor the qadi, but he himself be assigned jurisdiction.[76] Amiri's petition to the Porte, which supported the qadi's earlier request, can only have strengthened the view in Istanbul that these cases deserved special attention.

Amiri's actions came at a bad time for the British consulate, which was responsible for the bankrupt estate of Yusuf and Antun Sadir.

[75] BOA, A.DVN.DVE 138, doc. 20, end Şevval 1176/5–13 May 1763.
[76] Ibid., doc. 18. Cf. below, page 246.

The consul, Kinloch, had set out for Istanbul to act as *chargé d'affaires* after the ambassador, Henry Grenville, had been recalled. In Kinloch's absence the office of British consul was attended to by a council of four merchants, David Hays, Charles Smith, Jasper Shaw, and Henry Preston, the treasurer of the *nation*.[77] It was their intention to attend collectively to the tasks of the consul, but according to Grenville the central Ottoman chancery in Istanbul refused to issue a consular *berat* for four. Before his departure he had therefore applied for the *berat* to be granted to Preston. The Levant Company supported this initiative and appointed Preston "Pro-Consul" in Aleppo, until Kinloch returned or a successor was found.[78]

It was during this time when the English factory in Aleppo officially lacked a proper consul that it became known that Amiri had obtained a *ferman* which annulled the sale of the Sadirs' houses and enabled the local court to retrieve the dividends that had already been paid to the other creditors, despite the fact that the previous qadi had agreed with the procedures. According to English reports, officers of the *mahkema* in Aleppo immediately put pressure on the buyers of Yusuf Sadir's house to comply with the Imperial decree. They were soon ready to vacate the house and return the deed to the consulate, but only on the condition that the 2,500 *kuruş* they had paid be returned to them. Since the English were unwilling to reverse laborious procedures that had taken eighteen months and to start all over again under the supervision of the local court, they vainly confronted the qadi with his predecessor's approval. Amiri won the argument by stressing—as the imperial order he had obtained erroneously confirmed—that the Sadir brothers were not actually dragomans, and hence their estate was not protected by the capitulations. In light of this argument the qadi pronounced the con-

---

77 ENA, SP 110/29, f. 108r: Eleazar Edwards to George Baldwin, Acri, [ ] September 1765.

78 Provisional appointments by the English in this period were commonly marked by the prefix 'Pro-'. There is no trace of Preston's appointment in *ecnebi defteri* 35/1 in which William Clark (in office 1768–1770) is recorded as the immediate successor of William Kinloch (in office 1759–1766). ENA, SP 110/29, fos 118v–119r, Levant Company to Treasurer & Factory at Aleppo, 10 December 1765; BOA, ED 35/1, 116/389, 19 Gemaziyelevvel 1172/17 January 1759 (Francis Browne to Kinloch); Ibid., 122–123/422, 15 Rebiyülevvel 1182/30 July 1768 (Kinloch to Clark).

sular settlement procedures to be in contradiction with Islamic law, and ordered the implementation of the Imperial command.[79]

The English sought support against Amiri's actions both in Istanbul and in Aleppo. First they asked Kinloch at the British embassy to review the procedures once again, and intercede with the Porte if possible. This did lead to the issue of an Imperial decree of some sort, but the First Dragoman, Jirjis A'ida, considered it useless.[80] In Aleppo the help of the French and Dutch consuls was solicited on the grounds that the Imperial orders were detrimental to all European creditors of the Sadirs, and possibly to European privileges in general. The Dutch consul, Heemskerk's successor Van Maseijk, refused to get involved, probably because they were business associates. The French consul, Pierre Thomas, actively supported the English. With Thomas' help the English factors applied for an imperial command confirming the consular procedures. It was the Frenchman who explained to the chargé d'affaires in Istanbul, Kinloch, what kind of command was required:

> Le commandement [obtained by Amiri] étant contraire aux privilèges des Capitulations, il en résulte un tort considérable aux Francs qui se trouvent intéressés dans la Faillite des dits Saders et pour empêcher toutes les démarches qu'Hadgi Abdelkadir peut faire, on demande un commandement qui porte que le Defter des Dettes et des effets des susdits Sader (qui etoient alors Dragomans) & qui a été authorisé par un Bujurdi du Basha & par le scelle du Caddy, sera confirmé & que tous le créanciers ayent à s'y confirmer & que ce Procès ne pourra plus être entendu à Alep malgré tous les Commandements antérieurs ou postérieurs qu'il pourroit y avoir à ce sujet.[81]

Amiri challenged the applicability of the capitulations on the grounds that the Sadir brothers were not actually dragomans. He was right in the sense that Yusuf and Antun Sadir did not serve the British consulate as interpreters, but because they possessed dragoman's *berat*s the Sadir brothers legally were dragomans, even if they actually

---

[79] ENA, SP 110/29, fos 112–113, The Factory at Aleppo to Kinloch in Istanbul, 27 November 1765.

[80] Ibid., fos 110v–111v: Henry Preston, David Hays, Charles Smith, Jasper Shaw in Aleppo to Kinloch in Istanbul, 20 November 1765. I have not found this *ferman* in the Ottoman records.

[81] ENA, SP 110/29, fos 112r–113v, Preston, Hays, Smith and Shaw in Aleppo to Kinloch in Istanbul, 27 November 1765.

worked as warehousemen. Amiri turned to the Porte with his challenge, and it was also to the Porte that the British consulate turned to have its jurisdiction reaffirmed, after the local court had refused to confirm the approval of its procedures by both the previous governor-general and qadi of Aleppo. This appears to have resulted in a stalemate that lasted about a year, during which nothing was recorded about the case in the British chanceries in Istanbul and Aleppo. Many questions must therefore remain unanswered. For example, it is not clear how long Antun Sadir remained in the custody of the qadi after his escape from the British consular prison. Nor is the fate of his brother, Yusuf, in this period recorded in our sources. We only know that both died within a year and a half of their bankruptcy.[82]

Little else was recorded about the bankruptcy of the two brothers until 24 November 1766, when the consul and factory in Aleppo reported to the new English ambassador, John Murray, that the case was closed. Amiri had reportedly been appeased with the help of "Cheleby & Trabolsi Effendi" and a third mediator, one Ahmad Ghumaa.[83] Çelebi Effendi has already been introduced. The second identifiable mediator was Muhammad Trabulsi, a former mufti of Aleppo who, like Çelebi Effendi, was appointed *nekibüleşraf* of the city several times during this period.[84] Their silent diplomacy, which has left no further traces in the available sources, finally resolved the conflict at a cost of about 4,000 *kuruş*.[85]

It is not clear how much the Sadir brothers owed Amiri, but we know that he claimed their houses, which represented a value of some 2,500 *kuruş*. If Amiri had accepted the consular arrangements, he would only have received about 10% of this sum, amounting to little more than 250 *kuruş*. Some of the 4,000 *kuruş* that was paid for the mediation undoubtedly went to the three mediators. It seems likely that Amiri would have received a substantial part of it, but

[82] BOA, ED 35/1, 120/410, 9 Zilka'de 1177/10 May 1764 (Antun Sadir); Ibid., 120/412, 21 Cemaziyel'ahır 1178/16 December 1764 (Yusuf Sadir). These are the dates on which the transfer of their *berat*s was registered, so they probably died several months earlier.

[83] ENA, SP 110/29, f. 121, Consul & Factory at Aleppo to ambassador Murray, 24 November 1766. Murray was in office 1765–1775.

[84] Meriwether, *The Notable Families*, 25, 238, 249.

[85] ENA, SP 110/62 (i), 234.

even if the sum was split in four equal shares, one for each mediator and one for Amiri, the latter would still have recouped four times what the consulate had been able to offer. Challenging the jurisdiction of the English consulate via the Porte—even on the basis of false arguments—thus appears to have paid in this case.

Amiri's success in his use of the Porte is in stark contrast with Heemskerk's efforts to do the same. The two earliest reports from Aleppo to the Porte focused on the bankruptcy of Jarmanos Sadir and both mentioned the Dutch consul, Heemskerk, explicitly. The Islamic judge and administrator outright accused the Dutch consul of foul play. The consul, he wrote to Istanbul, considered the case to fall under the capitulations, but the qadi disagreed and asked to be assigned jurisdiction himself.[86] In his contemporaneous letter the governor-general of Aleppo, Mustafa Paşa, likewise blamed the bankruptcy of Jarmanos Sadir on Heemskerk, emphasizing that the Dutchman was also a creditor of his own warehousemen. The Paşa reported that the Dutch consul refused to have the case heard by the local court and implied that this might harm the interests of the Muslim creditors. The governor-general claimed that business had been good for the Sadir brothers, and that the unexpected bankruptcies must therefore have been fraudulent. Instead of allowing the Dutch to apply their own laws to the bankrupts, Mustafa Paşa asked the Porte to assign jurisdiction in the bankruptcies to him.[87]

The Dutch sources confirm that the local authorities in Aleppo had been in contact with the consul from the beginning. Soon after the French creditors had first openly accused him of embezzlement (within a week after Jarmanos Sadir's bankruptcy) Heemskerk had turned to the governor-general of Aleppo with repeated requests to uphold the capitulations and guarantee his consular privileges. At the same time he obtained letters of support from senior official at the Porte through the Dutch embassy in Istanbul.[88] Possibly encour-

[86] BOA, A.DVN.DVE 138, doc. 20, end Şevval 1176/5–13 May 1763.

[87] Ibid., doc. 18. The document is undated, but it refers to the qadi's report, which means that it was probably written around the same time. They even seem to have been composed jointly, since the wording is identical in several passages of the two documents. The pencil note dating Mustafa Paşa's petition to 1175 A.H. (1762–3) is therefore probably incorrect.

[88] The authors are identified as "Jusuf Effendi Rusnamesi and Arab Zade, first Ulema." The *ruznamçeci* was a high treasury official. The 'first of the *ulema*" was possibly the *Şeyhülislâm*. DNA, LH 165, Memorie van d'H[r] Heemskerk van Aleppo 1765 [Copia], 12, 20; DNA, LAT 602, Van Asten to Heemskerk, 3 March 1763.

aged by this sign of support from the Ottoman capital, Heemskerk announced to the authorities in Aleppo that he had decided to appeal directly to the Porte. The *beylerbeyi* advised against this step, saying the people of Aleppo might rise against the Dutchman, under the impression that he was trying to escape his responsibilities.[89] Heemskerk knew that at this time the *beylerbeyi* was awaiting the Porte's reply to his petition asking for the affairs of the Sadir brothers to be put in his own hands.[90] The governor-general reportedly used all means at his disposal to prevent Heemskerk leaving Aleppo, without actually arresting the consul, which was against the capitulations. The Dutchman wrote to the embassy that

> thinking I wanted to leave last night, the *tufenkçi başı* and the *serdar* [yesterday] had the order [of the governor-general] conveyed to the *odabaşı* of my khan and to the [consular] Janissaries, that they should not let me leave without warning them first, and this morning I heard that guards have been posted at all the [city] gates.[91]

The Dutch *chargé d'affaires* in Istanbul Van Asten was surprised that the consul's use of the capitulations was not just a tactic, but that his intentions were genuine. Van Asten thought it was inadvisable for Heemskerk to execute his plan, since it might do more harm than good to the consul personally, and to the Dutch community in Aleppo in general. Van Asten clearly stated he would not cooperate without first consulting the Dutch States-General about the issue.[92] This was not the answer Heemskerk had hoped for, and it delayed his decision to leave Aleppo.

The alarming reports from Aleppo's two most important administrators and the others petitions from the city eventually led to the issue of a *ferman* which ordered that the bankruptcies of the Sadir brothers and Antun Diyab be examined and adjudicated locally by the qadi. The imperial decree, which was addressed to Mustafa Paşa and the qadi, arrived in Aleppo in the second half of April 1763.[93]

---

[89] Ibid., Extract uyt een Brief... [3 March 1763].

[90] DNA, LAT 602: Van Asten to Heemskerk, 26 March 1763 (in Dutch).

[91] DNA, LH 165, folder 1763, Extract uyt een Brief... 3 March 1763 (in Dutch). The *tufenkçi başı* was the leader of the *beylerbeyi*'s personal infantry guard. The *odabaşı* was subordinate to the *ağa*, the superintendent of the khan on behalf of the owner.

[92] DNA, LAT 602, Van Asten to Heemskerk, 26 March 1763.

[93] BOA, ED 22/1, 383/1660, mid Ramazan 1176/26 March–4 April 1763; DNA, LH 165, folder 1763, Heemskerk to the Directors, 23 March 1763; Ibid., same to same, 23 April 1763 (both in Dutch).

The Porte thus had rejected Heemskerk's request to be heard by the *divan-ı hümayun*, preferring to let the local Islamic court deal with the case. At first glance this appears to be a violation of the capitulations, which, after all, gave the consul and his dragomans the right to appeal to the Imperial Council in cases involving more than 4,000 *akçe*. The context of this article in the capitulations, however, reveals that this privilege was intended to protect the consul and his dragomans against frivolous litigation. In this case it was clear that the allegations against the consul were not fabricated. The arguments in favour of adjudication in Aleppo were the same as in the previous chapter, where an investigator of the Porte had argued that reliable witnesses were easier to find there than in Istanbul.[94] Adjudication in Istanbul would inconvenience many, while only the Dutch consul claimed to suffer damage when legal procedures took place in Aleppo.

The Porte's involvement in these bankruptcies did not end with its decision to assign jurisdiction over them to the qadi in Aleppo. At the beginning of September 1763 the *reisülküttab* told a dragoman of the British embassy that the Ottoman authorities were paying close attention to the way the affairs of Yusuf and Antun Sadir and of Jarmanos Sadir and Antun Diyab were handled by their respective consulates. The Dutch were reportedly threatened with punitive measures, while the British were merely told to do everything in their power to clear up any form of "theft" concerning the bankruptcy of Yusuf and Antun Sadir.[95] All eyes were on the Islamic court in Aleppo.

c. *The Qadi Court*

Mediation between Abdalqadir Amiri and the British consulate ended the settlement of the bankrupt estate of Yusuf and Antun Sadir. In the case of Sadir and Diyab a number of Ottoman creditors, three tax collectors and the powerful Çelebi Effendi, managed to come to an agreement with the Dutch consulate at an early stage. All other claims had to wait until it was clear who had jurisdiction in this

[94] See Chapter Four, page 192–194.

[95] DNA, LH 165, folder 1763, Note de la Communication faite a Mons:r L'Ambassadeur d'Angeleterre & Mons:r Le Chargé des Affaires d'hollande par voije des Drogemans des susdites Nations ce 5:e 7bre 1763.

matter. Heemskerk had tried to have the case moved to Istanbul, but the Porte had decided otherwise. From this moment it was no longer the interested parties who determined how they might pursue their claims, but the local Islamic court that determined the course of events. For this reason the following section is not arranged by the individual strategies of the bankrupts and their creditors, but by the procedures the qadi dictated.

i. Court Supervision

The authorities in Aleppo did not take action immediately, but allowed two months to pass after the *ferman* had arrived. By that time Antun Sadir was no longer in the custody of the British consulate, because he had escaped and turned himself in at the *mahkema* in the second week of June 1763. Lansdown reported to one of his own creditors that

> [o]ne of my warehousemen has made his escape from the Consulary house & has told the Turk creditors that they may prove the debts before the Caddi & he is now a prisoner with him at the Mackamy [*mahkema*]. The Basha has likewise begun to intermeddle in their embroils & tis said he has with in these few days received a command from Stambole [Istanbul] to procure the Turk [Muslim] creditors payment for what is owing them by Useph & Antone Sader, so I fear the greatest part of what remains will be eaten up by the Basha & Caddi & little or nothing will be divided among the creditors & there is no knowing how long it may be before this unhappy affair will be ended.[96]

Antun Sadir had preferred the Islamic court to the English consulate from the start. Already at his arrest by the First Dragoman of the English consulate, Sadir had dramatically exclaimed: "O people of Muhammad, I want to turn to the law of Islam, but they won't let me!"[97] Some unnamed Muslim creditors reportedly supported Sadir's plea, but consul Kinloch refused to hand him over to the qadi. The fact that these creditors turned to the British consul in the first place indicates that they accepted his authority in the matter, which probably

[96] ENA, SP 110/37, f. 183: Lansdown to Benjamin Barker, Galata, 14 June 1763.

[97] ENA, SP 110/62 (i), 131: Statement by First Dragoman of the English consulate, Niqula Fakhr, dated 6 June 1763, also signed by Henry Preston, Charles Smith and al-Hamid [?] Ibrahim Ubari. In the Italian text only this quotation is noted in Arabic as well.

explains why the Ottoman authorities did not intervene at this stage. After having spent more than four months in prison, however, Antun Sadir directly involved the Islamic court of Aleppo by escaping from the consular gaol and turning to the qadi.

What could Sadir have hoped to achieve? Maybe he hoped that the qadi might help him come to some sort of agreement with his principal creditors that would allow him to continue in business under their supervision, which might enable him to repay them in full eventually. Or he may have hoped that being declared bankrupt by the qadi would wipe out his debts altogether. According to Joseph Schacht

> if the debtor is released from prison as being unable to pay, he is declared bankrupt (*muflis*); it is contested whether this wipes out his debts, or whether the creditor or creditors may still resort to self-help by watching over his person and taking from him the surplus of his earnings.[98]

In the absence of further evidence we can only speculate about Antun Sadir's motives, but it is clear that he had nothing to lose by taking this course of action. The impartiality of the Dutch consul was questionable, to say the least, and it was not in the interest of the British consulate to challenge another consulate's jurisdiction in a bankruptcy connected with one under its own authority. After all, the settlement of the bankrupt estate of Yusuf and Antun Sadir was proceeding relatively smoothly at this time. Moreover, William Kinloch was himself a creditor of Jarmanos Sadir for more than 3,000 *kuruş*, so it was also in his personal interest not to get involved in his capacity as British consul, too.[99] The 4,000 *akçe* clause in the capitulations also did not help the Sadir brothers. Invoking their capitulatory right to a trial in Istanbul was costly and there was little reason to expect a sympathetic ear from the Porte after the reports it had already received.[100] It is therefore not surprising that when Antun Sadir managed to escape from the British consulate's prison, it was to the qadi that he turned himself in.

Antun Sadir's escape to the Islamic court is significant because it provided the Ottoman authorities with first hand information about the course of events. Lansdown's warehouseman denounced the fraud-

---

[98] Schacht, *An Introduction to Islamic Law*, 197–198.
[99] See Table 9, page 164.
[100] See above, page 246.

ulent circumstances surrounding his brother's bankruptcy, incriminating Heemskerk and Diyab. Sadir thus gave the Ottoman authorities sufficient grounds to adjudicate the disputes over the bankruptcies themselves, but the qadi chose not to at this stage. Instead, he delegated further examinations of the evidence to a number of arbiters who operated under his supervision.

On 28 June 1763 the creditors of Sadir and Diyab held a closed meeting in the house of Thomas Lansdown at the Ottoman authorities' initiative. The meeting was led by unnamed "Turkish [i.e. Muslim] arbiters who have no interest as creditors" appointed by the qadi. Also present were the four bankrupts, the First, Second and Third Dragomans of the Dutch consulate, the Dutch chancellor, and the English First Dragoman, Jirjis A'ida. During this meeting, Jarmanos Sadir and Antun Diyab answered a number of allegations levelled against them on a previous occasion by Yusuf and Antun Sadir.[101] Fact-finding seems to have been the principal aim of the meeting.

The governor-general and the qadi of Aleppo subsequently ordered the creditors of Sadir and Diyab to examine the bankrupts' accounts on Saturday, 16 July 1763. This second meeting took place in the house of the merchant Abdullah Ağa "Mirozade", who appears to have been one of the arbiters.[102] On the orders of the local authorities the meeting was attended by a certain *Seyyid* Bakri, by Abdurrahman Ağa Qurna, the French merchants Reinaud and Bernard, and the English merchants David Hays, Charles Smith and Colvill Bridger. Also present were the Frenchmen Pons and Magy, as well as Lansdown, the First and Second Dragomans of the French, the English and the Dutch *nation*, and Antun Diyab and Jarmanos Sadir themselves.[103]

Although the meeting was called to examine the accounts of Sadir and Diyab, little seems to have come of this. Instead, the bankrupts were confronted with *Seyyid* Bakri's claim that they had made a profit

---

[101] DNA, LAT 1118, Estrato autentico della Cancellaria Neederlandese di questa Citta di Aleppo & le sue Dippendenze . . . [20 Iuglio 1763].

[102] Although Miro is neither a Turkish nor an Arabic name, this is how it appears in the European sources. I have found no Ottoman or Arabic text in which the man is mentioned.

[103] DNA, LAT 1118, Noi sottoscritti Mercanti Inglese . . . dated 16 July 1763. Although the document is unsigned, it is clear from surrounding documents that it was written by Smith and Bridger on Heemskerk's request. Their account of the meeting was confirmed by all four dragomans in Dutch service at the time.

of 7,000 *kuruş* on a load of unspecified textiles that he had sold to them. Sadir denied this, claiming that he could prove that they had suffered a loss of 1,137 *kuruş* on the transaction instead. The records of the buyers, the French merchants Jouve and Cuzin, would prove his case, he claimed. The creditors seem to have been insensitive to these arguments, however. Instead of examining the bankrupts' business records, they demanded an acceptable settlement. According to previous calculations the estate of Sadir and Diyab was worth 23,000 *kuruş* while their debts amounted to 190,000 *kuruş*. This meant the creditors could expect a 12.1% dividend, but they did not consider this satisfactory. They demanded 25% from the Dutch consul, who would have to supply the remaining 24,500 *kuruş*. It was thought that the bankrupts should be able to repay their employer over a period of two or three years. A dividend of 25% was justified according to the English first dragoman, Jirjis A'ida, who claimed that Yusuf and Antun Sadir would also pay their creditors this percentage.[104] The French also supported this demand, which was presented to the two dragomans of the Dutch consulate. The dragomans returned to the meeting with Heemskerk's reply, the translation of which was read aloud. According to the consul, the meeting had been called to examine the bankrupts' accounts in order to verify the consular investigation. He flatly refused to discuss the demand of a 25% dividend. By taking this position, Heemskerk further antagonized his warehousemen's creditors, who were already suspicious of his role in the scandal. As a result, the creditors sent a report to the governor-general and the qadi stating that Jarmanos Sadir and Antun Diyab were thieves and that they were guilty of embezzlement.[105]

Even after the Porte had assigned jurisdiction to the qadi in Aleppo, the Islamic court gave the interested parties several months to reach an agreement without its direct involvement. Only after this had failed did the qadi order a general session in his court in order to examine the numerous claims against the Dutch consul and his warehousemen.

---

[104] This was a (deliberate?) exaggeration. The creditors of Yusuf and Antun Sadir only recouped 10%.

[105] '. . . che questi Germanos Sader e Antonio Diab sono furbi, e che hanno mangiato il bene delli Genti . . .' DNA, LAT 1118, Noi sottoscritti Mercanti Inglese . . .

ii. A General Session in the Islamic Court

About a week after the meeting of 16 July, a hearing took place in Aleppo's *mahkema*.[106] The high-profile hearing was attended by several of the highest officers in Aleppo, including the *muhassıl*, Çündükürlü Effendi, the *serdar*, Umar Ağa, and Çelebi Effendi. Also present were creditors from several notable Muslim families. Shouts from the audience claimed that possessions of the *ummat Muhammad* ("the community of Muhammad", i.e. the Muslims) had been embezzled, loudly demanding justice.[107] Although this phrase was clearly meant to influence the Islamic judge, his judgement appears to have been unaffected by it. The case proceeded as follows. After the bankrupts had been identified, three creditors came forward with their claims. The first was Muhammad Ağa Kabkaboğlu, who claimed that Sadir and Diyab owed him in excess of 4,000 *kuruş*. If any evidence was referred to, it is not mentioned in the account of the hearing. The qadi relegated the second claimant, *el-hacc* Sulayman b. Muhammad Shaykh, to a separate lawsuit, despite protests from the audience. The third creditor who came forward was *el-hacc* Yahya Usays, who claimed to have sold white silk to the Dutchman for 17,000 *kuruş*, half of which had been paid to him by the consul, leaving 8,500 *kuruş* still due. Sadir replied that only half of the transaction had been for consul Heemskerk's account, the other half being for himself and his brothers. This was denied by both Yusuf and Antun Sadir and Usays. In the end the deed of sale was found and read out loud in court. Since it confirmed Jarmanos' claim, the qadi proclaimed that *el-hacc* Usays had no case against the Dutch consul.

The qadi subsequently asked the bankrupts where all their money had gone. Jarmanos replied that the preceding six years had been characterized by "illness, misery, death, adversity in trade, war in Europe, plague and similar circumstances." As a result, Sadir claimed that they had had to pay high interests, had lost many creditors, and suffered losses in trade. The qadi repeated the claim voiced by *Seyyid* Bakri at a previous meeting, that Sadir and Diyab had made

---

[106] An eyewitness account of this meeting is found in DNA, LAT 1118. The unsigned document is in Italian and is dated 23 July 1763. The following passages are based on this document.

[107] For other examples of unruly behaviour in court, see Amnon Cohen, "Le Rouge at le Noir—Jerusalem Style" *REMM* 55–56 (1990/1–2), 141–149; and Ergene, *Local Court, Provincial Society and Justice in the Ottoman Empire*, 133–138.

a profit of 7,000 *kuruş* on a transaction, involving textiles. In vain did Sadir again deny the claim. Apparently in response to shouts from the audience, the qadi summoned Yusuf and Antun Sadir, whose testimony would be crucial to the case.

On the stand Antun Sadir testified that in the week preceding the bankruptcy merchandise belonging to Sadir and Diyab had been removed from their storage rooms and transported to secured chambers belonging to Heemskerk under Diyab's supervision. Moreover, he claimed that goods entrusted to his brother Jarmanos and to Diyab by unidentified Muslims were hidden in the Honey Khan.[108] Antun Diyab acknowledged this nightly transport of goods to the consular storerooms, but denied any wrongdoing. He explained that he had calculated the balance between him and Sadir and their employer that evening. When the consul discovered how much he was owed by his warehousemen, he had ordered Diyab to settle their debts immediately. The warehouseman therefore consigned to Heemskerk the equivalent in kind of the sum he was owed. According to the testimony of the principal porter of the khan, that night he and his colleagues moved 160 bales of broadcloth, 20 barrels of sugar, 2 barrels of cochineal, the same quantity of indigo, 90 bales of unspecified textiles, 6 cases of hats, as well as three rooms full of wood. A similar statement was recorded from the *odabaşı* (supervisor) of the Dutch consular khan, and the consul's scribe. The total value of these goods was estimated at 120,000 *kuruş*.

Once the rumours of suspicious nocturnal movements of goods had been confirmed before the court, the Dutch consul was given three days to meet the creditors' demands for a fair financial settlement. If he failed to comply, the Porte would be notified of the court's damaging conclusions. Yet the Dutchman persisted in his refusal to accept the competence of the local court, demanding a hearing before the Grand Vizier to vindicate himself. After their ultimatum had lapsed, the local authorities thus sent a report to Istanbul

---

[108] Jarmanos Sadir and Antun Diyab later continued to deny that the transfer of these goods was illegal. In a *hüccet* (of which I have only found the Italian translation), they stated that "... ch'e Corso voce ne tempo del nostro fallimento che il Console sud:º Heemskerk aveva pigliato dal nostro Ben[e] certe mercanzie, non e di nulla verita ...". DNA, LAT 1118: Translazione del Hogget del Debito di Germano Sadir e Antonio Diab, 21 Giamadi Elawal 1177/27 November 1763.

to complain about the consul's actions.[109] At the beginning of September, the dragomans of the Dutch and British ambassadors were told by the *reisülküttab* that the Grand Vizier was favourably disposed towards the petition he had received from Aleppo. He ordered the Dutch to hand over the goods that had been moved at night on Heemskerk's orders, threatening to close Aleppo to Dutch trade if his orders were not followed.[110]

Some two months later, on 21 November 1763, a joint statement was registered in the local court of Aleppo on behalf of 30 creditors of Jarmanos, Jibrail, Antun and Yusuf Sadir and of Antun Diyab. This group consisted of most of the prominent Muslim creditors, the French and British merchants involved, and of the Christian and Jewish Ottoman creditors, including the British First Dragoman Jirjis A'ida. First they briefly mentioned the bankruptcies in question, and referred to both their report to the Porte and the Imperial Command they had received in reply. Then they declared that they had become convinced that the controversial nightly transportation of goods to the Dutch consul's storage rooms had concerned only his own goods, to which the creditors of Sadir and Diyab were not entitled. They renounced all previous claims against the consul and unequivocally stated that there were no disputes between them and the Dutchman. Heemskerk was given a lengthy *hüccet*, which was authenticated by the qadi's seal, and signed by the city's most important Ottoman officials. Among them were Çelebi Effendi, and *el-hacc* Ahmad Ağa, who was both *muhassil* and *mütesellim* at that moment, as well as one member each of the notable local Muslim Fansa, Tahazade, Trabulsi, Kawakibi and Imadi families. The *serdar* of Aleppo and several lesser officials, such as the dragoman of the *mahkema*, are also mentioned as witnesses.[111] Although the deed of quittance does not mention a

[109] A translation of this document is found in DNA, LAT 1118, Copia della translazione dei principali punti del Hailam [*i'lâm*] fatti nella Giustizia Turca . . . [undated], where the testimony of Shukri Diyab is given in full. Our estimate of the value of these goods is also from this document. Cf. DNA, LH 165, folder 1763, Estratto vicino del Hailam che hanno fatto nella Giustizia Turcha nel Mese di Iuglio 1763 e toccante l'Assemblea del 23 Iuglio dello Primati.

[110] DNA, LH 165, folder 1763, Note de la Communication . . . 5:[e] 7bre 1763.

[111] DNA, LAT 1092, doc. 1092/36, Ottoman *hüccet* dated 15 Cemaziyelevvel 1177/21 November 1763. DNA, LAT 1118 contains the Translazione del Hoggiet di differenzione del Sig:[r] Console delle Calunie che gli Erano fatte; e quietanza di tutti li Creditori di Germanos Sader, è Anton Diab Bancherotte.

financial settlement, Heemskerk claimed to have paid the creditors of his warehousemen the sum of 10,130.96 Lion dollars for it. He claimed to have done this in order to protect Dutch interests in Aleppo in general, and sent a request to the Dutch Directors of Levant Trade for reimbursement of his expenses. Heemskerk was convinced that the affair was qualified as a national *avania*, a crisis which affected the entire *nation* in Aleppo and which should therefore be paid by the Directors.[112]

The unsigned eyewitness account of this meeting, on which this discussion is largely based, is interesting because an image of the qadi court emerges from it that is seldom found in Western sources.[113] The court was evidently filled with people, Muslims, non-Muslims and foreigners alike, who all had an interest in the procedure. Some of the Muslims present made loud and emotional appeals to the qadi to punish the embezzlement of goods belonging to the *umma* of Muhammad. The qadi appears to have dealt with these outcries in a dispassionate manner, rejecting some claims after a brief inquiry, while relegating others to separate trials. Only when he had solid proof of embezzlement on the part of the Dutch consul did he sentence him to meet the creditors' demands. This contradicts the stock image of the unreliable qadi found all too often in Western diplomatic sources of the period. The adjudication of the remaining claims strengthens this conclusion.

iii. Individual Trails in the Islamic Court

While an agreement had now been reached with the majority of the creditors, three individual creditors remained. The first was *el-hacc* Sulayman b. Muhammad Shaykh, whose claim was relegated to a separate lawsuit by the qadi during the hearing at the end of July. Sadir and Diyab already owed 13,000 *kuruş* by August 1762 and the debt may well have increased later. The others were *el-hacc* Musa Amiri, and *el-hacc* Abdalwahhab Homsi Çelebi. Amiri was due at least 35,000 *kuruş*, which made him the second largest creditor of

[112] Bronnen III, 482–483, n. 2, referring to DNA, LH 165 (A copy of Heemskerk's request for reimbursement by the Directors of Levant Trade, in the folder for 1763). Also see LH 165, 29 April 1763, 24 September 1763, Heemskerk to the Directors. The claim does not seem to have been successful.

[113] DNA, LAT 1118.

Sadir and Diyab after Jirjis A'ida. Homsi Çelebi was owed almost 4,000 *kuruş*.

The case of *el-hacc* Sulayman b. Muhammad Shaykh involved a quantity of silk, which the Ottoman merchant initially denied having sold at all.[114] Instead, he claimed only to have left it with Jarmanos Sadir on deposit. During the hearing at the end of July, Sadir produced written evidence of the sale and when it appeared that Heemskerk had bought a substantial part of the silk from his warehouseman, the qadi decided that *el-hacc* Sulayman should take the consul to court instead of his warehouseman. The Dutchman refused to appear in court, however, asserting his capitulatory right to be tried only in Istanbul. *El-hacc* Sulayman then sent a petition to the Porte, in reply to which Heemskerk was ordered to accept the local court's authority in the matter. The case finally came before the court at the end of November 1763, when Heemskerk had already left Aleppo and the Ottoman claimant was not in Aleppo either. Although no procurator is mentioned for *el-hacc* Sulayman, at a previous stage he had apparently produced an extract from the registers of the collector of the *kassabiye* tax which mentioned Heemskerk as the buyer of the silk in question. Obviously, this document supported *el-hacc* Sulayman's claims against the Dutchman. Heemskerk was represented by his First Dragoman, Antun Bitar, who produced affidavits from the collector of the *kassabiye*, from a silk weigher, and from several Ottoman merchants. The tax collector testified that it was customary for merchants who had a *berat* to register transactions between them under the name of a foreigner, to avoid both parties having to pay duties on the sale. This was confirmed by the silk weigher's statement. Moreover, a group of merchants stated that *el-hacc* Sulayman had sold the silk to Jarmanos, Yusuf and Antun Sadir, and not to

[114] On the basis of *evamir-i sultaniyye* kept in the records of the *mahkema* of Aleppo, Rhoads Murphey notes that the precise quantity was 833.83 *batmans* of silk, sold at the current price of 22 *kuruş* per *batman*. Of the total value of 19,000 *kuruş*, Murphey claims only 'roughly one-quarter' had been paid. Rhoads Murphey, "Conditions of Trade in the Eastern Mediterranean: An Appraisal of Eighteenth-Century Ottoman Documents from Aleppo", *JESHO* 33 (1990), 38–39. Alternative quantities are mentioned in DNA, LH 165, folder 1763, 'Copije van een advijs gesonden door den Heer van Asten van Const. aen den Heer Consul Heemskerk in Aleppo' [undated (September 1763) in French and Italian.] and Ibid., LAT 1118, [unsigned account of the court session in Italian, dated 23 July 1763].

Heemskerk. On the basis of this testimony, the qadi denied the claim of *el-hacc* Sulayman, and issued a deed to this effect.[115]

Little is known about the circumstances of the final case against the former Dutch consul that came to court in Aleppo. *El-hacc* Musa Amiri was the brother of Abdalqadir Amiri, who attempted to have the consular settlement of the estate of Yusuf and Antun Sadir reversed. His name already appears on the list of creditors of Jarmanos and Jibrail Sadir and Antun Diyab in August of 1762, where a credit of 35,000 *kuruş* was registered. Homsi Çelebi also appears on this list, with 3,975 *kuruş* to his name. Together they filed a lawsuit the only evidence of which that has survived consists of the *hüccet* the qadi issued as a result. Although I have found no references to this case in the Dutch records, the consulate was certainly aware of it, because goods were kept sequestered in connection with the claims. These unspecified goods were kept under Heemskerk's seal in two rooms in the Khan of Ubayd Çelebi, in a room in the portal building of the Khan al-Harir, in four rooms in the house of Jarmanos Sadir and in three rooms and a safe in Antun Diyab's house. In court the two creditors proved that they were entitled to 38,941 *kuruş*, and they had also obtained an Imperial Command in support of their claim.[116] By this time Heemskerk had left Aleppo, and his business partner, Nicolaas van Maseijk had succeeded him as Dutch consul. Thus, on 5 December 1763, it was Van Maseijk who was ordered by Aleppo's *müsellim* and *muhassıl* to hand over the sequestered merchandise to *el-hacc* Ali Effendi, the *kahya* (steward) of the qadi.[117] The consul complied with this demand on the same day, and received a *hüccet* from the court as evidence.[118]

The Islamic court thus adjudicated the final two claims against the Dutch consul. In both cases the claimants were notable Muslims, but this did not mean that their case was automatically stronger than

---

[115] DNA, LAT 1118, 'No. 3', Ottoman text, dated mid Cemaziyelevvel 1177/26 March-4 April 1763. It is accompanied by a Translazione del Ilam contro Haggi Soliman figlio di Mehemed Scieke.

[116] According to the 'Nota delli debiti' they were owed 34 *kuruş* more.

[117] DNA, LAT 1092, doc. 44: Order by the qadi and the interim governor of Aleppo, in Ottoman Turkish, dated 29 C I [1]177/5 December 1763; See LAT 1118, for the 'Traduzione del Murassallé del Caddi'.

[118] DNA, LAT 1118, Translazione del Hogget del Chiaja del Cadi [Italian, without Ottoman text].

that of the Dutchman. The first claimant even lost his case, because it did not concern the consul, but his warehousemen. Here the qadi disregarded written evidence that supported the claim in favour of the testimony of witnesses that confirmed a common practice among merchants in Aleppo. It is not clear if the claimant pursued the matter further, for the sources are silent about all matters involving these bankruptcies from this point.

Conclusion

There were countless bankruptcies in the Ottoman Empire in the eighteenth century which only involved Westerners and protégés of their embassies or consulates. Some merchants simply limited their commercial relations to fellow Europeans, while others successfully used their brokers and warehousemen to create legal buffers between themselves and the Ottoman marketplace. The capitulations assigned jurisdiction in such matters to the consul concerned, or, if the bankruptcy occurred in Istanbul, to the ambassador. In those cases the consulate of the bankrupt was responsible for the sequestration of his estate, for the safe-keeping of any assets, and for collecting debts owed to the estate. All Western consulates and embassies in the Ottoman Empire followed the same standard procedures for bankruptcies, which had developed among the foreign *nations* there through the years.

Even when all creditors belonged to the same community, there were several possible complications. For example, bankrupts might try to escape their creditors by fleeing from their place of residence, or from the Ottoman Empire altogether. The ownership of consignments was generally difficult to establish, and often the subject of protracted disputes among the creditors. Such factors complicated matters for the consulate, but its jurisdiction was generally secure.

It is interesting that one seldom finds references in the eighteenth-century sources to the application of national laws, even when all creditors belonged to the same community as the bankrupt. These laws were probably only relevant when creditors pursued their claims in the native country of the bankrupt. This was the case, for example, with Thomas Lansdown. Most of the arrangements in connection with his bankruptcy were made in Aleppo, where the British consulate followed standard "Levantine" procedures. Only when several of his creditors from London decided to lay disputes among themselves before British courts in England did English law actually become important.

Consular jurisdiction over bankruptcies of Western merchants or Ottoman *beratlı*s was not always self-evident. The consul settled all bankruptcies and adjudicated ensuing disputes only as long as all interested parties belonged to the same consulate, or to other Western communities. The capitulations explicitly mentioned the jurisdiction of the qadi, as well as the *divan-ı hümayun*. In the eyes of the Ottoman authorities anyone—also foreign merchants—had the right to apply to the Islamic court in his place of residence or to the Imperial Council in Istanbul. Any of the interested parties could therefore attempt to circumvent or challenge consular jurisdiction by turning to the Ottoman authorities. In the eyes of most Western consuls and ambassadors this was a violation of the capitulations, but it was fully in accordance with the Ottoman legal system. In none of the *ahdnames* the Porte had ever relinquished its right to reassign jurisdiction, when this was in the interest of Ottoman subjects.

Jan Heemskerk jr. personified the common Western notion that consuls and ambassadors in this period enjoyed more extensive privileges than they actually had. Heemskerk thought that his dignity as consul would take precedence over the interest of the creditors of Jarmanos Sadir and Antun Diyab. The Dutchman was also the bankrupts' employer and one of their creditors, but the Dutchman denied this constituted a conflict of interests. Moreover, the consul had triggered the bankruptcy of his own warehousemen by extracting instant payment of their debts to him, taking away what assets they had left, whereby he effectively forced them to declare bankruptcy. The creditors of Sadir and Diyab considered the nocturnal transfer of the warehousemen's goods to the storage rooms of the consul, which Heemskerk considered legal payment, a form of embezzlement. In the Dutch consul's eyes none of these factors carried enough weight to affect his jurisdiction over the bankrupt estates of his own employees. The Ottoman authorities disagreed with the Dutchman and reassigned jurisdiction to the qadi in Aleppo, who appears to have acted conscientiously and even-handedly.

Even after the Islamic judge had been assigned jurisdiction he allowed the creditors to negotiate a settlement out of court. Only when this failed did the qadi hold a series of hearings during which he adjudicated several claims. Each case was examined individually and judged on its merits. As a result he rejected the claims of some creditors, while supporting those of others. The Dutch consul was alone considering the Porte's decision an injustice. None of his fellow consuls involved, the English and French, denounced the actions of the Ottoman government as a violation of their privileges. Neither forbade the members of their *nations* from laying their claims against Heemskerk before the Islamic court. On the contrary, the other Western consulates and the European creditors acted in concert with the Ottoman creditors, Muslims and non-Muslims, and welcomed the intervention of the Ottoman authorities.

Although these bankruptcies by themselves were not exceptional, the conduct of the Dutch consul was. Heemskerk thought his status as consul made him immune to the Ottoman legal system. It was this conviction that motivated his actions. By clinging to this misguided view without adjusting it out of pragmatism or self-preservation, the Dutch consul explored the limits of Western legal autonomy in the Ottoman Empire. Foreign *nations* did enjoy a degree of legal autonomy provided only Europeans or their protégés were involved, but they ultimately remained subject to the Ottoman legal system. When the interests of Ottoman subjects were at risk the Porte asserted its authority and imposed its own laws on foreign residents. This case shows that such drastic measures were not necessarily harmful to the interests of the Western creditors involved. There was also no sign of erosion of the capitulatory privileges. Heemskerk left Aleppo and the Levant, and his successor, Nicolaas van Maseijk, took over the consulate.[119] The capitulatory system continued to function as before, these bankruptcies had just revealed some of its limits, as well as its place within the Ottoman legal system.

[119] At his own request the Dutch States General dismissed Heemskerk from his office on 20 June 1763. The Dutchman left the Levant at the end of that year and returned to Amsterdam where he became a successful merchant and insurance agent. He died on 9 March 1799. Schutte, *Repertorium*, 353.

Table 9. 'Nota delli debiti di Germanos & Gibrail Sader & Anton Diab', 8 August 1762.

A Seid Dervis [b. sayyid Hasan]	Piaster	3.787,–
Seid Hassan Hamui		1.305,–
Seid Mehemet Gannam [Ghannam]		3.485,–
Seid Abdalla		1.250,–
Seid Juseph Entachi		1.363,–
Seid Arabi		1.100,–
Seid Ali [b. 'Ayrut?]		2.034,–
Seid Mehemed Diarbekirli		250,–
Haggi Musa [b. *el-hacc* Hasan] Emir [Amiri]		35.000,–
Hassan Cialabi [Çavuş başı?]		1.250,–
Haggi Abdelvahab [Homsi]		3.975,–
Mustafa Ağa		2.000,–
		56.808,–
A Haggi Jehje [Usays] Mussoli		8.540,–
Mahomed Aga [Kabkaboğlu]		4.284,–
Mmo. Sig. Console Inghilterra [William Kinloch]		3.180,–
Sig. Heemskerk, Maseyk & Co.		7.539,–
Sig. [Jean-François] Ponz		11.487,–
Sig. [Jean-Paul] Magy		8.677,–
Sig. [Michel] Gilly		2.244,–
Sig. [Jean-Pierre] Augier		3.636,–
Sig. Giorgio Ayde [Jirjis A'ida]		13.000,–
Sig. Giorgios Asiun [w. Khaccadur]		2.520,–
Elias & Anton Gadban [Ghadban]		636,–
Pietro ['figlio di Samaan'] Simonetti		407,–
Azar Cadid		834,–
		123.792,–
A Name Diarbekirli		2.170,–
Sig. Casia		196,–
Salamon Ragivan		3.407,–
Jacob Agiami		217,–
Sig. Namet pstr 39,– Haggi Ali 1.258,–		1.297,–
Haggi Solaiman pstr 13.000,– [*el-hacc* Sulayman b. Muhammad Shaykh]		
Michel Entaki 18.900,–		31.900,–
		162.979,–
A Sign Lansdown per sicurta a conto di Juseph & Anton Sader		17.623,–
A Sig. Aide per Sicurta a conto di detti		35.000,–
		215.602,–

Germano Sader
Anton Diab

sino 8 agosta 1762

Source: DNA, LAT 624.

CHAPTER SIX

THEFT

The third and final case study I propose to examine is different from the previous two. Deaths and bankruptcies of members of foreign communities and their Ottoman protégés occurred frequently enough to allow a preliminary survey of possible complications and other relevant aspects to precede each case that was studied in detail. That is not the case here. Although petty theft must have happened with some regularity, I have found precious few records of litigation over it. This does not mean that the present case study should be dismissed as unique, and therefore unrepresentative. What makes this case worth examining is the fact that it confronted several European consuls and ambassadors with a problem that was not mentioned in the capitulations. Although the Ottoman authorities did not intervene in the consular procedures, which took place in Aleppo and Istanbul, the qadi of Basra had a significant influence on their outcome, nevertheless. This case sheds valuable light on consular legal procedures in the Ottoman Empire in general, and the application of the principle of double jeopardy and the use of arbitration as an instrument for dispute resolution in particular. It also confirms the importance of the parties involved, whose individual strategies could seriously affect the course of justice.

Theft in the Ottoman Legal System

Amputation of the hand as the fixed penalty for stealing is probably the most well known rule of Islamic law outside the Islamic world. The fact that most Islamic jurists have systematically reduced the practical applicability of this Koranic injunction from an early age is not common knowledge. As Colin Imber has shown, in the Ottoman period the rule was removed from the sphere of practical law by defining theft in a way that obstructed its implementation. Taking the view that the fixed penalty was meant as a deterrent, the jurists formulated a very restrictive definition of theft, which virtually ruled out convictions. Imber points out that "the usual standard of proof in Hanafi law is two male eyewitnesses, or one man and two women, which would be very difficult to achieve for an offence which the jurists define as taking 'by stealth'." Moreover, the legal scholars distinguished two types of custody, the first "a place such as a house or a room, which is custody by definition, and custody by a guardian, such as when a person is sitting with his goods, or sleeping with them under his head." Theft from custody did not incur amputation.

There were other conditions that relegated the issue of theft to the realm of legal theory, too, divorcing it from practice to all intends and purposes. The Hanafi scholars preferred to define acts of theft as usurpation. Damage and redress became the central issues in cases of misappropriation, the principal aim being "to restore the status quo ante between the individuals concerned, by ensuring that the compensation given is precisely equivalent in value to the loss suffered." The theorists disregarded the issue of intent, reducing theft to a private matter between the two parties.[1] In practice theft was a matter of public order, too. Jurists therefore began tacitly to support the notion that governors had authority over cases of theft and usurpation, making them subject to discretionary punishment. This development is clearly reflected in Ottoman secular law, *kanun*, where fines and flogging were introduced as penalties for these offences. Moreover, criminal intent was developed as a legal principle.

The protagonist of Imber's study, the *Şeyhülislam* Ebu's-Suʿud (c. 1490–1574), determined that the normal standards of proof do not apply to theft. In response to a question about the proper way to question suspects of theft, Ebu's-Suʿud quoted an anecdote about Ali, the fourth Caliph. A group of people had taken the son of a Muslim to another district, but the boy had gone missing. When the judge questioned the people who had accompanied the boy, they denied being responsible for his disappearance. Unsure of how to proceed, the judge asked the Caliph for advice. Ali summoned the people involved and questioned them separately one by one, asking each to describe for every stage of the journey what the boy was

[1] Imber, *Ebu's-Suʿud*, 213–220. Imber lists many more such restrictions. I have limited my summary to aspects that are relevant to the principal case study of this chapter.

wearing, what the suspect himself ate, and other detailed questions. The Caliph had all contradictions in their statements written down and subsequently confronted the suspects with these contradictions in a joint hearing, whereupon they could no longer deny their guilt and confessed. "This kind of ingenuity is a requirement of the case", Ebu's-Suʿud added. Imber points out the two purposes of the story. First, it legitimised the transfer of such cases from the Islamic courts, personified in the story by the judge, to the administrative authorities, here in the person of Ali. Second, it introduced non-canonical methods of criminal investigation. Moreover, the story indicates that in cases of theft (or, in this case, abduction) it is no longer the victim who must produce evidence against suspects, but the administrative authorities on whom the responsibility of the investigation and punishment of thieves rests.[2]

Under the Ottomans theft was thus largely transferred from the competence of the *şeriat* courts to the jurisdiction of the administrative authorities. Compensation for damages remained the principal aim, but the authorities could impose additional punishment, too, in the form of fines or flogging. Thieves could even be executed by administrative decree for "fomenting corruption", a phrase from the Koran, which, as Ergene has shown, was occasionally used by the courts to convict, even if there was insufficient formal proof against the suspect.[3]

There are no provisions about theft in the capitulations. Several texts contain an article about murder, which may have stood for any kind of criminal case. The principal criterion seems to have been whether the parties were all technically foreigners, or Ottoman subjects were involved, as well. A provision about this matter is found for the first time in the French capitulations of 1673, which unambiguously assigned jurisdiction over murders committed among the French to the French ambassador and consuls. The English capitulation of 1675 stipulated that when an Englishman committed murder or any other crime, and a lawsuit was filed against him with the Ottoman authorities, the Ottoman officers should not proceed without the consul or consular dragoman, but adjudicate the mat-

[2] Ibid., 223–224.

[3] Ergene, *Local Court, Provincial Society and Justice in the Ottoman Empire*, 152–161, 225.

ter in concert with them.[4] The English text is not a contradiction of its French predecessor, but an addition to it. The privileges awarded the French were clearly limited to cases among members of the same nation. The English capitulation of 1675 was not, and should be interpreted as a provision in case foreigners murdered Ottoman subjects, or committed other criminal acts against them. This article also appears in the French capitulation of 1740 in a slightly different form. It is worth quoting Noradounghian's translation of this article (no. 65) here.

> Si un Français ou un protégé de France commettait quelque meurtre ou quelqu'autre crime, et qu'on voulût que la justice en prit connaissance, les juges de mon empire et les officiers ne pourront y procéder qu'en présence de l'ambassadeur et des consuls, ou de leurs substituts, dans les endroits ou ils se trouveront; et, enfin qu'il ne se fasse rien de contraire à la noble justice ni aux capitulations impériales, il sera procédé de part et d'autre avec attention aux perquisitions et recherches nécessaires.[5]

Bianchi has notes that in the nineteenth century this article was erroneously considered proof that the Ottoman tribunals had not jurisdiction over Frenchmen, because they could only take notice of cases involving them if the French wanted them to. According to Bianchi, "d'après le texte turc, la seule interprétation vraie et littérale est: «lorsque la justice voudra en prendre connaissance»." It thus was the Ottoman judiciary who decided whether or not to take notice of such cases, not the French, as this translation suggests.[6]

Other capitulatory stipulations concern the adjudication of disputes among members of different foreign *nations*. The Europeans had long established that appeals to consular verdicts could be filed with the ambassador, but this rule was only included in the capitulations in 1740.[7] The custom that disputes should be filed with, and adjudicated by the consul or ambassador of the plaintiff was also well established among Europeans in the Levant, despite the fact that it is not found in any of the *ahdnames*.

---

[4] Noradounghian, *Recueil* i, 139; Cf. Ibid., 156 (English capitulation of 1675, art. 42), 282 (French capitulation of 1740, art. 15).
[5] Ibid., 294.
[6] Ibid., 305.
[7] For the relevant article, see Chapter One.

Case Study: Legal Disputes in a Partnership of Beratlis *(1781–1788)*

In the third and final case study the activities of the protagonists focus on the overland trade from Aleppo to the east. At the beginning of the 1780s Yusuf Dwek Cohen, a Jewish dragoman of the Dutch consulate, and Minas Uskan, an Armenian protégé of the British consulate, engaged in trade with Baghdad and Basra together. Using the caravans that continued to cross the deserts, in 1781 they sent several loads of merchandize as well as specie to Iraq, but somewhere along the way part of the money disappeared. This resulted in litigation before the Islamic court in Basra, the Dutch consul in Aleppo, and, finally, the Dutch ambassador in Istanbul. The lawsuits over the missing money went hand in hand with a dispute between Uskan and Dwek Cohen over the conditions of one particular commercial transaction they had concluded with one another.

The two disputes offer a final illustration of the interaction between Ottoman and European mechanisms of justice in the Levant in the eighteenth century, offering rare information about rules of procedure, the application of the doctrine of double jeopardy, and the personal and local circumstances that influenced consular legal practices.

Interested Parties

Almost nothing is known about Minas Uskan, other than that he was an Armenian protégé of the English consulate in Aleppo with the status of *hizmetkâr*. It is not clear under whose *berat* he was registered, nor do we know when his connection with the British commenced. Uskan operated as an independent merchant, whose correspondents in Basra and Baghdad were fellow Armenians.[8] At no point do our sources allude to a *beratlı* with whom he may have been connected. It therefore seems likely that Minas Uskan was actually only the nominal servant of some British protégé. He appears never to have been in the active service of the English consulate, contrary to his business partner.

Yusuf w. Simeon Dwek Cohen probably settled in Aleppo at the beginning of the 1770s, coming from Damascus. He became a pro-

[8] On the Armenian communities in this period, see Avedis Sanjian, *The Armenian Communities in Syria under Ottoman Dominion* (Cambridge, 1965).

tégé of the Dutch consulate in Aleppo on 17 April 1772.[9] At the beginning of 1780 he was seconded to the Venetian consulate by the Dutch consul, but the objections of the Venetian ambassador against a Dutch protégé in the service of the Serenissima soon ended the arrangement. Dwek Cohen remained an honorary dragoman until 1795, when he became First Dragoman of the Dutch consulate in Aleppo.[10] His commercial activities were directed both west and east. He conducted his trade from an unknown khan in Aleppo, with the help of his *odabaşı*, Ishaq w. Harrari, who supervised his business in the khan. His official *hizmetkâr*s were the Syrian Christian Azzuz w. Azar Shami, and a Maronite called Jurji w. Ayyub, but it is not clear if there was actually any connection between Dwek Cohen and his "servants".[11]

The earliest record I have found of Dwek Cohen's business activities dates from 1775, when the English vessel *The Duke of Genoa* arrived in Istanbul from Iskenderun. Among its cargo were 22 bales of textiles from Bengal, which had been loaded by one Stefano Caleve in Iskenderun. The goods were marked ID and TS, the initials of the owners of the goods, Yusuf Dwek Cohen, and Thomas de Serpos, the addressee of the cargo in Istanbul. When the ship arrived in the Ottoman capital, it became clear that two bales had been drenched in seawater and were damaged. Of one bale belonging to Dwek Cohen, 67 pieces with a value of 296 *kuruş* and 38 *akçe* had become worthless, while De Serpos had lost only 17 pieces with a total value of some 37 *kuruş*. An Armenian and a Greek merchant inspected the goods and stated that the owners were entitled to compensation.[12] Although this is not stated explicitly, the two merchants were probably compensated for their loss either by the captain of the English vessel, John Chesell, or by its owner. After all, the transporters of the merchandize were responsible for its safety during the trip.

---

[9] BOA, ED 22/1, 405/1753, 14 Muharrem 1186/17 April 1772.

[10] DNA, LAT 774, N. van Maseijk to Van Haeften, 12 and 17 April 1780; DNA, LH 167 (file 1794–1795).

[11] BOA, ED 22/1, 428/1851, mid Receb 1193/25 July–3 August 1779. Cf. DNA, LAT 774, N. van Maseijk to Van Haeften, 9 December 1779, which speaks of Abdulaziz w. Azar Shami, "di Nazione Soriana"; BOA, ED 22/1, 432/1869, beginning Cemaziyelevvel 1194/5–14 May 1780.

[12] BNA, SP 105/186, 102–103, 20 July 1775 [in Italian].

In later years Dwek Cohen and De Serpos maintained a commercial correspondence while they also engaged in trade with other partners. One of Dwek Cohen's other associates was Minas Uskan. The Dutch *beratlı* and the English *hizmetkâr* were equal partners, and both conducted trade on their own account and in partnership with others at the same time. Each kept his own books and after every transaction the balance between them was calculated and settled. There was no common capital. Goods were acquired either by mutual consent or by one of the partners who bought them on his own account first, subsequently offering the merchandize for sale to the partnership. In those cases the conditions of the transfer of ownership, like the price of the goods, discounts, and exchange rates, were discussed beforehand. Only when both partners agreed, were the goods formally acquired by the partnership.

It is useful here also to introduce the Dutch consuls who eventually became involved in the disputes between Uskan and Dwek Cohen. Nicolaas van Maseijk had arrived in Aleppo in the spring of 1755.[13] He had close connections with the British community in the city. For example, in 1757 the English merchant Thomas Vernon lodged with Van Maseijk, also dining at his table.[14] He returned to the Dutch republic at an uncertain date. He was subsequently appointed consul at Aleppo in 1763, arriving there for the second time at the end of 1764. He would hold the office for twenty years. Despite the fact that the Dutch Republic and Great Britain were fighting the Fourth Anglo-Dutch War all over the world between 1780 and 1784, in Aleppo Nicolaas van Maseijk continued to maintain close relations with the English there, attending services in the British chapel with his wife on Sundays. Before the disputes between Uskan and Van Maseijk were concluded, Van Maseijk died on 28 February 1784.[15] His son, Jan, was his successor as Dutch consul.

Jan van Maseijk's connections with the British *nation* were even stronger than those of his father. He was born in Aleppo on Christmas

---

[13] Schutte seems to have been unaware of Nicolaas van Maseijk's first term in Aleppo, since his biography of him only starts after his return from the Dutch Republic, in 1763. Schutte, *Repertorium*, 354.

[14] BNA, SP 110/74 (ii), Van Maseijk to Vernon, 9 May 1757 (in English). Vernon annually paid 500 *kuruş* for board. It is neither clear when the arrangement began, nor when it ended.

[15] Schutte, *Repertorium*, 354.

Day 1758, the second son born in the town to Nicolaas and his English wife, Elizabeth. He was baptized in the British consular chapel on 16 September 1759, the English merchants Bridger and Kirkhouse being the sponsors. Before he was ten years old Jan van Maseijk spoke Dutch, French, English, Italian, Arabic, and Armenian. Soon after his father died, he called an assembly of the Dutch *nation* and had himself appointed Dutch consul pro-interim, an arrangement that was approved by the States-General at the end of 1784. He also acted as vice-consul for Naples, Sweden and Denmark in Aleppo.[16] The connections of Nicolaas and Jan van Maseijk are relevant for this case, because the British consulate was also involved in it, since Minas Uskan was its protégé.

Legal Issues and Strategies

In July 1781 Uskan and Dwek Cohen sent fifteen cases of merchandize and three cases of specie to Basra. Half the cargo consisted of tinsel (*lametta*), the other half of false coral.[17] The merchandize belonged to Uskan and Dwek Cohen, each owning 50%. The goods were gathered in Dwek Cohen's khan, where they were packed in bags, put in crates, nailed shut and secured by ropes and chains. Each crate contained two cases, making a total of nine loads. The Jewish dragoman arranged for packers, as well as porters who would transport the crates to the point of departure of the caravan to Basra in the company of a caravan conductor.[18] While Dwek Cohen took care of the practicalities in Aleppo, the correspondents of Uskan were responsible for the sale of the goods in Basra, the proceeds of which they would remit to Aleppo by caravan. Nine cases were addressed to Maghak w. Serkis and Kevork w. Der David, Uskan's business partners in Basra, while the remaining nine were addressed to other correspondents there. Uskan announced the shipment to them by letter, in which he revealed the Armenian abbreviations by which the crates could be distinguished from other cargo in the caravan.

---

[16] BNA, SP 110/74 (iv), John van Maseijk, Aleppo, to E. Edwards at Tripoly, 27 April 1768 (in English). Schutte, *Repertorium*, 354.

[17] The word *lametta* is translated as 'clincant' (Fr: *clinquant* = tinsel) in DNA, LAT 1266, Mokdevi Calostian to ambassador Van Dedem, 30 August 1786 (in French).

[18] DNA, LAT 774, Estratto del giornale del Sigr Jusef Dueck.

Before the cases left the khan Uskan supplied bags of money of various currencies, which were placed in the final three cases. It was customary for merchants in Aleppo to transport money in this way, and Dwek Cohen regularly organised the dispatch for others. At an unknown date he handed over the eighteen cases belonging to his company with Uskan to a caravan conductor called Muhammad al-Shai al-Makkari al-Najdi, a member of the Muntafik tribe.[19] The loads were transported with three horses supplied by someone in Dwek Cohen's service, and escorted by the caravan conductor and his assistants. Besides the eighteen cases belonging to his company with Dwek Cohen Uskan also sent a case and a half of silk with another conductor of the same caravan. The silk was addressed to two Armenian merchants, who had invested money in it.

Upon the arrival of the caravan in Basra, Maghak and Kevork received all the nine cases Uskan had sent to them, as well as the one and a half cases of silk. First, the silk was examined and sent on to the two investors. Then the cases transported by Muhammad al-Shai were inspected and opened. This took place in the presence of four Armenians from Julfa, and four Muslim packers who were frequently employed by William Digges La Touche, the agent of the East India Company (EIC) in Basra. According to Uskan's letter, the last three cases should contain money instead of merchandize. Case 16 should contain two purses, one belonging to Uskan, the other the property of Stefan Der Raphael. Case 17 was supposed to contain three purses, one of which was owned jointly by Uskan, Maghak and Kevork. The other two purses in case 17 belonged partly to Stefan Der Raphael, and partly to Mokdevi Calostian, a merchant living in Istanbul. Case 18 should contain two purses, one belonging to Uskan, the other to two other Armenian merchants. When the three cases were opened, however, number 16 turned out to be empty, except for a bundle of dried spices and some paper. What should have been in case number 16 was found in case 17. The final case, number 18, contained the two purses that it was supposed to. This meant that the three purses that should have been

[19] This man will henceforth be referred to as al-Shai. DNA, LAT 1266: Extra Aanwinsten 1894, No. 96: doc 9, David Hays to Nicolaas van Maseijk, 19 May 1783 (in Italian) refers to the 'Montefeek'. Redhouse, *Turkish and English Lexicon* locates this Bedouin tribe at the lower Euphrates.

in case 17 were missing. It is not clear how much money Uskan had been sent East in all, but detailed accounts of the missing sums have survived. In all, it amounted to some 9,140 *kuruş*, in which Minas Uskan had a 40% share, the remainder belonged to Maghak and Kevork.[20]

In legal terms the disappearance of the money constituted theft from custody by a guardian, so could this guardian be held liable? At first sight there appear to be analogies between the case of the missing money and the above-mentioned incident involving two bales of Indian textiles, which Dwek Cohen had sent to Istanbul via an agent in Iskenderun. The agent had consigned the cargo to an English captain, who took it to the Ottoman capital. Upon their arrival two bales turned out to be drenched in seawater, and the captain was held responsible. By analogy, in the case of the missing money it was Minas Uskan who sent it to Basra. Dwek Cohen acted as middleman, consigning the money to the caravan conductor. Part of the cargo was missing after the caravan's arrival in Basra, so it could be argued that the caravan conductor was responsible. This is the point where the analogy does not hold, however. When the two wet bales of textiles were unloaded in the docks of Istanbul, they were probably considerably heavier than the others, and water may even have dripped from them. Even if the water had dried by the time the ship was unloaded, it would probably have left considerable stains on the packaging cloth. In Basra there was no such external evidence of anything being amiss. When Muhammad al-Shai handed over the cases to the correspondents of Minas Uskan, they appeared to be in proper condition. The money had been dispatched in crates, which were nailed shut and secured with ropes and chains, so this did not raise any suspicions that anything might be amiss. In effect, there was no evidence of theft at all, let alone anything that pointed to the caravan leader.

The ensuing disputes over the missing money would focus on the question of who had stolen it. The possibilities were limited. Either the money had disappeared in Dwek Cohen's khan, or it had happened en route between his khan and Basra. If the first were true, the Jewish dragoman, his son or his *odabaşı* must have done it; if

[20] Ibid., doc. 7, 28 February 1783 (in Italian); BNA, SP 110/65, 167–172, 27 February 1783 (in Italian).

not, the caravan conductor must have been responsible. All parties seem to have accepted that there had been money in the first place, despite the fact that this, too, would probably have been impossible to prove in court because the money had been handed over in the privacy of Dwek Cohen's khan without witnesses to support Uskan's version of events. The dragoman of the Dutch consulate never adopted this used this argument, however, and there is no point speculating how it might have effected the case if he had.

Which strategies could, and did, the interested parties adopt?

The first priority for Maghak and Kevork was to register the discrepancy between what they had expected to receive and what had actually arrived. They did this in an affidavit written in Armenian on 14 September 1781 and signed by witnesses. They sent the document by the first messenger to Uskan in Aleppo, along with an Italian translation made in Basra.[21] The merchants could immediately have turned to the Islamic court, but they probably did not do so, because it was possible that there was some misunderstanding, or a change of plans about they had not been notified on time.

When the news reached Aleppo, in October 1781, Uskan confronted Dwek Cohen with it. The British protégé was not only convinced that the money had been stolen, but also that it could only have taken place in Aleppo, since the recipients of the cases had noticed nothing untoward about the packaging. Dwek Cohen questioned his son and his *odabaşı* about the matter, and vouched for their conduct. Uskan suggested that they put further pressure on the warehouse supervisor in order to establish the truth, but Dwek Cohen would not allow it, arguing that the man was a protégé of the Venetian consulate. This meant that the Venetian consul would have to give his permission if Uskan wanted to question him. When Uskan asked Dwek Cohen what he thought had happened, he answered that he had been told that the caravan conductor to whom they had entrusted the eighteen cases had stolen the money. A Muslim inhabitant of the Bab al-Nurayb area, one Abdalqadir b. Shaykh al-Jub, had told Dwek Cohen that Muhammad al-Shai had taken the

[21] DNA, LAT 1266, doc. 1 (in Armenian, with witness clauses in Arabic). An Italian translation of the document was made by 'Giuseppe Bethlehem', an Armenian graduate of the Sagra Congregazione De Propaganda Fide in Rome, who seems to have been the brother of one of the witnesses. Two other Roman Catholic Armenian priests confirmed the accuracy of the translation.

cargo to a house in Aleppo, where a carpenter had opened and resealed the cases for him. Abdalqadir had heard this from the wife of the owner of the house where it had allegedly taken place. Dwek Cohen had been told this in the presence of two Muslim witnesses.[22] Uskan gave Dwek Cohen three days to find the carpenter in question, but the man had reportedly left Aleppo with the caravan to Mecca immediately after having helped Muhammad al-Shai. The two witnesses were useless, because they had only witnessed the rumour being spread, not the crime involved.

Several things about Uskan's conduct are interesting. He evidently did not completely trust his business partner, for he instantly assumed that Dwek Cohen or his personnel had stolen the money. This is confirmed by the fact he took a witness with him to the meeting with Dwek Cohen. Uskan had asked Stefan Ajami to accompany him. Ajami was a *beratlı* of the Dutch, but his loyalties lay with the English community in Aleppo.[23] Moreover, by forcing his partner to substantiate the rumour about the caravan conductor, he placed the burden of proof on Dwek Cohen's shoulders. This was not the behaviour of a merchant who trusted his business partner implicitly until he had good reason to do otherwise. Furthermore, despite the fact that the rumour about the caravan conductor was unconfirmed and there were no witnesses anymore, both Uskan and Dwek Cohen passed it on to others, including the Armenian merchant's correspondents in Basra. It is also interesting to consider what Uskan did *not* do. If he instantly suspected his partner of theft, he should, according to the customs of Western communities in the Ottoman Empire, have filed a complaint with the Dutch consul in Aleppo. He did not do this until much later, and he also did not attempt to get permission to question Dwek Cohen's *odabaşı* further.

The lack of any proof concerning the disappearance of the money did not prevent Uskan's associates in Iraq considering Dwek Cohen

---

[22] Ibid., doc. 14, Account by Ilyas Antun A'ida and Stefan Ajami of the meeting with Dwek Cohen, dated October 1781 (in Arabic, with Italian translation No. 3); For the official record of the rumour, see ibidem, doc. 22, Statement dated 9 S 1198/3 June 1784 (in Arabic). The authors dated the encounter with Abdalqadir ibn Shaykh al-Jub in the month Zilkade 1195/19 October–17 November 1781.

[23] DNA, LAT 1125: Van Haeften to Meerman Van Goes, Advocate General of the VOC in Amsterdam, 14 April 1781; Ibid., extract from a letter by Matlub Rahamim in Aleppo to De Serpos in Istanbul concerning the overland mail (undated, in French).

guilty of theft. In the second week of February 1782 Dwek Cohen received a letter from Stefan Der Raphael, an agent of the EIC in Baghdad. The author had sent it to Uskan via an agent of Stefan Ajami, with orders to pass it on to Dwek Cohen. The EIC agent had come to the conclusion that Dwek Cohen had committed the theft, and threatened him with protracted lawsuits unless he reimbursed the money immediately. Der Raphael warned that he would use both his official and personal connections to ruin Dwek Cohen. If necessary, he would also instruct his brother, Ovanes, who lived in Trieste, to travel to Istanbul and sue the Dutch dragoman there. Ovanes, who was said to have had experience in English courts after suing an English general stationed in Bengal, was even prepared to go on to the Dutch Republic to seek redress for his brother if he did not return the missing money.[24]

There was little Dwek Cohen could do against these developments. As a protégé of the Dutch consulate he was entitled to legal aid, but the jurisdiction of the consul did not extend to Baghdad, where the author of the threats resided. The dragoman turned to the consulate, nevertheless. On the assumption that only Uskan could have fanned Der Raphael's suspicions, Dwek Cohen filed a complaint against his former business partner with his consul. The Dutch dragoman considered the treatment by the EIC agent an unwarranted insult to his reputation, especially because Uskan had not filed any official suit against him.[25] The Armenian protégé answered that it was only logical that Der Raphael be upset, because he had suffered a great financial loss. He admitted that he had not yet filed a formal suit against his Jewish partner, because he was still preparing his case. A copy of this response was sent to the Dutch consulate, along with a letter from the English consul, John Abbott, in which he stated that he had read the covering letter from Der Raphael to Uskan, where the EIC agent had threatened Uskan with legal procedures if he refused to pass on the principal message to Dwek

[24] DNA, LAT 774, Traduzione del Vero Senso di Lettere in Idioma e Carattere Arabo dal Sig.r Stephan Der Raphael, e diretta a Jusef Duek Turcimanno Barattario d'Ollanda in Aleppo, consegat' aperta, e senza sigillo dal Sig.r Azzarià, servitore del Sig.r Stefan Ajemi Turcimanno Barattario d'Ollanda, il di 13. Febr.ro 1782.

[25] BNA, SP 110/65, 1–7 contain a copy of the Italian translation of Dwek Cohen's protest. It was registered on 15 February 1782, and Uskan was notified of it three days later.

Cohen. In light of this threat, Abbott considered Uskan's decision to hand over the letter to the Jewish dragoman justifiable.[26] The English consul's opinion ended this particular matter, but many similar skirmishes followed in the course of the conflict.

Sometime in the course of the disputes the correspondents of Uskan in Iraq laid a sequestration on the goods the partnership of Dwek Cohen and Uskan had sent to Basra. The reason for the sequestration was their suspicion of Dwek Cohen's involvement in the disappearance of the money, and the measure indicates their expectation that the dragoman would be proven guilty in due course. By putting a formal claim on his share of the goods at an early stage, Uskan's correspondents must have hoped to secure reimbursement for their losses. Once Dwek Cohen had been convicted, they probably expected to be assigned ownership of his goods. Dwek Cohen held Uskan responsible for the sequestration, which prevented the goods from being sold and which seriously tarnished his reputation, as it was a formal indication of the suspicions against him. Uskan denied having ordered the measure, however, suggesting that his correspondents had acted on their own initiative.[27]

By this time Uskan and Dwek Cohen communicated through their respective consulates only. Statements and documents of Uskan were first filed with the English consul, who would order the chancellor to register them in the chancery records and pass on a copy to the Dutch consulate. The Dutch consul, Nicolaas van Maseijk, then ordered his own chancellor to register the in-coming letter and to have a copy delivered to Dwek Cohen. The Jewish protégé's response followed the same route in reverse. The advantage of this procedure was that both consulates gathered similar dossiers of relevant documents on the basis of which the dispute would eventually be settled, but the chancery expenses for Dwek Cohen and Uskan increased with each statement that was registered and every copy that was issued.

A second dispute between the two business partners further stimulated the flow of petitions and complaints. It concerned the costs

[26] BNA, SP 110/65, 7–10, 22 February 1782, reaction by Uskan with Abbott's message attached, dated 25 February.

[27] BNA, SP 110/65, 105–106, continued on 162–165, 5 February 1783 (Dwek Cohen's proposal); Ibid., 167–172 (Uskan's reaction).

of the merchandize they had sent to Basra on account of their company. On 16 April 1782 Uskan filed a petition with his consulate, openly accusing Dwek Cohen of having lied to him about the terms on which he had originally acquired the goods.[28] The deals by which Dwek Cohen had obtained the goods he later offered to his partnership with Uskan were complicated. They were barter transactions in which the goods exchanged were not valued with legal precision, as Islamic law prescribes to ensure that commodities bartered were of equal value. Furthermore, Dwek Cohen had bartered these goods together with another business associate, who worked for a French firm as a warehouseman. They had exchanged a quantity of cotton they jointly owned for a variety of merchandize, including tinsel and false coral, owned by a British merchant, David Hays. They received a 15% discount on the deal, having paid 6% *agio*. Six months later the Dutch protégé sold the tinsel and some pieces of false coral to his company with Minas Uskan, offering them at a discount of 10% and 5.5% *agio*. Uskan accepted the terms, and the goods were transferred to the company without a written sales contract. Both partners registered the transaction in their own account books.[29]

According to Uskan his partner had offered the goods to their company, saying that he had bought them at the same terms he was offering to their company. When the English protégé later heard from Hays that this was not the case, he accused Dwek Cohen of lying and demanded that his account books be examined. According to Islamic law the legitimacy of sales depends largely upon the disclosure by the seller of the terms on which he has bought the goods on offer. The emphasis on openness between the parties of a sale, which should prevent illegitimate gain, was relevant for all merchants—Muslims, non-Muslims, and Europeans alike—in the period studied here.[30] In terms of Islamic law Uskan accused his partner of acting in bad faith, and not fully disclosing all information relevant to the transaction. For unknown reasons he did not bring the case

[28] Ibid., 11–13, 16 April 1782, petition by Uskan (in Italian).

[29] Ibid., 19 April 1782, reponse by Dwek Cohen to Uskan's petition of 16 April [= BNA, SP 110/72 (i), fos 47r–50r] (in Italian).

[30] A. Udovitch, 'Islamic Law and the Social Context of Exchange in the Medieval Middle East', *History and Anthropology* 1 (1985), 445–465.

before the Islamic court, however, preferring to pursue the matter through the consular justice system.

Neither of the disputes between Yusuf Dwek Cohen and Minas Uskan was ever heard by the qadi in Aleppo. A Muslim court had a profound influence on the settlement of some of their conflicts, nevertheless, because Uskan's business associates in Iraq went to the qadi in Basra in connection with the missing money.

Outcome: The Caravan Conductor

Kevork and Maghak filed a suit against the caravan conductor, Muhammad al-Shai, in the Islamic court in Basra on 31 December 1781, three and a half months after the theft had been discovered. This was before Uskan had officially accused Dwek Cohen of being the culprit, and after the rumour from Aleppo about the involvement of the caravan conductor had spread. In court the two Armenian merchants concisely recounted the circumstances of the case, mentioning the partnership between Dwek Cohen and Uskan, the three numbered cases, and the discovery that the contents of one case were missing. They explicitly stated that it was Dwek Cohen who had voiced suspicions against the defendant, who had allegedly opened the cases in Aleppo with the help of a carpenter.

> According to the aforementioned Yusuf, the Jew, after he had collected the cases from the khan, Hammad [sic] b. Shai al-Nadji al-Makkari went to a house where he [stayed] in Aleppo, bringing with him a carpenter to do what it is he [i.e. the carpenter] does. The aforementioned Hammad subsequently took the three cases to Basra, and handed them to us. Then a group gathered, which included the Muslims Rajab b. Farhan and Sabar b. Shihab, the porters of the consul, and the three aforementioned cases were inspected and examined in the presence of the Armenian Christians *khawaja* Ovanes, the assistant of *al-khawaja* Arutin, and *khawaja* Ilyas al-Sarraf. [They stated:] "We opened the three cases, taking notice of the firmness of the ropes, the nails, and the chains which had been applied in Aleppo. [When the cases had been opened] we saw that the Dirhams that should have been in case number 16 had been transferred to case number 17, and that those that should have been in case number 17 had disappeared without a trace. [. . .]"
>
> The judge (*hakim*), whose name is recorded [Ismail al-Qadi], questioned al-Makkari about the [disappeared] sum, and he answered: "When I collected the cases from the khan of Yusuf w. Dwek, the Jew, they were sealed and secured with iron nails and rope, and I

> have taken them directly to the tent, and not to my house, nor to any other place." Then he was asked to present evidence for his claim, whereupon he presented two reliable witnesses, Husayn b. Hafiz and Sulayman b. Ariti. When they were questioned, they stated: "We declare before God, that the defendant, Hammad b. Shai al-Makkari al-Najdi, when he collected the aforementioned three cases from the khan of the aforementioned Jew, directly went to the tent in our company. To this we testify. That morning we loaded the cases [on the camels] together, and we set off for Basra, and we did not unload them anywhere."

The qadi accepted the witnesses as reliable, ruling that no evidence had been produced to show that Muhammad al-Shai was responsible for the disappearance of the money. He issued a *hüccet* to this effect, a copy of which was dispatched to Aleppo, probably by Uskan's correspondents.[31]

The fact that the qadi heard this case was probably because the plaintiffs chose to file their suit in his court. The Ottoman jurists may have transferred theft from the realm of *şeriat* to that of *siyaset*, but the qadi represented both. Moreover, it was qadi who heard the case and ruled on it, but the secular authorities were also well represented, because the highest administrators of Basra attended the court session. The interim-governor of the city, the chief of customs, the head of Basra's treasury, and a representative of the military even acted as the court's witnesses (*şuhud al-hal*) on this occasion. The Shafiite mufti also attended the court session in this capacity. Their names were duly recorded in the right-hand margin of the record of the proceedings.[32]

It is noteworthy that neither the word theft (*sarika*), nor thief (*sarik*) is mentioned in the document. The caravan conductor is merely accused of taking a carpenter with him to his place of residence in Aleppo "so that he [i.e. the carpenter] would do what it is that he does" (A: *li-ya*ʿ*mal fiha ma ya*ʿ*malu*). The role of the qadi is of interest,

---

[31] DNA, LAT 1266, Extra Aanwinsten 1894, No. 96, Doc. 2: Uncertified copy of a *hüccet* issued by the Islamic judge of Basra on 15 Muḥarrem 1196/31 December 1781. It is accompanied by a translation in Italian made by one 'Giuseppe di Giabur', an *odabaşı* (supervisor of a khan), on 3 August 1784.

[32] Ibid.; their names were Ismail Ağa, *kaimmakam balad al-Basra*; Mustafa Paşa, *emin gümrük al-Basra*; *el-hacc* Muhammad Efendi, *defterdar-i Basra*; Hüseyin Ağa ibn Ali, *ser ayanı serdenkeçdi* (a corps of voluntary storm-troopers, belonging to the Janissary corps); and Yaşin Efendi, *mufti al-Shafiyya bi-madinat Basra.*

too. Apart from listening to the veiled accusation and summoning the suspect, the qadi appears to have remained rather passive. On the authority of Ebu's-Suʿud he could have exercised greater ingenuity in his questioning of the witnesses, instead of accepting their reliability at face value. After all, they could just have easily been the caravan conductor's accomplices to the crime. Maybe the case was simply too weak, having been filed by two non-Muslims in Basra solely on the basis of a rumour heard by another non-Muslim in Aleppo, but in the absence of further evidence this remains conjectural.

The qadi's verdict left few possibilities for subsequent litigation against Muhammad al-Shai, whose lack of connections with the Dutch and English consulates in Aleppo made him immune to the consuls' authority. Moreover, the Europeans honoured the doctrine of double jeopardy, the legal principle that no one could be tried for the same offence twice. Although some continued to suspect him of the crime, the caravan conductor was thus excluded from further litigation.

Outcome: Yusuf Dwek Cohen

The fact that Dwek Cohen was the only suspect left who could be sued in connection with the missing money did not expedite matters. It seems Uskan's principal tactic was to delay procedures, keeping suspicions against Dwek Cohen alive without actually acting on them. His aim was probably to tarnish the Jewish dragoman's reputation over such a prolonged period, that it was more expedient for him to pay off a charge he was innocent of than to have doubts cast on his trustworthiness any longer. In the controversy over the conditions of one particular transaction it was not Uskan who was responsible for the delay, however, but the Dutch consul.

According to Dwek Cohen Uskan had no reason to "whine" about the terms of the deal, which were fair in his opinion.[33] Despite the Dutch dragoman's protests, he had to show his account books to a delegation consisting of the chancellors and First Dragomans of the Dutch and English consuls. Since Dwek Cohen kept his accounts in Hebrew, the dragomans made Italian translations of them. These

[33] BNA, SP 110/65, 19 April 1782. The Italian verb "lagnare" is used.

confirmed that Dwek Cohen had sold the goods to his partnership with Uskan on terms different from those on which he had procured them. The crucial question remained of whether or not Dwek Cohen had told this to Uskan. The Armenian merchant claimed that he had, while Dwek Cohen denied it. Both sides reiterated arguments in support of their claims, but produced no proof.[34]

Through the summer of 1782 Minas Uskan and Yusuf Dwek Cohen continued to file petitions, responses, and new recriminations with their respective consulates. In view of the mounting chancery expenses, on 27 August Dwek Cohen proposed to his consul that the disputes be settled by arbitration. He suggested that he and Uskan each appoint two jurors, the fifth to be nominated by the Dutch consul, if necessary.[35] Consul Van Maseijk did not adopt Dwek Cohen's proposal, but asked two French merchants to review the evidence instead. On 24 September 1782 Jean François Pons and a countryman called Belleville advised the Dutch consul that they agreed with Minas Uskan. In their opinion Dwek Cohen should be forced to recalculate the costs of his deal with Uskan and compensate him. Moreover, the Jewish dragoman should pay all chancery expenses incurred by Uskan in the course of the dispute.[36] Nicolaas van Maseijk rejected the French verdict, however, judging it too harsh on Dwek Cohen. The first attempt at arbitration thus failed, because the Ducth consul refused to implement the outcome.

On 5 February 1783 Dwek Cohen repeated his request for arbitration of all his quarrels with Uskan. Preparations for the procedure had already been made in Istanbul. One of the other owners of the missing money, Mokdevi Calostian, had filed a petition with the Dutch ambassador asking him to arrange the arbitration. The ambassador had entrusted the Danish chargé d'affaires, Hübsch and Timoni, with the preparations, and two dates had already been proposed. Dwek Cohen had appointed Thomas de Serpos as his agent, and emphasized that he wanted all disputes to be decided at once. Uskan rejected the procedures in Istanbul that Calostian had initiated on his own accord without consulting him. According to the

[34] Ibid., pages 32–34, and DNA, LAT 774, 15–22, 34–42.
[35] BNA, SP 110/65, 77–79.
[36] DNA, LAT 774, 'Verdict' of Belleville and Pons, 24 September 1782 (in French).

English protégé the case of the theft of their money was a criminal offence, which could not be resolved by arbitration. More importantly, he still had not yet filed an official complaint against Dwek Cohen, so formally there was no dispute between them on account of the stolen money.[37] In light of the complications of the disputes and the difficulties in obtaining the cooperation of both parties, the ambassadors of the Dutch Republic and of Great Britain sent the cases back to Aleppo where the Dutch consul should adjudicate them.

In May 1783 the English Pro-consul in Aleppo, took the initiative in the disputes between Uskan and his partner, ignoring the fact that the matters were not under his jurisdiction. He called an assembly of merchants to convene in his own residence on 19 May. The Englishman asked Van Maseijk to bring Dwek Cohen to the meeting as well. The Dutchman was not certain how to respond. He had received orders from his ambassador to settle the affair with the British consul, Abbott, but he was not sure if the home authorities would approve of cooperation with the Englishman. Dwek Cohen, who had found out about the assembly before the Dutchman could inform him of it officially, ended Van Maseijk's dilemma by announcing that he had no intention of appearing before the council. The consul attempted to persuade Dwek Cohen to change his mind by promising that he would not pass sentence against him if he attended the assembly, but to no avail.[38]

Minas Uskan continued to take his time to prepare his case. In the process the Dutch dragoman's early suspicions of the caravan conductor had come under close scrutiny. The rumour on which he had based his accusation had proved unreliable. Uskan even claimed to have evidence that unnamed persons had offered money for false testimonies incriminating the caravan conductor.[39] The statements were meant to undermine Dwek Cohen's reputation, but they kept alive the suspicions against Muhammad al-Shai at the same time.

[37] BNA, SP 110/65, 105–106, continued on 162–165, 5 February 1783 (Dwek Cohen's proposal); Ibid., 167–172 (Uskan's reaction).

[38] DNA, LAT 774, N. van Maseijk to Ambassador Van Haeften, 18 May 1783 (in Dutch).

[39] BNA, SP 110/65, 243 (Arabic text), 244–245 (Italian translation), Statement by one *seyyid el-hacc* Qasim ibn Junayd Tuma describing how he had been offered money for a false testimony, which he had refused. The names of three witnesses (*shuhud al-hal*) were also registered.

The caravan conductor was aware of this, and he confronted the Jewish *berath* with it a year and a half after the case had come before the court in Basra. Personally appearing in Dwek Cohen's khan, the caravan conductor demanded the dragoman either voice his suspicions formally, or stop inciting people against him. In fact Uskan's investigation was responsible for the continuing rumours, but Dwek Cohen's refusal to answer his unexpected guest and to appear before the council probably strengthened suspicions against him.[40]

Only on 21 June 1783, some twenty months after the money belonging to the Armenian merchants had disappeared, and sixteen months after registering his protest against Dwek Cohen, did Minas Uskan officially accuse his partner of being responsible for the disappearance of the money.[41] Contrary to common procedure, he filed his complaint with the British Pro-Consul instead of his Dutch colleague. Uskan accused Dwek Cohen of having stolen the money he had entrusted him with. He reasoned that the cargo had reached Basra in proper condition, since his correspondents had noticed nothing untoward when they had collected the cases, nor when they had opened them. The caravan conductor had proved his innocence by producing two witnesses before the court of the qadi in Basra. Uskan reasoned that the theft could thus only have taken place in the khan of Dwek Cohen in Aleppo. It was even reported that Dwek Cohen had acknowledged his responsibility for the disappearance of the money in a letter to his correspondent in Istanbul, Thomas de Serpos. The dragoman allegedly admitted to De Serpos that he might have sent the money to Bengal instead of Basra by mistake. Mokdevi Calostian, the representative of Uskan at the appeal, had personally heard this from De Serpos, and he had notified Uskan.[42]

The charge of theft was difficult to prove. The plaintiff needed witnesses who would testify that Dwek Cohen had engineered the

[40] DNA, LAT 1266, Extra Aanwinsten 1894 No. 96, doc. 11: 'Estratta dai Registri della Cancellaria Brittanica in Aleppo', attestazione No. 4; Ibid., doc. 12: Attestazione No. 5: [Translation of a declaration by two witnesses of the confrontation between al-Nadji and Dwek, 29 C II 1197/1 June 1783.]

[41] Ibid., doc. 1, [Memorial by Uskan addressed to the ambassador of the Dutch Republic and Great Britain], 21 June 1783 (in Italian).

[42] BNA, SP 110/65, 251, Undated letter by Calostian to Uskan (Arabic text), 251–252 (Italian translation). The translation was made by Niqula Fakhr on 6 April 1783, and registered in the chancery on 3 October 1783.

disappearance of his partner's money. In the previous case study the supervisor of the Dutch consul's khan had witnessed the illicit removal of goods, and was willing to testify to this. Dwek Cohen, however, refused to let his opponents interrogate the *odabaşı* of his khan on the grounds that he was a protégé of the Venetian consulate. If Uskan wanted to interrogate the warehouse supervisor he needed to apply to the Venetian consul for permission first. Dwek Cohen's son also worked for him, but he was protected by the Dutch consulate on the basis of his father's *berat*, and could also only be questioned with his consul's permission. Uskan incorrectly claimed that Dwek Cohen's *odabaşı* had long been a British *beratlı*, who had been forced by his principal to exchange his patent for a *berat* from the Venetians specially to elude British consular jurisdiction in this matter.[43] This accusation would later backfire on Uskan.

The Armenian protégé further emphasized that Dwek Cohen had initially accused Muhammad al-Shai of the theft, claiming that the caravan conductor had returned to Aleppo to answer the suspicions that Dwek Cohen was sustaining against him. As soon as the man had arrived in town, however, the Jewish *beratlı* had denied continuing to believe that he was guilty of the theft. The plaintiff considered this contradiction an indication of Dwek Cohen's guilt.[44] In a similar fashion, Uskan tried to make the most of alleged contradictions in other statements by the defendant. For example, Dwek Cohen maintained that he had personally placed the first four purses of money in cases 16 and 17 in Uskan's presence, and that he had also witnessed their sealing. According to Stefan Ajami and Ilyas Antun A'ida, however, Dwek Cohen had told them that Uskan had not been present when he put money in cases 16 and 17. This was in line with Uskan's own version of events. The Armenian therefore reasoned that the theft could only have taken place in the khan of Dwek Cohen, and that his suspect behaviour—the contradicting statements, the accusation of the caravan conductor, which was later retracted—proved his guilt. The formal accusation finally made it possible for the Dutch consul in Aleppo to adjudicate the protracted dispute, but again it was the British Pro-Consul who took the first step in order to end the conflict.

[43] DNA, LAT 664, 'Mémoire justificatif', 13.
[44] Ibid., 5.

Hays organised another hearing before a council of merchants. This time his Dutch colleague would not take no for an answer. Acting more forcefully than earlier, Van Maseijk obliged Dwek Cohen to attend the hearing in Hays' house on 3 September 1783. Hays had chosen the ten members of the council, which consisted of two local non-Muslim merchants, six notable Muslim merchants, and two Frenchmen.[45] Also in attendance were Nicolaas van Maseijk and Minas Uskan. The meeting was presided over by David Hays, the new British Pro-Consul, who was fluent enough in Arabic to conduct the entire meeting in this language. The first question to the merchants was whether or not there remained any accusations against Muhammad al-Shai. The caravan conductor was also present at the hearing, having been assured beforehand that he could not be tried twice for the same crime. The council answered that Dwek Cohen had voiced such accusations, but that the council considered al-Shai free and beyond reproach. The council was then asked whether or not they thought it was possible for a thief to open the crates in a house, as Dwek Cohen had claimed the caravan leader had done. The merchants stated that they thought this was impossible. Finally, Dwek Cohen was questioned about the packaging process. While the Dutch protégé claimed that Minas Uskan had been present when the first two crates had been sealed, others had testified to the contrary. Dwek Cohen repeated his own version of events, pointing out that the cases had been marked with Armenian signs. Since Uskan had notified his correspondents about these identifying marks, only he could have placed them on the crates, Dwek Cohen argued. The foreign consulates had no jurisdiction over the caravan conductor, and even if this had been different, the principle of double jeopardy prevented a retrial. By publicly supporting the acquittal of the caravan conductor, the council prevented him turning to the Ottoman authorities, clearing the way for further consular litigation at the same time.

Yusuf Dwek Cohen had been forced to attend the hearing against

---

[45] Their names of the non-Muslims were Yusuf Turra and Stefan Ajami. The Muslims were *el-hacc* Muhammad Qurna Çelebi, *el-hacc* Bakr Miri Çelebi, *seyyid* Yusuf Arabi Katib Çelebi, *al-hacc* Ibrahim Çelebi, *al-hacc* Umar Walid, and *el-hacc* Ahmad Hashim Çelebi. The French merchants were Jean-François Pons and Michel Germain. See Meriwether, *The Notable Families of Aleppo*, 322, 350–356 for genealogies of the Miri and Qurna families respectively.

his will by his own consul, after initially refusing to appear because the arrangement was in contravention of the normal procedures. After all, in disputes between members of different foreign communities, the conflict was always brought before the consul of the defendant. By allowing the hearing to take place in the British Pro-Consul's house under his own chairmanship, and by leaving the selection of the members of the council to Hays, Van Maseijk had abandoned a number of basic principles. Standard procedures emphasized that the burden of proof lay with the plaintiff, forcing him to convince with legal arguments a consul who presumed the defendant innocent in principle. Van Maseijk may have wanted to prevent a dispute between protégés from disturbing peaceful Anglo-Dutch relations in the city, but by relinquishing his own consular jurisdiction the Dutch consul failed to meet his obligations toward his protégé. Van Maseijk's presence during the hearing had offered Dwek Cohen no guarantee of consular intervention on his behalf because Van Maseijk did not understand Arabic.[46] The Dutchman also ignored another strong argument of Dwek Cohen, notably that several of the council's members were his opponents. Stefan Ajami, for example, was a known supporter of Uskan. Moreover, the British Pro-Consul himself, as well as the two Frenchmen, had been involved in the dispute over the commercial transaction.

By this time the disputes had dragged on for almost three years. Several factors had slowed down the mechanisms of justice. The litigants themselves were partly responsible for the delays, since months often passed between petitions, responses and new petitions. Whenever one of the parties made a concrete proposal to end the disputes, the other rejected the plan without negotiation. Dwek Cohen continued to refuse to cooperate with any initiative taken by the British consul, even when his own consul supported it. Most importantly of all Uskan's tactic of letting twenty months pass between his protest and the complaint proper considerably extended the duration of the procedures. The conduct of the Dutch consul, Nicolaas van Maseijk, also influenced the course of justice in this case. As the consul of the defendant he had the authority to separate the dispute over the missing money from the one concerning the terms of an earlier trans-

---

[46] DNA, LAT 774, Yusuf Dwek Cohen to the Dutch ambassador, Van Haeften, 12 September 1783 [in Italian, with Dwek Cohen's signature and seal in Hebrew].

action. Both parties had asked Van Maseijk to solve the disputes several times, but he took no action. When he finally consulted two French merchants about the conflict over the barter transaction, he did not accept their verdict against his own protégé, allowing the dispute to drag on. The Dutchman had allowed his British colleague, Abbott, to undertake a number of initiatives in order to settle the conflicts, but when it came to the cooperation of Dwek Cohen, he claimed that he could not force his protégé to accept the authority of the Englishman. Van Maseijk could also have put pressure on Uskan to file his official complaint against Dwek Cohen sooner. Although he would have been unable to force Uskan to do anything, his close friend and colleague John Abbott certainly could have done so.

Abbott's death, on 25 March 1783, made the cooperation with the English and Dutch consulates more complicated.[47] Abbott and Van Maseijk had trusted one another completely, but the candidates for the British consul's succession were less impartial in the eyes of Van Maseijk. Charles Smith, for example, had a good reputation, but a number of his employees were somehow involved in the dispute between Uskan and Dwek Cohen.[48] The fact that the consulate went to David Hays was equally complicating, since he was the merchant with whom Dwek Cohen had concluded the transaction over which the dispute with Uskan had arisen. For the Jewish *berath* of the Dutch consulate Hays' appointment must have been an unpleasant surprise, because Dwek Cohen had called him a liar in several of his official statements, copies of which had all been registered in the English chancery records.[49]

The pace of procedures finally quickened after Jan van Maseijk had succeeded his father as Dutch consul in 1784. The new consul was already familiar with the disputes between Uskan and Dwek Cohen, having been his father's most trusted interpreter during the last years of his life. Already in March 1782 Nicolaas van Maseijk had sent his son to Istanbul to report about the conflicts to the

[47] BNA, SP 110/65, 174–175, Report signed by Charles Smith, Robert Abbott, Gian Stefano Vesetti, and Ilyas Antun A'ida.

[48] DNA, LAT 774, N. van Maseijk to Van Haeften, 24 April 1783.

[49] BNA, SP 110/65, 34–42, 8 May 1782, reaction by Dwek Cohen to Uskan's statement of 19 April.

Dutch ambassador.[50] On 20 August 1784, within six months of his father's death and before he had even been confirmed as consul by the Dutch authorities, Jan van Maseijk passed a verdict.

Van Maseijk junior addressed both disputes between Yusuf Dwek Cohen and Minas Uskan at the same time. With regard to the conflict about the terms of sale, the Dutch consul first ordered his protégé again to show his accounts. On the basis of the evidence, Jan van Maseijk then accepted the opinion of the two French merchants who had reviewed the case earlier, ordering Dwek Cohen to recalculate the transaction and to pay Uskan what he owed him. He also obliged him to pay all costs of the litigation, as the French arbiters had recommended.[51] Minas Uskan thus won the first dispute, but he lost the second.

Although Jan van Maseijk was already familiar with the litigation over the missing sums of money before becoming Dutch consul, he nevertheless examined the documents extensively once he was in office. This was not an easy task, because the chancery records of the period were in disarray. While the disputes between Dwek Cohen and Uskan continued, Nicolaas van Maseijk had suspended the chancellor of the Dutch consulate, Alexander Laars. Relations between the two Dutchmen had been strained from the beginning, but the consul only took steps against him after 25 protégés of the Dutch consulate had filed a formal complaint, accusing Laars of being a drunk and a liar, whose Muslim creditors formed a potential danger to the entire Dutch *nation*. They explicitly declared him unfit for his office, urging the consul to dismiss him. In response to the petition, Van Maseijk suspended Laars, who had been chancellor from 1772. Three months later the consul changed his mind, however, reinstating Laars and withdrawing his recommendation to the home authorities to fire him.[52] During the suspension of the Dutch chancellor his office was attended to by Vincenzo Ottonelli, the Italian vice-chancellor of the British consulate. After Jan van Maseijk had taken over the consulate it appeared that some relevant documents

---

[50] DNA, LAT 774, Nicolaas van Maseijk to Van Haeften, 11 September 1781; Ibid., same to same, 9 March 1782.

[51] DNA, LAT 1266, doc. 8, Jan van Maseijk to Kroll, chargé d'affaires, 1 September 1784.

[52] DNA, LAT 774, Petition dated 15 April 1783, signed by 25 protégés. In Arabic with Italian translation. Bronnen IV/i, 335, N. van Maseijk to the Directors, 19 April 1782, n. 2. Laars' reinstatement is not mentioned in Schutte, *Repertorium*, 356.

had not been registered during the period of the suspension of Laars. The chaotic state of the records of this period even made Van Maseijk believe the rumour that Ottonelli was the driving force behind Uskan's complaints.[53] But Ottonelli's failure to register two crucial documents eventually worked in Dwek Cohen's favour.

Uskan's case was based on his reasoning that the theft could only have taken place in his partner's khan, and on apparent contradictions in Dwek Cohen's statements about the crucial question of who had actually handled the purses that had gone missing. The testimonies of Stefan Ajami were central to this question. Ajami had filed three statements that cast serious doubts on the consistency of Dwek Cohen's declarations, but they had never been registered properly in either the British or Dutch chancery at the time of their issue.[54] Jan van Maseijk noted that none of the testimonies were dated, and that the copies the Dutch consulate had been given did not indicate when they had been originally registered in the British chancery. Van Maseijk repeatedly asked Hays to be allowed to inspect the original documents, but the Englishman evaded his colleague's requests. Eventually Hays informed Van Maseijk that Uskan had only produced the crucial affidavits at the hearing of 3 September 1783, and that they had been copied in the British chancery records even later.[55] Van Maseijk's investigation of these statements led him to declare them inadmissible as evidence on the grounds that they had not been filed in conformity with consular guidelines, i.e. that they lacked the original dates and the dates of registration.[56]

---

[53] Ibid., Extra aanwinsten 1894, no. 90: No. 7. Jan van Maseijk to Kroll, chargé d'affaires, 12 August 1784: 'Je suis beaucoup avancé dans l'examen du differend entre les Srs Doek & Vascan don't j'ai eu l'honneur de vous ecrire le 12 du mois passé & ayant trouvé parmi les pièces les plus essentielles du procés un désordre frappant, qui m'a donné des soupçons fondés sur la conduite de l'ancien Pro Chancellier d'Angleterre le Sr Ottonelli, qui l'on assure être le directeur de toutes les écritures presentés par le Sr Vascan [. . .]'

[54] DNA, LAT 1266, undated statement by Ajami and A'ida (Arabic, with Italian translation); BNA, SP 110/65, f. 242v., I: statement by Mikhail Tutunji dated 19 September 1783 (Arabic, with Italian translation on f. 243).

[55] DNA, LAT 1266, Extra aanwinsten 1894, no. 90: No. 26, Hays to Van Maseijk, 4 August 1784 (in Italian); The documents preceding this one form the correspondence between the two consuls on the subject. A copy of the declaration by A'ida and Ajami handed over by to the Dutch consul by his British colleague was dated 20 December 1783. Ibid., doc. 14, Attestazione No. 3.

[56] Ibid., Registramento della sentenza emanata dall'Ill.mo Sig.re Gio. Van Maseijk Pro-Console Generale &ca nella causa fra Sig.re Juseph Doek baratario d'olanda ed il Sig.re Minas Vascan firmanlino Britanico, 20 August 1784 (in French).

The Dutch consul found another inaccuracy in Uskan's accusations. Soon after he had heard that part of the money was missing, Uskan had intended to interrogate the *odabaşı* in the service of Dwek Cohen, but the dragoman had refused to cooperate on the grounds that the warehouse supervisor was a protégé of the Venetian consulate. In his formal complaint of 21 June 1783, Uskan claimed that Dwek Cohen had had his employee exchange his British *berat* for one from the Venetians so as to elude British consular jurisdiction in this matter.[57] In order to verify this, Van Maseijk made inquiries with the collector of the poll tax in Aleppo, Hasan Efendi. On 6 August 1784 this officer issued a document, which stated that Harrari had been a protégé of the Venetian consulate since the beginning of 1780, long before the conflicts between his employer and Uskan arose.[58] Uskan's claims thus were proven incorrect. Finally, Van Maseijk rejected Uskan's claim that the theft could only have taken place in Aleppo. It was not clear, for example, when exactly the caravan had reached Basra, because Uskan's correspondents had failed to mention the date. They had also failed to supply the date on which they had collected the cases, and the day on which they had opened them. It was therefore impossible to exclude the possibility that the cases had been left unopened and unattended in Basra for some time, during which the money could have been stolen.

The Dutch consul had suggested that he and Hays adjudicate the disputes together, to lend the verdict the maximum authority. Hays had rejected the offer on the grounds that he did not want to go beyond his formal jurisdiction.[59] Jan van Maseijk thus had to give a sentence on his own, which he did on 20 August 1784. Considering the evidence produced by Uskan insufficient grounds for a conviction, he acquitted Dwek Cohen, and ordered that the sequestration of his possessions in Basra be lifted. Van Maseijk also entitled his protégé to sue anyone who continued illegitimately to hold his goods.[60]

---

[57] DNA, LAT 1266, Extra aanwinsten 1894, no. 90: [Memorial], 21 June 1783.

[58] Ibid., Arabic document issued by Hasan Efendi *el-haracci* on 19 Ramazan 1198/6 August 1784. Ishaq Harrari had been a Venetian protégé since the month of Muharrem 1194/8 January–6 February 1780. The document was issued at the request of Jan van Maseijk, who is referred to in the text by his nickname, Jacky.

[59] Ibid., doc. 23, Jan van Maseijk to David Hays, 9 July 1784 (the proposal); Ibid., doc. 24, Hays to Van Maseijk, 10 July 1784 (its rejection). Both documents are in Italian.

[60] Ibid., Registramento della sentenza . . ., 20 August 1784.

Moreover, Jan van Maseijk ordered Dwek Cohen to swear under oath that he and his employees were not responsible for the disappearance of the money. In order further to legitimise his verdict, Van Maseijk asked his Venetian colleague, Salessio Rizzini, to comment on it. The consul of Venice fully agreed with the Dutchman's decision, explicitly declaring that he also considered the two controversial statements inadmissible as evidence, and that it was indeed unknown what had happened to the goods in Basra.[61] Minas Uskan appealed against the verdict immediately.

The Appeal and its Aftermath

Uskan filed his appeal with the British and Dutch ambassadors in Istanbul within weeks of Van Maseijk's verdict, again violating juridical protocol among Europeans in the Levant, as it was impossible to appeal against the verdict of a consul of one *nation* to the ambassador of another. Although the *faux pas* did not prevent the Dutch *chargé d'affaires*, George Ferdinand Kroll, accepting the appeal, he had little time to deal with it further, matters of international politics taking up most of his time. Peace with Great Britain had just been signed in Paris, and Ottoman relations with Russia and the Habsburg Emperor were turbulent. Dutch Levant trade had suffered dramatically from British maritime supremacy during the war, and Kroll's priority lay with restoring Dutch commerce in the Ottoman Empire. Although the Dutch Republic was no longer an international power to be reckoned with, Kroll attempted to keep up with the competition with regard to commercial privileges, and the appeal therefore had to wait until the new ambassador, baron Frederik Gijsbert van Dedem van de Gelder arrived in the Ottoman capital in 1785.

A year after Van Dedem had reached the port of Istanbul, Mokdevi Calostian presented Uskan's case to the ambassador on 30 August 1786. He repeated all the arguments put forward personally by Uskan in Aleppo without introducing any new evidence. Calostian ended his plea by criticizing Van Maseijk's verdict. In the eyes of Uskan's agent the verdict was "irregular" for the following reasons. Firstly,

---

[61] DNA, LAT 1266, Extra aanwinsten 1894, no. 90: Doc. II, Salessio Rizzini to Van Maseijk, 13 January 1785. He had been asked for his opinion in Ibid., Van Maseijk to Rizzini, 10 January 1785 (both in Italian).

it was based on and referred to allegations Uskan denied ever having made. Secondly, the plaintiff considered Dwek Cohen's oath worthless, because it was easy for him to take an oath concerning a crime of which he was not the principle perpetrator. Thirdly, because the consul had accepted the oath of a Jew against a score of circumstances that pointed to his guilt. Fourthly, strictly speaking it was not permissible to accept oaths in criminal cases, unless the plaintiff had requested it.[62]

Yusuf Dwek Cohen was represented at the appeal by Sylvester de Serpos, a Swedish honorary dragoman, and brother of Dwek Cohen's late business partner, Thomas de Serpos. The defence presented its case on 19 November 1786.[63] De Serpos first summarized the events leading to the disputes, beginning with the caravan of July 1781, the discovery of that money was missing, the accusations against and trial of the caravan conductor, and the suspicions against Dwek Cohen. With regard to the missing purses Uskan had to "prove clearly that it was him [Dwek Cohen] who had stolen them before consigning them" to the caravan conductor, as De Serpos stated. He began the defence by emphasizing that the plaintiff's claim that the theft must have taken place in Dwek Cohen's khan since the cases had arrived in Basra unscathed was based on assumption, not evidence.

It was De Serpos' task to create reasonable doubt about the claims levelled against his principal, and he did this by systematically countering Uskan's accusations. He even rejected the reliability of material not referred to by Calostian in the appeal, but which was nevertheless found among the documents handed over to the Dutch embassy. For example, there was an unconfirmed report that Dwek Cohen had acknowledged his responsibility for the disappearance of the money in a letter to his correspondent in Istanbul, Thomas de Serpos. The dragoman allegedly admitted to De Serpos that he might have sent the money to Bengal instead of Basra by mistake. Mokdevi Calostian, the representative of Uskan at the appeal, had personally heard this from De Serpos. It was the word of the agent of Dwek Cohen against that of Uskan. Mokdevi Calostian claimed personally

[62] DNA, LAT 1266, 'Muksi' Calostian to Van Dedem, 30 August 1786 (in French).

[63] BOA, HH 9779-C lists Sylvester de Serpos son of Ağob as a *beratlı* of Sweden in Istanbul from 6 Ramazan 1199/13 July 1785. Thomas de Serpos, who was also under Swedish protection, is not mentioned in this document. It is possible that Thomas' *berat* was passed on to Sylvester after his death.

to have heard Thomas de Serpos talk about it, but Sylvester de Serpos denied that Dwek Cohen had ever sent the confession to his brother. In the end Uskan had been unable to produce a copy of the letter from Dwek Cohen to Thomas de Serpos, and the report remained unsubstantiated. Sylvester de Serpos also reiterated the arguments of Jan van Maseijk against the admissibility of the testimonies of Stefan Ajami individually, and in combination with Ilyas Antun A'ida, a subject ignored by Calostian.[64]

Although it was not for the defendant to prove who had committed the crime he was accused of, it was useful for De Serpos to discuss the other suspects anyway. Muhammad al-Shai had been acquitted by the qadi in Basra, but it was still possible that he had been involved in the theft. Without contesting the legitimacy of the qadi's verdict, De Serpos pointed out that the two witnesses who had confirmed the caravan conductor's version of events could just as easily have been his accomplices. After all, it may have been difficult for an individual to open two sealed crates in the desert and to steal part of their contents, but three men could probably do the job, De Serpos argued. Provided they had brought the right materials for sealing the crates again, it could not have been very difficult for the caravan conductors to copy the original packing methods. Dwek Cohen's agent was merely speculating, but it helped undermine Uskan's argument that the theft could only have taken place in Aleppo. For the same reason Sylvester de Serpos also criticized the conduct of Uskan's correspondents in Basra, adopting the argument of Jan van Maseijk's verdict. They had failed to provide the date of arrival of the caravan, of the day on which they collected the goods, and when they opened the cases. De Serpos also wondered why they had not immediately suspected the caravan conductor, who was the most obvious suspect in his eyes. Dwek Cohen's representative concluded that the verdict of the Dutch consul had been just, and that there was no evidence for the accusations against

[64] DNA, LAT 664, Mémoire justificatif pour le Sieur Joseph Doek drogman barataire de Hollande à Alep en son proces avec le Sieur Minas Vascan firmanli d'Angleterre porté en appel devant le tribunal de S. E. Monsieur l'Ambassadeur de Hollande à Constantinople, 4; BNA, SP 110/65, 251, Undated letter by Calostian to Uskan (Arabic text), 251–252 (Italian translation). The translation was made by Niqula Fakhr on 6 April 1783, and it was registered in the British chancery on 3 October 1783.

his principal. He therefore asked for a confirmation of the verdict, so that the sequestration of Dwek Cohen's goods in Basra could finally be lifted.

The sources do not spell out which law the Dutch ambassador should apply. Formally his jurisdiction was based on regulations and resolutions passed by the Dutch States-General, but in practice an ill-defined system of legal customs developed among Western ambassadors in Istanbul in combination Van Dedem's own sense of prudence and justice determined his actions. He chose not to rule on the matter personally, but to leave it to four merchants from different European nations to examine the evidence one last time. Within three weeks of Sylvester de Serpos' plea, on 7 December 1786, these merchants wrote to the ambassador that, in their opinion, Uskan could not prove that the theft had taken place in Dwek Cohen's khan.[65] The acceptance of this advice and its confirmation as verdict by the ambassador were merely formalities, but almost two more years passed before Van Dedem finalized the details. Only on 3 August 1788 did he confirm the verdict by Jan van Maseijk, on the basis of the advice of the four merchants in Istanbul:

> puisqu'en aucune manière il n'a paru ni à nous ni aux susdits Aviseurs comme il est évident par la pièce ci jointe *sub. Lit. A.* que l'accusation du vol portée contre *Joseph Doek* a été prouvée clairement, ou que dans les formes de justice elle ait été prouvée d'une manière convaincante: ce que cependant pour pouvoir être condamné juridiquement suivant le principe du droit connu *qu'un accusateur est obligé de prouver* auroit dû précéder nécessairement.
>
> Nous entendons et décidons que le Consul de Leurs Hautes Puissances à Alep *Jean van Maseijk* à la première instance a bien et duement jugé, et par conséquent l'appelant *Minas Vascan* a illégalement et sans raison appellé, que pour cet effet, sa demande et conclusion soient totalement rejetées, et au contraire entièrement approuvée et confirmée la sentence qu'en date *20* Août 1784 a été prononcé contre lui par le dit *Consul de Maseijk*: que *Joseph Doek* finalement selon ses conditions y arrêtés, est déclaré absous de toute accusation, demande et action quelconque.[66]

---

[65] They were the German merchant B. Ahrens, the Frenchman Paul Thoron, the Dutchman Jan Pieter Panchaud, and the Englishman Peter Tooke. DNA, LAT 1266, 'Nous soussignés ayant examine le process existant entre les sieurs Minas Vaskan & Josep Doëk au sujet de quelque groups perdue, dont le premier réclame la valeur [. . .]'

[66] Ibid.: "Nous Fréderik Gijsbert Baron de Dedem . . .' Verdict by the Dutch

Van Dedem's verdict had little effect. Since the Dutch ambassador's authority did not extend beyond the boundaries of his own *nation*, he could not compel members or protégés of other *nations* to respect and implement his sentence. The verdict thus did not lead to the lifting of the sequestration in Iraq.

It seems that the British consulate in Basra had had some role in the sequestration of the goods in Basra, because already in April 1788 Dwek Cohen asked Van Dedem to apply to the British ambassador in this matter. It is also possible, however, that Dwek Cohen wanted to rally support from as many foreign consulates in Basra as possible. The Dutch ambassador does not appear to have acted on the dragoman's request, because, at the beginning of 1789, the entire consular dossier of the disputes was sent to the embassy from Aleppo, probably in another attempt to persuade the ambassador to act in Dwek Cohen's favour.[67] Whether or not Van Dedem ever endeavoured to help his dragoman is not clear. His ability to assist was, in any case, limited. If the British consulate in Basra was indeed involved, all the Dutch ambassador could do was request the help of his colleague in Istanbul. If the sequestration had been put in place by the Ottoman authorities in Basra, the Dutchman's verdict did not have any authority. It is clear from our sources that the Ottoman legal authorities did not accept consular verdicts, simply treating disputes that had already been adjudicated by Westerners as new cases they were entitled to hear throughout the eighteenth century.

The sequestration of these goods lasted until the end of 1789, when they were released and sold.[68] Uskan, who appears to have made a habit of personally escorting his goods between Aleppo and Basra, probably invested the proceeds in Iraq by buying merchandize he planned to sell in Syria. Dwek Cohen claimed that Uskan subsequently refused to pay him his share of the profit. The Dutch

---

ambassador, in Dutch and French. Although the French version is said to be a translation of the Dutch, the former is dated 1 August 1788, two days before the Dutch version.

[67] DNA, LAT 1266, Dwek Cohen to Van Dedem, 21 April 1788 (in Italian); Ibid., Jan van Maseijk to Van Dedem, 4 February 1789 (in French). In Istanbul all the documents had to be translated into French for the ambassador's benefit, for which Dwek Cohen was willing to pay.

[68] The following is based on DNA, LAT 1266, Traduction de la Requête du S:[r] *Juseph Doek Cohen* Barattaire de Hollande. Alep le 18[e] Janvier 1790.

dragoman was entitled to this share because the goods had, some eight years earlier, been sent to Basra by Uskan and Dwek Cohen jointly, each owning half of the cargo. His original investment had amounted to 4,620 *kuruş*, which, if he had invested them in a different manner, Dwek Cohen believed would certainly have yielded 12,000 *kuruş* over the eight years during which the disputes dragged on. Moreover, the dragoman demanded reimbursement of all the expenses of litigation, in conformity with the verdict of the Dutch ambassador.

Further litigation was prevented by the death of Minas Uskan, after a sickbed of several days, on Christmas Day, 1789. He had recently returned to Aleppo with the Basra caravan, bringing with him a cargo of textiles from Bengal and coffee. After Uskan's death the qadi of Aleppo ordered his house and warehouse sealed, in order to levy the customary duties. Dwek Cohen subsequently learned that Uskan's parents had removed some of their son's possessions during the night of his death, including the coffee and Bengali textiles. The dragoman instantly reported this to the Dutch consul, who reported the event to the qadi. Around the same time—the chronology of Dwek Cohen's account is not clear at this point—the dragoman filed suit before the qadi, demanding his share of the profit of the goods he had expedited to Basra together with Uskan. The Dutch dragoman won the case, partly on the basis of the testimony of the chancellor of the Venetian consulate and the First Dragoman of the Dutch consulate. Unfortunately I have not found any additional records of this court case, in which the qadi evidently accepted the testimony of a Venetian.[69] According to Dwek Cohen's account, the Islamic judge awarded him 5,591 and a half *kuruş*, 4,620 for the original investment, the remainder a compensation for the chancery fees he had paid to the Dutch consulate, the receipts of which he was able to show as evidence in court. Dwek Cohen did not receive cash, but was assigned ownership of five bales of textiles, instead. The estimated value of these textiles had been fixed at the sum owed to the dragoman.

Still the case was not over. To his "great mortification" Dwek Cohen discovered that the bales did not contain the valuable tex-

[69] This contradicts Heyd, *Studies in Old Ottoman Criminal Law*, 245: "The testimony . . . of a non-Muslim foreign resident [is accepted] only against another *müste'min*, not even against a *zimmī*."

tiles he had expected. Instead of the Bengali cloth Uskan had recently brought with him from Basra, Dwek Cohen had been given inferior materials that had remained unsold for a considerable period. When he finally found a buyer for them, the dragoman only got some 3,222 for the textiles. The dragoman thus went back to the Islamic court, where Uskan's parents reportedly attempted to bribe the qadi with 1,500 *kuruş*. In order to prevent a further travesty of justice, Dwek Cohen decided to bribe the qadi pre-emptively by offering the same sum. As a result he was left with only about 1,722 *kuruş*, only a fraction of the money he claimed to be entitled to.

The qadi in Aleppo had ruled in Dwek Cohen's favour, but still he felt defrauded of his investment in the ill-fated consignment by his former partner's heirs. The Islamic judge had not awarded him a share of the profits on the sale, which Dwek Cohen estimated at 2,000 *kuruş*, but the dragoman clearly did not want to pursue the matter further in the courts. Instead, he chose a different strategy altogether to attempt once again to obtain compensation for the losses he had suffered. In Dwek Cohen's own words

> J'ai réussi d'obtenir un *Fetva* du *Mufti* qui explique clairement qui si quelque sujet du Grand Seigneur sous protection Européenne auroit été condamné par une sentence d'un Juge Franc à payer une certaine somme à quelqu'autre sujet, et qu'il viendroit de mourir avant de s'être acquitté de la dite dette, les héritiers du décédé seront obligés de se soumettre à ce qui aura été jugé auparavant.

Dwek Cohen sent this fatwa to the Dutch ambassador in Istanbul, asking him to obtain a confirmation of this legal opinion, first from the *Şeyhülislam*, and subsequently from the Porte, in the form of a *ferman*. He calculated that he had lost a total of 28,342 *kuruş* in "capital, interest, expenses, and damages". We know from the qadi's verdict that the original investment, the capital of the quotation, amounted to 4,620 *kuruş*, and that Dwek Cohen had receipts for only 971.5 *kuruş* in chancery fees. Add to this subtotal of 5,591.5 *kuruş* the 1,000 *kuruş* Dwek Cohen claimed had been his share of the profits on the sale of the tinsel and false coral he and Uskan had sent to Basra in 1781, and we arrive at 6,591.5 *kuruş*. From this we can deduce that Dwek Cohen was suing for damages to the amount of some 21,750 *kuruş*.[70] He specified this as the loss of his

[70] If the ambassador considered this too much, Dwek Cohen wrote, the diplo-

good name, and, consequently, the inability to conduct trade with Iraq, because he was unable to find people there who would do business with him.

Whether or not the embassy did what the dragoman in Aleppo had asked it to, is not clear, and I have not found any evidence that corroborates the fatwa's existence. The embassy officers may well have wondered why Dwek Cohen had gone through the trouble of obtaining it in the first place. After all, the estates of Ottoman protégés of foreign embassies and consulates always fell under the jurisdiction of these institutions. As Chapter Four has shown, the capitulations confirmed this unequivocally.

This takes us back to the legal status Minas Uskan. Our sources consistently refer to him as the "fermanli" (*hizmetkâr*) of the English consulate, and it was because of this circumstance that the fatwa favoured Dwek Cohen's cause. But if this were the case, why was Uskan's estate after his death not sealed and administrated by the British consulate? Chapter Four has shown that this was standard procedure in the case of dragomans and their "servants", but Dwek Cohen himself informs us that it was the qadi who seized the estate, levied the customary duties on it, and ruled on the dragoman's claim against Uskan's heirs, instead. If Uskan remained a British protégé until his death, the seizure of his estate by the qadi would almost certainly have led to protests from the English consulate. I have found none. If Uskan had lost his privileged status before he died, the fatwa obtained by his former business partner would have been less useful, because the text—as far as we can tell—exclusively concerned those still under foreign protection at the time of their death. Without conclusive evidence about Uskan's legal status this apparent contradiction cannot be explained.

The final twist in the case is interesting, nevertheless. It is striking that Dwek Cohen never referred to the capitulations in any of his letters to the Dutch consul or embassy. He could have pointed, for example, to the article in the French capitulation of 1740, which made it possible for him to appeal against the qadi's verdict before the *divan-ı hümayun*.[71] This is clearly not what he was after, however.[72]

mat should feel free to adjust the claim "analogue aux principes de l'équité et de la justice."

[71] See Chapter One, pages 33–34.

[72] DNA, LAT 1266, Traduction de la Requête.

This Jewish dragoman of the Dutch consulate in Aleppo obtained the fatwa as an instrument in a legal dispute with the heirs of his former business partner, not to use it in court or to overturn a verdict with it, but to solicit support from the Porte. Maybe Dwek Cohen was more familiar with the Islamic legal infrastructure than with the capitulations, which already contained the privilege he sought to secure by obtaining a fatwa.

Conclusion

The disputes between Yusuf Dwek Cohen and Minas Uskan are illustrative of consular legal procedures in the Levant in the eighteenth century. The conflict with regard to the terms of one transaction between them was purely commercial, while the case of the missing money could be considered a criminal matter. Uskan, a protégé of the British consulate in Aleppo, filed a complaint against his former partner, Dwek Cohen, who was a dragoman of the Dutch. Procedure among the Europeans in the Levant dictated that disputes should be adjudicated by the consul of the accused. In this case that was the Dutch consul, Nicolaas van Maseijk. The consular verdict was eventually passed by his successor, his son, Jan van Maseijk, while the Dutch ambassador in Istanbul ruled on the appeal. During both stages the Dutch sought the advice of knowledgeable outsiders. In Aleppo Nicolaas van Maseijk asked two French merchants to examine the dispute over the terms of a transaction between Uskan and Dwek Cohen, and his son later asked the Venetian consul to review his verdict in the case of the missing money. Van Maseijk father and son also cooperated with the British consulate in both matters. In Istanbul the Dutch ambassador later asked the advice of four disinterested European merchants, whose opinion he accepted and confirmed.

The case was not an exclusively consular matter, however, and several circumstances and elements are noteworthy. Most importantly, the dispute over the missing money began in the Islamic court in Basra with the lawsuit against the Bedouin caravan conductor who had supervised the transport of the crates with merchandize and money from Aleppo. The man was quickly acquitted by the qadi on the basis of the testimony of two witnesses who confirmed the alibi of the accused. The court's verdict notwithstanding, suspicions against the caravan conductor continued to exist. The Dutch and British consuls in Aleppo did not have jurisdiction over him, however, so that legal action against him before a consular tribunal was impossible. At this point the consuls inventively organized a hearing of the case on 3 September 1783, during which the caravan conductor was declared to be free of debt and above suspicion.

From a strictly legal point of view the hearing was superfluous, and it must thus have served other purposes. The composition of the council of merchants who participated in the proceedings is probably significant in this context. The majority were Muslims, and of the non-Muslims only two were westerners, apart from the British Pro-consul, who chaired the session, and his Dutch colleague who was merely an observer. By having this council confirm that the caravan conductor was above suspicion, the consuls tacitly acknowledged the verdict of the qadi in Basra, while reaffirming their own jurisdiction over the disputes between Uskan and Dwek Cohen at the same time. This satisfied the caravan conductor, whose complaints that the Europeans were questioning his acquittal could have caused trouble with the Ottoman authorities for the consuls at some point. The hearing also cleared the way for purely consular procedures between Uskan and Dwek Cohen, which pleased both the plaintiff and the consuls. By organizing the hearing the British and Dutch consuls thus managed to remove the only party who was not under their jurisdiction from the procedure, eliminating a possible pretext for the Ottoman authorities to interfere in the case.

The hearing is also evidence of another extraordinary circumstance in Aleppo at this time, the intimate relations between the Dutch and British consulates. While the Fourth Anglo-Dutch War was being fought elsewhere, relations between the two communities in Aleppo had never been better. This was largely due to the fact that the Dutch consul, Nicolaas van Maseijk, had an English wife, and was a devout Protestant, who attended services in the British consular chapel regularly. Van Maseijk went to great lengths to maintain his personal friendship with the English, often disregarding formal procedures in the disputes of Uskan and Dwek Cohen in the process. In principle this went against the interests of his dragoman, who was entitled to a proper trial in accordance with standard consular practice. The Dutchman's lenience in relation to procedures and the practices of the interim-chancellor, Ottonelli, eventually worked to Dwek Cohen's advantage, when Jan van Maseijk rejected some important evidence because it did not conform to formal requirements, but this did not compensate for the inefficiency of the Dutch consulate during the first years of the conflicts.

The fact that the case only ended formally in 1788 was due to the low priority the settlement of the dispute evidently had for the Dutch *chargé d'affaires*, Kroll, and the next ambassador, Van Dedem. The former was operating in difficult times, when the Dutch Republic was trying to regain its former position as a commercial power in the Levant, but why the latter delayed ending the conflicts for two years remains unknown. In any case, the Dutch consuls and ambassadors who were involved in the disputes between Yusuf Dwek Cohen and Minas Uskan show that the practical efficiency of the protection system also partly depended on these officers' willingness to maintain it.

This case makes one final important point. Despite the theoretical importance of the capitulations in all matters involving foreigners in the Ottoman Empire, they appear to have been irrelevant in these disputes. The *ahdnames* guaranteed that these conflicts could be tried by foreign judges in the first place, but that is also where their application ended in this case. Dwek Cohen's procurement of a fatwa to obtain a privilege that was already codified in emphasizes their lack of practical value for him. Did this dragoman in the active service of the Dutch consulate not know of the capitulatory privilege? Or did he not trust the consulate to ensure its implementation? Answers to these questions must remain conjectural. More importantly, it reminds us that even at the end of the eighteenth century in an age-old centre of international trade, the practical importance of the capitulations simply cannot be taken for granted.

CHAPTER SEVEN

CONCLUSION

In the past legal scholars predominantly studied the legal status of Westerners in the Ottoman Empire on the basis of the capitulations, which they tended to consider instruments of international law. These texts were important codifications of privileges, but the *ahdname*s offer little evidence about their practical implementation. By contrast, historians uninterested in legal niceties have tended to consult almost exclusively those sources that reflect practice, without consulting normative texts. The present work aimed to combine these two approaches in order to examine the legal position of Western communities vis-à-vis the Ottoman legal system in the eighteenth century.

A critical comparison of the normative texts (the capitulations, as well as other, predominantly Ottoman, types of decrees) with contemporary accounts of the Ottoman legal practice (usually the official reports of Western ambassadors, consuls, and travelogues) brings to light many discrepancies. Privileges listed prominently in the *ahdname*s appear to have had little relevance on the ground, while in practice mechanisms of dispute resolution that were not even mentioned in the capitulations appear to have been common. The capitulations formed a framework of privileges that was not designed to offer solutions for every imaginable problem the foreigners might be confronted with. General rules had to be applied to specific situations, a process that required discussion and negotiation between the Ottoman authorities and the Western representatives. The inherent uncertainty of this situation is generally disregarded or denied in the European sources from the eighteenth century, which emphasize the primacy of the "sacred" capitulations. The exaggerated expectations of the Western ambassadors and consuls created a problem they subsequently had to explain over and over again to their home authorities: the difference between the theory and practice of their capitulatory status. By the eighteenth century the word *avania* had become a blanket explanation that implicitly laid the blame for the problem with the capriciousness of the Ottoman legal administration.

A careful examination of the *ahdname*s reveals that they distinguished three jurisdictions, two of which were Ottoman; under certain conditions the consul or ambassador could adjudicate disputes, but otherwise conflicts were resolved by the qadi or the *divan-ı hümayun*. This suggests that the European communities were not isolated from the Ottoman legal system—they were subject to it, except under specific circumstances and conditions. The *ahdname*s were instruments of Ottoman state law that created space for a limited foreign jurisdiction within the Ottoman legal system on the basis of the foreigners' own legal customs. The juridical status of Westerners thus was not divorced from the other two major components of Buskens' Islamic legal triangle, state law and Islamic law. On the contrary, it was in constant negotiation with them.

If we apply this model to case studies of incidents labelled *avania*s in the Western sources, we find that they were often not clear-cut examples of Ottoman injustice, or the unreliability of the Ottoman legal system at all. The only common denominator of these cases is the European perception of injustice. A different light is often shed on these incidents by taking into account that the conduct of Ottoman officers was not only—or even predominantly—determined by their personal interests, but also by decrees from the Porte, the prescripts of Islamic law, the maintenance of public order, and local circumstances like the involvement of political factions. Certainly not all incidents the Europeans considered extortionate can be explained in this way. Undeniably there were Ottoman officials who abused their office for personal gain. Western reports of Ottoman injustice should not be taken at face value, however. At the same time these biased descriptions can be valuable for the historian of Islamic law in the Ottoman period, because they contain information about aspects of mechanisms of justice that lie outside the scope of the Ottoman sources.

The *ahdname*s do not mention the Islamic legal concepts of *sulh*, or *musalaha*, which Heyd translates as "composition".[1] This method of dispute resolution based on negotiation between the interested parties appears to have been common, nevertheless, also when foreigners were involved. The procedure allowed the parties to reach a mutually acceptable settlement, which was subsequently registered

[1] Heyd, *Studies in Old Ottoman Criminal Law*, 247–250.

in the Islamic court. When Westerners were involved, dragomans generally conducted the negotiations on their behalf. The process seems to have taken place openly, and official accounts of payments or damages were kept. In the eyes of many Europeans these procedures may have been blatant examples of corruption, because they considered themselves innocent, but in the Ottoman context it was commonplace. In the Ottoman courts, too, parties who continued to proclaim their innocence agreed to pay damages. We can only speculate about their reasons for agreeing to this. Heyd suggests that the party was in fact guilty and preferred to settle before the plaintiff found actual proof of his guilt. Fear of false witnesses testifying against him, is another possible motive he has suggested, or to prevent being tortured in the course of further investigations.[2] Our case studies suggest another possibility. When merchants were involved in protracted litigation this could eventually damage their reputation. Apart from short-term financial effects—the costs of litigation, capital tied up in good sequestered that thus could not be reinvested—the loss of one's good name was a dangerous prospect. It was therefore sometimes more pragmatic to settle, even when innocent.

Arbitration was also a favourite method of resolving conflicts, both among the Ottoman authorities and the Western ambassadors and consuls in the Ottoman Empire. This procedure did not entail negotiations directly between the parties involved, but the examination of their claims by a council of arbiters. They were either appointed by the parties involved themselves, or by the authorities who could impose arbitration on them. Arbitration councils appear often to have been mixed, even those appointed by the Ottoman authorities. Muslims and non-Muslims, Ottoman subjects and Westerners could take part in these procedures as arbiters. The authorities generally converted the recommendation of the arbiters into a sentence, and guaranteed its implementation. Because the instruments of power of ambassadors and consuls were limited, arbitration was the most effective if it had the support of the Ottoman authorities, as well. This form of dispute resolution thus was based essentially on consensus building.

Local circumstances also influenced the Ottoman legal system. For example, in Aleppo, where most of the case studies in this study are

[2] Ibid.

situated, the existence of a large community of *eşraf* had a traceable effect on the legal position of foreigners. The prominence of this group increased what we might call the Islamic sensibilities of the Muslim population. This meant that Europeans had to be careful not to give offence. An arrogant glance, or the public display of green clothing could easily lead to (threats of) litigation, something that was probably facilitated by the fact that the descendants of the Prophet Muhammad were a well-organised and politically powerful faction in Aleppo.

Finally, the influence of individual parties is impossible to capture in theoretical models, but it must be mentioned, nevertheless. The Ottoman authorities could have a central role in the division of the inheritance of a locally recruited dragoman of a Dutch consulate (Chapter Four) because one of his heirs preferred to employ his connections in the Ottoman administration, instead of following consular procedures. The fact that he was *beratlı* of another consulate made no difference. At the same time, when the consular system gave them the liberty to divided part of the estate as they saw fit, it was the Islamic system of shares of inheritance they adopted. The disputes that arose from the bankruptcies in Chapter Five can partly be attributed to the inflexible behaviour of the consul-cum-employer of two of the bankrupts. Strategic stalling by the Armenian plaintiff in Chapter Six largely accounts for the long duration of the case. Personal preferences may explain the Dutch consul's conduct in the same case, which deviated from standard procedures significantly at several points. The case was eventually ended only when his son strictly applied the rules of consular procedure. These particularities may complicate the formulation of general theory, but by disregarding them altogether we risk oversimplification.

ARCHIVAL SOURCES

Başbakanlık Osmanlı Arşivi (Archives of the Prime Minister's Office, Ottoman Branch), Istanbul
- Ecnebi defterleri 22/1 (Dutch Republic), 27/2 (France), 34–2/11 (France), 35/1 (England), 51 (Register of travel permits), 96/1 (Sicily)
- Bab-i Asafi Divan-i Hümayun Düvel-I Ecnebiye Kalemi, 81, 99, 100, 101, 138
- Cevdet Tasnifi Hariciye 264, 1140, 1246, 1309, 1666, 1791, 1807, 6594, 9594
- Hatt-ı Hümayun 9779–B, C, D, E, F, G, H, I, J, K

Nationaal Archief, The Hague
- Legatiearchief Turkije (*Archives of the Legation in Istanbul*): 168, 176, 177, 238, 382, 596, 602, 664, 752, 774, 784, 1010, 1083, 1084, 1086, 1088, 1090, 1091, 1096, 1097, 1101, 1118, 1124, 1125, 1130, 1236, 1260, 1266
- Familiearchief Van Dedem (*Family Archives Van Dedem*), 108
- Liassen Levantse Handel (*Files on Levant Trade*), 105, 165, 221, 222, 235, 239, 572
- Consulaatarchief Smyrna (*Archives of the Consulate in Izmir*), 320

National Archives, Kew (London)
- State Papers
  - Series 105: 102, 104, 118–121, 177–187, 190, 216, 334, 343
  - Series 110: 27, 29, 37, 58–66, 70, 72, 74, 86, 87

Archivum General Cappucini, Rome
- AD 106 I (1626–1834)

SELECTED BIBLIOGRAPHY

Abbott, G.F., *Under the Turk in Constantinople. A Record of Sir John Finch's Embassy 1674–1681* (Oxford, 1920), 266.

Abi-Chahla, Habib, *L'extinction des capitulations en Turquie et dans les régions arabes* (Paris, 1924).

Almkvist, Herman, *Ein türkisches Dragoman-Diplom aus dem vorigen Jahrhundert* (Upsala, 1894).

Anastasopoulos, Antonis, "Building Alliances: a Christian Merchant in Eighteenth-Century Karaferya" (Forthcoming).

Arvieux, Laurent Chevalier d', *Mémoires du Chevalier d'Arvieux* (Paris, 1735).

Bacqué-Grammont, Jean-Louis, 'Un *berāt* de Mahmūd Ier portant nomination du consul général de France en Égypte en 1736', *Tarih Enstitüsü Dergisi* XII (1981–1982), 259–278.

Bağış, Ali İhsan, *Osmanlı ticaretinde gayri müslimler. Kapitülasyonlar—beratlı tüccârlar—Avrupa ve Hayriye tüccârları (1750–1839)* (Ankara, 1983).

Binswanger, Karl, *Untersuchungen zum Status der Nichtmuslime im osmanischen Reich des 16. Jahrhunderts mit einer Neudefinition des Begriffes "Dimma"* (Munich, 1977).

Belin, F.A., *Des capitulations et des traités de la France en Orient* (Paris, 1870).

Bianchi, M., 'Recueil de Fetvas, écrit en turk et en arabe, par Hafiz Mohammed ben Ahmed ben Elcheikh Moustafa Elkedousy, imprimée à Constantinople en 1822', *Journal Asiatique* IV (1824), 171–184.

Boogert, Maurits H. van den, 'Redress for Ottoman Victims of European Privateering. A Case against the Dutch in the *Divan-i Hümayun* (1708–1715)', *Turcica* 33 (2001), 91–118.

——, 'Tussen consul en qâdî: De juridische positie van dragomans in theorie en praktijk', *Sharqiyyât* 9/1 (1997), 37–53.

——, 'European Patronage in the Ottoman Empire: Anglo-Dutch Conflicts of Interest in Aleppo (1703–1755)' in Hamilton et al. (eds) *Friends and Rivals in the East,* 187–221.

Bosscha-Erdbrink, G.R., *At the Threshold of Felicity: Ottoman-Dutch Relations during the Embassy of Cornelis Calkoen at the Sublime Porte 1726–1744* (Amsterdam, 1977).

Bulut, Mehmet, *Ottoman-Dutch Economic Relations in the Early Modern Period 1571–1699* (Hilversum, 2001).

Buskens, Léon, 'An Islamic Triangle. Changing Relationships between *Sharīʿa,* State Law, and Local Customs', *ISIM Newsletter* 5/00, 8.

Charles-Roux, F., *Les Echelles de Syrie et de Palestine au 18ème siècle* (Paris, 1928).

Charrière, E., (ed.), *Négociations de la France dans le Levant* I (Paris, 1848).

Cohen, Amnon, 'Communal Legal Entities in a Muslim Setting; Theory and Practice: The Jewish Community in Sixteenth-Century Jerusalem', *Islamic Law and Society* 3/1 (February 1996), 75–90.

——, "Le Rouge at le Noir—Jerusalem Style" *REMM* 55–56 (1990/1–2), 141–149.

Constantini, Vera, 'Il commercio veneziano ad Aleppo nel settocento', *Studi Veneziani* XLII (2001), 143–211.

Dam van Isselt, W.E. van, 'Avaniën in de Levant (1662–1688)', *De Navorscher* 56 (1906), 525–577.

Davis, Ralph, *Aleppo and Devonshire Square: English Merchants in the Levant in the Eighteenth Century* (London, 1967).

Davison, Roderic H., "'Russian Skill and Turkish Imbecility': The Treaty of Kuchuk Kainardji Reconsidered", Roderic H. Davison, *Essays in Ottoman and Turkish History, 1774–1923. The Impact of the West* (London, 1990), 29–50.

Duparc, Pierre, *Recueil des instructions données aux ambassadeurs et ministres de France depuis les traités de Westphale jusqu'à la Révolution Française* (Paris, 1969).

Ekrem, Reşat, *Osmanlı muahdeleri ve kapitülâsiyonlar 1300–1920* (Istanbul, 1934).

Eldem, Edhem, *French Trade in Istanbul in the Eighteenth Century* (Leiden, 1999).

——, Daniel Goffman, and Bruce Masters, *The Ottoman City between East and West. Aleppo, Izmir, and Istanbul* (Cambridge, 1999).

Ergene, Boğaç A., *Local Court, Provincial Society and Justice in the Ottoman Empire. Legal Practice and Dispute Resolution in Çankırı and Kastamonu* (Leiden, 2003).

Essad, Mahmoud, *Des capitulations ottomanes: Leur caractère juridique d'après l'histoire et les textes* (Istanbul, 1928).

Feridun Beg, *Münşeat-i Selatin* (Istanbul, 174–1275/1858).

Fleet, Kate, *European and Islamic Trade in the Early Ottoman State. The Merchants of Genoa and Turkey* (Cambridge, 1999).

——, 'Turkish-Latin Diplomatic Relations in the Fourteenth Century: The Case of the Consul', in van den Boogert and Fleet (eds), *The Ottoman Capitulations*, 605–611.

Foster, William (ed.), *The Travels of John Sanderson in the Levant 1584–1602* (London, 1931).

Frangakis-Syrett, Elena, *The Commerce of Smyrna in the Eighteenth Century (1700–1820)* (Athens, 1992).

——, "Networks of Friendship, Networks of Kinship: Eighteenth-Century Levant Merchants", *Eurasian Studies* I/2 (2002), 183–205.

Fukasawa, Katsumi, *Toilerie et commerce du levant au XVIII*[e] *siècle d'Alep à Marseille* (Paris, 1987).

Gallotta, Aldo, Alessio Bombaci, "The History of *avania*" in Barbera Kellner-Heinkele and Peter Zieme (eds), *Studia Ottomanica. Festgabe für György Hazai zum 65. Geburtstag* (Wiesbaden, 1997), 53–73.

Ghazzī, Kāmil al-, *Nahr al-dhahab fī ta'rīkh Ḥalab* (Aleppo, 1923–1926).

Gerber, Haim, *Islamic Law and Culture* (Leiden, 1999).

Goffman, Daniel, 'Ottoman *Millets* in the Early Seventeenth Century', *New Perspectives on Turkey* 11/1994.

——, *Britons in the Ottoman Empire, 1642–1660* (Seattle/London, 1998).

Gökbilgin, M. Tayyib, 'Venedik devlet arşivindeki Türkçe belgeler koleksiyonu ve bizimle ilgile diğer belgeler', *Belgeler* V–VIII (1968–1971) 9–12, 1–152.

Grenville, Henry, *Observations sur l'etat actuel de l'empire ottoman* Andrew S. Ehrenkreuz (ed.) (Ann Arbor, 1965).

Groot, A.H. de *The Ottoman Empire and the Dutch Republic. A History of the Earliest Diplomatic Relations 1610–1630* (Leiden/Istanbul, 1978).

——, 'Dragomans' Careers: The Change of Status in some Families connected with the British and Dutch Embassies at Istanbul 1785–1829', Hamilton, et al. (eds), *Friends and Rivals*, 223–246.

——, 'The Dragomans of the Embassies in Istanbul, 1785–1834', Geert Jan van Gelder and Ed de Moor (eds), *Eastward Bound. Dutch Ventures and Adventures in the Middle East.* (Amsterdam/Atlanta GA, 1994), 130–158.

Heyberger, Bernard, *Les chrétiens du Proche-Orient au temps de la réforme catholique* (Rome, 1994).

Heyd, Uriel, *Studies in Old Ottoman Criminal Law*, V.L. Ménage (ed.), (Oxford, 1973), 224–226.

——, *Ottoman Documents on Palestine 1552–1615. A Study of the Firman according to the Mühimme Defteri* (Oxford, 1960).

Heywood, Colin 'The Kapudan Pasha, the English Ambassador and the *Blackham* Galley: An Episode in Anglo-Ottoman Maritime Relations (1697)' in: Elizabeth

Zachariadou (ed.), *The Kapudan Pasha, His Office and His Domain* (Crete, 2002), 409–438.

——, 'All for Love?: Lucca della Rocca and the betrayal of Grabusa (1691) (Documents from the British Library *Nāme-i Hümāyūn Defteri*', Jan Schmidt (ed.), *Essays in Jonour of Barbara Flemming* (Cambridge, MA, 2002) [= *Journal of Turkish Studies/Türklük Bilgisi Araştırmaları* 26/I (2002)], 353–372, esp. 366.

——, 'A *buyuruldu* of A.H. 1100/A.D. 1689 for the Dragomans of the English Embassy at Istanbul (Notes and Documents on the English Dragomanate, I)', Çiğdem Balım-Harding and Colin Imber (eds), *The Balance of Truth. Essays in Honour of Professor Geoffrey Lewis* (Istanbul, 2000), 124–144.

Historical Manuscript Commission, *Report on the Manuscripts of Allen George Finch, Esq. of Burley-On-The-Hill, Rutland* i (London, 1913).

Holt, P.M., *Early Mamluk Diplomacy (1260–1290): Treaties of Baybars and Qalāwūn with Christian Rulers* (Leiden, 1995).

Howard, John, *An Account of the Principal Lazarettos in Europe with various papers relative to the Plague; together with further observations on some foreign prisons and hospitals; and additional remarks on the present state of those in Great Britain and Ireland* (2nd edition with additions, London, 1791).

Hurewitz, J.C., *Diplomacy in the Near and Middle East. A Documentary Record. Volume 1: 1535–1914*, (Princeton, 1975).

Imber, Colin, *Ebu's-su'ud. The Islamic Legal Tradition* (Edinburgh, 1997).

——, "Why You Should Poison Your Husband. A Note on Liability in *Hanafī* Law in the Ottoman Period", in Colin Imber, *Studies in Ottoman History and Law* (Istanbul, 1996), 253–261.

——, "Four Documents From John Ryland's Turkish MS No. 145", *Tarih Dergisi*, XXXII (1979), 173–186; reprinted in Colin Imber, *Studies in Ottoman History and Law* (Istanbul: The Isis Press, 1996), 161–174.

İnalcık, Halil, 'Ottoman Galata, 1453–1553', in: Edhem Eldem (ed.), *Première Rencontre Internationale sur l'Empire Ottoman et la Turquie Moderne* (Istanbul, Paris, 1991), 17–105—reprinted in his *Essays in Ottoman History* (Istanbul, 1998), 271–376.

——, 'The Status of the Greek Orthodox Patriarch under the Ottomans', *Essays in Ottoman History*, 195–214, esp. 204 (reprinted from *Turcica* XXI–XXIII (1991), 407–436).

——, with Donald Quataert (eds), *An Economic and Social History of the Ottoman Empire 1300–1914* (Cambridge, 1994).

Ivanova, Svetlana,'The Empire's "own" Foreigners: Armenians and *Acem tüccar* in Rumeli in the seventeenth and eighteenth centuries', in: Maurits H. van den Boogert and Kate Fleet (eds.) *The Ottoman Capitulations: Text and Context* (Rome, 2003), 681–703.

Jamgocyan, Onnik, "Une famille de financiers arméniens au XVIIIe siècle: les Serpos" in Daniel Panzac (ed.), *Les villes dans l'empire ottoman: Activités et sociétés* I (Paris, 1991), 365–391.

Khadduri, Majid, *The Islamic Law of Nations. Shaybānī's Siyar* (Baltimore, 1966).

Kołodziejczyk, Dariusz, *Ottoman-Polish Diplomatic Relations (15th–18th Century). An Annotated Edition of* 'Ahdnames *and Other Documents* (Leiden, 2000).

Krüger, Hilmar, *Fetwa und Siyar. Zur internationalrechtlichen Gutachtenspraxis der osmanischen Seyh il-Islām vom 17. bis 19. Jahrhundert undert besonderer Berücksichtigung des 'Behcet ül-Fetāvā'* (Wiesbaden, 1978).

Marcus, Abraham, *The Middle East on the Eve of Modernity. Aleppo in the Eighteenth Century* (New York, 1989).

Masson, Paul, *Histoire du commerce français dans le Levant au XVIIe siècle* (Paris, 1896)—reprinted New York, 1967.

——, *Histoire du commerce français dans le Levant au XVIIIe siècle* (Paris, 1911)—reprinted New York, 1967.

Masters, Bruce, 'The Sultan's Entrepeneurs: The *Avrupa Tüccaris* and the *Hayriye Tüccaris* in Syria', *IJMES* (1992), 579–597.
——, *Christians and Jews in the Ottoman Arab World. The Roots of Sectarianism* (Cambridge, 2001).
——, *The Origins of Western Economic Dominance in the Middle East* (New York, 1988).
——, 'The Sultan's Entrepreneurs: The *Avrupa Tüccaris* and the *Hayriye Tüccaris* in Syria', *IJMES* 24 (1992), 579–597.
Matuz, J., 'A propos de la validité des capitulations de 1536 entre l'empire ottoman et la France', *Turcica* XXIV (1992), 183–192.
Meriwether, Margaret L., *The Kin Who Count. Family and Society in Ottoman Aleppo, 1770–1840* (Austin, 1999).
——, *The Notable Families of Aleppo, 1770–1830: Networks and Social Structure.* Unpublished PhD dissertation, University of Pennsylvania, 1981.
Murphy, Rhoads, "Merchants, Nations and Free-Agency: An Attempt at a Qualitative Characterization of Trade on the Eastern Mediterranean", in Alastair Hamilton, Alexander H. de Groot and Maurits H. van den Boogert (eds), *Friends and Rivals in the East. Studies in Anglo-Dutch Relations in the Levant from the Seventeenth to the Early Nineteenth Century* (Leiden, 2000), 25–58.
——, "Conditions of Trade in the Eastern Mediterranean: An Appraisal of Eighteenth-Century Ottoman Documents from Aleppo", *JESHO* 33 (1990), 35–50.
Noradounghian, Gabriel Effendi, *Recueil d'actes internationaux de l'empire ottoman I: 1300–1789* (Paris, 1897).
d'Ohsson, Mouradgea, *Tableau général de l'empire othoman: divisé en deux parties dont l'une comprend la legislation mahométane, l'autre l'histoire de l'empire othoman* (Paris, 1788–1820).
Olnon, Merlijn, "Towards Classifying *Avanias*: A Study of Two cases involving the English and Dutch Nations in Seventeenth-Century Izmir", in Hamilton et al. (eds), *Friends and Rivals in the East,* 25–58.
Oordt, Johannes van, *De privaatrechterlijke toestand van den Nederlandschen koopman in de landen van den Islam* (Leiden, 1899).
Panaite, Viorel, *The Ottoman Law of War and Peace. The Ottoman Empire and Tribute Payers* (Boulder, 2000).
——, 'Islamic Tradition and Ottoman Law of Nations', *Archæus* IV/4 (2000), 123–140; Ibid., 'The Status of Trade and Merchants in the Ottoman-Polish *'Ahdnāmes* (1607–1699)', *Archív orientální. Supplementa VIII* (1998), 275–298.
Pélissié du Rausas, G., *Le régime des capitulations dans l'Empire Ottoman* (Paris, 1910–1911).
Russell, Alexander, *The Natural History of Aleppo*—Patrick Russell ed. (London, 1791).
Saint-Priest, M. le Comte de, *Mémoires sur l'ambassade de France en Turquie et sur le commerce des Français dans le Levant,* (Paris, 1877).
Schacht, Joseph, *An Introduction to Islamic Law* (Oxford, 1964).
Scheel, Helmuth, 'Die Schreiben der türkischen Sultane an die preußischen Könige in der Zeit von 1721 bis 1774 und die ersten preußischen Kapitulationen vom Jahre 1761', *Mitteilungen des Seminars für Orientalische Sprachen zu Berlin. Zweite Abteilung, Westasiatische Studien* XXXIII (1930), 1–82.
Schlicht, Alfred, *Frankreich und die syrische Christen 1759–1861: Minoritäten und europäischer Imperialismus im Vorderen Orient* (Berlin, 1981).
Schmidt, Jan, "French-Ottoman Relations in the Early Modern Period and the John Rylands Library MSS Turkish 45 & 46", *Turcica,* 31 (1999), 375–436.
——, "Dutch Merchants in 18th-Century Ankara", *Anatolica* XXII (1996), 237–260.
Schopoff, A., *Les réformes et la protection des chrétiens en Turquie 1673–1904: Firmans, bérats, protocoles, traités, capitulations, conventions, arrangements, notes, circulaires, règlements, lois, mémorandums, etc.* (Paris, 1904).

Schutte, O., *Repertorium der Nederlandse vertegenwoordigers residerende in het buitenland 1584–1810* (The Hague, 1979).

Shalit, Yoram, *Nicht-Muslime und Fremde in Aleppo und Damaskus im 18. und in der ersten Hälfte des 19. Jahrhunderts* (Berlin, 1996).

Skilliter, S.A., *William Harborne and the Trade with Turkey 1578–1582. A Documentary Study of the First Anglo-Ottoman Relations* (Oxford, 1977).

Sonyel, Salâhi R., 'The Protégé System in the Ottoman Empire and its Abuses', *Belleten* LV/214 (1991), 675–686.

——, *Minorities and the Destruction of the Ottoman Empire* (Ankara, 1993).

Svoronos, N.G., *Le commerce de Salonique au XVIIIe siècle* (Paris, 1956).

Testa, Ignace baron de, *Recueil des traités de la Porte Ottomane avec les Puissances étrangers depuis le premier traité conclu en 1536* (Paris, 1864–1898).

Theunissen, Hans, *Ottoman-Venetian Diplomatics: The* 'Ahd-Names. *The Historical Background and the Development of a Category of Political-Commercial Instruments together with an Annotated Edition of a Corpus of Relevant Documents*; published on the Internet. See the Electronic Journal of Oriental Studies of Utrecht University, the Netherlands, at www.let.uu.nl/oosters/EJOS/EJOS-1.2.html.

Tongas, Gérard, *Les relations de la France avec l'empire ottoman durant la première moitié du XVIIe siècle. L'ambassade a Constantinople de Philippe de Harlay, Comte de Césy (1619–1640)* (Toulouse, 1942).

Udovitch, A., 'Islamic Law and the Social Context of Exchange in the Medieval Middle East', *History and Anthropology* 1 (1985), 445–465.

Ülker, Necmi, 'XVII. Yüzyılın ikinci yarısında İzmir'deki İngiliz tüccarına dair ticarî problemlerle ilgili belgeler', *Belgeler* XIV, 18 (1989–1992), 261–320.

——, *XVII. ve XVIII. yüzyıllarda İzmir şehri tarihi I. Ticaret tarihi araştırmaları* (Izmir, 1994).

Volney, C.F., *Voyage en Syrie et en Egypte pendant les années 1783, 1784 & 1785* (Paris, 1790).

Wakin, Jeanette, *The Function of Documents in Islamic Law: The Chapters on Sale from Tahāwī's* Kitāb al-shurūt al-kabīr (Albany, 1972).

Wertheim, Jac., *Manuel a l'usage des consuls des Pays-Bas précédé d'un aperçu historique sur l'établissement du consulat néerlandais a l'étranger et de la législation depuis son origine jusqu'à nos jours suivi d'un recueil de documents officiels* (Amsterdam, 1861).

Wood, Alfred C., *A History of the Levant Company* (Oxford, 1935).

INDEX

www.ingramcontent.com/pod-product-compliance
Lightning Source LLC
Chambersburg PA
CBHW031320230926
51848CB00001B/30
* 9 7 8 9 0 0 4 4 2 8 6 2 1 *